Study Guide

Principles of Microeconomics

Third Edition

N. Gregory Mankiw
Harvard University

Prepared by

David R. Hakes
University of Northern Iowa

Australia · Canada · Mexico · Singapore · Spain · United Kingdom · United States

Study Guide to accompany

Principles of Microeconomics, 3e

N. Gregory Mankiw

Prepared by

David R. Hakes

Vice President, Editorial Director:
Jack W. Calhoun

Vice President, Editor-in-Chief:
Michael P. Roche

Publisher of Economics:
Michael B. Mercier

Senior Acquisitions Editor:
Peter Adams

Developmental Editor:
Jane Tufts

Contributing Editors:
Jeff Gilbreath
Sarah K. Dorger
Susanna C. Smart

Senior Marketing Manager:
Janet Hennies

Senior Marketing Coordinator:
Jenny Fruechtenicht

Production Editor:
Daniel C. Plofchan

Manufacturing Coordinator:
Sandee Milewski

Senior Media Technology Editor:
Vicky True

Media Developmental Editor:
Peggy Buskey

Media Production Editor:
Pam Wallace

Compositor:
Graphic Arts Center Indianapolis

Project Management:
OffCenter Concept House
Soldotna, AK

Printer:
Globus Printing, Inc.
Minster, Ohio

Senior Design Project Manager:
Mike Stratton

Internal/Cover Designer:
Mike Stratton

Cover Illustration:
"Market Scene"
19th century French watercolor
Artist unknown
From a private collection

Cover Images:
PhotoDisc, Inc.

Printed in the United States of America
1 2 3 4 5 06 05 04 03

For more information contact South-Western, 5191 Natorp Boulevard, Mason, Ohio 45040.
Or you can visit our Internet site at: http://www.swlearning.com

Book ISBN: 0-324-17461-6

One must learn by doing the thing;
For though you think you know it
You have no certainty, until you try.

Sophocles, c. 496–406 B.C.
Greek playwright
Trachiniae

Preface

This *Study Guide* accompanies N. Gregory Mankiw's *Principles of Economics,* Third Edition. It was written with only one audience in mind—you, the student.

Your time is scarce. To help you use it efficiently, this *Study Guide* focuses strictly on the material presented in Mankiw's *Principles of Microeconomics,* Third Edition. It does not introduce extraneous material.

Objectives of the Study Guide

There are three broad objectives to the *Study Guide*. First, the *Study Guide* reinforces the text and improves your understanding of the material presented in the text. Second, it provides you with experience in using economic theories and tools to solve actual economic problems. That is, this *Study Guide* bridges the gap between economic concepts and economic problem solving. This may be the most important objective of the *Study Guide* because those students who find economics inherently logical often think that they are prepared for exams just by reading the text or attending lectures. However, it is one thing to watch an economist solve a problem in class and another thing altogether to solve a problem alone. There is simply no substitute for hands-on experience. Third, the *Study Guide* includes a self-test to validate areas of successful learning and to highlight areas needing improvement.

It is unlikely that you will truly enjoy any area of study if you fail to understand the material or if you lack confidence when taking tests over the material. It is my hope that this *Study Guide* improves your understanding of economics and improves your test performance so that you are able to enjoy economics as much as I do.

Organization of the Study Guide

Each chapter in the *Study Guide* corresponds to a chapter in Mankiw's *Principles of Microeconomics.* Each chapter is divided into the following sections:

- The Chapter Overview begins with a description of the purpose of the chapter and how it fits into the larger framework of the text. Following this context and purpose section are learning objectives, a section-by-section Chapter Review, and some helpful hints for understanding the material. The Chapter Overview ends with terms and definitions. This part is particularly important because it is impossible for the text to communicate information to you or for you to communicate information to your instructor on your exams without the use of a common economic vocabulary.

- Problems and Short-Answer Questions provide hands-on experience with problems based on the material presented in the text. The practice problems are generally multiple-step problems while the short-answer questions are generally based on a single issue.

- The Self-Test is composed of 15 True/False questions and 20 Multiple-Choice questions.
- The Advanced Critical Thinking section is a real-world problem that employs the economic reasoning and tools developed in the chapter. It is an applied story problem.
- Solutions are provided for all questions in the *Study Guide*. Explanations are also provided for false responses to True/False questions in the Self-Test.

Use of the Study Guide

I hesitate to suggest a method for using this *Study Guide* because how one best uses a study guide is largely a personal matter. It depends on your preferences and talents and on your instructor's approach to the material. I will, however, discuss a few possible approaches, and trial and error may help you sort out an approach that best suits you.

Some students prefer to read an entire chapter in the text prior to reading the *Study Guide*. Others prefer to read a section in the text and then read the corresponding section in the Chapter Overview portion of the *Study Guide*. This second method may help you focus your attention on the most important aspects of each section in the text. Some students who feel particularly confident after reading the text may choose to take the Self-Test immediately. I do not generally support this approach. I suggest that you complete all of the Practice Problems and Short-Answer Questions before you attempt the Self-Test. You will receive more accurate feedback from the Self-Test if you are well prepared prior to taking it.

A study guide is not a substitute for a text any more than *Cliff Notes* is a substitute for a classic novel. Use this *Study Guide* in conjunction with Mankiw's *Principles of Microeconomics*, not in place of it.

Final Thoughts

All of the problems and questions in this *Study Guide* have been checked by a number of accuracy reviewers. However, if you find a mistake, or if you have comments or suggestions for future editions, please feel free to contact me via e-mail at hakes@uni.edu.

Acknowledgments

I would like to thank Greg Mankiw for having written such a well thought-out text that it made writing the *Study Guide* a truly enjoyable task. I thank Sarah Dorger, the Developmental Editor, for keeping in close contact with me throughout the project. Our regular conversations kept me on schedule and made the entire project a pleasant experience. Sheryl Nelson and Greg Sallee copy-edited the manuscript and also offered many helpful suggestions. Daniel Flores-Guri reviewed the chapters that are new to this edition. Ken McCormick, a friend and colleague, provided constructive counsel throughout the project.

Finally, I would like to thank my family for being patient and understanding during the many months I spent working on this *Study Guide.*

David R. Hakes
University of Northern Iowa

March 2003

Comparative Table of Contents

Contents

1

TEN PRINCIPLES OF ECONOMICS

GOALS

In this chapter you will

- Learn that economics is about the allocation of scarce resources
- Examine some of the tradeoffs that people face
- Learn the meaning of opportunity cost
- See how to use marginal reasoning when making decisions
- Discuss how incentives affect people's behavior
- Consider why trade among people or nations can be good for everyone
- Discuss why markets are a good, but not perfect, way to allocate resources
- Learn what determines some trends in the overall economy

OUTCOMES

After accomplishing these goals, you should be able to

- Define scarcity
- Explain the classic tradeoff between "guns and butter"
- Add up your particular opportunity cost of attending college
- Compare the marginal costs and marginal benefits of continuing to attend school indefinitely
- Consider how a quadrupling of your tuition payments would affect your decision to educate yourself
- Explain why specialization and trade improve people's choices
- Give an example of an externality
- Explain the source of large and persistent inflation

CHAPTER OVERVIEW

Context and Purpose

Chapter 1 is the first chapter in a three-chapter section that serves as the introduction to the text. Chapter 1 introduces ten fundamental principles on which the study of economics is based. In a broad sense, the rest of the text is an elaboration on these ten principles. Chapter 2 will develop how economists approach problems while Chapter 3 will explain how individuals and countries gain from trade.

The purpose of Chapter 1 is to lay out ten economic principles that will serve as building blocks for the rest of the text. The ten principles can be grouped into three categories: how people make decisions, how people interact, and how the economy works as a whole. Throughout the text, references will be made repeatedly to these ten principles.

CHAPTER REVIEW

Introduction

Households and society face decisions about how to allocate scarce resources. Resources are **scarce** in that we have fewer resources than we wish. **Economics** is the study of how society manages its scarce resources. Economists study how people make decisions about buying and selling, and saving and investing. We study how people interact with one another in markets where prices are determined and quantities are exchanged. We also study the economy as a whole when we concern ourselves with total income, unemployment, and inflation.

This chapter addresses ten principles of economics. The text will refer to these principles throughout. The ten principles are grouped into three categories: how people make decisions, how people interact, and how the economy works as a whole.

How People Make Decisions

People face tradeoffs. Economists often say, "There is no such thing as a free lunch." This means that there are always tradeoffs—to get more of something we like, we have to give up something else that we like. For example, if you spend money on dinner and a movie, you won't be able to spend it on new clothes. Socially, we face tradeoffs as a group. For example, there is the classic tradeoff between "guns and butter." That is, if we decide to spend more on national defense (guns), then we will have less to spend on social programs (butter). There is also a social tradeoff between **efficiency** (getting the most from our scarce resources) and **equity** (benefits being distributed fairly across society). Policies such as taxes and welfare make incomes more equal but these policies reduce returns to hard work and, thus, the economy doesn't produce as much. As a result, when the government tries to cut the pie into more equal pieces, the pie gets smaller.

The cost of something is what you give up to get it. The **opportunity cost** of an item is what you give up to get that item. It is the true cost of the item. The opportunity cost of going to college obviously includes your tuition payment. It also includes the value of your time that you could have spent working, valued at your potential wage. It would exclude your room and board payment because you have to eat and sleep whether you are in school or not.

Rational people think at the margin. **Marginal changes** are incremental changes to an existing plan. Rational decision-makers only proceed with an action if the *marginal benefit* exceeds the *marginal cost*. For example, you should only go to another year of school if the benefits from that year of schooling exceed the cost of attending that year. A farmer should produce another bushel of corn only if the benefit (price received) exceeds the cost of producing it.

People respond to incentives. Since rational people weigh marginal costs and marginal benefits of activities, they will respond when these costs or benefits change. For example, when the price of automobiles rises, buyers have an incentive to buy fewer cars while automobile producers have an incentive to hire more workers and produce more autos. Public policy can alter the costs or benefits of activities. For example, a luxury tax on expensive boats raises the price and discourages purchases. Some policies have unintended consequences because they alter behavior in a manner that was not predicted.

How People Interact

Trade can make everyone better off. Trade is not a contest where one wins and one loses. Trade can make each trader better off. Trade allows each trader to specialize in what they do best, whether it be farming, building, or manufacturing, and trade their output for the output of other efficient producers. This is as true for countries as it is for individuals.

Markets are usually a good way to organize economic activity. In a **market economy,** the decisions about what goods and services to produce, how much to produce, and who gets to consume them, are made by millions of firms and households. Firms and households, guided by self-interest, interact in the marketplace where prices and quantities are determined. While this may appear like chaos, Adam Smith made the famous observation in the Wealth of Nations in 1776 that self-interested households and firms interact in markets and generate desirable social outcomes as if guided by an "invisible hand." These optimal social outcomes were not their original intent. The prices generated by their competitive activity signal the value of costs and benefits to producers and consumers, whose activities unknowingly maximize the welfare of society. Alternatively, the prices dictated by central planners contain no information on costs and benefits and, therefore, these prices fail to efficiently guide economic activity. Prices also fail to efficiently guide economic activity when governments distort prices with taxes or restrict price movements with price controls.

Governments can sometimes improve market outcomes. Government must first protect property rights in order for markets to work. In addition, government sometimes can intervene in the market to improve efficiency or equity. When markets fail to allocate resources efficiently, there has been **market failure.** There are many different sources of market failure. An **externality** is when the actions of one person affect the well-being of a bystander. Pollution is a standard example. **Market power** is when a single person or group can influence the price. In these cases, the government may be able to intervene and improve economic efficiency. The government may also intervene to improve equity with income taxes and welfare. Sometimes well-intentioned policy intervention has unintended consequences.

How the Economy as a Whole Works

A country's standard of living depends on its ability to produce goods and services. There is great variation in average incomes across countries at a point in time and within the same country over time. These differences in incomes and standards of living are largely attributable to differences in productivity. **Productivity** is the amount of goods and services produced by each hour of a worker's time. As a result, public policy intended to improve standards of living should improve education, generate more and better tools, and improve access to current technology.

Prices rise when the government prints too much money. **Inflation** is an increase in the overall level of prices in the economy. High inflation is costly to the economy. Large and persistent inflation is caused by rapid growth in the quantity of money. Policymakers wishing to keep inflation low should maintain slow growth in the quantity of money.

Society faces a short-run tradeoff between inflation and unemployment. An increase in inflation tends to reduce unemployment. The short-run tradeoff between inflation and unemployment is known as the **Phillips curve.** The tradeoff is temporary but can last for several years. Understanding this tradeoff is important for understanding the fluctuations in economic activity known as the **business cycle.** In the short run, policymakers may be able to affect the mix of inflation and unemployment by changing government spending, taxes, and the quantity of money.

HELPFUL HINTS

1. Place yourself in the story. Throughout the text, most economic situations will be composed of economic actors—buyers and sellers, borrowers and lenders, firms and workers, and so on. When you are asked to address how any economic actor would respond to economic incentives, place yourself in the story as the buyer or the seller, the borrower or the lender, the producer or the consumer. Don't think of yourself always as the buyer (a natural tendency) or always as the seller. You will find that your role-playing will usually produce the right response once you learn to think like an economist—which is the topic of the next chapter.

2. Trade is not a zero-sum game. Some people see an exchange in terms of winners and losers. Their reaction to trade is that, after the sale, if the seller is happy the buyer must be sad because the seller must have taken something from the buyer. That is, they view trade as a *zero-sum game* where what one gains the other must have lost. They fail to see that both parties to a voluntary transaction gain because each party is allowed to specialize in what it can produce most efficiently, and then trade for items that are produced more efficiently by others. Nobody loses, because trade is voluntary. Therefore, a government policy that limits trade reduces the potential gains from trade.

3. An externality can be positive. Because the classic example of an externality is pollution, it is easy to think of an externality as a cost that lands on a bystander. However, an externality can be positive in that it can be a benefit that lands on a bystander. For example, education is often cited as a product that emits a positive externality because when your neighbor educates herself, she is likely to be more reasonable, responsible, productive, and politically astute. In short, she is a better neighbor. Positive externalities, just as much as negative externalities, may be a reason for the government to intervene to promote efficiency.

TERMS AND DEFINITIONS

Choose a definition for each key term.

Key terms:

_____ Scarcity

_____ Economics

_____ Efficiency

_____ Equity

_____ Opportunity cost

_____ Marginal changes

_____ Market economy

_____ "Invisible hand"

_____ Market failure

_____ Externality

_____ Market power

_____ Monopoly

_____ Productivity

_____ Inflation

_____ Phillips curve

_____ Business cycle

Definitions:

1. The property of distributing output fairly among society's members
2. A situation in which the market fails to allocate resources efficiently
3. Limited resources and unlimited wants
4. The amount of goods and services produced per hour by a worker
5. The case in which there is only one seller in the market
6. The principle that self-interested market participants may unknowingly maximize the welfare of society as a whole
7. The property of society getting the most from its scarce resources
8. An economic system where interaction of households and firms in markets determine the allocation of resources
9. Fluctuations in economic activity
10. When one person's actions have an impact on a bystander
11. An increase in the overall level of prices
12. Incremental adjustments to an existing plan
13. Study of how society manages its scarce resources
14. Whatever is given up to get something else
15. The ability of an individual or group to substantially influence market prices
16. The short-run tradeoff between inflation and unemployment

PROBLEMS AND SHORT-ANSWER QUESTIONS

Practice Problems

1. People respond to incentives. Governments can alter incentives and, hence, behavior with public policy. However, sometimes public policy generates unintended consequences by producing results that were not anticipated. Try to find an unintended consequence of each of the following public policies.
   a. To help the "working poor," the government raises the minimum wage to $25 per hour.

   b. To help the homeless, the government places rent controls on apartments restricting rent to $10 per month.

   c. To reduce the deficit and limit consumption of gasoline, the government raises the tax on gasoline by $2.00 per gallon.

   d. To reduce the consumption of drugs, the government makes drugs illegal.

   e. To raise the population of wolves, the government prohibits the killing of wolves.

f. To improve the welfare of American sugar beet growers, the government bans imports of sugar from South America.

____

____

____

2. Opportunity cost is what you give up to get an item. Since there is no such thing as a free lunch, what would likely be given up to obtain each of the items listed below?
   a. Susan can work full time or go to college. She chooses college.

   ____

   ____

   b. Susan can work full time or go to college. She chooses work.

   ____

   ____

   c. Farmer Jones has 100 acres of land. He can plant corn, which yields 100 bushels per acre, or he can plant beans, which yield 40 bushels per acre. He chooses to plant corn.

   ____

   ____

   d. Farmer Jones has 100 acres of land. He can plant corn, which yields 100 bushels per acre, or he can plant beans, which yield 40 bushels per acre. He chooses to plant beans.

   ____

   ____

   e. In (a) and (b) above, and (c) and (d) above, which is the opportunity cost of which—college for work or work for college? Corn for beans or beans for corn?

   ____

   ____

Short-Answer Questions

1. Is air scarce? Is clean air scarce?

2. What is the opportunity cost of saving some of your paycheck?

3. Why is there a tradeoff between equity and efficiency?

4. Water is necessary for life. Diamonds are not. Is the marginal benefit of an additional glass of water greater or lesser than an additional one carat diamond? Why?

5. Your car needs to be repaired. You have already paid $500 to have the transmission fixed, but it still doesn't work properly. You can sell your car "as is" for $2000. If your car were fixed, you could sell it for $2500. Your car can be fixed with a guarantee for another $300. Should you repair your car? Why?

6. Why do you think air bags have reduced deaths from auto crashes less than we had hoped?

7. Suppose one country is better at producing agricultural products (because they have more fertile land) while another country is better at producing manufactured goods (because they have a better educational system and more engineers). If each country produced their specialty and traded, would

there be more or less total output than if each country produced all of their agricultural and manufacturing needs? Why?

8. In the *Wealth of Nations* Adam Smith said, "It is not from the benevolence of the butcher, the brewer, or the baker that we expect our dinner, but from their regard to their own interest." What do you think he meant?

9. If we save more and use it to build more physical capital, productivity will rise and we will have rising standards of living in the future. What is the opportunity cost of future growth?

10. If the government printed twice as much money, what do you think would happen to prices and output if the economy were already producing at maximum capacity?

11. A goal for a society is to distribute resources equitably or fairly. How would you distribute resources if everyone were equally talented and worked equally hard? What if people had different talents and some people worked hard while others did not?

12. Who is more self-interested, the buyer or the seller?

SELF-TEST

True/False Questions

_____ 1. When the government redistributes income with taxes and welfare, the economy becomes more efficient.

_____ 2. When economists say, "There is no such thing as a free lunch," they mean that all economic decisions involve tradeoffs.

_____ 3. Adam Smith's "invisible hand" concept describes how corporate business reaches into the pockets of consumers like an "invisible hand."

_____ 4. Rational people act only when the marginal benefit of the action exceeds the marginal cost.

_____ 5. The United States will benefit economically if we eliminate trade with Asian countries because we will be forced to produce more of our own cars and clothes.

_____ 6. When a jet flies overhead, the noise it generates is an externality.

_____ 7. A tax on liquor raises the price of liquor and provides an incentive for consumers to drink more.

_____ 8. An unintended consequence of public support for higher education is that low tuition provides an incentive for many people to attend state universities even if they have no desire to learn anything.

_____ 9. Sue is better at cleaning and Bob is better at cooking. It will take fewer hours to eat and clean if Bob specializes in cooking and Sue specializes in cleaning than if they share the household duties evenly.

_____10. High and persistent inflation is caused by excessive growth in the quantity of money in the economy.

_____11. In the short run, a reduction in inflation tends to cause a reduction in unemployment.

_____12. An auto manufacturer should continue to produce additional autos as long as the firm is profitable, even if the cost of the additional units exceed the price received.

_____13. An individual farmer is likely to have market power in the market for wheat.

_____14. To a student, the opportunity cost of going to a basketball game would include the price of the ticket and the value of the time that could have been spent studying.

_____15. Workers in the United States have a relatively high standard of living because the United States has a relatively high minimum wage.

Multiple-Choice Questions

1. Which of the following involve a tradeoff?
   a. buying a new car
   b. going to college
   c. watching a football game on Saturday afternoon
   d. taking a nap
   e. All of the above involve tradeoffs.

2. Tradeoffs are required because wants are unlimited and resources are
   a. efficient.
   b. economical.
   c. scarce.
   d. unlimited.
   e. marginal.

3. Economics is the study of how
   a. to fully satisfy our unlimited wants.
   b. society manages its scarce resources.
   c. to reduce our wants until we are satisfied.
   d. to avoid making tradeoffs.
   e. society manages its unlimited resources.

4. A rational person does not act unless the action
   a. makes money for the person.
   b. is ethical.
   c. produces marginal costs that exceed marginal benefits.
   d. produces marginal benefits that exceed marginal costs.
   e. none of the above

5. Raising taxes and increasing welfare payments
   a. proves that there is such a thing as a free lunch.
   b. reduces market power.
   c. improves efficiency at the expense of equity.
   d. improves equity at the expense of efficiency.
   e. none of the above

6. Suppose you find $20. If you choose to use the $20 to go to the football game, your opportunity cost of going to the game is
   a. nothing, because you found the money.
   b. $20 (because you could have used the $20 to buy other things).
   c. $20 (because you could have used the $20 to buy other things) plus the value of your time spent at the game.
   d. $20 (because you could have used the $20 to buy other things) plus the value of your time spent at the game, plus the cost of the dinner you purchased at the game.
   e. none of the above

7. Foreign trade
   a. allows a country to have a greater variety of products at a lower cost than if it tried to produce everything at home.
   b. allows a country to avoid tradeoffs.
   c. makes a country more equitable.
   d. increases the scarcity of resources.
   e. none of the above

8. Since people respond to incentives, we would expect that, if the average salary of accountants increases by 50 percent while the average salary of teachers increases by 20 percent,
   a. students will shift majors from education to accounting.
   b. students will shift majors from accounting to education.
   c. fewer students will attend college.
   d. none of the above

9. Which of the following activities is most likely to produce an externality?
   a. A student sits at home and watches T.V.
   b. A student has a party in her dorm room.
   c. A student reads a novel for pleasure.
   d. A student eats a hamburger in the student union.

10. Which of the following products would be *least* capable of producing an externality?
   a. cigarettes
   b. stereo equipment
   c. inoculations against disease
   d. education
   e. food

11. Which of the following situations describes the greatest market power?
   a. a farmer's impact on the price of corn
   b. Volvo's impact on the price of autos
   c. Microsoft's impact on the price of desktop operating systems
   d. a student's impact on college tuition

12. Which of the following statements is true about a market economy?
   a. Market participants act as if guided by an "invisible hand" to produce outcomes that maximize social welfare.
   b. Taxes help prices communicate costs and benefits to producers and consumers.
   c. With a large enough computer, central planners could guide production more efficiently than markets.
   d. The strength of a market system is that it tends to distribute resources evenly across consumers.

13. Workers in the United States enjoy a high standard of living because
   a. unions in the United States keep the wage high.
   b. we have protected our industry from foreign competition.
   c. the United States has a high minimum wage.
   d. workers in the United States are highly productive.
   e. none of the above

14. High and persistent inflation is caused by
    a. unions increasing wages too much.
    b. OPEC raising the price of oil too much.
    c. governments increasing the quantity of money too much.
    d. regulations raising the cost of production too much.

15. The Phillips curve shows that
    a. an increase in inflation temporarily increases unemployment.
    b. a decrease in inflation temporarily increases unemployment.
    c. inflation and unemployment are unrelated in the short run.
    d. the business cycle has been eliminated.
    e. none of the above.

16. An increase in the price of beef provides information which
    a. tells consumers to buy more beef.
    b. tells consumers to buy less pork.
    c. tells producers to produce more beef.
    d. provides no information because prices in a market system are managed by planning boards.

17. You have spent $1000 building a hot dog stand based on estimates of sales of $2000. The hot dog stand is nearly completed but now you estimate total sales to be only $800. You can complete the hot dog stand for another $300. Should you complete the hot dog stand? (Assume that the hot dogs are costless to you.)
    a. Yes.
    b. No.
    c. There is not enough information to answer this question.

18. Referring to Question 17, your decision rule should be to complete the hot dog stand as long as the cost to complete the stand is less than
    a. $100.
    b. $300.
    c. $500.
    d. $800.
    e. none of the above.

19. Which of the following is *not* part of the opportunity cost of going on vacation?
    a. the money you could have made if you had stayed home and worked
    b. the money you spent on food
    c. the money you spent on airplane tickets
    d. the money you spent on a Broadway show

20. Productivity can be increased by
    a. raising minimum wages.
    b. raising union wages.
    c. improving the education of workers.
    d. restricting trade with foreign countries.

ADVANCED CRITICAL THINKING

Suppose your university decides to lower the cost of parking on campus by reducing the price of a parking permit from $200 per semester to $5 per semester.

1. What do you think would happen to the number of students desiring to park their cars on campus?

____

____

2. What do you think would happen to the amount of time it would take to find a parking place?

____

____

3. Thinking in terms of opportunity cost, would the lower price of a parking permit necessarily lower the true cost of parking?

____

____

4. Would the opportunity cost of parking be the same for students with no outside employment and students with jobs earning $15 per hour?

____

____

____

SOLUTIONS

Terms and Definitions

3 Scarcity
13 Economics
7 Efficiency
1 Equity
14 Opportunity cost
12 Marginal changes
8 Market economy
6 "Invisible hand"
2 Market failure
10 Externality
15 Market power
5 Monopoly
4 Productivity
11 Inflation
16 Phillips curve
9 Business cycle

Practice Problems

1. a. Many would want to work at $25/hour but few firms would want to hire low productivity workers at this wage; therefore it would simply create unemployment.
   b. Many renters would want to rent an apartment at $10/month, but few landlords could produce an apartment at this price, therefore this rent control would create more homelessness.
   c. Higher gas prices would reduce the miles driven. This would lower auto accidents, put less wear and tear on roads and cars, and reduce the demand for cars and road repairs.
   d. This raises the price of drugs and makes selling them more profitable. This creates more gangs and gang warfare.
   e. Restrictions on killing wolves reduces the population of animals upon which wolves may feed—rabbits, deer, etc.
   f. South American growers have difficulty repaying their bank loans to U.S. banks. They turn to more profitable crops such as coca leaves and marijuana.

2. a. She gives up income from work (and must pay tuition).
   b. She gives up a college degree and the increase in income through life that it would have brought her (but doesn't have to pay tuition).
   c. He gives up 4000 bushels of beans.
   d. He gives up 10,000 bushels of corn.
   e. Each is the opportunity cost of the other because each decision requires giving something up.

Short-Answer Questions

1. No, you don't have to give up anything to get it. Yes, you can't have as much as you want without giving up something to get it (pollution equipment on cars, etc.)

2. The items you could have enjoyed had you spent it (current consumption).

3. Taxes and welfare make us more equal but reduce incentives for hard work, lowering total output.

4. The marginal benefit of another glass of water is generally lower because we have so much water that one more glass is of little value. The opposite is true for diamonds.

5. Yes, because the marginal benefit of fixing the car is $2500 – $2000 = $500 and the marginal cost is $300. The original repair payment is not relevant.

6. The cost of an accident was lowered. This changed incentives so people drive faster and have more accidents.

7. There would be more total output if they specialize and trade because each is doing what it does most efficiently.

8. The butcher, brewer, and baker produce the best food possible, not out of kindness, but because it is in their best interest to do so. Self-interest can maximize social welfare.

9. We must give up consumption today.

10. Spending would double but since the quantity of output would remain the same, prices would double.

11. Fairness would require that everyone get an equal share. Fairness would require that people not get an equal share.

12. They are equally self-interested. The seller will sell to the highest bidder and the buyer will buy from the lowest offer.

True/False Questions

1. F; the economy becomes less efficient because it decreases the incentive to work hard.

2. T

3. F; the "invisible hand" refers to how markets guide self-interested people to create desirable social outcomes.

4. T

5. F; all countries gain from voluntary trade.

6. T

7. F; higher prices reduce the quantity demanded.

8. T

9. T

10. T

11. F; a reduction in inflation tends to raise unemployment.

12. F; a manufacturer should produce as long as the marginal benefit exceeds the marginal cost.

13. F; a single farmer is too small to influence the market.

14. T

15. F; workers in the United States have a high standard of living because they are productive.

Multiple-Choice Questions

1. e	5. d	9. b	13. d	17. a
2. c	6. c	10. e	14. c	18. d
3. b	7. a	11. c	15. b	19. b
4. d	8. a	12. a	16. c	20. c

Advanced Critical Thinking

1. More students would wish to park on campus.
2. It would take much longer to find a parking place.
3. No, because we would have to factor in the value of our time spent looking for a parking place.
4. No. Students who could be earning money working are giving up more while looking for a parking place. Therefore, their opportunity cost is higher.

2

THINKING LIKE AN ECONOMIST

GOALS

In this chapter you will

See how economists apply the methods of science

Consider how assumptions and models can shed light on the world

Learn two simple models—the circular-flow and the production possibilities frontier

Distinguish between microeconomics and macroeconomics

Learn the difference between positive and normative statements

Examine the role of economists in making policy

Consider why economists sometimes disagree with one another

OUTCOMES

After accomplishing these goals, you should be able to

Describe the scientific method

Understand the art of making useful assumptions

Explain the slope of a production possibilities frontier

Place economic issues into the categories of microeconomics or macroeconomics

Place economic statements into the categories of normative or positive.

See the link between policymaking and normative statements

List two reasons why economists disagree

CHAPTER OVERVIEW

Context and Purpose

Chapter 2 is the second chapter in a three-chapter section that serves as the introduction of the text. Chapter 1 introduced ten principles of economics that will be revisited throughout the text. Chapter 2 develops how economists approach problems while Chapter 3 will explain how individuals and countries gain from trade.

The purpose of Chapter 2 is to familiarize you with how economists approach economic problems. With practice, you will learn how to approach similar problems in this dispassionate systematic way. You will see how economists employ the scientific method, the role of assumptions in model building, and the application of two specific economic models. You will also learn the important distinction between two roles economists can play: as scientists when we try to explain the economic world and as policymakers when we try to improve it.

CHAPTER REVIEW

Introduction

Like other fields of study, economics has its own jargon and way of thinking. It is necessary to learn the special language of economics because knowledge of the economic vocabulary will help you communicate with precision to others about economic issues. This chapter will also provide an overview of how economists look at the world.

The Economist as Scientist

While economists don't use test tubes or telescopes, they are scientists because they employ the *scientific method*—the dispassionate and objective development and testing of theories.

The scientific method: observation, theory, and more observation Just as in other sciences, an economist observes an event, develops a theory, and collects data to test the theory. An economist observes inflation, creates a theory that excessive growth in money causes inflation, and then collects data on money growth and inflation to see if there is a relationship. Collecting data to test economic theories is difficult, however, because economists usually cannot create data from experiments. That is, economists cannot manipulate the economy just to test a theory. Therefore, economists often use data gathered from historical economic events.

The role of assumptions Assumptions are made to make the world easier to understand. A physicist assumes an object is falling in a vacuum when measuring acceleration due to gravity. This assumption is reasonably accurate for a marble but not for a beachball. An economist may assume that prices are fixed (can't be changed) or may assume that prices are flexible (can move up or down in response to market pressures). Since prices often cannot be changed quickly (the menu in a restaurant is expensive to change) but can be changed easily over time, it is reasonable for economists to assume that prices are fixed in the short run but flexible in the long run. The art of scientific thinking is deciding which assumptions to make.

Economic models Biology teachers employ plastic models of the human body. They are simpler than the actual human body but that is what makes them useful. Economists use economic models that are composed of diagrams and equations. Economic models are based on assumptions and are simplifications of economic reality.

Our first model: the circular-flow diagram The **circular-flow diagram** shows the flow of goods and services, factors of production, and monetary payments between households and firms. Households sell the factors of production, such as land, labor, and capital to firms, in the market for factors of production. In exchange, the households receive wages, rent, and profit. Households use these dollars to buy goods and services from firms in the market for goods and services. The firms use this revenue to pay for the factors of production, and so on. This is a simplified model of the entire economy. This version of the circular flow diagram has been simplified because it excludes international trade and the government.

Our second model: the production possibilities frontier A **production possibilities frontier** is a graph that shows the combinations of output the economy can possibly produce given the available factors of production and the available production technology. It is drawn assuming the economy produces only two goods. This model demonstrates the following economic principles:

- If the economy is operating on the production possibilities frontier, it is operating *efficiently* because it is producing a mix of output that is the maximum possible from the resources available.

- Points inside the curve are therefore *inefficient.* Points outside the curve are currently unattainable.

- If the economy is operating on the production possibilities frontier, we can see the *tradeoffs* society faces. To produce more of one good, it must produce less of the other. The amount of one good given up when producing more of another good is the *opportunity cost* of the additional production.

- The production possibilities frontier is bowed outward because the opportunity cost of producing more of a good increases as we near maximum production of that good. This is because we use resources better suited toward production of the other good in order to continue to expand production of the first good.

- A technological advance in production shifts the production possibilities frontier outward. This is a demonstration of *economic growth.*

Microeconomics and macroeconomics Economics is studied on various levels. **Microeconomics** is the study of how households and firms make decisions and how they interact in specific markets. **Macroeconomics** is the study of economy-wide phenomena such as the federal deficit, the rate of unemployment, and policies to improve our standard of living. Microeconomics and macroeconomics are related because changes in the overall economy arise from decisions of millions of individuals. Although related, the methods employed in microeconomics and macroeconomics differ enough that they are often taught in separate courses.

The Economist as Policy Advisor

When economists attempt to explain the world as it is, they act as scientists. When economists attempt to improve the world, they act as policy advisors. Correspondingly, **positive statements** describe the world *as it is,* while **normative statements** prescribe how the world *ought to be.* Positive statements can be confirmed or refuted with evidence. Normative statements involve values (ethics, religion, political philosophy) as well as facts.

For example, "Money growth causes inflation" is a positive statement (of a scientist). "The government ought to reduce inflation" is a normative statement (of a policy advisor). The two statements are related because evidence about whether money causes inflation might help us decide what tool the government should use if it chooses to reduce inflation.

Economists act as policy advisors to the government in many different areas. The president is advised by economists on the Council of Economic Advisers, the Department of Treasury, the Department of Labor, and the Department of Justice. Congress is advised by economists from the Congressional Budget Office and the Federal Reserve.

Why Economists Disagree

There are two reasons why economists have a reputation for giving conflicting advice to policymakers.

- Economists may have different scientific judgments. That is, economists may disagree about the validity of alternative positive theories about how the world works. For example, economists differ in their views of the sensitivity of household saving to changes in the after-tax return to saving.

- Economists may have different values. That is, economists may have different normative views about what policy should try to accomplish. For example, economists differ in their views of whether taxes should be used to redistribute income.

In reality, although there are legitimate disagreements among economists on many issues, there is tremendous agreement on many basic principles of economics.

Let's Get Going

In the next chapter, we will begin to apply the ideas and methods of economics. As you begin to think like an economist, you will use a variety of skills—mathematics, history, politics, philosophy—with the objectivity of a scientist.

HELPFUL HINTS

1. Opportunity costs are usually not constant along a production possibilities frontier. Notice that the production possibilities frontier shown in Exhibit 1 is bowed outward. It shows the production tradeoffs for an economy that produces only paper and pencils.

   If we start at the point where the economy is using all of its resources to produce paper, producing 100 units of pencils only requires a tradeoff or an

EXHIBIT 1

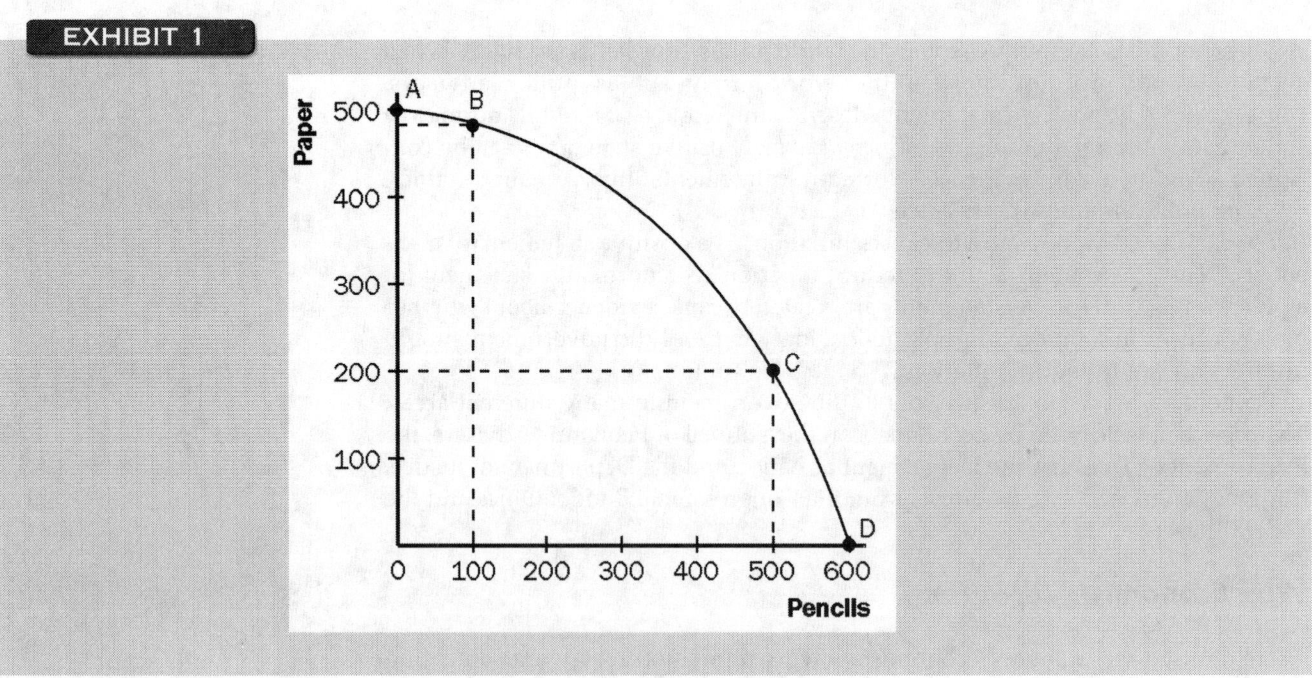

opportunity cost of 25 units of paper (point A to point B). This is because when we move resources from paper to pencil production, we first move those resources best suited for pencil production and poorly suited for paper production. Therefore, pencil production increases with very little decrease in paper production. However, if the economy were operating at point C, the opportunity cost of an additional 100 pencils (point C to D) is 200 units of paper. This is because we now move resources toward pencil production that were extremely well suited for paper production and are poorly suited for pencil production. Therefore, as we produce more and more of any particular good, the opportunity cost per unit tends to rise because resources are specialized. That is, resources are not equally well suited for producing each output.

The argument above applies when moving either direction on the production possibilities frontier. For example, if we start at point D (maximum production of pencils) a small reduction in pencil production (100 units) releases enough resources to increase production of paper by a large amount (200 units). However, moving from point B to point A only increases paper production by 25 units.

2. A production possibilities frontier only shows the choices available—not which point of production is best. A common mistake made by students when using production possibilities frontiers is to look at a production possibilities frontier and suggest that a point somewhere near the middle "looks best." Students make this subjective judgment because the middle point appears to provide the biggest total number of units of production of the two goods. However, ask yourself the following question. Using the production possibilities frontier in Exhibit 1, what production point would be best if paper were worth $10 per sheet and pencils were worth 1 cent per dozen? We would move our resources toward paper production. What if paper were worth 1 cent per sheet and pencils were worth $50 each? We would move our resources toward pencil production. Clearly, what we actually choose to produce depends on the price of each good. Therefore, a production possibilities frontier only provides the choices available; it alone cannot determine which choice is best.

3. Economic disagreement is interesting but economic consensus is more important. Economists have a reputation for disagreeing with one another because we tend to highlight our differences. While our disagreements are interesting to us, the matters on which we agree are more important to you. There are a great number of economic principles for which there is near unanimous support within the economics profession. The aim of this text is to concentrate on the areas of agreement within the profession as opposed to the areas of disagreement.

TERMS AND DEFINITIONS

Choose a definition for each key term.

Key terms:

_____Scientific method

_____Economic models

_____Circular-flow diagram

_____Factors of production

_____Production possibilities frontier

_____Opportunity cost

_____Efficiency

_____Microeconomics

_____Macroeconomics

_____Positive statements

_____Normative statements

Definitions:

1. Inputs such as land, labor, and capital
2. The study of economy-wide phenomena
3. Objective development and testing of theories
4. Whatever is given up to get something else
5. Prescription for how the world ought to be
6. Getting maximum output from the resources available
7. Descriptions of the world as it is
8. Simplifications of reality based on assumptions
9. A graph that shows the combinations of output the economy can possibly produce given the available factors of production and the available production technology
10. The study of how households and firms make decisions and how they interact in markets
11. A diagram of the economy that shows the flow of goods and services, factors of production, and monetary payments between households and firms.

PROBLEMS AND SHORT-ANSWER QUESTIONS

Practice Problems

1. Identify the parts of the circular-flow diagram immediately involved in the following transactions.
   a. Mary buys a car from General Motors for $20,000.

____

____

____

____

b. General Motors pays Joe $5,000/month for work on the assembly line.

____

____

____

c. Joe gets a $15 hair cut.

____

____

____

d. Mary receives $10,000 of dividends on her General Motors stock.

____

____

____

2. The following table provides information about the production possibilities frontier of Athletic Country.

Bats	Rackets
0	420
100	400
200	360
300	300
400	200
500	0

a. In Exhibit 2, plot and connect these points to create Athletic Country's production possibilities frontier.

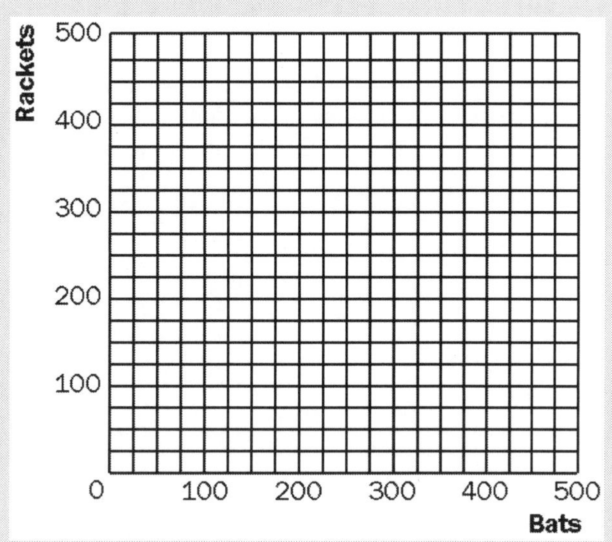

b. If Athletic Country currently produces 100 bats and 400 rackets, what is the opportunity cost of an additional 100 bats?

c. If Athletic Country currently produces 300 bats and 300 rackets, what is the opportunity cost of an additional 100 bats?

d. Why does the additional production of 100 bats in part (c) cause a greater tradeoff than the additional production of 100 bats in part (b)?

e. Suppose Athletic Country is currently producing 200 bats and 200 rackets. How many additional bats could they produce without giving up any rackets? How many additional rackets could they produce without giving up any bats?

f. Is the production of 200 bats and 200 rackets efficient? Explain.

3. The production possibilities frontier in Exhibit 3 shows the available tradeoffs between consumption goods and capital goods. Suppose two countries face this identical production possibilities frontier.
   a. Suppose Party Country chooses to produce at point A while Parsimonious Country chooses to produce at point B. Which country will experience more growth in the future? Why?

EXHIBIT 3

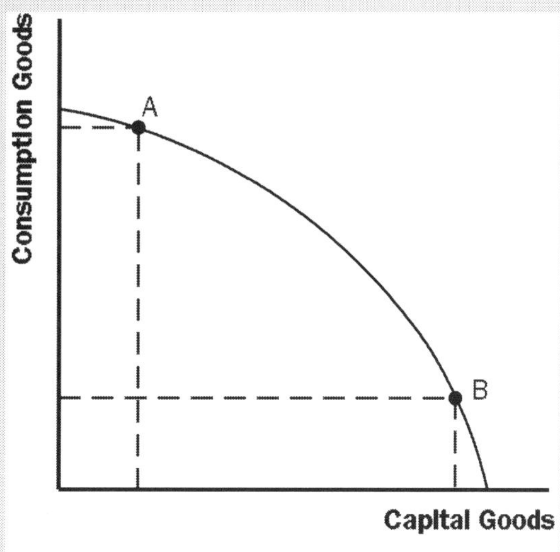

b. In this model, what is the opportunity cost of future growth?

____

____

c. Demonstrate in Exhibit 4 the impact of growth on a production possibilities frontier such as the one shown above. Would the production possibilities frontier for Parsimonious Country shift more or less than that for Party Country? Why?

____

____

EXHIBIT 4

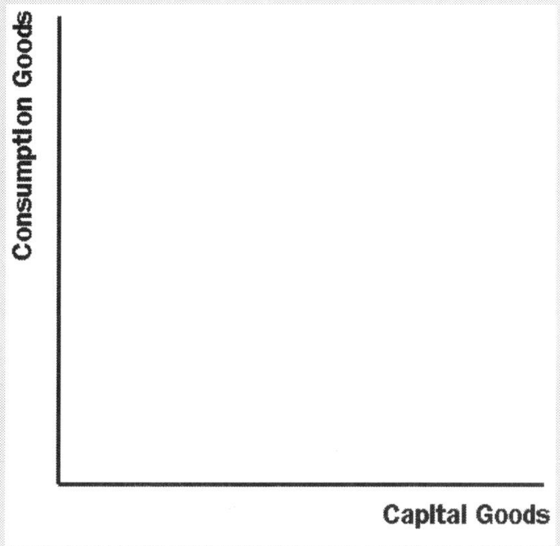

Consumption Goods

Capital Goods

EXHIBIT 5

d. On the graph in Exhibit 5, show the shift in the production possibilities curve if there were an increase in technology that only affected the production of capital goods.
e. Does the shift in part (d) above imply that all additional production must be in the form of capital goods? Why?

____

____

Short-Answer Questions

1. Describe the scientific method.

____

____

2. What is the role of assumptions in any science?

____

____

3. Is a more realistic model always better?

____

____

____

4. Why does a production possibilities frontier have a negative slope (slope down and to the right)?

____

____

5. Why is the production possibilities frontier bowed outward?

____

____

____

6. What are the two subfields within economics? Which is more likely to be a building block of the other? Why?

____

____

____

7. When an economist makes a normative statement, is she more likely to be acting as a scientist or a policy advisor? Why?

____

____

____

8. Which statements are testable: positive statements or normative statements? Why?

____

____

9. Name two reasons why economists disagree.

____

____

10. Name two economic propositions for which more than 90 percent of economists agree.

____

____

____

SELF-TEST

True/False Questions

_____ 1. Economic models must mirror reality or they are of no value.

_____ 2. Assumptions make the world easier to understand because they simplify reality and focus our attention.

_____ 3. It is reasonable to assume that the world is composed of only one person when modeling international trade.

_____ 4. When people act as scientists, they must try to be objective.

_____ 5. If an economy is operating on its production possibilities frontier, it must be using its resources efficiently.

_____ 6. If an economy is operating on its production possibilities frontier, it must produce less of one good if it produces more of another.

_____ 7. Points outside the production possibilities frontier are attainable but inefficient.

_____ 8. If an economy were experiencing substantial unemployment, the economy is producing inside the production possibilities frontier.

_____ 9. The production possibilities frontier is bowed outward because the tradeoffs between the production of any two goods are constant.

_____10. An advance in production technology would cause the production possibilities curve to shift outward.

_____11. Macroeconomics is concerned with the study of how households and firms make decisions and how they interact in specific markets.

_____12. The statement, "An increase in inflation tends to cause unemployment to fall in the short run," is normative.

_____13. When economists make positive statements, they are more likely to be acting as scientists.

_____14. Normative statements can be refuted with evidence.

_____15. Most economists believe that tariffs and import quotas usually reduce general economic welfare.

Multiple-Choice Questions

1. The scientific method requires that
   a. the scientist use test tubes and have a clean lab.
   b. the scientist be objective.
   c. the scientist use precision equipment.
   d. only incorrect theories are tested.
   e. only correct theories are tested.

2. Which of the following is most likely to produce scientific evidence about a theory?
   a. An economist employed by the AFL/CIO doing research on the impact of trade restrictions on workers' wages.
   b. A radio talk show host collecting data on how capital markets respond to taxation.
   c. A tenured economist employed at a leading university analyzing the impact of bank regulations on rural lending.
   d. A lawyer employed by General Motors addressing the impact of air bags on passenger safety.

3. Which of the following statements regarding the circular-flow diagram is true?
   a. The factors of production are owned by households.
   b. If Susan works for IBM and receives a paycheck, the transaction takes place in the market for goods and services.
   c. If IBM sells a computer, the transaction takes place in the market for factors of production.
   d. The factors of production are owned by firms.
   e. None of the above.

4. In which of the following cases is the assumption most reasonable?
   a. To estimate the speed at which a beach ball falls, a physicist assumes that it falls in a vacuum.
   b. To address the impact of money growth on inflation, an economist assumes that money is strictly coins.
   c. To address the impact of taxes on income distribution, an economist assumes that everyone earns the same income.
   d. To address the benefits of trade, an economist assumes that there are two people and two goods.

5. Economic models are
   a. created to duplicate reality.
   b. built with assumptions.
   c. usually made of wood and plastic.
   d. useless if they are simple.

6. Which of the following is not a factor of production?
   a. land
   b. labor
   c. capital
   d. money
   e. All of the above are factors of production.

7. Points on the production possibilities frontier are
   a. efficient.
   b. inefficient.
   c. unattainable.
   d. normative.
   e. none of the above.

8. Which of the following will not shift a country's production possibilities frontier outward?
   a. an increase in the capital stock
   b. an advance in technology
   c. a reduction in unemployment
   d. an increase in the labor force

9. Economic growth is depicted by
   a. a movement along a production possibilities frontier toward capital goods.
   b. a shift in the production possibilities frontier outward.
   c. a shift in the production possibilities frontier inward.
   d. a movement from inside the curve toward the curve.

Use Exhibit 6 to answer questions 10–13.

EXHIBIT 6

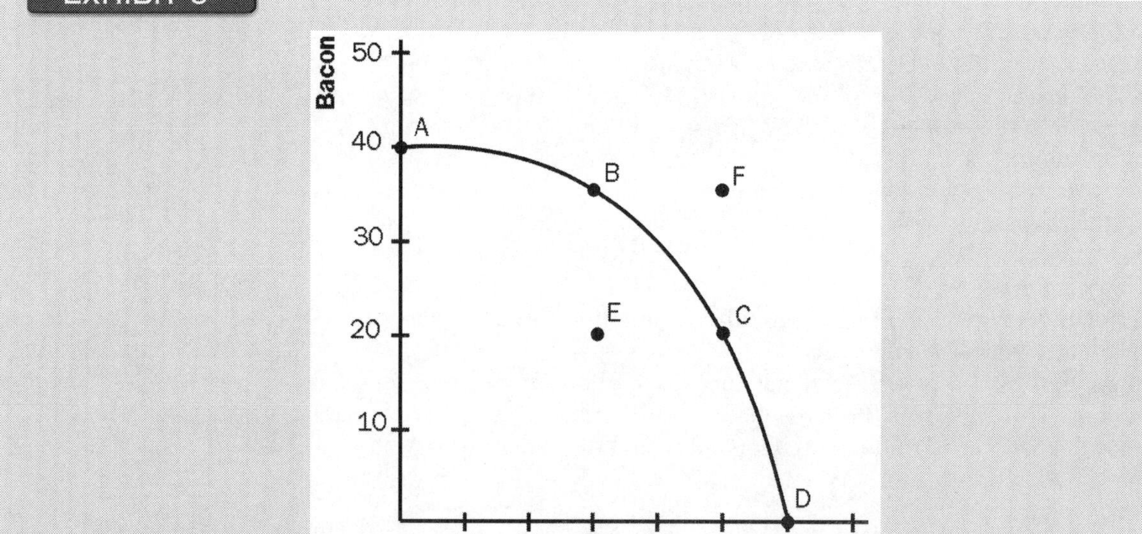

10. If the economy is operating at point C, the opportunity cost of producing an additional 15 units of bacon is
    a. 10 units of eggs.
    b. 20 units of eggs.
    c. 30 units of eggs.
    d. 40 units of eggs.
    e. 50 units of eggs.

11. If the economy were operating at point E,
    a. the opportunity cost of 20 additional units of eggs is 10 units of bacon.
    b. the opportunity cost of 20 additional units of eggs is 20 units of bacon.
    c. the opportunity cost of 20 additional units of eggs is 30 units of bacon.
    d. 20 additional units of eggs can be produced with no impact on bacon production.

12. Point F represents
    a. a combination of production that can be reached if we reduce the production of eggs by 20 units.
    b. a combination of production that is inefficient because there are unemployed resources.
    c. a combination of production that can be reached if there is a sufficient advance in technology.
    d. none of the above.

13. As we move from point A to point D,
    a. the opportunity cost of eggs in terms of bacon is constant.
    b. the opportunity cost of eggs in terms of bacon falls.
    c. the opportunity cost of eggs in terms of bacon rises.
    d. the economy becomes more efficient.
    e. the economy becomes less efficient.

14. Which of the following issues is related to microeconomics?
    a. the impact of money on inflation
    b. the impact of technology on economic growth
    c. the impact of the deficit on saving
    d. the impact of oil prices on auto production

15. Which of the following statements about microeconomics and macroeconomics is not true?
    a. The study of very large industries is a topic within macroeconomics.
    b. Macroeconomics is concerned with economy-wide phenomena.
    c. Microeconomics is a building block for macroeconomics.
    d. Microeconomics and macroeconomics cannot be entirely separated.

16. Which of the following statements is normative?
    a. Printing too much money causes inflation.
    b. People work harder if the wage is higher.
    c. The unemployment rate should be lower.
    d. Large government deficits cause an economy to grow more slowly.

17. In making which of the following statements is an economist acting more like a scientist?
    a. A reduction in unemployment benefits will reduce the unemployment rate.
    b. The unemployment rate should be reduced because unemployment robs individuals of their dignity.
    c. The rate of inflation should be reduced because it robs the elderly of their savings.
    d. The state should increase subsidies to universities because the future of our country depends on education.

18. Positive statements are
    a. microeconomic.
    b. macroeconomic.
    c. statements of prescription that involve value judgments.
    d. statements of description that can be tested.

19. Suppose two economists are arguing about policies that deal with unemployment. One economist says, "The government should fight unemployment because it is the greatest social evil." The other economists responds, "Hogwash. Inflation is the greatest social evil." These economists
    a. disagree because they have different scientific judgments.
    b. disagree because they have different values.
    c. really don't disagree at all. It just looks that way.
    d. none of the above

20. Suppose two economists are arguing about policies that deal with unemployment. One economist says, "The government could lower unemployment by one percentage point if it would just increase government spending by 50 billion dollars." The other economist responds, "Hogwash. If the government spent an additional 50 billion dollars, it would reduce unemployment by only one tenth of one percent, and that effect would only be temporary!" These economists
    a. disagree because they have different scientific judgments.
    b. disagree because they have different values.
    c. really don't disagree at all. It just looks that way.
    d. none of the above

ADVANCED CRITICAL THINKING

You are watching the McNeil News Hour on public television. The first focus segment is a discussion of the pros and cons of free trade (lack of obstructions to international trade). For balance, there are two economists present—one in support of free trade and one opposed. Your roommate says, "Those economists have no idea what's going on. They can't agree on anything. One says free trade makes us rich. The other says it will drive us into poverty. If the experts don't know, how is the average person ever going to know whether free trade is best?"

1. Can you give your roommate any insight into why economists might disagree on this issue?

    ____

    ____

    ____

2. Suppose you discover that 93 percent of economists believe that free trade is generally best (which is the greatest agreement on any single issue). Could you now give a more precise answer as to why economists might disagree on this issue?

____

____

____

3. What if you later discovered that the economist opposed to free trade worked for a labor union. Would that help you explain why there appears to be a difference of opinion on this issue?

____

____

____

SOLUTIONS

Terms and Definitions

_3_ Scientific method

_8_ Economic models

_11_ Circular-flow diagram

_1_ Factors of production

_9_ Production possibilities frontier

_4_ Opportunity cost

_6_ Efficiency

_10_ Microeconomics

_2_ Macroeconomics

_7_ Positive Statements

_5_ Normative Statements

Practice Problems

1. a. $20,000 of spending from households to market for goods and services. Car moves from market for goods and services to household. $20,000 of revenue from market for goods and services to firms while car moves from firm to market for goods and services.
   b. $5,000 of wages from firms to market for factors of production. Inputs move from market for factors of production to firms. Labor moves from households to market for factors of production while $5,000 income moves from market for factors to households.
   c. $15 of spending from households to market for goods and services. Service moves from market for goods and services to household. Service moves from firms to market for goods and services in return for $15 revenue.
   d. $10,000 of profit from firms to market for factors of production. Inputs move from market for factors of production to firms. Capital services move from households to market for factors of production in return for $10,000 income.

2. a. See Exhibit 7.
   b. 40 rackets
   c. 100 rackets
   d. Because as we produce more bats, the resources best suited for making bats are already being used. Therefore it takes even more resources to produce 100 bats and greater reductions in racket production.
   e. 200 bats; 160 rackets
   f. No. Resources were not used efficiently if production can be increased with no opportunity cost.

3. a. Parsimonious country. Capital (plant and equipment) is a factor of production and producing more of it now will increase future production.
   b. Fewer consumption goods are produced now.
   c. See Exhibit 8. The production possibilities curve will shift more for Parsimonious Country because they have experienced a greater increase in factors of production (capital).
   d. See Exhibit 9.
   e. No, the outward shift improves choices available for both consumption and capital goods.

EXHIBIT 7

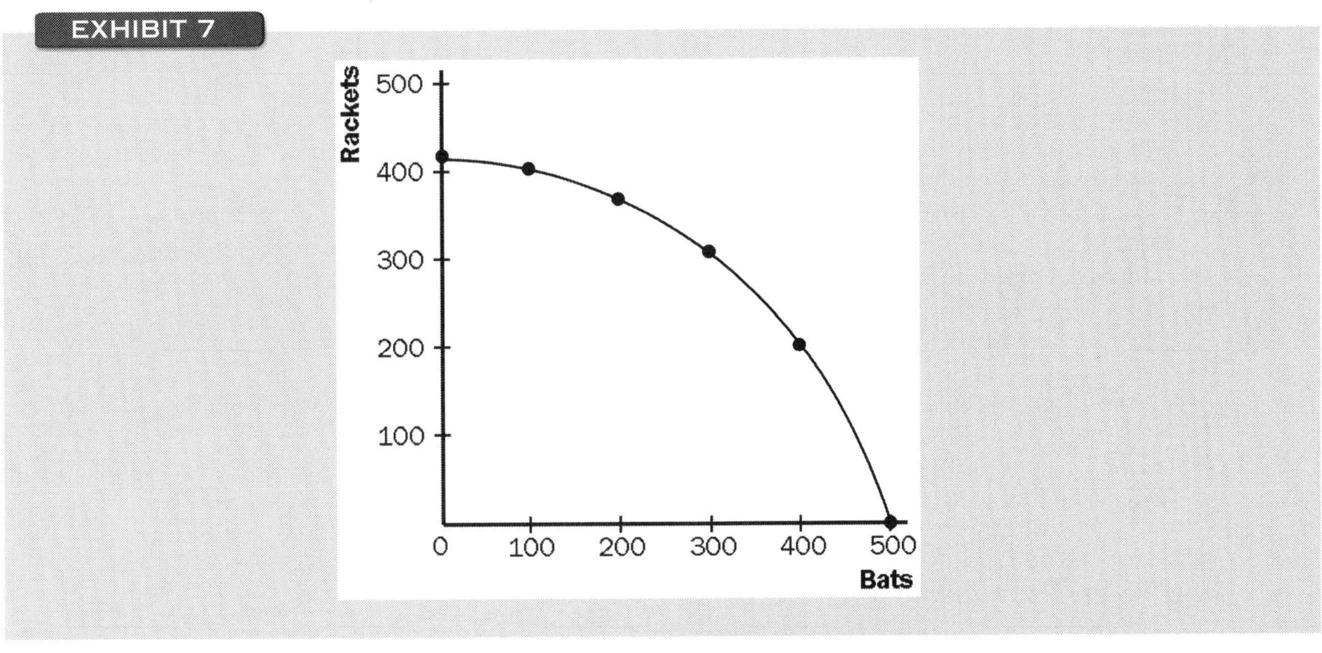

EXHIBIT 8

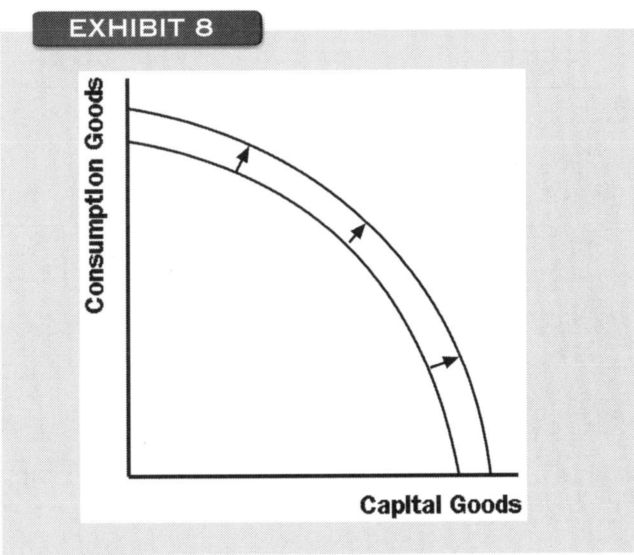

EXHIBIT 9

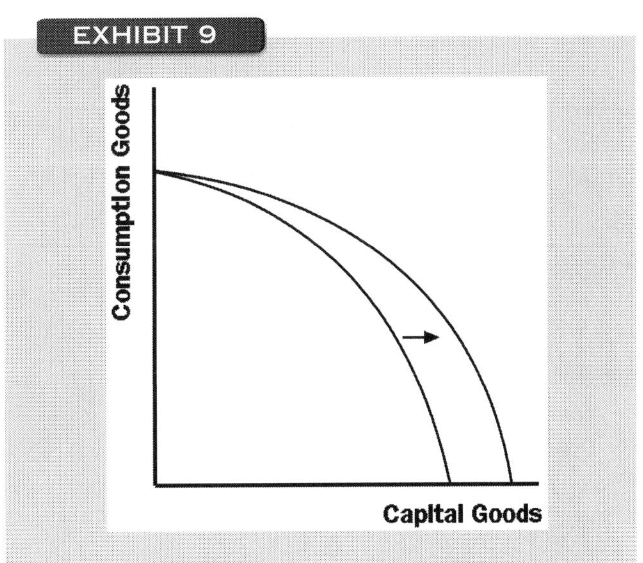

Short-Answer Questions

1. The dispassionate development and testing of theory by observing, testing, and observing again.
2. To simplify reality so that we can focus our thinking on what is actually important.
3. Not necessarily. Realistic models are more complex. They may be confusing and they may fail to focus on what is important.
4. Because if an economy is operating efficiently, production choices have opportunity costs. If we want more of one thing, we must have less of another.

5. Because resources are specialized and, thus, are not equally well-suited for producing different outputs.

6. Microeconomics and macroeconomics. Microeconomics is more of a building block of macro because when we address macro issues (say unemployment) we have to consider how individuals respond to work incentives such as wages and welfare.

7. As a policy advisor because normative statements are prescriptions about what ought to be and are somewhat based on value judgments.

8. Positive statements are statements of fact and are refutable by examining evidence.

9. Economists may have different scientific judgments. Economists may have different values.

10. A ceiling on rents reduces the quantity and quality of housing available. Tariffs and import quotas usually reduce general economic welfare.

True/False Questions

1. F; economic models are simplifications of reality.

2. T

3. F; there must be at least two individuals for trade.

4. T

5. T

6. T

7. F; points outside the production possibilities frontier cannot yet be attained.

8. T

9. F; it is bowed outward because the tradeoffs are not constant.

10. T

11. F; macroeconomics is the study of economy-wide phenomena.

12. F; this statement is positive.

13. T

14. F; normative statements cannot be refuted.

15. T

Multiple-Choice Questions

1. b	6. d	11.d	16. c
2. c	7. a	12. c	17. a
3. a	8. c	13. c	18. d
4. d	9. b	14. d	19. b
5. b	10. b	15. a	20. a

Advanced Critical Thinking

1. Economists may have different scientific judgments. Economists may have different values. There may not really be any real disagreement because the majority of economists may actually agree.

2. Those opposed to free trade are likely to have different values than the majority of economists. There is not much disagreement on this issue among the mainstream economics profession.

3. Yes. It suggests that impediments to international trade may benefit some groups (organized labor) but these impediments are unlikely to benefit the public in general. Supporters of these policies are promoting their own interests.

APPENDIX

Practice Problems

1. The following ordered pairs of price and quantity demanded describe Joe's demand for cups of gourmet coffee.

Price per Cup of Coffee	Quantity Demanded of Coffee
$5	2 cups
4	4 cups
3	6 cups
2	8 cups
1	10 cups

a. Plot and connect the ordered pairs on the graph in Exhibit 10.

EXHIBIT 10

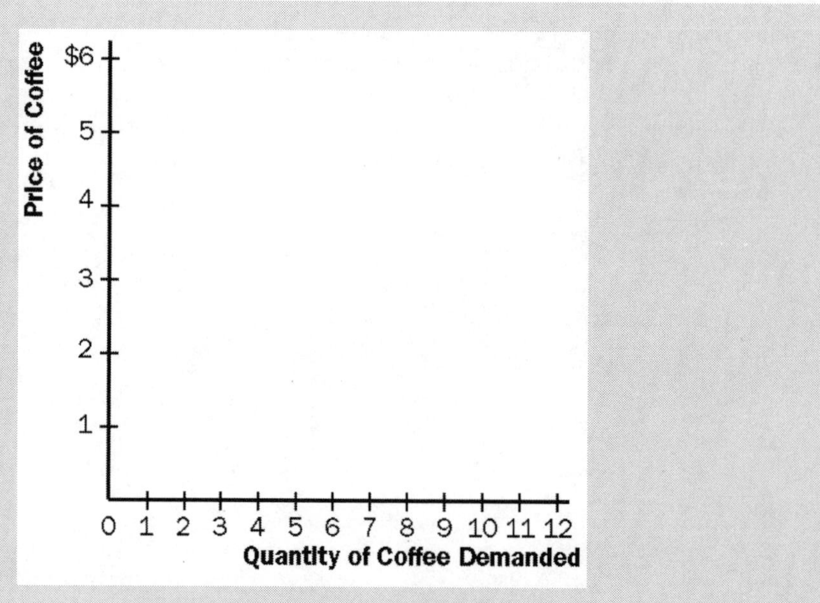

b. What is the slope of Joe's demand curve for coffee in the price range of $5 and $4?

____

c. What is the slope of Joe's demand curve for coffee in the price range of $2 and $1?

____

d. Are the price of coffee and Joe's quantity demanded of coffee positively correlated or negatively correlated? How can you tell?

____

____

e. If the price of coffee moves from $2 per cup to $4 per cup, what happens to the quantity demanded? Is this a movement along a curve or a shift in the curve?

____

____

f. Suppose Joe's income doubles from $20,000 per year to $40,000 per year. Now the following ordered pairs describe Joe's demand for gourmet coffee. Plot these ordered pairs on the graph provided in part (a) above.

Price per cup of coffee	Quantity demanded of coffee
$5	4 cups
4	6 cups
3	8 cups
2	10 cups
1	12 cups

g. Did the doubling of Joe's income cause a movement along his demand curve or a shift in his demand curve? Why?

____

____

2. An alien lands on earth and observes the following: on mornings when people carry umbrellas, it tends to rain later in the day. The alien concludes that umbrellas cause rain.
   a. What error has the alien committed?

   ____

   b. What role did *expectations* play in the alien's error?

   ____

   ____

   c. If rain is truly caused by humidity, temperature, wind currents, and so on, what additional type of error has the alien committed when it decided that umbrellas cause rain?

   ____

True/False Questions

_____ 1. When graphing in the coordinate system, the x-coordinate tells us the horizontal location while the y-coordinate tells us the vertical location of the point.

_____ 2. When a line slopes upward in the x, y coordinate system, the two variables measured on each axis are positively correlated.

_____ 3. Price and quantity demanded for most goods are positively related.

_____ 4. If three variables are related, one of them must be held constant when graphing the other two in the x, y coordinate system.

_____ 5. If three variables are related, a change in the variable not represented on the x, y coordinate system will cause a movement along the curve drawn in the x, y coordinate system.

_____ 6. The slope of a line is equal to the change in y divided by the change in x along the line.

_____ 7. When a line has negative slope, the two variables measured on each axis are positively correlated.

_____ 8. There is a positive correlation between lying down and death. If we conclude from this evidence that it is unsafe to lie down, we have an *omitted variable* problem because critically ill people tend to lie down.

_____ 9. Reverse causality means that while we think A causes B, B may actually cause A.

_____10. Since people carry umbrellas to work in the morning and it rains later in the afternoon, carrying umbrellas must cause rain.

SOLUTIONS FOR APPENDIX

Practice Problems

1. a. See Exhibit 11.
   b. –1/2
   c. –1/2
   d. Negatively correlated, because an increase in price is associated with a decrease in quantity demanded. That is, the demand curve slopes negatively.
   e. Decrease by 4 cups. Movement along curve.
   f. See Exhibit 12.
   g. Shift in curve because a variable changed (income) which is not measured on either axis.

2. a. Reverse causality.
   b. Since rain can be predicted, people's expectation of rain causes them to carry umbrellas *before* it rains, making it appear as if umbrellas cause rain.
   c. Omitted variables.

EXHIBIT 11

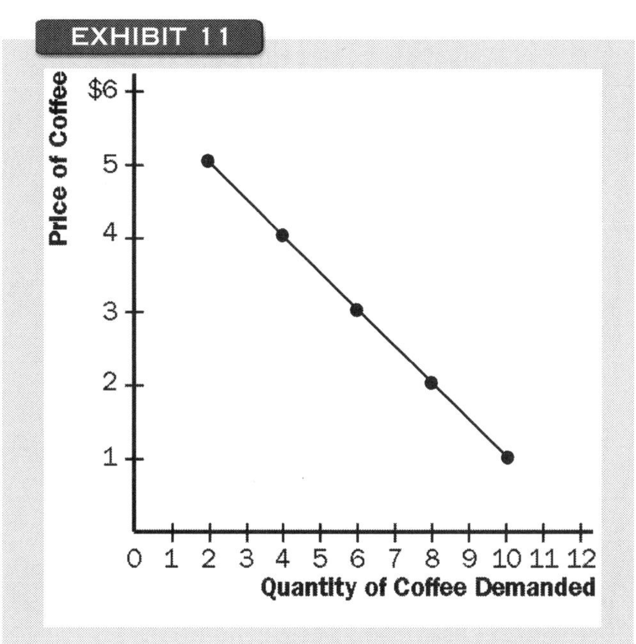

EXHIBIT 12

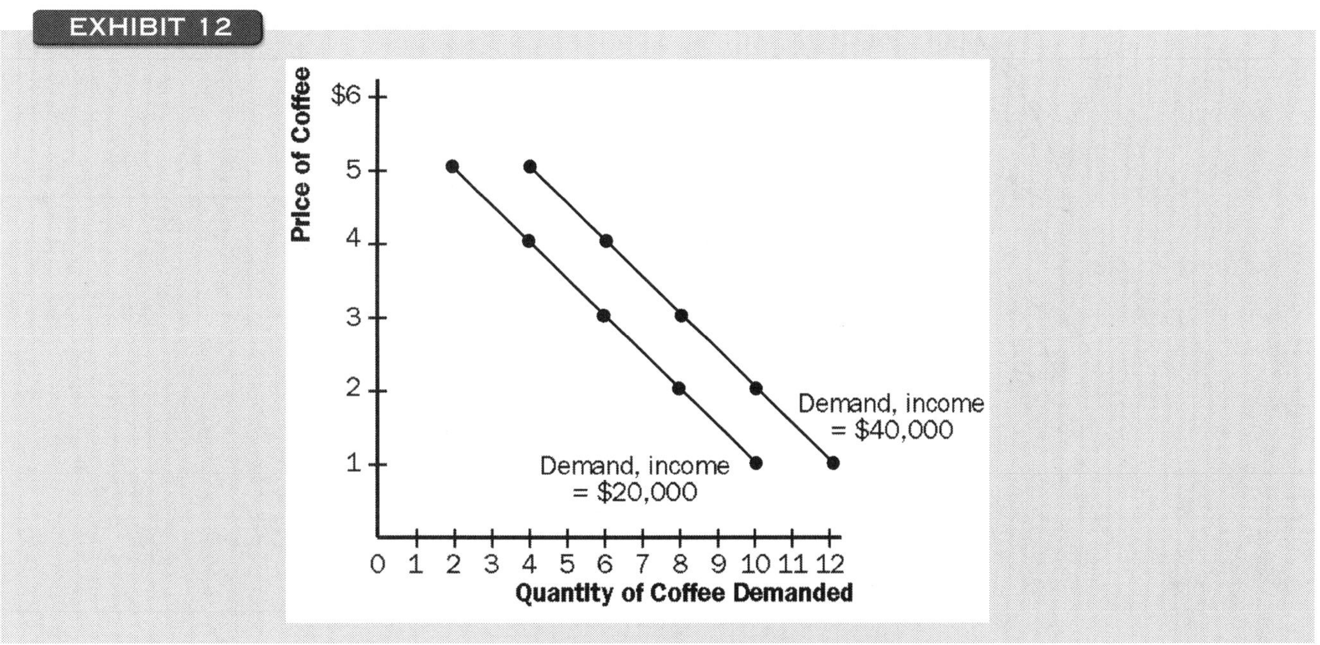

True/False Questions

1. T

2. T
3. F; they are negatively correlated.
4. T
5. F; a change in a variable not represented on the graph will cause a shift in the curve.
6. T
7. F; negative slope implies negative correlation.
8. T
9. T
10. F; this is an example of reverse causation.

3

INTERDEPENDENCE AND THE GAINS FROM TRADE

GOALS

In this chapter you will

Consider how everyone can benefit when people trade with one another

Learn the meaning of absolute advantage and comparative advantage

See how comparative advantage explains the gains from trade

Apply the theory of comparative advantage to everyday life and national policy

OUTCOMES

After accomplishing these goals, you should be able to

Define scarcity

Show how total production rises when individuals specialize in the production of goods for which they have a comparative advantage

Explain why all people have a comparative advantage even if they have no absolute advantage

Demonstrate the link between comparative advantage and opportunity cost

Explain why people who are good at everything still tend to specialize

CHAPTER OVERVIEW

Context and Purpose

Chapter 3 is the third chapter in the three-chapter section that serves as the introduction of the text. The first chapter introduced ten fundamental principles of economics. The second chapter developed how economists approach problems. This chapter shows how people and countries gain from trade (which is one of the ten principles discussed in Chapter 1).

The purpose of Chapter 3 is to demonstrate how everyone can gain from trade. Trade allows people to specialize in the production of goods for which they have a comparative advantage and then trade for goods other people produce. Because of specialization, total output rises and through trade we are all able to share in the bounty. This is as true for countries as it is for individuals. Since everyone can gain from trade, restrictions on trade tend to reduce welfare.

CHAPTER REVIEW

Introduction

Each of us consumes products every day that were produced in a number of different countries. Complex products contain components that were produced in many different countries so these products have no single country of origin.

Those who produce are neither generous nor ordered by government to produce. People produce because they wish to trade and get something in return. Hence, trade makes us interdependent.

A Parable for the Modern Economy

Imagine a simple economy. There are two people—a cattle rancher and a potato farmer. There are two goods—meat and potatoes.

- If each can produce only one product (the rancher can produce only meat and the farmer potatoes) they will trade just to increase the variety of products they consume. Each benefits because of increased variety.

- If each can produce both goods, but each is more efficient than the other at producing one good, then each will specialize in what he or she does best (again the rancher produces meat and the farmer produces potatoes), total output will rise, and they will trade. Trade allows each to benefit because trade allows for specialization, and specialization increases the total production available to share.

- If one producer is better than the other at producing *both* meat and potatoes, there are the same advantages to trade but it is more difficult to see. Again, trade allows each to benefit because trade allows for specialization, and specialization increases the total production available to share. To understand the source of the gains from trade when one producer is better at producing both products, we must understand the concept of comparative advantage.

The Principle of Comparative Advantage

To understand **comparative advantage,** we begin with the concept of **absolute advantage.** Absolute advantage compares the quantity of inputs required to produce a good. The producer that requires fewer resources (say fewer hours worked) to produce a good is said to have an absolute advantage in the production of that good. That is, the most efficient producer (the one with the highest productivity) has an absolute advantage.

While absolute advantage compares the actual cost of production for each producer, *comparative advantage* compares **opportunity costs** of production for each producer. The producer with the lower opportunity cost of production is said to have a comparative advantage. Regardless of absolute advantage, if producers have *different opportunity costs* of production for each good, each should specialize in the production of the good for which their opportunity cost of production is lower. That is, each producer should produce the item for which they have a comparative advantage. They can then trade some of their output for the other good. Trade makes both producers better off because trade allows for specialization, and specialization increases the total production available to be shared.

The decision to specialize and the resulting gains from trade are based on comparative advantage, not absolute advantage. Although a single producer can have an absolute advantage in the production of both goods, he/she cannot have a comparative advantage in the production of both goods because a low opportunity cost of producing one good implies a high opportunity cost of producing the other good.

In summary, trade allows producers to exploit the differences in their opportunity costs of production. Each specializes in the production of the good for which they have the lower opportunity cost of production and, thus, a comparative advantage. This increases total production and makes the economic pie larger. Everyone can benefit. The additional production generated by specialization is the gain from trade.

Adam Smith in his 1776 book, *An Inquiry into the Nature and Causes of the Wealth of Nations,* and David Ricardo in his 1817 book, *Principles of Political Economy and Taxation,* both recognized the gains from trade through specialization and the principle of comparative advantage. Current arguments for free trade are still based on their work.

Applications of Comparative Advantage

The principle of comparative advantage applies to individuals as well as countries.

Recall, absolute advantage does not determine specialization in production. For example, Tiger Woods may have an absolute advantage in both golf and lawn mowing. However, because he can earn $5,000/hour playing golf, he is better off paying someone to mow his lawn (even if they do it more slowly than he) as long as he can get someone to do it for less than $5,000/hour. This is because the opportunity cost of an hour of mowing for Tiger Woods is $5,000. Tiger Woods will likely specialize in golf and trade for other services. He does this because he has a comparative advantage in golf and a comparative disadvantage in lawn mowing even though he has an absolute advantage in both.

Trade between countries is subject to the same principle of comparative advantage. Goods produced abroad and sold domestically are called **imports.** Goods produced domestically and sold abroad are called **exports.** Even if the United States has an absolute advantage in the production of both cars and food, it should specialize in the production of the item for which it has a comparative advantage. Since the opportunity cost of food is low in the United States (better land) and high in Japan, the United States should produce more food and export it to Japan in exchange for imports of autos from Japan. While the U.S. gains from trade, the impact of trade on U.S. autoworkers is different from the impact of trade on U.S. farmers.

A reduction in barriers to free trade improves the welfare of the importing country *as a whole* but it does not improve the welfare of the domestic producers in the importing country. For this reason, domestic producers lobby their governments to maintain (or increase) barriers to free trade. For example, the American Sheep Industry Association has been able to maintain barriers to the importing of lamb to the detriment of the American consumer.

HELPFUL HINTS

1. A step by step example of comparative advantage will demonstrate most of the concepts discussed in Chapter 3. It will give you a pattern to follow when answering questions at the end of the chapter in your text and for the problems that follow in this Study Guide.

   Suppose we have the following information about the productivity of industry in Japan and Korea. The data are the units of output per hour of work.

	Steel	Televisions
Japan	6	3
Korea	8	2

EXHIBIT 1

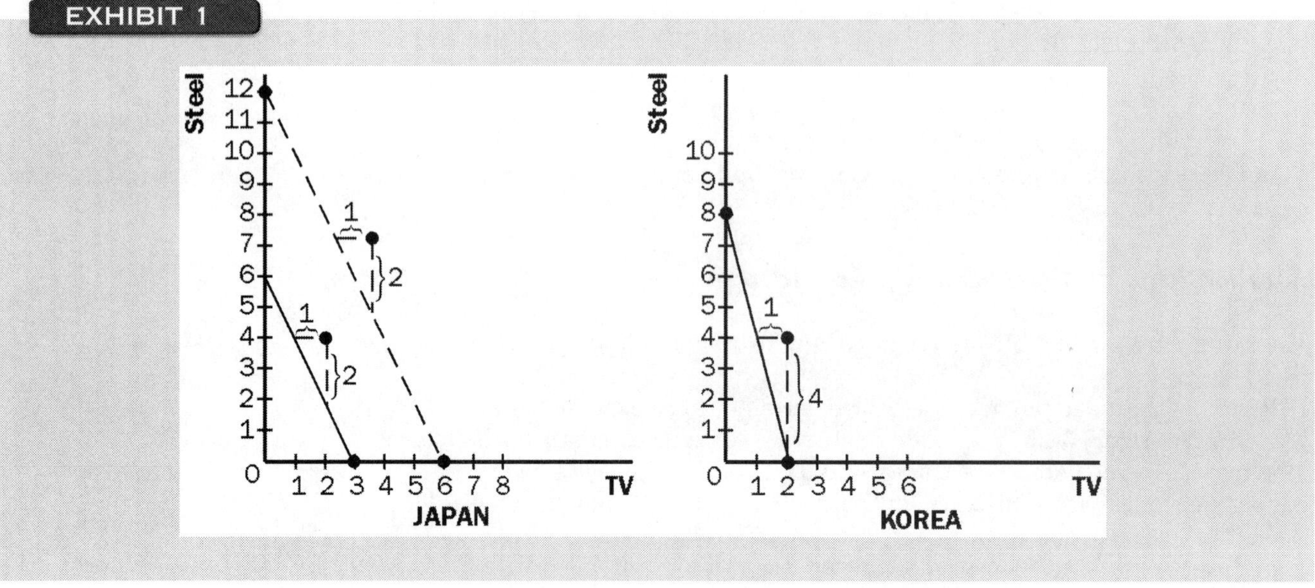

A Japanese worker can produce 6 units of steel or 3 TVs per hour. A Korean worker can produce 8 units of steel or 2 TVs per hour.

We can plot the production possibilities frontier for each country assuming each country has only one worker and the worker works only one hour. To plot the frontier, plot the end points and connect them with a line. For example, Japan can produce 6 units of steel with its worker or 3 TVs. It can also allocate one half hour to the production of each and get 3 units steel and 1 1/2 TVs. Any other proportion of the hour can be allocated to the two productive activities. The production possibilities frontier is linear in these cases because the labor resource can be moved from the production of one good to the other at a constant rate. We can do the same for Korea. Without trade, the production possibilities frontier is the consumption possibilities frontier, too.

Comparative advantage determines specialization and trade. The opportunity cost of a TV in Japan is 2 units of steel, which is shown by the slope of the production possibilities frontier in Exhibit 1. Alternatively, the opportunity cost of one unit of steel in Japan is 1/2 of a TV. In Korea, the opportunity cost of a TV is 4 units of steel and the cost of a unit of steel is 1/4 of a TV. Since the opportunity cost of a TV is lower in Japan, Japan has a comparative advantage in TV production and should specialize in TVs. Since the opportunity cost of steel is lower in Korea, Korea has a comparative advantage in steel production and should specialize in steel.

What is the range of prices at which each country would be willing to exchange? If Japan specializes in TV production and produces 3 televisions, it would be willing to trade TVs for steel as long as the price of steel is below 1/2 TV per unit of steel because that was the Japanese price for a unit of steel prior to trade. Korea would be willing to specialize in steel production and trade for TVs as long as the price of a TV is less than 4 units of steel because that was the Korean price of a TV prior to trade. In short, the final price must be between the original tradeoffs each faced in the absence of trade. One TV will cost between 2 and 4 of units of steel. One unit of steel will cost between 1/2 and 1/4 of a TV.

2. Trade allows countries to consume outside their original production possibilities frontier. Suppose that Japan and Korea settle on a trading price of 3 units of steel for 1 TV (or 1/3 of a TV for 1 unit of steel). (I am giving you this price. There is nothing in the problem that would let you calculate the final trading price. You can only calculate the range in which it must lie.) This price is halfway between the two prices that each faces in the absence of trade. The range for the trading price is 4 units of steel for 1 TV to 2 units of steel for 1 TV.

   If Japan specializes in TV production, produces 3 televisions, and exports 1 TV for 3 units of steel, Japan will be able to consume 2 TVs and 3 units of steel. If we plot this point (2 TVs and 3 steel) on Japan's graph, we see that it lies outside its production possibilities frontier. If Korea specializes, produces 8 units of steel, and exports 3 units for 1 TV, Korea will be able to consume 5 units of steel and 1 TV. If we plot this point (5 steel and 1 TV) on Korea's graph, we see that it also lies outside its production possibilities frontier.

   This is the gain from trade. Trade allows countries (and people) to specialize. Specialization increases world output. After trading, countries consume outside their individual production possibilities frontiers. In this way, trade is like an improvement in technology. It allows countries to move beyond their current production possibilities frontiers.

3. Only comparative advantage matters—absolute advantage is irrelevant. In the previous example, Japan had an absolute advantage in the production of TVs because it could produce 3 per hour while Korea could only produce 2. Korea had an absolute advantage in the production of steel because it could produce 8 units per hour compared to 6 for Japan.

   To demonstrate that comparative advantage, not absolute advantage, determines specialization and trade, we alter the previous example so that Japan has an absolute advantage in the production of both goods. To this end, suppose Japan becomes twice as productive as in the previous table. That is, a worker can now produce 12 units of steel or 6 TVs per hour.

	Steel	**Televisions**
Japan	12	6
Korea	8	2

Now Japan has an absolute advantage in the production of both goods. Japan's new production possibilities frontier is the dashed line in Exhibit 1. Will this change the analysis? Not at all. The opportunity cost of each good within Japan is the same—2 units of steel per TV or 1/2 TV per unit of steel (and Korea is unaffected). For this reason, Japan still has the identical comparative advantage as before and it will specialize in TV production while Korea will specialize in steel. However, since productivity has doubled in Japan, its entire set of choices has improved and, thus, its material welfare has improved.

TERMS AND DEFINITIONS

Choose a definition for each key term.

Key terms:

______Absolute advantage

______Comparative advantage

______Gains from trade

______Opportunity cost

______Imports

______Exports

Definitions:

1. Whatever is given up to obtain some item
2. The comparison among producers of a good based on their opportunity cost
3. Goods produced domestically and sold abroad
4. Goods produced abroad and sold domestically
5. The comparison among producers of a good based on their productivity
6. The increase in total production due to specialization allowed by trade

PROBLEMS AND SHORT-ANSWER QUESTIONS

Practice Problems

1. Angela is a college student. She takes a full load of classes and has only 5 hours per week for her hobby. Angela is artistic and can make 2 clay pots per hour or 4 coffee mugs per hour.
   a. Draw Angela's production possibilities frontier for pots and mugs.

EXHIBIT 2

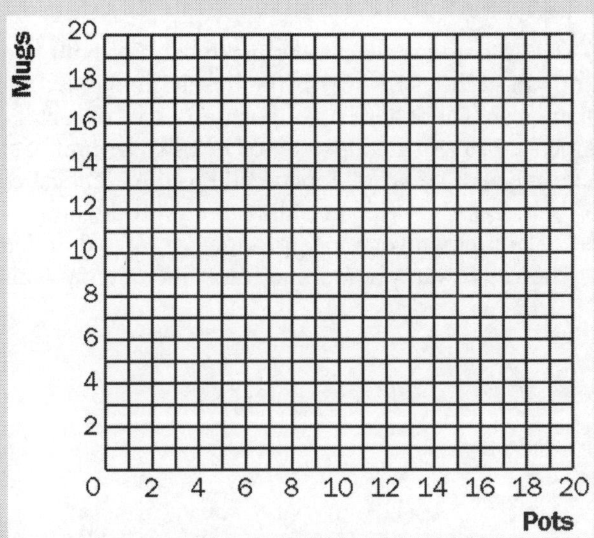

b. What is Angela's opportunity cost of 1 pot? 10 pots?

____

c. What is Angela's opportunity cost of 1 mug? 10 mugs?

____

d. Why is her production possibilities frontier a straight line instead of bowed out like those presented in Chapter 2?

____

____

2. Suppose a worker in Germany can produce 15 computers or 5 tons of grain per month. Suppose a worker in Poland can produce 4 computers or 4 tons of grain per month. For simplicity, assume that each country has only one worker.

a. Fill out the following table:

	Computers	Grain
Germany	______	______
Poland	______	______

EXHIBIT 3

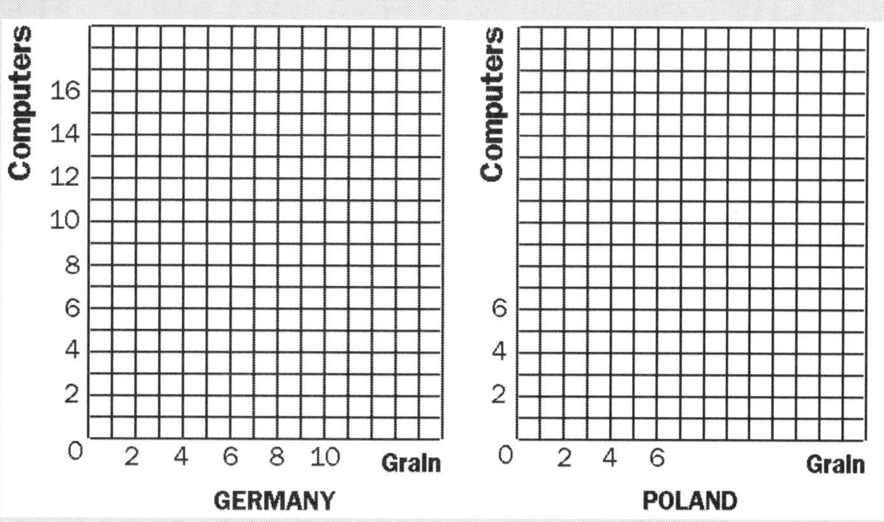

b. Graph the production possibilities frontier for each country in Exhibit 3.

c. What is the opportunity cost of a computer in Germany? What is the opportunity cost of a ton of grain in Germany?

____

____

d. What is the opportunity cost of a computer in Poland? What is the opportunity cost of a ton of grain in Poland?

e. Which country has the absolute advantage in producing computers? Grain?

f. Which country has the comparative advantage in producing computers? Grain?

g. Each country should tend toward specialization in the production of which good? Why?

h. What is the range of prices for computers and grain for which both countries would benefit?

i. Suppose Germany and Poland settle on a price of 2 computers for 1 ton of grain or 1/2 ton of grain for a computer. Suppose each country specializes in production and they trade 4 computers for 2 tons of grain. Plot the final consumption points on the graphs you made in part (b) above. Are these countries consuming inside or outside of their production possibilities frontier?

j. Suppose the productivity of a worker in Poland doubles so that a worker can produce 8 computers or 8 tons of grain per month. Which country has the absolute advantage in producing computers? Grain?

____

____

k. After the doubling of productivity in Poland, which country has a comparative advantage in producing computers? Grain? Has the comparative advantage changed? Has the material welfare of either country changed?

____

____

____

____

l. How would your analysis change if you assumed, more realistically, that each country had 10 million workers?

____

____

____

3. Suppose a worker in the United States can produce 4 cars or 20 computers per month while a worker in Russia can produce 1 car or 5 computers per month. Again, for simplicity, assume each country has only one worker.
a. Fill out the following table:

	Cars	Computers
United States	______	______
Russia	______	______

b. Which country has the absolute advantage in the production of cars? Computers?

____

____

c. Which country has the comparative advantage in the production of cars? Computers?

____

____

____

d. Are there any gains to be made from trade? Why?

e. Does your answer in (d) above help you pinpoint a source for gains from trade?

f. What might make two countries have different opportunity costs of production? (Use your imagination. This was not directly discussed in Chapter 3.)

SHORT-ANSWER QUESTIONS

1. Why do people choose to become interdependent as opposed to self-sufficient?

2. Why is comparative advantage important in determining trade instead of absolute advantage?

3. What are the gains from trade?

4. Why is a restriction of trade likely to reduce material welfare?

____

____

5. Suppose a lawyer that earns $200 per hour can also type at 200 words per minute. Should the lawyer hire a secretary who can only types 50 words per minute? Why?

____

____

____

6. Evaluate this statement: A technologically advanced country, which is better than its neighbor at producing everything, would be better off if it closed its borders to trade because the less productive country is a burden to the advanced country.

____

____

____

____

SELF-TEST

True/False Questions

_____ 1. If Japan has an absolute advantage in the production of an item, it must also have a comparative advantage in the production of that item.

_____ 2. Comparative advantage, not absolute advantage, determines the decision to specialize in production.

_____ 3. Absolute advantage is a comparison based on productivity.

_____ 4. Self-sufficiency is the best way to increase one's material welfare.

_____ 5. Comparative advantage is a comparison based on opportunity cost.

_____ 6. If a producer is self-sufficient, the production possibilities frontier is also the consumption possibilities frontier.

_____ 7. If a country's workers can produce 5 hamburgers per hour or 10 bags of French fries per hour, absent trade, the price of 1 bag of fries is 2 hamburgers.

_____ 8. If producers have different opportunity costs of production, trade will allow them to consume outside their production possibilities frontiers.

_____ 9. If trade benefits one country, its trading partner must be worse off due to trade.

_____10. Talented people that are the best at everything have a comparative advantage in the production of everything.

_____11. The gains from trade can be measured by the increase in total production that comes from specialization.

_____12. When a country removes a specific import restriction, it always benefits every worker in that country.

_____13. If Germany's productivity doubles for everything it produces, this will not alter its prior pattern of specialization because it has not altered its comparative advantage.

_____14. If an advanced country has an absolute advantage in the production of everything, it will benefit if it eliminates trade with less developed countries and becomes completely self-sufficient.

_____15. If gains from trade are based solely on comparative advantage, and if all countries have the same opportunity costs of production, then there are no gains from trade.

Multiple-Choice Questions

1. If a nation has an absolute advantage in the production of a good,
   a. it can produce that good at a lower opportunity cost than its trading partner.
   b. it can produce that good using fewer resources than its trading partner.
   c. it can benefit by restricting imports of that good.
   d. it will specialize in the production of that good and export it.
   e. none of the above.

2. If a nation has a comparative advantage in the production of a good,
   a. it can produce that good at a lower opportunity cost than its trading partner.
   b. it can produce that good using fewer resources than its trading partner.
   c. it can benefit by restricting imports of that good.
   d. it must be the only country with the ability to produce that good.
   e. none of the above.

3. Which of the following statements about trade is true?
   a. Unrestricted international trade benefits every person in a country equally.
   b. People that are skilled at all activities cannot benefit from trade.
   c. Trade can benefit everyone in society because it allows people to specialize in activities in which they have an absolute advantage.
   d. Trade can benefit everyone in society because it allows people to specialize in activities in which they have a comparative advantage.

4. According to the principle of comparative advantage,
   a. countries with a comparative advantage in the production of every good need not specialize.
   b. countries should specialize in the production of goods that they enjoy consuming.
   c. countries should specialize in the production of goods for which they use fewer resources in production than their trading partners.
   d. countries should specialize in the production of goods for which they have a lower opportunity cost of production than their trading partners.

5. Which of the following statements is true?
   a. Self-sufficiency is the road to prosperity for most countries.
   b. A self-sufficient country consumes outside its production possibilities frontier.
   c. A self-sufficient country can, at best, consume on its production possibilities frontier.
   d. Only countries with an absolute advantage in the production of every good should strive to be self-sufficient.

6. Suppose a country's workers can produce 4 watches per hour or 12 rings per hour. If there is no trade,
   a. the domestic price of 1 ring is 3 watches.
   b. the domestic price of 1 ring is 1/3 of a watch.
   c. the domestic price of 1 ring is 4 watches.
   d. the domestic price of 1 ring is 1/4 of a watch.
   e. the domestic price of 1 ring is 12 watches.

7. Suppose a country's workers can produce 4 watches per hour or 12 rings per hour. If there is no trade,
   a. the opportunity cost of 1 watch is 3 rings.
   b. the opportunity cost of 1 watch is 1/3 of a ring.
   c. the opportunity cost of 1 watch is 4 rings.
   d. the opportunity cost of 1 watch is 1/4 of a ring.
   e. the opportunity cost of 1 watch is 12 rings.

The following table shows the units of output a worker can produce per month in Australia and Korea. Use this table for questions 8 through 15.

	Food	Electronics
Australia	20	5
Korea	8	4

8. Which of the following statements about absolute advantage is true?
   a. Australia has an absolute advantage in the production of food while Korea has an absolute advantage in the production of electronics.
   b. Korea has an absolute advantage in the production of food while Australia has an absolute advantage in the production of electronics.
   c. Australia has an absolute advantage in the production of both food and electronics.
   d. Korea has an absolute advantage in the production of both food and electronics.

9. The opportunity cost of 1 unit of electronics in Australia is
   a. 5 units of food.
   b. 1/5 of a unit of food.
   c. 4 units of food.
   d. 1/4 of a unit of food.

10. The opportunity cost of 1 unit of electronics in Korea is
    a. 2 units of food.
    b. 1/2 of a unit of food.
    c. 4 units of food.
    d. 1/4 units of food.

11. The opportunity cost of 1 unit of food in Australia is
    a. 5 units of electronics.
    b. 1/5 of a unit of electronics.
    c. 4 units of electronics.
    d. 1/4 of a unit of electronics.

12. The opportunity cost of 1 unit of food in Korea is
    a. 2 units of electronics.
    b. 1/2 of a unit of electronics.
    c. 4 units of electronics.
    d. 1/4 units of electronics.

13. Which of the following statements about comparative advantage is true?
    a. Australia has a comparative advantage in the production of food while Korea has a comparative advantage in the production of electronics.
    b. Korea has a comparative advantage in the production of food while Australia has a comparative advantage in the production of electronics.
    c. Australia has a comparative advantage in the production of both food and electronics.
    d. Korea has a comparative advantage in the production of both food and electronics.
    e. Neither country has a comparative advantage.

14. Korea should
    a. specialize in food production, export food, and import electronics.
    b. specialize in electronics production, export electronics, and import food.
    c. produce both goods because neither country has a comparative advantage.
    d. produce neither good because it has an absolute disadvantage in the production of both goods.

15. Prices of electronics can be stated in terms of units of food. What is the range of prices of electronics for which both countries could gain from trade?
    a. The price must be greater than 1/5 of a unit of food but less than 1/4 of a unit of food.
    b. The price must be greater than 4 units of food but less than 5 units of food.
    c. The price must be greater than 1/4 of a unit of food but less than 1/2 of a unit of food.
    d. The price must be greater than 2 units of food but less than 4 units of food.

16. Suppose the world consists of two countries—the U.S. and Mexico. Further, suppose there are only two goods—food and clothing. Which of the following statements is true?
    a. If the U.S. has an absolute advantage in the production of food, then Mexico must have an absolute advantage in the production of clothing.
    b. If the U.S. has a comparative advantage in the production of food, then Mexico must have a comparative advantage in the production of clothing.
    c. If the U.S. has a comparative advantage in the production of food, it must also have a comparative advantage in the production of clothing.
    d. If the U.S. has a comparative advantage in the production of food, Mexico might also have a comparative advantage in the production of food.
    e. none of the above.

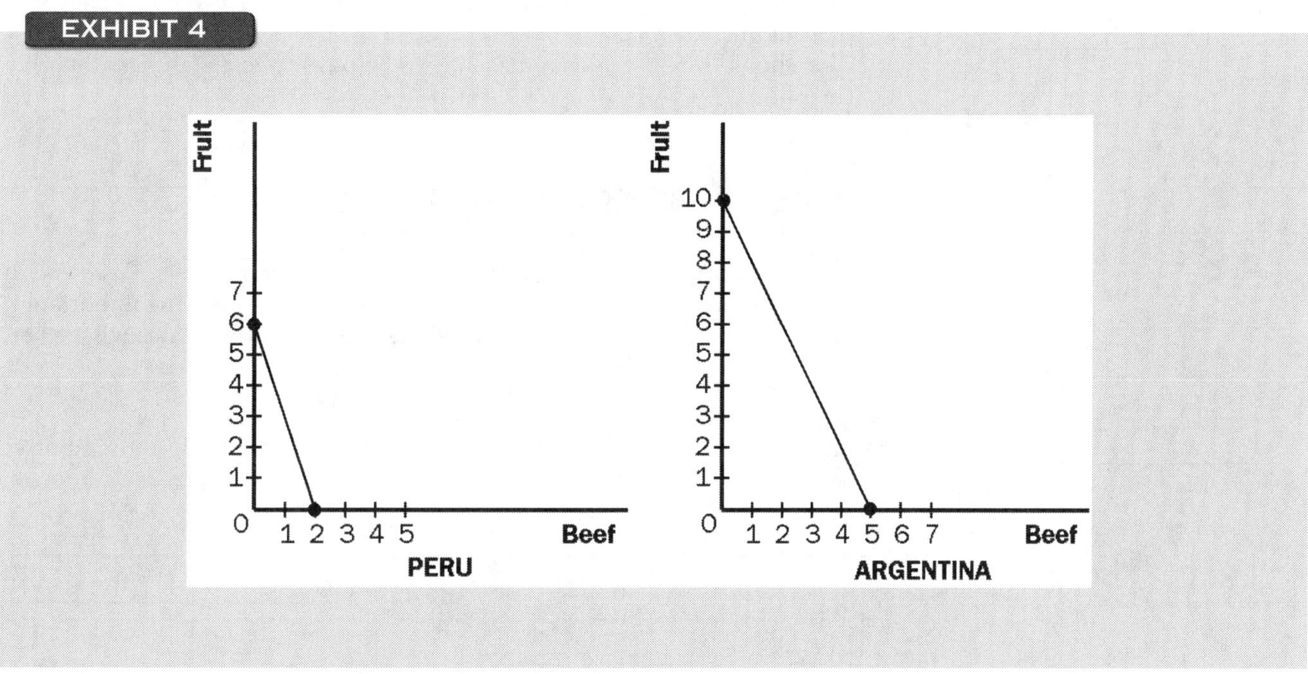

Use the production possibilities frontiers in Exhibit 4 to answer questions 17 through 19. Assume each country has the same number of workers, say 20 million, and that each axis is measured in metric tons per month.

17. Argentina has a comparative advantage in the production of
    a. both fruit and beef.
    b. fruit.
    c. beef.
    d. neither fruit nor beef.

18. Peru will export
    a. both fruit and beef.
    b. fruit.
    c. beef.
    d. neither fruit nor beef.

19. The opportunity cost of producing a metric ton of beef in Peru is
    a. 1/3 ton of fruit.
    b. 1 ton of fruit.
    c. 2 tons of fruit.
    d. 3 tons of fruit.
    e. 6 tons of fruit.

20. Joe is a tax accountant. He receives $100 per hour doing tax returns. He can type 10,000 characters per hour into spreadsheets. He can hire an assistant who types 2,500 characters per hour into spreadsheets. Which of the following statements is true?
    a. Joe should not hire an assistant because the assistant cannot type as fast as he.
    b. Joe should hire the assistant as long as he pays the assistant less than $100 per hour.
    c. Joe should hire the assistant as long as he pays the assistant less than $25 per hour.
    d. none of the above.

ADVANCED CRITICAL THINKING

You are watching an election debate on television. A candidate says, "We need to stop the flow of foreign automobiles into our country. If we limit the importation of autos, our domestic auto production will rise and the United States will be better off."

1. Is it likely that the *United States* will be better off if we limit auto imports? Explain.

   ____

   ____

   ____

   ____

2. Will anyone in the United States be better off if we limit auto imports? Explain.

   ____

   ____

   ____

   ____

3. In the real world, does every person in the country gain when restrictions on imports are reduced? Explain.

___

___

___

___

SOLUTIONS

Terms and Definitions

5 Absolute advantage

2 Comparative advantage

6 Gains from trade

1 Opportunity cost

4 Imports

3 Exports

Practice Problems

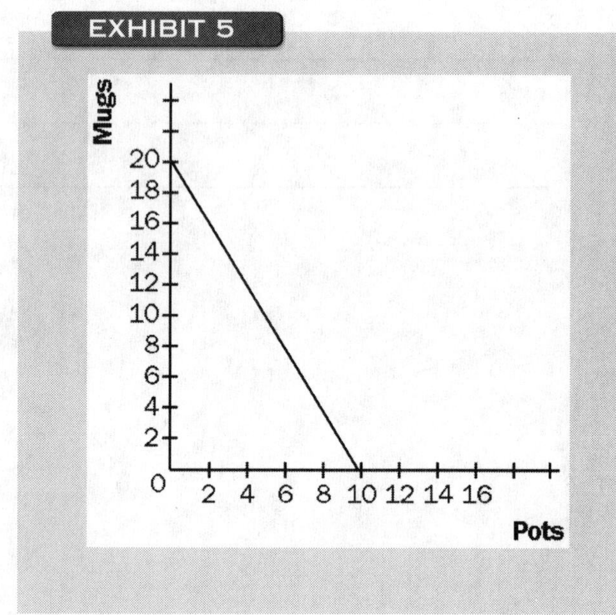

1. a. See Exhibit 5.
   b. 2 mugs. 20 mugs.
   c. 1/2 pot. 5 pots.
   d. Because here resources can be moved from the production of one good to another at a constant rate.

2. a.

	Computers	Grain
Germany	15	5
Poland	4	4

   b. See Exhibit 6.
   c. 1/3 ton grain. 3 computers.

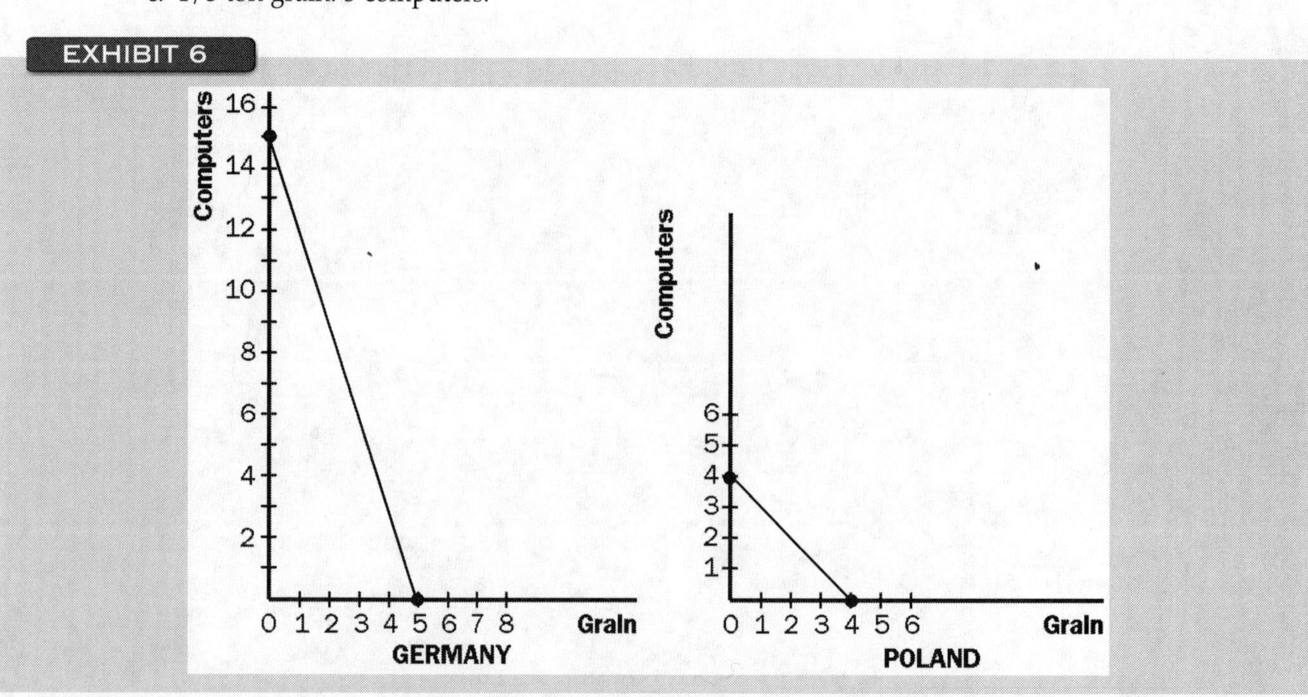

d. 1 ton grain. 1 computer.
e. Germany because one worker can produce 15 computers compared to 4. Germany because one worker can produce 5 tons of grain compared to 4.
f. Germany because a computer has the opportunity cost of only 1/3 ton of grain compared to 1 ton of grain in Poland. Poland because a ton of grain has the opportunity cost of only 1 computer compared to 3 computers in Germany.
g. Germany should produce computers while Poland should produce grain because the opportunity cost of computers is lower in Germany and the opportunity cost of grain is lower in Poland. That is, each has a comparative advantage in those goods.
h. Grain must cost less than 3 computers to Germany. Computers must cost less than 1 ton of grain to Poland.
i. See Exhibit 7. They are consuming outside their production possibilities frontier.

EXHIBIT 7

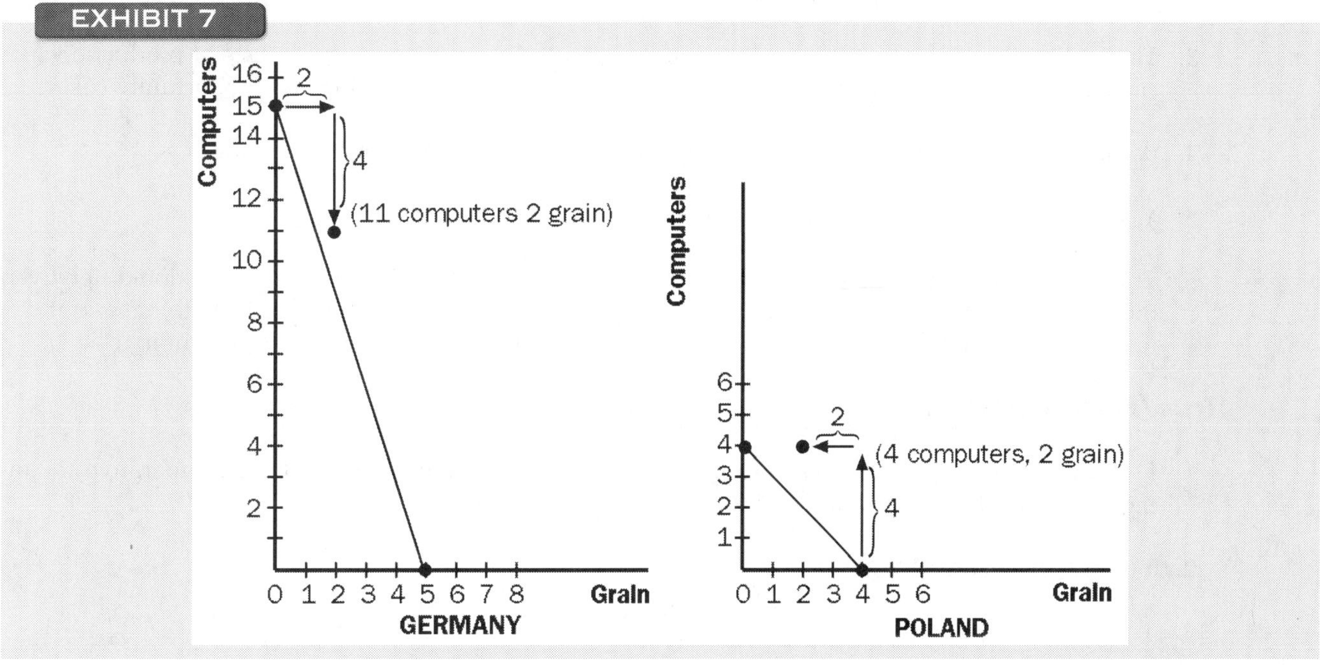

j. Germany because one worker can produce 15 compared to 8. Poland because one worker can produce 8 compared to 5.
k. Germany has comparative advantage in computers. Poland has comparative advantage in grain. No change in comparative advantage. Poland is better off, however, because it now has a larger set of choices.
l. It would not change absolute advantage or comparative advantage. It would change the scale in the previous two graphs by a factor of 10 million.

3. a.

	Cars	Computers
United States	4	20
Russia	1	5

b. United States because one worker can produce 4 cars compared to 1. The United States because one worker can produce 20 computers compared to 5.
c. In both, the opportunity cost of 1 car is 5 computers. In both, the opportunity cost of 1 computer is 1/5 of a car. Therefore, neither has a comparative advantage in either good.
d. No. Each can get the same tradeoff between goods domestically.

e. Yes. There needs to be differences in opportunity costs of producing goods across countries for there to be gains from trade.
f. The availability of resources or technology might be different across countries. That is, workers could have different levels of education, land could be of different quality, capital could be of different quality, or the available technology might be different.

Short-Answer Questions

1. Because a consumer gets a greater variety of goods at a much lower cost than they could produce by themselves. That is, there are gains from trade.

2. What is important in trade is how a country's costs without trade differ from each other. This is determined by the relative opportunity costs across countries.

3. The additional output that comes from countries with different opportunity costs of production specializing in the production of the item for which they have the lower domestic opportunity cost.

4. Because it forces people to produce at a higher cost than they pay when they trade.

5. Yes, as long as the secretary earns less than $50/hour, the lawyer is ahead.

6. This is not true. All countries can gain from trade if their opportunity costs of production differ. Even the least productive country will have a comparative advantage at producing something, and it can trade this good to the advanced country for less than the advanced country's opportunity cost.

True/False Questions

1. F; absolute advantage compares the quantities of inputs used in production while comparative advantage compares the opportunity costs.

2. T

3. T

4. F; restricting trade eliminates gains from trade.

5. T

6. T

7. F; the price of 1 bag of fries is 1/2 of a hamburger.

8. T

9. F; voluntary trade benefits both traders.

10. F; a low opportunity cost of producing one good implies a high opportunity cost of producing the other good.

11. T

12. F; it may harm those involved in that industry.

13. T

14. F; voluntary trade benefits all traders.

15. T

Multiple-Choice Questions

1. b	5. c	9. c	13. a	17. c
2. a	6. b	10. a	14. b	18. b
3. d	7. a	11. d	15. d	19. d
4. d	8. c	12. b	16. b	20. c

Advanced Critical Thinking

1. No. If we import autos, it is because the opportunity cost of producing them elsewhere is lower than in the United States.
2. Yes. Those associated with the domestic auto industry—stockholders of domestic auto producers and auto workers.
3. No. When we reduce restrictions on imports, the country gains from the increased trade but individuals in the affected domestic industry may lose.

4

GOALS

In this chapter you will

Learn what a competitive market is

Examine what determines the demand for a good in a competitive market

Examine what determines the supply of a good in a competitive market

See how supply and demand together set the price of a good and the quantity sold

Consider the key role of prices in allocating scarce resources in market economies

OUTCOMES

After accomplishing these goals, you should be able to

Define scarcity

List the two characteristics of a competitive market

List the factors that affect the amount that consumers wish to buy in a market

List the factors that affect the amount that producers wish to sell in a market

Draw a graph of supply and demand in a market and find the equilibrium price and quantity

Shift supply and demand in response to an economic event and find the new equilibrium price and quantity

THE MARKET FORCES OF SUPPLY AND DEMAND

CHAPTER OVERVIEW

Context and Purpose

Chapter 4 is the first chapter in a three-chapter sequence that deals with supply and demand and how markets work. Chapter 4 shows how supply and demand for a good determines both the quantity produced and the price at which the good sells. Chapter 5 will add precision to our discussion of supply and demand by addressing the concept of elasticity—the sensitivity of the quantity supplied and quantity demanded to changes in economic variables. Chapter 6 will address the impact of government policies on prices and quantities in markets.

The purpose of Chapter 4 is to establish the model of supply and demand. The model of supply and demand is the foundation for our discussion for the remainder of this text. For this reason, time spent studying the concepts in this chapter will return benefits to you throughout your study of economics. Many instructors would argue that this chapter is the most important chapter in the text.

CHAPTER REVIEW

Introduction

In a market economy, supply and demand determine both the quantity of each good produced and the price at which each good is sold. In this chapter, we develop the determinants of supply and demand. We also address how changes in supply and demand alter prices and change the allocation of the economy's resources.

Markets and Competition

A **market** is a group of buyers and sellers of a particular good or service. It can be highly organized like a stock market or less organized like the market for ice cream. A **competitive market** is a market in which there are many buyers and sellers so that each has a negligible impact on the market price.

A *perfectly competitive* market has two main characteristics:

- The goods offered for sale are all the same.
- The buyers and sellers are so numerous that no one buyer or seller can influence the price.

If a market is perfectly competitive, both buyers and sellers are said to be *price takers* because they cannot influence the price. The assumption of perfect competition applies well to agricultural markets because the product is similar and no individual buyer or seller can influence the price.

There are other types of markets. If a market has only one seller, the market is known as a *monopoly*. If there are only a few sellers, the market is known as an *oligopoly*. If there are many sellers but each product is slightly different so that each seller has some ability to set its own price, the market is called *monopolistically competitive*.

Demand

The behavior of buyers is captured by the concept of demand. The **quantity demanded** is the amount of a good that buyers are willing and able to purchase. While many things determine the quantity demanded of a good, the *price* of the good plays a central role. Other things equal, an increase in the price of a good reduces the quantity demanded. This negative relationship between the price of a good and the quantity demanded of a good is known as the **law of demand.**

The **demand schedule** is a table that shows the relationship between the price of a good and the quantity demanded. The **demand curve** is a graph of this relationship with the price on the vertical axis and the quantity demanded on the horizontal axis. The demand curve is downward sloping due to the law of demand.

Market demand is the sum of the quantities demanded for each individual buyer at each price. That is, the market demand curve is the horizontal sum of the individual demand curves. The market demand curve shows the total quantity demanded of a good at each price, while all other factors that affect how much buyers wish to buy are held constant.

Shifts in the demand curve When people change how much they wish to buy at each price, the demand curve shifts. If buyers increase the quantity demanded at each price, the demand curve shifts right which is called an *increase in demand*. Alternatively, if buyers decrease the quantity demanded at each price, the demand curve shifts left which is called a *decrease in demand*. The most important factors that shift demand curves are:

- *Income:* A **normal good** is a good for which an increase in income leads to an increase in demand. An **inferior good** is a good for which an increase in income leads to a decrease in demand.

- *Prices of Related Goods:* If two goods can be used in place of one another, they are known as **substitutes.** When two goods are substitutes, an increase in the price of one good leads to an increase in the demand for the other good. If two goods are used together, they are known as **complements.** When two goods are complements, an increase in the price of one good leads to a decrease in the demand for the other good.

- *Tastes:* If your preferences shift toward a good, it will lead to an increase in the demand for that good.

- *Expectations:* Expectations about future income or prices will affect the demand for a good today.

- *Number of Buyers:* An increase in the number of buyers will lead to an increase in the market demand for a good because there are more individual demand curves to horizontally sum.

A demand curve is drawn with price on the vertical axis and quantity demanded on the horizontal axis while holding other things equal. Therefore, a change in the price of a good represents a movement along the demand curve while a change in income, prices of related goods, tastes, expectations, and the number of buyers causes a shift in the demand curve.

Supply

The behavior of sellers is captured by the concept of supply. The **quantity supplied** is the amount of a good that sellers are willing and able to sell. While many things determine the quantity supplied of a good, the *price* of the good is central. Other things equal, an increase in the price makes production more profitable and increases the quantity supplied. This positive relationship between the price of a good and the quantity supplied is known as the **law of supply.**

The **supply schedule** is a table that shows the relationship between the price of a good and the quantity supplied. The **supply curve** is a graph of this relationship with the price on the vertical axis and the quantity supplied on the horizontal axis. The supply curve is upward sloping due to the law of supply.

Market supply is the sum of the quantity supplied for each individual seller at each price. That is, the market supply curve is the horizontal sum of the individual supply curves. The market supply curve shows the total quantity supplied of a good at each price, while all other factors that affect how much producers wish to sell are held constant.

Shifts in the supply curve When producers change how much they wish to sell at each price, the supply curve shifts. If producers increase the quantity supplied at each price, the supply curve shifts right, which is called an *increase in supply*. Alternatively, if producers decrease the quantity suppled at each price, the supply curve shifts left, which is called a *decrease in supply*. The most important factors that shift supply curves are:

- *Input Prices:* A decrease in the price of an input makes production more profitable and increases supply.

- *Technology:* An improvement in technology reduces costs, makes production more profitable, and increases supply.

- *Expectations:* Expectations about the future will affect the supply of a good today.

- *Number of Sellers:* An increase in the number of sellers will lead to an increase in the market supply for a good because there are more individual supply curves to horizontally sum.

A supply curve is drawn with price on the vertical axis and quantity supplied on the horizontal axis while holding other things equal. Therefore, a change in the price of a good represents a movement along the supply curve while a change in input prices, technology, expectations, and the number of sellers causes a shift in the supply curve.

Supply and Demand Together

When placed on the same graph, the intersection of supply and demand is called the market's **equilibrium.** Equilibrium is a situation in which the price has reached the level where quantity supplied equals quantity demanded. The **equilibrium price,** or the market-clearing price, is the price that balances the quantity demanded and the quantity supplied. When the quantity supplied equals the quantity demanded at the equilibrium price, we have determined the **equilibrium quantity.**

The market naturally moves toward its equilibrium. If the price is above the equilibrium price, the quantity supplied exceeds the quantity demanded and there is a **surplus,** or an excess supply of the good. A surplus causes the price to fall until it reaches equilibrium. If the price is below the equilibrium price, the quantity demanded exceeds the quantity supplied and there is a **shortage,** or an excess demand for the good. A shortage causes the price to rise until it reaches equilibrium. This natural adjustment of the price to bring the quantity supplied and the quantity demanded into balance is known as the **law of supply and demand.**

When an economic event shifts the supply or the demand curve, the equilibrium in the market changes. The analysis of this change is known as *comparative statics* because we are comparing the initial equilibrium to the new equilibrium. When analyzing the impact of some event on the market equilibrium, employ the following three steps:

- Decide whether the event shifts the supply curve or demand curve or both.

- Decide which direction the curve shifts.

- Use the supply-and-demand diagram to see how the shift changes the equilibrium price and quantity.

A shift in the demand curve is called a "change in demand." It is caused by a change in a variable that affects the amount people wish to purchase of a good *other than the price of the good.* A change in the price of a good causes a movement along a given demand curve and is called a "change in the quantity demanded." Likewise, a shift in the supply curve is called a "change in supply." It is caused by a change in a variable that affects the amount producers wish to supply of a good *other than the price of the good.* A change in the price of a good causes a movement along a supply curve and is called a "change in the quantity supplied."

For example, a frost that destroys much of the orange crop causes a decrease in the supply of oranges (supply of oranges shifts to the left). This increases the price of oranges and decreases the quantity demanded of oranges. In other words, a decrease in the supply of oranges increases the price of oranges and decreases the quantity of oranges purchased.

If both supply and demand shift at the same time, there may be more than one possible outcome for the changes in the equilibrium price and quantity. For example, if demand were to increase (shift right) while supply were to decrease (shift left), the price will certainly rise but the impact on the equilibrium quantity is ambiguous. In this case, the change in the equilibrium quantity depends on the magnitudes of the shifts in supply and demand.

Conclusion: How Prices Allocate Resources

Markets generate equilibrium prices. These prices are the signals that guide the allocation of scarce resources. Prices of products rise to the level necessary to allocate the products to those who are willing to pay for them. Prices of inputs (say labor) rise to the level necessary to induce people to do the jobs that need to get done. In this way, no jobs go undone, and there is no shortage of goods and services for those willing and able to pay for them.

HELPFUL HINTS

1. Equilibrium in a market is a static state. That is, once a market is in equilibrium, there are no further forces for change. That is why economists use the term *comparative statics* to describe the analysis of comparing an initial static equilibrium to a new static equilibrium.

2. By far, the greatest difficulty students have when studying supply and demand is distinguishing between a "change in demand" and a "change in the quantity demanded" and between a "change in supply" and a "change in the quantity supplied." It helps to remember that "demand" is the entire relationship between price and quantity demanded. That is, demand is the entire demand curve, not a point on a demand curve. Therefore, a change in demand is a shift in the entire demand curve, which can only be caused by a change in a determinant of demand other than the price of the good. A change in the quantity demanded is a movement along the demand curve and is caused by a change in the price of the good. Likewise, "supply" refers to the entire supply curve, not a point on the supply curve. Therefore, a change in supply is a shift in the entire supply curve, which can only be caused by a change in a determinant of supply other than the price of the good. A change in the quantity supplied is a movement along the supply curve and is caused by a change in the price of the good.

3. If both supply and demand shift at the same time and we do not know the magnitude of each shift, then the change in either the price or the quantity must be ambiguous. For example, if there is an increase in supply (supply shifts right) and an increase in demand (demand shifts right), the equilibrium quantity must certainly rise, but the change in the equilibrium price is ambiguous. Do this for all four possible combinations of changes in supply and demand. You will find that if you know the impact on the equilibrium price with certainty, then the impact on the equilibrium quantity must be ambiguous. If you know the impact on the equilibrium quantity with certainty, then the impact on the equilibrium price must be ambiguous.

TERMS AND DEFINITIONS

Choose a definition for each key term.

Key terms:

_____ Market

_____ Competitive market

_____ Monopoly

_____ Oligopoly

_____ Monopolistically competitive

_____ Quantity demanded

_____ Law of demand

_____ Demand schedule

_____ Demand curve

_____ Normal good

_____ Inferior good

_____ Substitutes

_____ Complements

_____ Quantity supplied

_____ Law of supply

_____ Supply schedule

_____ Supply curve

_____ Equilibrium

_____ Equilibrium price

_____ Equilibrium quantity

_____ Surplus

_____ Shortage

_____ The law of supply and demand

Definitions:

1. The quantity supplied and the quantity demanded at the equilibrium price
2. A table that shows the relationship between the price of a good and the quantity demanded
3. A table that shows the relationship between the price of a good and the quantity supplied
4. Market with sellers offering slightly different products
5. A group of buyers and sellers of a particular good or service
6. Market with only one seller
7. A good for which, other things equal, an increase in income leads to a decrease in demand
8. A situation in which quantity demanded is greater than quantity supplied
9. A situation in which quantity supplied is greater than quantity demanded
10. The amount of a good that buyers are willing and able to purchase
11. A situation in which the price has reached the level where quantity supplied equals quantity demanded
12. A market in which there are many buyers and sellers so that each has a negligible impact on the market price
13. The claim that, other things equal, the quantity demanded of a good falls when the price of the good rises
14. Market with only a few sellers
15. The price that balances quantity supplied and quantity demanded
16. The amount of a good that sellers are willing and able to sell
17. The claim that, other things equal, the quantity supplied of a good rises when the price of the good rises
18. The claim that the price of any good adjusts to bring the quantity supplied and quantity demanded for that good into balance
19. Two goods for which an increase in the price of one leads to a decrease in the demand for the other
20. A good for which, other things equal, an increase in income leads to an increase in demand
21. A graph of the relationship between the price of a good and the quantity supplied
22. Two goods for which an increase in the price of one leads to an increase in the demand for the other
23. A graph of the relationship between the price of a good and the quantity demanded

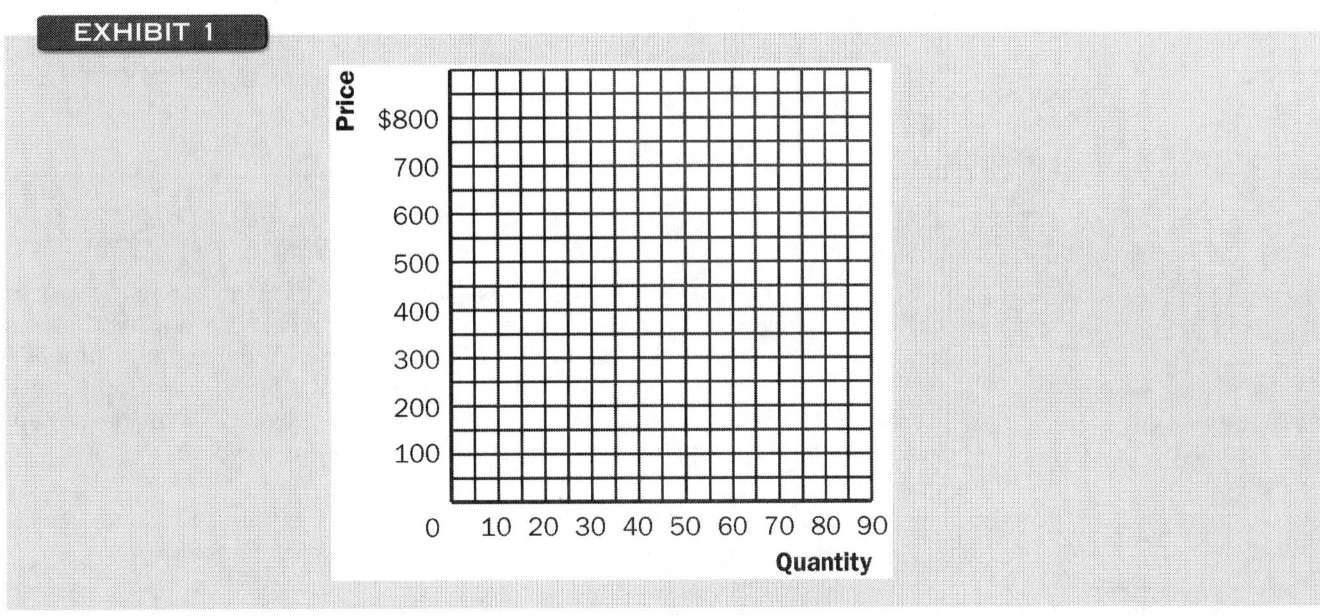

PROBLEMS AND SHORT-ANSWER QUESTIONS

Practice Problems

1. Suppose we have the following market supply and demand schedules for bicycles:

Price	Quantity Demanded	Quantity Supplied
$100	70	30
200	60	40
300	50	50
400	40	60
500	30	70
600	20	80

a. Plot the supply curve and the demand curve for bicycles in Exhibit 1.

b. What is the equilibrium price of bicycles?

____

c. What is the equilibrium quantity of bicycles?

____

d. If the price of bicycles were $100, is there a surplus or a shortage? How many units of surplus or shortage are there? Will this cause the price to rise or fall?

____

____

e. If the price of bicycles were $400, is there a surplus or a shortage? How many units of surplus or shortage are there? Will this cause the price to rise or fall?

f. Suppose that the bicycle maker's labor union bargains for an increase in its wages. Further, suppose this event raises the cost of production, makes bicycle manufacturing less profitable, and reduces the quantity supplied of bicycles by 20 units at each price of bicycles. Plot the new supply curve and the original supply and demand curves in Exhibit 2. What is the new equilibrium price and quantity in the market for bicycles?

EXHIBIT 2

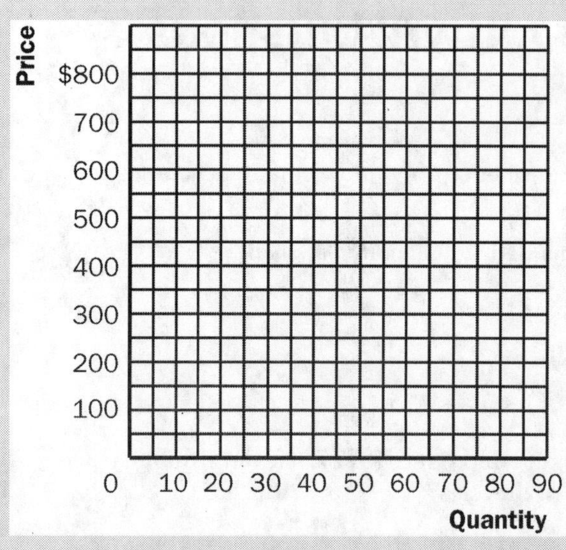

2. Each of the events listed below has an impact on the market for bicycles. For each event, which curve is affected (supply or demand for bicycles), what direction is it shifted, and what is the resulting impact on the equilibrium price and quantity of bicycles?
   a. The price of automobiles increases.

   b. Consumers' incomes decrease, and bicycles are a normal good.

c. The price of steel used to make bicycle frames increases.

d. An environmental movement shifts tastes toward bicycling.

e. *Consumers* expect the price of bicycles to fall in the future.

f. A technological advance in the manufacture of bicycles occurs.

g. The price of bicycle helmets and shoes falls.

h. Consumers' incomes decrease, and bicycles are an inferior good.

3. The following questions address a market when both supply and demand shift.
   a. What would happen to the equilibrium price and quantity in the bicycle market if there is an increase in both the supply and the demand for bicycles?

   b. What would happen to the equilibrium price and quantity in the bicycle market if the demand for bicycles increases more than the increase in the supply of bicycles?

Short-Answer Questions

1. What are the two main characteristics of a perfectly competitive market?

2. Explain the law of demand.

3. What are the variables that should affect the amount of a good that consumers wish to buy, other than its price?

4. What is the difference between a normal good and an inferior good?

5. Explain the law of supply.

6. What are the variables that should affect the amount of a good that producers wish to sell, other than its price?

7. Suppose *suppliers* of corn expect the price of corn to rise in the future. How would this affect the supply and demand for corn and the equilibrium price and quantity of corn?

8. If there is a surplus of a good, is the price above or below the equilibrium price for that good?

9. Suppose there is an increase in consumers' incomes. In the market for automobiles (a normal good), does this event cause an increase in demand or an increase in quantity demanded? Does this cause an increase in supply or an increase in quantity supplied? Explain.

____

____

____

____

____

10. Suppose there is an advance in the technology employed to produce automobiles. In the market for automobiles, does this event cause an increase in supply or an increase in the quantity supplied? Does this cause an increase in demand or an increase in the quantity demanded? Explain.

____

____

____

____

____

SELF-TEST

True/False Questions

_____ 1. A perfectly competitive market consists of products that are all slightly different from one another.

_____ 2. An oligopolistic market has only a few sellers.

_____ 3. The law of demand states that an increase in the price of a good decreases the demand for that good.

_____ 4. If apples and oranges are substitutes, an increase in the price of apples will decrease the demand for oranges.

_____ 5. If golf clubs and golf balls are complements, an increase in the price of golf clubs will decrease the demand for golf balls.

_____ 6. If consumers expect the price of shoes to rise, there will be an increase in the demand for shoes today.

_____ 7. The law of supply states that an increase in the price of a good increases the quantity supplied of that good.

_____ 8. An increase in the price of steel will shift the supply of automobiles to the right.

_____ 9. When the price of a good is below the equilibrium price, it causes a surplus.

_____10. The market supply curve is the horizontal summation of the individual supply curves.

_____11. If there is a shortage of a good, then the price of that good tends to fall.

_____12. If pencils and paper are complements, an increase in the price of pencils causes the demand for paper to decrease or shift to the left.

_____13. If Coke and Pepsi are substitutes, an increase in the price of Coke will cause an increase in the equilibrium price and quantity in the market for Pepsi.

_____14. An advance in the technology employed to manufacture roller blades will result in a decrease in the equilibrium price and an increase in the equilibrium quantity in the market for roller blades.

_____15. If there is an increase in supply accompanied by a decrease in demand for coffee, then there will be a decrease in both the equilibrium price and quantity in the market for coffee.

Multiple-Choice Questions

1. A perfectly competitive market has
   a. only one seller.
   b. at least a few sellers.
   c. many buyers and sellers.
   d. firms that set their own prices.
   e. none of the above.

2. If an increase in the price of blue jeans leads to an increase in the demand for tennis shoes, then blue jeans and tennis shoes are
   a. substitutes.
   b. complements.
   c. normal goods.
   d. inferior goods.
   e. none of the above.

3. The *law of demand* states that an increase in the price of a good
   a. decreases the demand for that good.
   b. decreases the quantity demanded for that good.
   c. increases the supply of that good.
   d. increases the quantity supplied of that good.
   e. none of the above.

4. The *law of supply* states that an increase in the price of a good
   a. decreases the demand for that good.
   b. decreases the quantity demanded for that good.
   c. increases the supply of that good.
   d. increases the quantity supplied of that good.
   e. none of the above.

5. If an increase in consumer incomes leads to a decrease in the demand for camping equipment, then camping equipment is
   a. a complementary good.
   b. a substitute good.
   c. a normal good.
   d. an inferior good.
   e. none of the above.

6. A monopolistic market has
   a. only one seller.
   b. at least a few sellers.
   c. many buyers and sellers.
   d. firms that are price takers.
   e. none of the above.

7. Which of the following shifts the demand for watches to the right?
   a. a decrease in the price of watches
   b. a decrease in consumer incomes if watches are a normal good
   c. a decrease in the price of watch batteries if watch batteries and watches are complements
   d. an increase in the price of watches
   e. none of the above

8. All of the following shift the supply of watches to the right except
   a. an increase in the price of watches.
   b. an advance in the technology used to manufacture watches.
   c. a decrease in the wage of workers employed to manufacture watches.
   d. manufacturers' expectation of lower watch prices in the future.
   e. All of the above cause an increase in the supply of watches.

9. If the price of a good is above the equilibrium price,
   a. there is a surplus and the price will rise.
   b. there is a surplus and the price will fall.
   c. there is a shortage and the price will rise.
   d. there is a shortage and the price will fall.
   e. the quantity demanded is equal to the quantity supplied and the price remains unchanged.

10. If the price of a good is below the equilibrium price,
    a. there is a surplus and the price will rise.
    b. there is a surplus and the price will fall.
    c. there is a shortage and the price will rise.
    d. there is a shortage and the price will fall.
    e. the quantity demanded is equal to the quantity supplied and the price remains unchanged.

11. If the price of a good is equal to the equilibrium price,
   a. there is a surplus and the price will rise.
   b. there is a surplus and the price will fall.
   c. there is a shortage and the price will rise.
   d. there is a shortage and the price will fall.
   e. the quantity demanded is equal to the quantity supplied and the price remains unchanged.

12. An increase (rightward shift) in the demand for a good will tend to cause
   a. an increase in the equilibrium price and quantity.
   b. a decrease in the equilibrium price and quantity.
   c. an increase in the equilibrium price and a decrease in the equilibrium quantity.
   d. a decrease in the equilibrium price and an increase in the equilibrium quantity.
   e. none of the above.

13. A decrease (leftward shift) in the supply for a good will tend to cause
   a. an increase in the equilibrium price and quantity.
   b. a decrease in the equilibrium price and quantity.
   c. an increase in the equilibrium price and a decrease in the equilibrium quantity.
   d. a decrease in the equilibrium price and an increase in the equilibrium quantity.
   e. none of the above.

14. Suppose there is an increase in both the supply and demand for personal computers. In the market for personal computers, we would expect
   a. the equilibrium quantity to rise and the equilibrium price to rise.
   b. the equilibrium quantity to rise and the equilibrium price to fall.
   c. the equilibrium quantity to rise and the equilibrium price to remain constant.
   d. the equilibrium quantity to rise and the change in the equilibrium price to be ambiguous.
   e. the change in the equilibrium quantity to be ambiguous and the equilibrium price to rise.

15. Suppose there is an increase in both the supply and demand for personal computers. Further, suppose the supply of personal computers increases more than demand for personal computers. In the market for personal computers, we would expect
   a. the equilibrium quantity to rise and the equilibrium price to rise.
   b. the equilibrium quantity to rise and the equilibrium price to fall.
   c. the equilibrium quantity to rise and the equilibrium price to remain constant.
   d. the equilibrium quantity to rise and the change in the equilibrium price to be ambiguous.
   e. the change in the equilibrium quantity to be ambiguous and the equilibrium price to fall.

16. Which of the following statements is true about the impact of an increase in the price of lettuce?
    a. The demand for lettuce will decrease.
    b. The supply of lettuce will decrease.
    c. The equilibrium price and quantity of salad dressing will rise.
    d. The equilibrium price and quantity of salad dressing will fall.
    e. Both (a) and (d).

17. Suppose a frost destroys much of the Florida orange crop. At the same time, suppose consumer tastes shift toward orange juice. What would we expect to happen to the equilibrium price and quantity in the market for orange juice?
    a. Price will increase; quantity is ambiguous.
    b. Price will increase; quantity will increase.
    c. Price will increase; quantity will decrease.
    d. Price will decrease; quantity is ambiguous.
    e. The impact on both price and quantity is ambiguous.

18. Suppose consumer tastes shift toward the consumption of apples. Which of the following statements is an accurate description of the impact of this event on the market for apples?
    a. There is an increase in the demand for apples and an increase in the quantity supplied of apples.
    b. There is an increase in the demand and supply of apples.
    c. There is an increase in the quantity demanded of apples and in the supply for apples.
    d. There is an increase in the demand for apples and a decrease in the supply of apples.
    e. There is a decrease in the quantity demanded of apples and an increase in the supply for apples.

19. Suppose both buyers and sellers of wheat expect the price of wheat to rise in the near future. What would we expect to happen to the equilibrium price and quantity in the market for wheat today?
    a. The impact on both price and quantity is ambiguous.
    b. Price will increase; quantity is ambiguous.
    c. Price will increase; quantity will increase.
    d. Price will increase; quantity will decrease.
    e. Price will decrease; quantity is ambiguous.

20. An inferior good is one for which an increase in income causes
    a. an increase in supply.
    b. a decrease in supply.
    c. an increase in demand.
    d. a decrease in demand.

ADVANCED CRITICAL THINKING

You are watching a national news broadcast. It is reported that a typhoon is heading for the Washington coast and that it will likely destroy much of this year's apple crop. Your roommate says, "If there are going to be fewer apples available, I'll bet that apple prices will rise. We should buy enormous quantities of apples now and put them in storage. Later we will sell them and make a killing."

1. If this information about the storm is publicly available so that all buyers and sellers in the apple market expect the price of apples to rise in the future, what will happen immediately to the supply and demand for apples and the equilibrium price and quantity of apples?

2. Can you "beat the market" with public information? That is, can you use publicly available information to help you buy something cheap and quickly sell it at a higher price? Why or why not?

3. Suppose a friend of yours works for the U.S. Weather Bureau. She calls you and provides you with inside information about the approaching storm—information not available to the public. Can you "beat the market" with inside information? Why?

SOLUTIONS

Terms and Definitions

5 Market

12 Competitive market

6 Monopoly

14 Oligopoly

4 Monopolistically competitive

10 Quantity demanded

13 Law of demand

2 Demand schedule

23 Demand curve

20 Normal good

7 Inferior good

22 Substitutes

19 Complements

18 The law of supply and demand

16 Quantity supplied

17 Law of supply

3 Supply schedule

21 Supply curve

11 Equilibrium

15 Equilibrium price

1 Equilibrium quantity

9 Surplus

8 Shortage

18 The law of supply and demand

Practice Problems

1. a. See Exhibit 3.

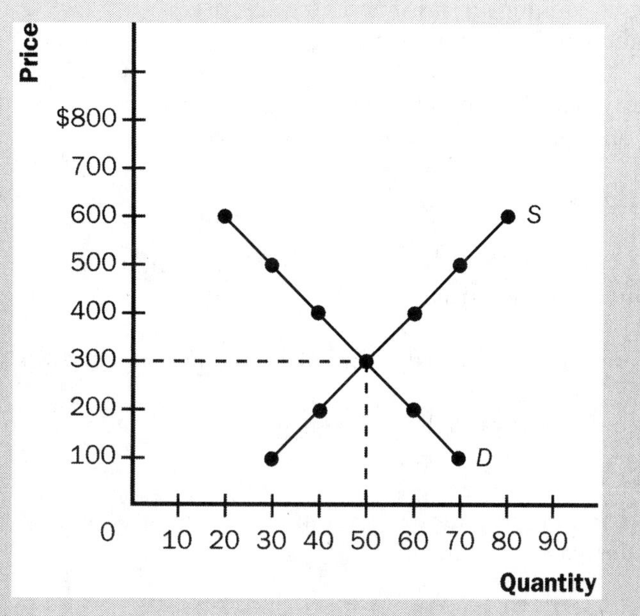

b. $300
c. 50 bicycles
d. Shortage, 70 – 30 = 40 units, the price will rise
e. Surplus, 60 – 40 = 20 units, the price will fall
f. See Exhibit 4. equilibrium price = $400, equilibrium quantity = 40 bicycles

EXHIBIT 4

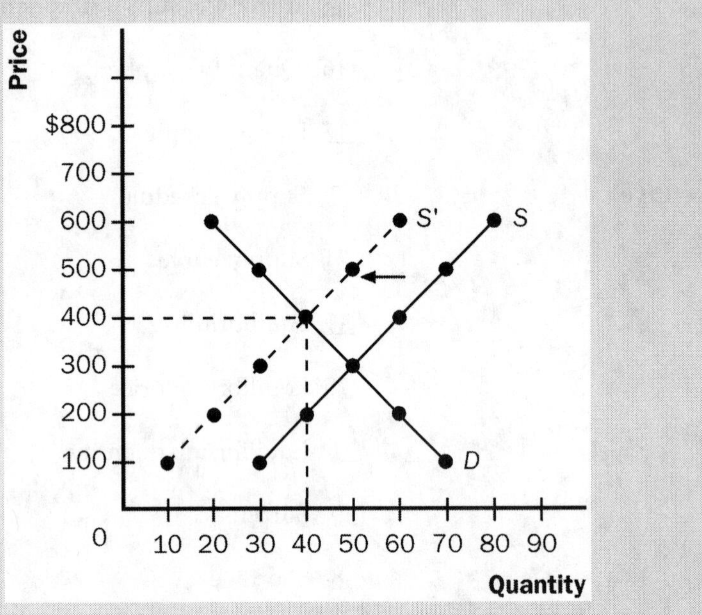

2. a. demand, shifts right, equilibrium price and quantity rise
   b. demand, shifts left, equilibrium price and quantity fall
   c. supply, shifts left, equilibrium price rises, equilibrium quantity falls
   d. demand, shifts right, equilibrium price and quantity rise
   e. demand, shifts left, equilibrium price and quantity fall
   f. supply, shifts right, equilibrium price falls, equilibrium quantity rises
   g. demand, shifts right, equilibrium price and quantity rise
   h. demand, shifts right, equilibrium price and quantity rise

3. a. equilibrium quantity will rise, equilibrium price is ambiguous
   b. equilibrium price and quantity will rise

Short-Answer Questions

1. The goods offered for sale are all the same and the buyers and sellers are so numerous that no one buyer or seller can influence the price.

2. Other things equal, price and quantity demanded of a good are negatively related.

3. The variables are income, prices of related goods, tastes, expectations, and number of buyers in the market.

4. When income rises, demand for a normal good increases or shifts right. When income rises, demand for an inferior good decreases or shifts left.

5. Other things equal, price and quantity supplied of a good are positively related.

6. The variables are input prices, technology, expectations, and number of sellers in the market.

7. The supply of corn in today's market would decrease (shift left) as sellers hold back their offerings in anticipation of greater profits if the price rises in the future. If only suppliers expect higher prices, demand would be unaffected. The equilibrium price would rise and the equilibrium quantity would fall.

8. The price must be above the equilibrium price.

9. There would be an *increase in the demand* for automobiles, which means that the entire demand curve shifts to the right. This implies a movement along the fixed supply curve as the price rises. The increase in price causes an *increase in the quantity supplied* of automobiles but there is no increase in the supply of automobiles.

10. There would be an *increase in the supply* of automobiles, which means that the entire supply curve shifts to the right. This implies a movement along the fixed demand curve as the price falls. The decrease in price causes an *increase in the quantity demanded* of automobiles but there is no increase in the demand for automobiles.

True/False Questions

1. F; a perfectly competitive market consists of goods offered for sale that are all the same.

2. T

3. F; the law of demand states that an increase in the price of a good decreases the *quantity demanded* of that good (a movement along the demand curve).

4. F; it will increase the demand for oranges.

5. T

6. T

7. T

8. F; an increase in the price of an input shifts the supply curve for the output to the left.

9. F; it causes an excess demand.

10. T

11. F; an excess demand causes the price to rise.

12. T

13. T

14. T

15. F; there will be a decrease in the equilibrium price, but the impact on the equilibrium quantity is ambiguous.

Multiple-Choice Questions

1. c	5. d	9. b	13. c	17. a
2. a	6. a	10. c	14. d	18. a
3. b	7. c	11. e	15. b	19. b
4. d	8. a	12. a	16. d	20. d

Advanced Critical Thinking

1. Sellers reduce supply (supply shifts left) in the hope of selling apples later at a higher price and buyers increase demand (demand shifts right) in the hope of buying apples now before the price goes up. The price will immediately rise and the quantity exchanged is ambiguous.

2. No. Usually the market immediately adjusts so that the price has already moved to its new equilibrium value before the amateur speculator can make his or her purchase.

3. Yes. In this case, you can make your purchase before the market responds to the information about the storm.

5

ELASTICITY AND ITS APPLICATION

GOALS

In this chapter you will

Learn the meaning of the elasticity of demand

Examine what determines the elasticity of demand

Learn the meaning of the elasticity of supply

Examine what determines the elasticity of supply

Apply the concept of elasticity in three very different markets

OUTCOMES

After accomplishing these goals, you should be able to

Define scarcity

Calculate the price and income elasticity of demand

Distinguish between the price elasticity of demand for necessities and luxuries

Calculate the price elasticity of supply

Distinguish between an inelastic and elastic supply curve

Demonstrate the impact of the price elasticity of demand on total revenue

CHAPTER OVERVIEW

Context and Purpose

Chapter 5 is the second chapter of a three-chapter sequence that deals with supply and demand and how markets work. Chapter 4 introduced supply and demand. Chapter 5 shows how much buyers and sellers respond to changes in market conditions. Chapter 6 will address the impact of government polices on competitive markets.

The purpose of Chapter 5 is to add precision to our supply and demand model. We introduce the concept of elasticity, which measures the responsiveness of buyers and sellers to changes in economic variables such as prices and income. The concept of elasticity allows us to make quantitative observations about the impact of changes in supply and demand on equilibrium prices and quantities.

CHAPTER REVIEW

Introduction

In Chapter 4, we learned that an increase in price reduces the quantity demanded and increases the quantity supplied in a market. In this chapter, we will develop the concept of elasticity so that we can address how much the quantity demanded and the quantity supplied responds to changes in market conditions such as price.

The Elasticity of Demand

To measure the response of demand to its determinants, we use the concept of **elasticity. Price elasticity of demand** measures how much the quantity demanded responds to a change in the price of that good, computed as the percentage change in quantity demanded divided by the percentage change in price.

If the quantity demanded changes substantially from a change in price, demand is *elastic*. If the quantity demanded changes little from a change in price, demand is *inelastic*. Whether a demand curve tends to be price elastic or inelastic depends on the following:

- *Availability of close substitutes:* The demand for goods with close substitutes is more sensitive to changes in prices and, thus, is more price elastic.

- *Necessities versus luxuries:* The demand for necessities is inelastic while the demand for luxuries is elastic. Since one cannot do without a necessity, an increase in the price has little impact on the quantity demanded. However, an increase in price greatly reduces the quantity demanded of a luxury.

- *Definition of the market:* The more narrowly we define the market, the more likely there are to be close substitutes and the more price elastic the demand curve.

- *Time horizon:* The longer the time period considered, the greater the availability of close substitutes and the more price elastic the demand curve.

The formula for computing the price elasticity of demand is:

$$\text{Price elasticity of demand} = \frac{\text{Percentage change in quantity demanded}}{\text{Percentage change in price}}$$

Since price elasticity of demand is always negative, it is customary to drop the negative sign.

When we compute price elasticity between any two points on a demand curve, we get a different answer depending on which point we choose to start and which point we choose to finish if we take the change in price and quantity as a percent of the starting value for each. To avoid this problem, economists often employ the *midpoint method* to calculate elasticities. With this method, the percentage changes in quantity and price are calculated by dividing the change in the variable by the *average* or midpoint value of the two points on the curve, not the starting point on the curve. Thus, the formula for the price elasticity of demand using the midpoint method is:

$$\text{Price elasticity of demand} = \frac{(Q_2 - Q_1)/[(Q_2 + Q_1)/2]}{(P_2 - P_1)/[(P_2 + P_1)/2]}$$

If price elasticity of demand is greater than one, demand is elastic. If elasticity is less than one, demand is inelastic. If elasticity is equal to one, demand is said to have unit elasticity. If elasticity is zero, demand is perfectly inelastic (vertical). If elasticity is infinite, demand is perfectly elastic (horizontal). In general, the flatter the demand curve, the more elastic. The steeper the demand curve, the more inelastic.

Total revenue is the amount paid by buyers and received by sellers, computed simply as price times quantity. The elasticity of demand determines the impact of a change in price on total revenue:

- If demand is price inelastic (less than 1) an increase in price increases total revenue because the price increase is proportionately larger than the reduction in quantity demanded.
- If demand is price elastic (greater than 1) an increase in price decreases total revenue because the decrease in the quantity demanded is proportionately larger than the increase in price.
- If demand is unit price elastic (exactly equal to 1) a change in price has no impact on total revenue because the increase in price is proportionately equal to the decrease in quantity.

Along a linear demand curve, price elasticity is not constant. When price is high and quantity low, price elasticity is large because a change in price causes a larger *percentage* change in quantity. When price is low and quantity high, price elasticity is small because a change in price causes a smaller *percentage* change in quantity.

There are additional demand elasticities. The **income elasticity of demand** is a measure of how much the quantity demanded responds to a change in consumers' income, computed as the percentage change in quantity demanded divided by the percentage change in income or:

$$\text{Income elasticity of demand} = \frac{\text{Percentage change in quantity demanded}}{\text{Percentage change in income}}$$

For *normal goods*, income elasticity is positive. For *inferior goods*, income elasticity is negative. Within the group of normal goods, necessities like food have small income elasticities because the quantity demanded changes little when income changes. Luxuries have larger income elasticities.

The **cross-price elasticity of demand** is a measure of the response of the quantity demanded of one good to a change in the price of another good, computed as the percentage change in the quantity demanded of one good divided by the percentage change in the price of another good or:

$$\text{Cross-price elasticity of demand} = \frac{\text{Percentage change in quantity demanded of good 1}}{\text{Percentage change in the price of good 2}}$$

The cross-price elasticity of demand is positive for *substitutes* and *negative* for complements.

The Elasticity of Supply

Price elasticity of supply measures how much the quantity supplied responds to a change in the price of that good, computed as the percentage change in quantity supplied divided by the percentage change in price.

If the quantity supplied changes substantially from a change in price, supply is *elastic*. If the quantity supplied changes little from a change in price, supply is *inelastic*. Supply is more elastic when the sellers have greater flexibility to change the amount of a good they produce in response to a change in price. Generally, the shorter the time period considered, the less flexibility the seller has in choosing how much to produce, and the more inelastic the supply curve.

The formula for computing the price elasticity of supply is:

$$\text{Price elasticity of supply} = \frac{\text{Percentage change in quantity supplied}}{\text{Percentage change in price.}}$$

If price elasticity of supply is greater than one, supply is elastic. If elasticity is less than one, supply is inelastic. If elasticity is equal to one, supply is said to have unit elasticity. If elasticity is zero, supply is perfectly inelastic (vertical). If elasticity is infinite, supply is perfectly elastic (horizontal). In general, the flatter the supply curve, the more elastic. The steeper the supply curve, the more inelastic.

Price elasticity of supply may not be constant along a given supply curve. At low quantities, a small increase in price may stimulate a large increase in quantity supplied because there is excess capacity in the production facility. Therefore, price elasticity is large. At high quantities, a large increase in price may cause only a small increase in quantity supplied because the production facility is at full capacity. Therefore, price elasticity is small.

Three Applications of Supply, Demand, and Elasticity

- *The market for agricultural products:* Advances in technology have shifted the supply curve for agricultural products to the right. The demand for food, however, is generally inelastic (steep) because food is inexpensive and a necessity. As a result, the rightward shift in supply has caused a great reduction in the equilibrium price and a small increase in the equilibrium quantity. Thus, ironically, technological advances in agriculture reduce total revenue paid to farmers as a group.

- *The market for oil:* In the 1970s, the Organization of Petroleum Exporting Countries (OPEC) reduced the supply of oil in order to raise its price. In the short run, the demand for oil tends to be inelastic (steep) because consumers cannot easily find substitutes. Thus, the decrease in supply raised the price substantially and increased total revenue to the producers. In the long run, however, consumers found substitutes and drove more fuel efficient cars causing the demand for oil to become more elastic, and producers searched for more oil causing supply to become more elastic. As a result, while the price of oil rose a great deal in the short run, it did not rise much in the long run.

- *The market for illegal drugs:* In the short run, the demand for illegal addictive drugs is relatively inelastic. As a result, drug interdiction policies that reduce the supply of drugs tend to greatly increase the price of drugs while reducing the quantity consumed very little and, thus, total revenue paid by drug users increases. This need for additional funds by drug users may cause drug-related crime to rise. This increase in total revenue and in crime is likely to be smaller in the long run because the demand for illegal drugs becomes more elastic as time passes. Alternatively, policies aimed at reducing the demand for drugs reduce total revenue in the drug market and reduce drug-related crime.

Conclusion

The tools of supply and demand allow you to analyze the most important events and policies that shape the economy.

HELPFUL HINTS

1. An easy way to remember the difference between the terms elastic and inelastic is to substitute the word *sensitivity* for elasticity. For example, price elasticity of demand becomes price *sensitivity* of demand. If the quantity demanded is sensitive to a change in price (demand is relatively flat), demand is elastic. If the quantity demanded is insensitive to a change in price (demand is relatively steep), demand is inelastic. The same is true for

the price elasticity of supply. If the quantity supplied is sensitive to a change in price, supply is elastic. If the quantity supplied is insensitive to a change in price, supply is inelastic.

2. While elasticity and slope are similar, they are not the same. Along a straight line, slope is constant. Slope (rise over run) is the same anywhere on the line and is measured as the change in the dependent variable divided by the change in the independent variable. Elasticity, however, is measured as the *percent* change in the dependent variable divided by the *percent* change in the independent variable. This value changes as we move along a line because a one-unit change in a variable is a larger percentage change when the initial values are small as opposed to when they are large. In practice, however, it is still reasonable to suggest that flatter curves tend to be more elastic and steeper curves tend to be more inelastic.

3. The term "elasticity" is used to describe how much the quantity stretches (or changes) in response to some economic event such as a change in price or income. If the quantity stretches a great deal in response to a change in price or income, it is considered elastic. This mental picture should also help you to remember how to calculate an elasticity—in the numerator you will always find the percent change in quantity and in the denominator you will always find the percent change in the variable that is the source of the change in quantity.

TERMS AND DEFINITIONS

Choose a definition for each key term.

Key terms:

_____ Elasticity

_____ Price elasticity of demand

_____ Elastic

_____ Inelastic

_____ Total revenue

_____ Income elasticity of demand

_____ Cross-price elasticity of demand

_____ Price elasticity of supply

_____ Normal good

_____ Inferior good

Definitions:

1. A measure of how much the quantity demanded of a good responds to a change in consumers' income.
2. When the quantity demanded or supplied responds substantially to a change in one of its determinants.
3. A good characterized by a negative income elasticity.
4. A measure of the responsiveness of the quantity demanded or quantity supplied to one of its determinants.
5. A good characterized by a positive income elasticity.
6. A measure of how much the quantity supplied of a good responds to a change in the price of that good.
7. When the quantity demanded or supplied responds only slightly to a change in one of its determinants.
8. The amount paid by buyers and received by sellers of a good computed as P ¥ Q.
9. A measure of how much the quantity demanded of a good responds to a change in the price of that good.
10. A measure of how much the quantity demanded of one good responds to a change in the price of another good.

PROBLEMS AND SHORT-ANSWER QUESTIONS

Practice Problems

1. For each pair of goods listed below, which good would you expect to have the more elastic demand? Why?
   a. cigarettes; a trip to Florida over spring break

   b. an AIDS vaccine over the next month; an AIDS vaccine over the next five years

   c. beer; Budweiser

   d. insulin; aspirin

2. Suppose the *Daily Newspaper* estimates that if it raises the price of its newspaper from $1.00 to $1.50 then the number of subscribers will fall from 50,000 to 40,000.
   a. What is the price elasticity of demand for the *Daily Newspaper* when elasticity is calculated using the midpoint method?

   b. What is the advantage of using the midpoint method?

c. If the *Daily Newspaper*'s only concern is to maximize total revenue, should it raise the price of a newspaper from $1.00 to $1.50? Why or why not?

____

____

3. The table below provides the demand schedule for motel rooms at Small Town Motel. Use the information provided to complete the table. Answer the following questions based on your responses in the table. Use the midpoint method to calculate the percentage changes used to generate the elasticities.

Price	Quantity Demanded	Total Revenue	% Change in Price	% Change in Quantity	Elasticity
$20	24	_______			
			_______	_______	_______
40	20	_______			
			_______	_______	_______
60	16	_______			
			_______	_______	_______
80	12	_______			
			_______	_______	_______
100	8	_______			
			_______	_______	_______
120	4	_______			

a. Over what range of prices is the demand for motel rooms elastic? To maximize total revenue, should Small Town Motel raise or lower the price within this range?

____

____

b. Over what range of prices is the demand for motel rooms inelastic? To maximize total revenue, should Small Town Motel raise or lower the price within this range?

____

____

c. Over what range of prices is the demand for motel rooms unit elastic? To maximize total revenue, should Small Town Motel raise or lower the price within this range?

____

____

4. The demand schedule from question 3 above is reproduced below along with another demand schedule when consumer incomes have risen to $60,000 from $50,000. Use this information to answer the following questions. Use the midpoint method to calculate the percentage changes used to generate the elasticities.

Price	Quantity Demanded When Income is $50,000	Quantity Demanded When Income is $60,000
$ 20	24	34
40	20	30
60	16	26
80	12	22
100	8	18
120	4	14

a. What is the income elasticity of demand when motel rooms rent for $40?

____

____

b. What is the income elasticity of demand when motel rooms rent for $100?

____

____

c. Are motel rooms normal or inferior goods? Why?

____

____

d. Are motel rooms likely to be necessities or luxuries? Why?

____

____

5. For each pair of goods listed below, which good would you expect to have the more elastic supply? Why?

a. televisions; beach front property

____

____

b. crude oil over the next week; crude oil over the next year

____

____

c. a painting by van Gogh; a print of the same painting by van Gogh

Short-Answer Questions

1. What are the four major determinants of the price elasticity of demand?

2. If demand is inelastic, will an increase in price raise or lower total revenue? Why?

3. If the price of soda doubles from $1.00 per can to $2.00 per can and you buy the same amount, what is your price elasticity of demand for soda and is it considered elastic or inelastic?

4. If the price of Pepsi increases by one cent and this induces you to stop buying Pepsi altogether and to switch to Coke, what is your price elasticity of demand for Pepsi and is it considered elastic or inelastic?

5. Suppose your income rises by 20 percent and your quantity demanded of eggs falls by 10 percent. What is the value of your income elasticity of demand for eggs? Are eggs normal or inferior goods to you?

6. Suppose a firm is operating at half capacity. Is its supply curve for output likely to be relatively elastic or inelastic? Why?

7. Is the price elasticity of supply for fresh fish likely to be elastic or inelastic when measured over the time period of one day? Why?

___

___

8. If a demand curve is linear, is the elasticity constant along the demand curve? Which part tends to be elastic and which part tends to be inelastic? Why?

___

___

___

___

9. Suppose that at a price of $2.00 per bushel, the quantity supplied of corn is 25 million metric tons. At a price of $3.00 per bushel, the quantity supplied is 30 million metric tons. What is the elasticity of supply for corn? Is supply elastic or inelastic?

___

___

10. Suppose that when the price of apples rises by 20 percent, the quantity demanded of oranges rises by 6 percent. What is the cross-price elasticity of demand between apples and oranges? Are these two goods substitutes or complements?

___

___

SELF-TEST

True/False Questions

_____ 1. If the quantity demanded of a good is sensitive to a change in the price of that good, demand is said to be price inelastic.

_____ 2. Using the midpoint method to calculate elasticity, if an increase in the price of pencils from 10 cents to 20 cents reduces the quantity demanded from 1000 pencils to 500 pencils, then the demand for pencils is unit price elastic.

_____ 3. The demand for tires should be more inelastic than the demand for Goodyear brand tires.

_____ 4. The demand for aspirin this month should be more elastic than the demand for aspirin this year.

_____ 5. The price elasticity of demand is defined as the percentage change in the price of that good divided by the percentage change in quantity demanded of that good.

_____ 6. If the cross-price elasticity of demand between two goods is positive, the goods are likely to be complements.

_____ 7. If the demand for a good is price inelastic, an increase in its price will increase total revenue in that market.

_____ 8. The demand for a necessity such as insulin tends to be elastic.

_____ 9. If a demand curve is linear, the price elasticity of demand is constant along it.

_____10. If the income elasticity of demand for a bus ride is negative, then a bus ride is an inferior good.

_____11. The supply of automobiles for this week is likely to be more price inelastic than the supply of automobiles for this year.

_____12. If the price elasticity of supply for blue jeans is 1.3, an increase in the price of blue jeans of 10 percent would increase the quantity supplied of blue jeans by 13 percent.

_____13. The price elasticity of supply tends to be more inelastic as the firm's production facility reaches maximum capacity.

_____14. An advance in technology that shifts the market supply curve to the right always increases total revenue received by producers.

_____15. The income elasticity of demand for luxury items, such as diamonds, tends to be large (greater than 1).

Multiple-Choice Questions

1. If a small percentage increase in the price of a good greatly reduces the quantity demanded for that good, the demand for that good is
   a. price inelastic.
   b. price elastic.
   c. unit price elastic.
   d. income inelastic.
   e. income elastic.

2. The price elasticity of demand is defined as
   a. the percentage change in price of a good divided by the percentage change in the quantity demanded of that good.
   b. the percentage change in income divided by the percentage change in the quantity demanded.
   c. the percentage change in the quantity demanded of a good divided by the percentage change in the price of that good.
   d. the percentage change in the quantity demanded divided by the percentage change in income.
   e. none of the above.

3. In general, a flatter demand curve is more likely to be
   a. price elastic.
   b. price inelastic.
   c. unit price elastic.
   d. none of the above.

4. In general, a steeper supply curve is more likely to be
   a. price elastic.
   b. price inelastic.
   c. unit price elastic.
   d. none of the above.

5. Which of the following would cause a demand curve for a good to be price inelastic?
   a. There are a great number of substitutes for the good.
   b. The good is inferior.
   c. The good is a luxury.
   d. The good is a necessity.

6. The demand for which of the following is likely to be the most price inelastic?
   a. airline tickets
   b. bus tickets
   c. taxi rides
   d. transportation

7. If the cross-price elasticity between two goods is negative, the two goods are likely to be
   a. luxuries.
   b. necessities.
   c. complements.
   d. substitutes.

8. If a supply curve for a good is price elastic, then
   a. the quantity supplied is sensitive to changes in the price of that good.
   b. the quantity supplied is insensitive to changes in the price of that good.
   c. the quantity demanded is sensitive to changes in the price of that good.
   d. the quantity demanded is insensitive to changes in the price of that good.
   e. none of the above.

9. If a fisherman must sell all of his daily catch before it spoils for whatever price he is offered, once the fish are caught the fisherman's price elasticity of supply for fresh fish is
   a. zero.
   b. one.
   c. infinite.
   d. unable to be determined from this information.

10. A decrease in supply (shift to the left) will increase total revenue in that market if
    a. supply is price elastic.
    b. supply is price inelastic.
    c. demand is price elastic.
    d. demand is price inelastic.

11. If an increase in the price of a good has no impact on the total revenue in that market, demand must be
    a. price inelastic.
    b. price elastic.
    c. unit price elastic.
    d. all of the above.

12. If consumers always spend 15 percent of their income on food, then the income elasticity of demand for food is
    a. 0.15.
    b. 1.00.
    c. 1.15.
    d. 1.50.
    e. none of the above.

13. Technological improvements in agriculture that shift the supply of agricultural commodities to the right tend to
    a. reduce total revenue to farmers as a whole because the demand for food is inelastic.
    b. reduce total revenue to farmers as a whole because the demand for food is elastic.
    c. increase total revenue to farmers as a whole because the demand for food is inelastic.
    d. increase total revenue to farmers as a whole because the demand for food is elastic.

14. If supply is price inelastic, the value of the price elasticity of supply must be
    a. zero.
    b. less than 1.
    c. greater than 1.
    d. infinite.
    e. none of the above.

15. If there is excess capacity in a production facility, it is likely that the firm's supply curve is
    a. price inelastic.
    b. price elastic.
    c. unit price elastic.
    d. none of the above.

Use the following information to answer the next two questions. Suppose that at a price of $30 per month, there are 30,000 subscribers to cable television in Small Town. If Small Town Cablevision raises its price to $40 per month, the number of subscribers will fall to 20,000.

16. Using the midpoint method for calculating the elasticity, what is the price elasticity of demand for cable TV in Small Town?
    a. 0.66
    b. 0.75
    c. 1.0
    d. 1.4
    e. 2.0

17. At which of the following prices does Small Town Cablevision earn the greatest total revenue?
    a. Either $30 or $40 per month because the price elasticity of demand is 1.0.
    b. $30 per month
    c. $40 per month
    d. $0 per month

18. If demand is linear (a straight line), then price elasticity of demand is
    a. constant along the demand curve.
    b. inelastic in the upper portion and elastic in the lower portion.
    c. elastic in the upper portion and inelastic in the lower portion.
    d. elastic throughout.
    e. inelastic throughout.

19. If the income elasticity of demand for a good is negative, it must be
    a. a luxury good.
    b. a normal good.
    c. an inferior good.
    d. an elastic good.

20. If consumers think that there are very few substitutes for a good, then
    a. supply would tend to be price elastic.
    b. supply would tend to be price inelastic.
    c. demand would tend to be price elastic.
    d. demand would tend to be price inelastic.
    e. none of the above.

ADVANCED CRITICAL THINKING

In order to reduce teen smoking, the government places a $2 per pack tax on cigarettes. After one month, while the price to the consumer has increased a great deal, the quantity demanded of cigarettes has been reduced only slightly.

1. Is the demand for cigarettes over the period of one month elastic or inelastic?

____

____

2. Suppose you are in charge of pricing for a tobacco firm. The president of your firm suggests that the evidence received over the last month demonstrates that the cigarette industry should get together and raise the price of cigarettes further because total revenue to the tobacco industry will certainly rise. Is the president of your firm correct? Why?

____

____

____

3. As an alternative, suppose the president of your tobacco firm suggests that your firm should raise the price of your cigarettes independent of the other tobacco firms because the evidence clearly shows that smokers are insensitive to changes in the price of cigarettes. Is the president of your firm correct if it is his/her desire to maximize total revenue? Why?

____

____

____

SOLUTIONS

Terms and Definitions

4 Elasticity

9 Price elasticity of demand

2 Elastic

7 Inelastic

8 Total revenue

1 Income elasticity of demand

10 Cross-price elasticity of demand

6 Price elasticity of supply

5 Normal good

3 Inferior good

Practice Problems

1. a. a trip to Florida because it is a luxury while cigarettes are a necessity (to smokers)
   b. an AIDS vaccine over the next five years because there are likely to be more substitutes (alternative medications) developed over this time period and consumers' behavior may be modified over longer time periods
   c. Budweiser because it is a more narrowly defined market than beer so there are more substitutes for Budweiser than for beer
   d. aspirin because there are many substitutes for aspirin but few substitutes for insulin

2. a. (10,000/45,000)/($.50/$1.25) = 0.56
   b. With the midpoint method, the value of the elasticity is the same whether you begin at a price of $1.00 and raise it to $1.50 or begin at a price of $1.50 and reduce it to $1.00.
   c. Yes. Since the price elasticity of demand is less than one (inelastic), an increase in price will increase total revenue.

3.

Price	Quantity Demanded	Total Revenue	% Change In Price	% Change In Quantity	Elasticity
$ 20	24	480			
			0.67	0.18	0.27
40	20	800			
			0.40	0.22	0.55
60	16	960			
			0.29	0.29	1.00
80	12	960			
			0.22	0.40	1.82
100	8	800			
			0.18	0.67	3.72
120	4	480			

a. $80 to $120; lower its prices
b. $20 to $60; raise its prices
c. $60 to $80; it doesn't matter. For these prices, a change in price proportionately changes the quantity demanded so total revenue is unchanged.

4. a. (10/25)/($10,000/$55,000) = 2.2
   b. (10/13)/($10,000/$55,000) = 4.2
   c. Normal goods, because the income elasticity of demand is positive.
   d. Luxuries, because the income elasticity of demand is large (greater than 1). In each case, an 18 percent increase in income caused a much larger increase in quantity demanded.

5. a. Televisions because the production of televisions can be increased in response to an increase in the price of televisions while the quantity of beach front property is fixed.
   b. Crude oil over the next year because production of oil over the next year can more easily be increased than the production of oil over the next week.
   c. A van Gogh print because more of them can be created in response to an increase in price while the quantity of an original work is fixed.

Short-Answer Questions

1. Whether the good is a necessity or a luxury, the availability of close substitutes, the definition of the market, and the time horizon over which demand is measured.

2. It will increase total revenue because a large increase in price will be accompanied by only a small reduction in the quantity demanded if demand is inelastic.

3. Zero, therefore it is considered perfectly inelastic.

4. Infinite, therefore it is considered perfectly elastic.

5. – 0.10/0.20 = –1/2. Eggs are inferior goods.

6. Elastic because a small increase in price will induce the firm to increase production a large amount.

7. Inelastic (nearly vertical) because once the fish are caught, the quantity offered for sale is fixed and must be sold before it spoils, regardless of the price.

8. No. The upper part tends to be elastic while the lower part tends to be inelastic. This is because on the upper part, for example, a one unit change in the price is a small percentage change while a one unit

change in quantity is a large percentage change. This effect is reversed on the lower part of the demand curve.

9. $\dfrac{(30 - 25)/[(25 + 30)/2]}{(3 - 2)/[(2 + 3)/2]} = 0.45$, therefore supply is inelastic.

10. $0.06/0.20 = 0.30$, apples and oranges are substitutes because the cross-price elasticity is positive (an increase in the price of apples increases the quantity demanded of oranges).

True/False Questions

1. F; demand would be price elastic.
2. T
3. T
4. F; the longer the time period considered, the more price elastic the demand curve because consumers have an opportunity to substitute or change their behavior.
5. F; the price elasticity of demand is defined as the percentage change in the quantity demanded of a good divided by the percentage change in the price of that good.
6. F; the two goods are likely to be substitutes.
7. T
8. F; the demand for necessities tends to be inelastic.
9. F; demand will be price elastic in its upper portion and price inelastic in its lower portion.
10. T
11. T
12. T
13. T
14. F; it will increase total revenue only if demand is price elastic.
15. T

Multiple-Choice Questions

1. b
2. c
3. a
4. b
5. d
6. d
7. c
8. a
9. a
10. d
11. c
12. b
13. a
14. b
15. b
16. d
17. b
18. c
19. c
20. d

Advanced Critical Thinking

1. Inelastic.

2. Not necessarily. Demand tends to be more elastic over longer periods. In the case of cigarettes, some consumers will substitute toward cigars and pipes. Others may quit or never start to smoke.

3. No. While the demand for cigarettes (the market broadly defined) may be inelastic, the demand for any one brand (market narrowly defined) is likely to be much more elastic because consumers can substitute toward other lower priced brands.

6

SUPPLY, DEMAND, AND GOVERNMENT POLICIES

GOALS

In this chapter you will

Examine the effects of government policies that place a ceiling on prices

Examine the effects of government policies that put a floor under prices

Consider how a tax on a good affects the price of the good and the quantity sold

Learn that taxes levied on buyers and taxes levied on sellers are equivalent

See how the burden of a tax is split between buyers and sellers

OUTCOMES

After accomplishing these goals, you should be able to

Describe the conditions necessary for a price ceiling to be a binding constraint

Explain why a binding price floor creates a surplus

Demonstrate why a tax placed on a good generally reduces the quantity of the good sold

Demonstrate why the results are the same when a tax is placed on the buyers or sellers of a good

Show whether the buyers or sellers of a good bear the burden of the tax when demand is inelastic and supply is elastic

CHAPTER OVERVIEW

Context and Purpose

Chapter 6 is the third chapter in a three-chapter sequence that deals with supply and demand and how markets work. Chapter 4 developed the model of supply and demand. Chapter 5 added precision to the model of supply and demand by developing the concept of elasticity—the sensitivity of the quantity supplied and quantity demanded to changes in economic conditions. Chapter 6 addresses the impact of government policies on competitive markets using the tools of supply and demand that you learned in Chapters 4 and 5.

The purpose of Chapter 6 is to consider two types of government policies—price controls and taxes. Price controls set the maximum or minimum price at which a good can be sold while a tax creates a wedge between what the buyer pays and the seller receives. These policies can be analyzed within the model of supply and demand. We will find that government policies sometimes produce unintended consequences.

CHAPTER REVIEW

Introduction

In Chapters 4 and 5, we acted as scientists because we built the model of supply and demand to describe the world as it is. In Chapter 6, we act as policy advisors because we address how government policies are used to try to improve the world. We address two policies—price controls and taxes. Sometimes these policies produce unintended consequences.

Controls on Prices

There are two types of controls on prices: price ceilings and price floors. A **price ceiling** sets a legal maximum on the price at which a good can be sold. A **price floor** sets a legal minimum on the price at which a good can be sold.

Price ceilings Suppose the government is persuaded by buyers to set a price ceiling. If the price ceiling is set above the equilibrium price, it is *not binding*. That is, it has no impact on the market because the price can move to equilibrium without restriction. If the price ceiling is set below the equilibrium price, it is a *binding constraint* because it does not allow the market to reach equilibrium. A binding price ceiling causes the quantity demanded to exceed the quantity supplied, or a shortage. Since there is a shortage, methods develop to ration the small quantity supplied across a large number of buyers. Buyers willing to wait in long lines might get the good, or sellers could sell only to their friends, family, or same race. Lines are inefficient and discrimination is both inefficient and unfair. Free markets are impersonal and ration goods with prices.

Price ceilings are commonly found in the markets for gasoline and apartments. When OPEC restricted the quantity of petroleum in 1973, the supply of gasoline was reduced and the equilibrium price rose above the price ceiling and the price ceiling became binding. This caused a shortage of gas and long lines at the pump. In response, the price ceilings were later repealed. Price ceilings on apartments are known as rent controls. Binding rent controls create a shortage of housing. Both the demand and supply of housing are inelastic in the short run so the initial shortage is small. In the long run, however, the supply and demand for housing become more elastic and the shortage is more apparent. This causes waiting lists for apartments, bribes to landlords, unclean and unsafe buildings, and lower quality housing.

When the government does not allow the price of water to rise during a drought, it acts as a price ceiling and a water shortage develops.

Price floors Suppose the government is persuaded by sellers to set a price floor. If the price floor is set below the equilibrium price, it is *not binding*. That is, it has no impact on the market because the price can move to equilibrium without restriction. If the price floor is set above the equilibrium price, it is a *binding constraint* because it does not allow the market to reach equilibrium. A binding price floor causes the quantity supplied to exceed the quantity demanded, or a surplus. In order to eliminate the surplus, sellers may appeal to the biases of the buyers and sell to family or same race buyers. Free markets are impersonal and ration goods with prices.

An important example of a price floor is the minimum wage. The minimum wage is a binding constraint in the market for young and unskilled workers. When the wage is set above the market equilibrium wage, the quantity supplied of labor exceeds the quantity demanded. The result is unemployment. Studies show that a 10 percent increase in the minimum wage depresses teenage employment by 1 to 3 percent. The minimum wage also causes teenagers to look for work and drop out of school.

Price controls often hurt those they are trying to help—usually the poor. The minimum wage may help those who find work at the minimum wage but harm those who become unemployed as a result of the minimum wage. Rent controls reduce the quality and availability of housing.

Taxes

Governments use taxes to raise revenue. A tax on a good will affect the quantity sold and both the price paid by buyers and the price received by sellers. If the tax is collected from the buyers, demand shifts downward by the size of the tax per unit. As a result of the decrease in demand, the quantity sold decreases, the price paid by the buyer increases, and the price received by the seller decreases. If the tax is collected from the sellers, supply shifts upward by the size of the tax per unit. As a result of the decrease in supply, the quantity sold decreases, the price paid by the buyer increases, and the price received by the seller decreases. Therefore, a tax collected from buyers has the same effect as a tax collected from sellers. After a tax has been placed on a good, the difference between what the buyer pays and the seller receives is the tax per unit and is known as the *tax wedge*. In summary:

- A tax discourages market activity. That is, the quantity sold is reduced.
- Buyers and sellers share the burden of a tax because the price paid by the buyers increases while the price received by the sellers decreases.
- The effect of a tax collected from buyers is equivalent to a tax collected from sellers.
- The government cannot legislate the relative burden of the tax between buyers and sellers. The relative burden of a tax is determined by the elasticity of supply and demand in that market.

Tax incidence is the manner in which the burden of a tax is shared among participants in a market. When a tax wedge is placed between buyers and sellers, the tax burden falls more heavily on the side of the market that is less elastic. That is, the tax burden falls more heavily on the side of the market that is less willing to leave the market when price movements are unfavorable to them. For example, in the market for cigarettes, since cigarettes are addictive, demand is likely to be less elastic than supply. Therefore, a tax on cigarettes tends to raise the price paid by buyers more than it reduces the price received by sellers and, as a result, the burden of a cigarette tax falls more heavily on the buyers of cigarettes. With regard to the payroll tax (Social Security and Medicare tax), since labor supply is less elastic than labor demand, most of the tax burden is born by the workers as opposed to the 50-50 split intended by lawmakers.

Conclusion

Supply and demand can be utilized to analyze the impact of government policies such as price controls and taxes.

HELPFUL HINTS

1. Price ceilings and price floors only matter if they are binding constraints. Price ceilings do not automatically cause a shortage. A price ceiling only causes a shortage if the price ceiling is set below the equilibrium price. In a similar manner, a price floor only causes a surplus if the price floor is set above the equilibrium price.

2. It is useful to think of taxes as causing vertical shifts in demand and supply. Since demand is the maximum buyers are willing to pay for each quantity, a tax imposed on the buyers in a market reduces or shifts downward the demand *faced by sellers* by precisely the size of the tax per unit. That is, the buyers now offer the sellers an amount that has been reduced by precisely the size of the tax per unit. Alternatively, since supply is the minimum sellers are willing to accept for each quantity, a tax imposed on the sellers in a market reduces or shifts upward the supply *faced by buyers* by precisely the size of the tax per unit. This is because the sellers now require an additional amount from the buyers that is precisely the size of the tax per unit.

TERMS AND DEFINITIONS

Choose a definition for each key term.

Key terms:

_____ Price ceiling

_____ Price floor

_____ Tax incidence

_____ Tax wedge

Definitions:

1. The manner in which the burden of a tax is shared among participants in a market
2. A legal maximum on the price at which a good can be sold
3. The difference between what the buyer pays and the seller receives after a tax has been imposed
4. A legal minimum on the price at which a good can be sold

PROBLEMS AND SHORT-ANSWER QUESTIONS

Practice Problems

1. Use the following supply and demand schedules for bicycles to answer the questions below.

Price	Quantity demanded	Quantity supplied
$300	60	30
400	55	40
500	50	50
600	45	60
700	40	70
800	35	80

a. In response to lobbying by the Bicycle Riders Association, Congress places a price ceiling of $700 on bicycles. What effect will this have on the market for bicycles? Why?

____

____

____

____

b. In response to lobbying by the Bicycle Riders Association, Congress places a price ceiling of $400 on bicycles. Use the information provided above to plot the supply and demand curves for bicycles in Exhibit 1. Impose the price ceiling. What is the result of a price ceiling of $400 on bicycles?

____

____

____

____

EXHIBIT 1

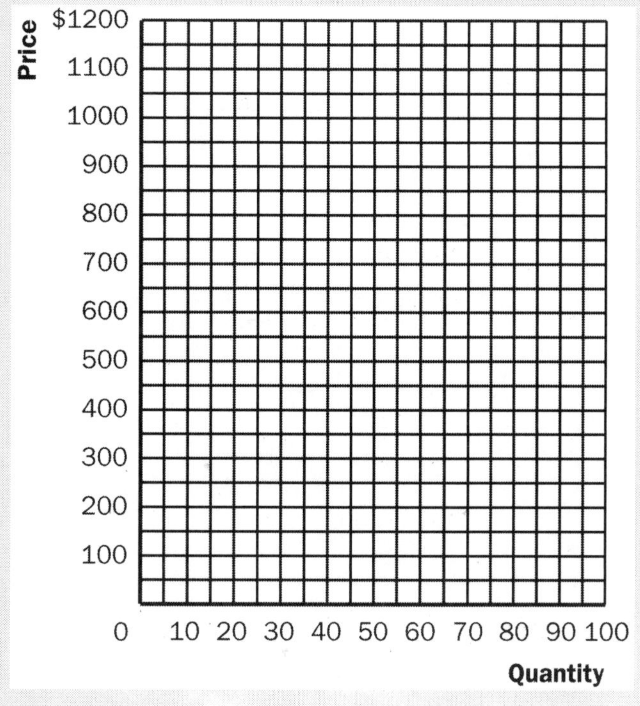

c. Does a price ceiling of $400 on bicycles make all bicycle buyers better off? Why or why not?

____

____

____

____

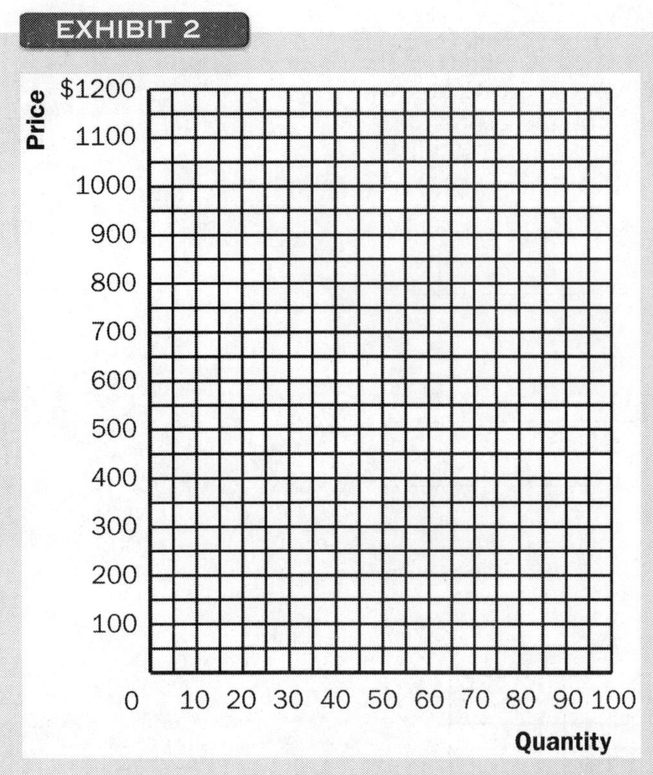

d. Suppose instead, in response to lobbying by the Bicycle Manufactures Association, Congress imposes a price floor on bicycles of $700. Use the information provided above to plot the supply and demand curves for bicycles in Exhibit 2. Impose the $700 price floor. What is the result of the $700 price floor?

____

____

____

____

____

____

____

____

____

____

2. Use the following supply and demand schedules for bicycles to answer the questions below.

Price	Quantity demanded	Quantity supplied
$300	60	30
400	55	40
500	50	50
600	45	60
700	40	70
800	35	80

a. Plot the supply and demand curves for bicycles in Exhibit 3. On the graph, impose a tax of $300 per bicycle to be collected from the sellers. After the tax, what has happened to the price paid by the buyers, the price received by the sellers, and the quantity sold when compared to the free market equilibrium?

EXHIBIT 3

Price: $1200, 1100, 1000, 900, 800, 700, 600, 500, 400, 300, 200, 100

0 10 20 30 40 50 60 70 80 90 100

Quantity

b. Again, plot the supply and demand curves for bicycles in Exhibit 4. On the graph, impose a tax of $300 per bicycle to be collected from the buyers. After the tax, what has happened to the price paid by the buyers, the price received by the sellers, and the quantity sold when compared to the free market equilibrium?

EXHIBIT 4

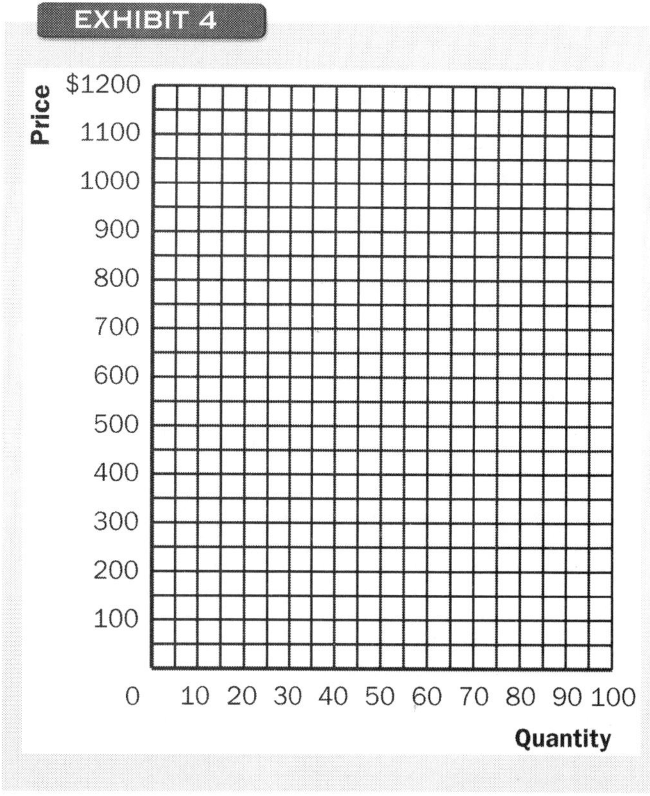

c. Compare your answers to questions (a) and (b) above. What conclusion do you draw from this comparison?

d. Who bears the greater burden of this tax, the buyers or the sellers? Why?

Short-Answer Questions

1. What is the impact on the price and quantity in a market if a price ceiling is set above the equilibrium price? Why?

2. What is the impact on the price and quantity in a market if a price ceiling is set below the equilibrium price?

3. What are some of the problems created by a binding price ceiling?

4. Is the impact of a binding price ceiling greater in the short run or the long run? Why?

5. What is the impact on the price and quantity in a market if a price floor is set below the equilibrium price? Why?

6. What is the impact on the price and quantity in a market if a price floor is set above the equilibrium price?

7. When we use the model of supply and demand to analyze a tax that is collected from the buyers, which way do we shift the demand curve? Why?

____

____

____

8. When we use the model of supply and demand to analyze a tax that is collected from the sellers, which way do we shift the supply curve? Why?

____

____

____

9. Why is a tax collected from the buyers equivalent to a tax collected from the sellers?

____

____

____

10. Suppose a gas-guzzler tax is placed on luxury automobiles. Who will likely bear the greater burden of the tax, the buyers of luxury autos or the sellers? Why?

____

____

____

____

SELF-TEST

True/False Questions

_____ 1. If the equilibrium price of gasoline is $1.00 per gallon and the government places a price ceiling on gasoline of $1.50 per gallon, the result will be a shortage of gasoline.

_____ 2. A price ceiling set below the equilibrium price causes a surplus.

_____ 3. A price floor set above the equilibrium price is a binding constraint.

_____ 4. The shortage of housing caused by a binding rent control is likely to be more severe in the long run when compared to the short run.

_____ 5. The minimum wage helps all teenagers because they receive higher wages than they would otherwise.

_____ 6. A 10 percent increase in the minimum wage causes a 10 percent reduction in teenage employment.

_____ 7. A price ceiling that is not a binding constraint today could cause a shortage in the future if demand were to increase and raise the equilibrium price above the fixed price ceiling.

_____ 8. A price floor in a market always creates a surplus in that market.

_____ 9. A $10 tax on baseball gloves will always raise the price that the buyers pay for baseball gloves by $10.

_____10. The ultimate burden of a tax lands most heavily on the side of the market that is less elastic.

_____11. If medicine is a necessity, the burden of a tax on medicine will likely land more heavily on the buyers of medicine.

_____12. When we use the model of supply and demand to analyze a tax collected from the buyers, we shift the demand curve upward by the size of the tax.

_____13. A tax collected from buyers has an equivalent impact to a same size tax collected from sellers.

_____14. A tax creates a tax wedge between a buyer and a seller. This causes the price paid by the buyer to rise, the price received by the seller to fall, and the quantity sold to fall.

_____15. The government can choose to place the burden of a tax on the buyers in a market by collecting the tax from the buyers rather than the sellers.

Multiple-Choice Questions

1. For a price ceiling to be a binding constraint on the market, the government must set it
   a. above the equilibrium price.
   b. below the equilibrium price.
   c. precisely at the equilibrium price.
   d. at any price because all price ceilings are binding constraints.

2. A binding price ceiling creates
   a. a shortage.
   b. a surplus.
   c. an equilibrium.
   d. a shortage or a surplus depending on whether the price ceiling is set above or below the equilibrium price.

3. Suppose the equilibrium price for apartments is $500 per month and the government imposes rent controls of $250. Which of the following is *unlikely* to occur as a result of the rent controls?
   a. There will be a shortage of housing.
   b. Landlords may discriminate among apartment renters.
   c. Landlords may be offered bribes to rent apartments.
   d. The quality of apartments will improve.
   e. There may be long lines of buyers waiting for apartments.

4. A price floor
   a. sets a legal maximum on the price at which a good can be sold.
   b. sets a legal minimum on the price at which a good can be sold.
   c. always determines the price at which a good must be sold.
   d. is not a binding constraint if it is set above the equilibrium price.

5. Which of the following statements about a binding price ceiling is true?
   a. The surplus created by the price ceiling is greater in the short run than in the long run.
   b. The surplus created by the price ceiling is greater in the long run than in the short run.
   c. The shortage created by the price ceiling is greater in the short run than in the long run.
   d. The shortage created by the price ceiling is greater in the long run than in the short run.

6. Which side of the market is more likely to lobby government for a price floor?
   a. Neither buyers or sellers desire a price floor.
   b. Both buyers and sellers desire a price floor.
   c. the sellers
   d. the buyers

7. The surplus caused by a binding price floor will be greatest if
   a. both supply and demand are elastic.
   b. both supply and demand are inelastic.
   c. supply is inelastic and demand is elastic.
   d. demand is inelastic and supply is elastic.

8. Which of the following is an example of a price floor?
   a. rent controls
   b. restricting gasoline prices to $1.00 per gallon when the equilibrium price is $1.50 per gallon
   c. the minimum wage
   d. All of the above are price floors.

9. Which of the following statements is true if the government places a price ceiling on gasoline at $1.50 per gallon and the equilibrium price is $1.00 per gallon?
   a. There will be a shortage of gasoline.
   b. There will be a surplus of gasoline.
   c. A significant increase in the supply of gasoline could cause the price ceiling to become a binding constraint.
   d. A significant increase in the demand for gasoline could cause the price ceiling to become a binding constraint.

10. Studies show that a 10 percent increase in the minimum wage
    a. decreases teenage employment by about 10 to 15 percent.
    b. increases teenage employment by about 10 to 15 percent.
    c. decreases teenage employment by about 1 to 3 percent.
    d. increases teenage employment by about 1 to 3 percent.

11. Within the supply and demand model, a tax collected from the buyers of a good shifts the
    a. demand curve upward by the size of the tax per unit.
    b. demand curve downward by the size of the tax per unit.
    c. supply curve upward by the size of the tax per unit.
    d. supply curve downward by the size of the tax per unit.

12. Within the supply and demand model, a tax collected from the sellers of a good shifts the
    a. demand curve upward by the size of the tax per unit.
    b. demand curve downward by the size of the tax per unit.
    c. supply curve upward by the size of the tax per unit.
    d. supply curve downward by the size of the tax per unit.

13. Which of the following takes place when a tax is placed a good?
    a. an increase in the price buyers pay, a decrease in the price sellers receive, and a decrease in the quantity sold
    b. an increase in the price buyers pay, a decrease in the price sellers receive, and an increase in the quantity sold
    c. a decrease in the price buyers pay, an increase in the price sellers receive, and a decrease in the quantity sold
    d. a decrease in the price buyers pay, an increase in the price sellers receive, and an increase in the quantity sold

14. When a tax is collected from the buyers in a market,
    a. the buyers bear the burden of the tax.
    b. the sellers bear the burden of the tax.
    c. the tax burden on the buyers and sellers is the same as an equivalent tax collected from the sellers.
    d. the tax burden falls most heavily on the buyers.

15. A tax of $1.00 per gallon on gasoline
    a. increases the price the buyers pay by $1.00 per gallon.
    b. decreases the price the sellers receive by $1.00 per gallon.
    c. increases the price the buyers pay by precisely $.50 and reduces the price received by sellers by precisely $.50.
    d. places a tax wedge of $1.00 between the price the buyers pay and the price the sellers receive.

16. The burden of a tax falls more heavily on the sellers in a market when
    a. demand is inelastic and supply is elastic.
    b. demand is elastic and supply is inelastic.
    c. both supply and demand are elastic.
    d. both supply and demand are inelastic.

17. A tax placed on a good that is a necessity for consumers will likely generate a tax burden that
    a. falls more heavily on buyers.
    b. falls more heavily on sellers.
    c. is evenly distributed between buyers and sellers.
    d. falls entirely on sellers.

18. The burden of a tax falls more heavily on the buyers in a market when
    a. demand is inelastic and supply is elastic.
    b. demand is elastic and supply is inelastic.
    c. both supply and demand are elastic.
    d. both supply and demand are inelastic.

19. Which of the following statements about the burden of a tax is correct?
    a. The tax burden generated from a tax placed on a good consumers perceive to be a necessity will fall most heavily on the sellers of the good.
    b. The tax burden falls most heavily on the side of the market (buyers or sellers) that is most willing to leave the market when price movements are unfavorable to them.
    c. The burden of a tax lands on the side of the market (buyers or sellers) from which it is collected.
    d. The distribution of the burden of a tax is determined by the relative elasticities of supply and demand and is not determined by legislation.

20. For which of the following products would the burden of a tax likely fall more heavily on the sellers?
    a. food
    b. entertainment
    c. clothing
    d. housing

ADVANCED CRITICAL THINKING

Suppose that the government needs to raise tax revenue. A politician suggests that the government place a tax on food because everyone must eat and, thus, a food tax would surely raise a great deal of tax revenue. However, since the poor spend a large proportion of their income on food, the tax should be collected only from the sellers of food (grocery stores) and not from the buyers of food. The politician argues that this type of tax would place the burden of the tax on corporate grocery store chains and not on poor consumers.

1. Can the government legislate that the burden of a food tax will fall only on the sellers of food? Why or why not?

____

____

____

____

2. Do you think the burden of a food tax will tend to fall on the sellers of food or the buyers of food. Why?

____

____

____

____

SOLUTIONS

Terms and Definitions

_2_ Price ceiling

_4_ Price floor

_1_ Tax incidence

_3_ Tax wedge

Practice Problems

1. a. It will have no effect. The price ceiling is not binding because the equilibrium price is $500 and the price ceiling is set at $700.
   b. See Exhibit 5. The quantity demanded rises to 55 units, the quantity supplied falls to 40 units, and there is a shortage of 15 units.
   c. No. It may make those bicycle buyers better off that actually get a bicycle. However, some buyers are unable to get a bike, must wait in line, pay a bribe, or accept a lower quality bicycle.
   d. See Exhibit 6. The quantity supplied rises to 70 units, the quantity demanded falls to 40 units, and there is a surplus of 30 units.

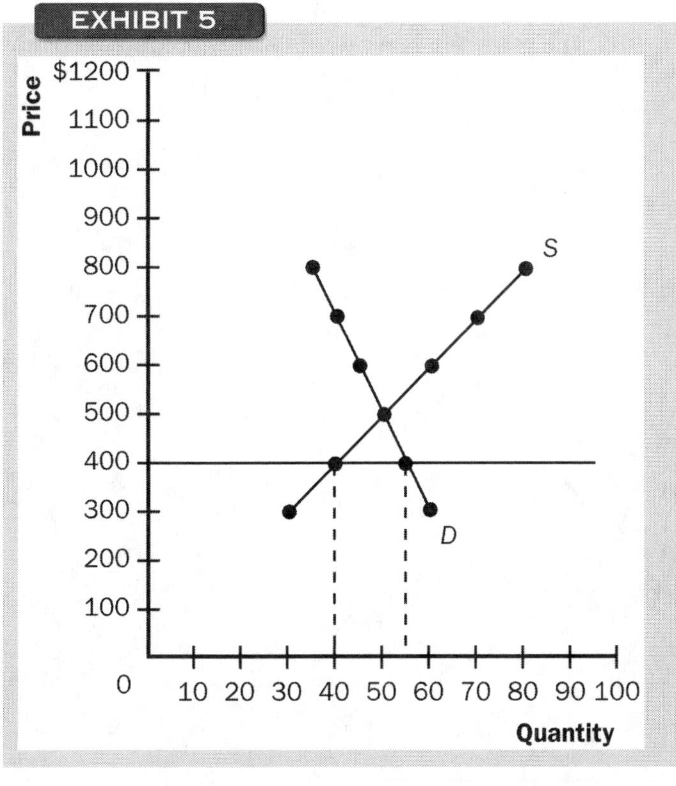

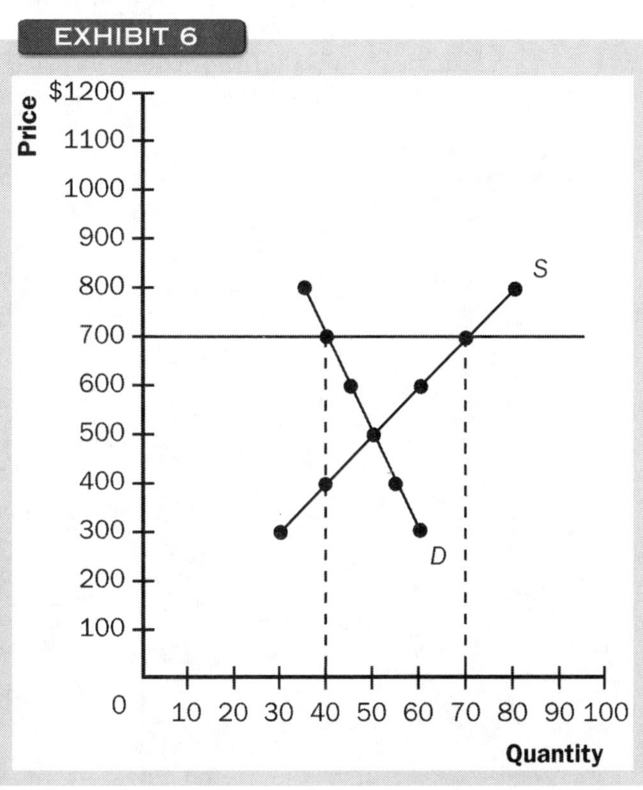

EXHIBIT 7

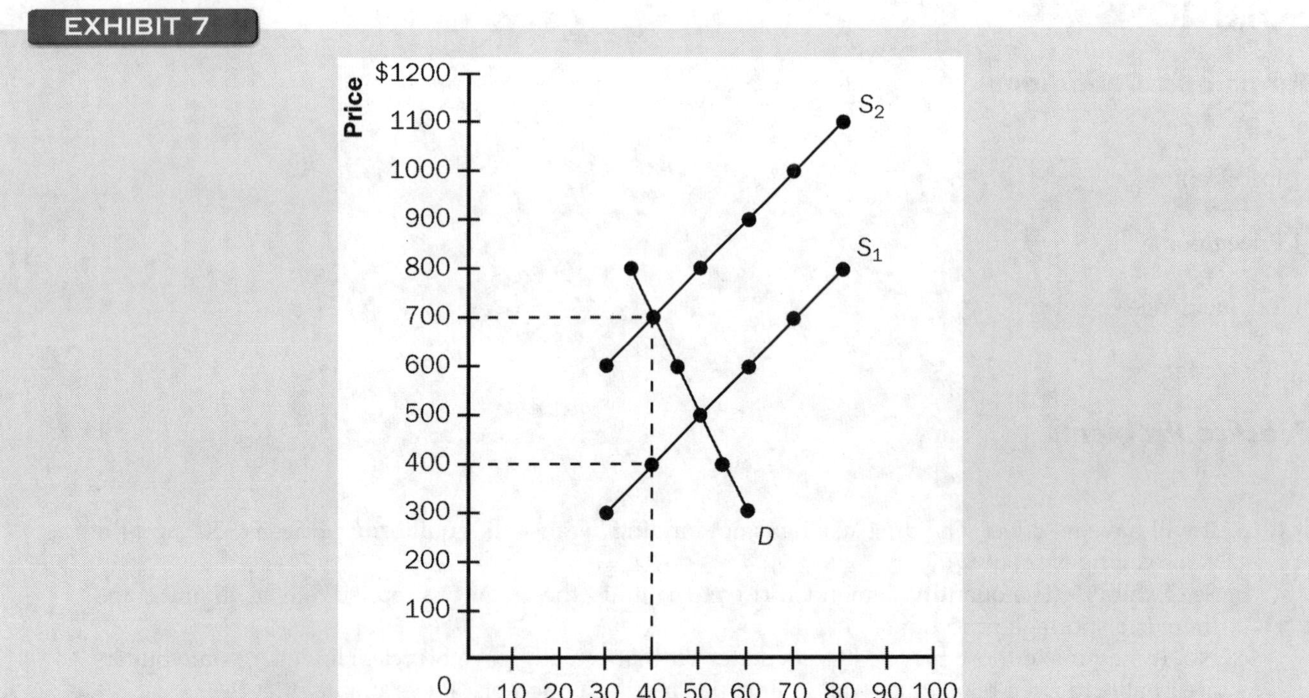

2. a. See Exhibit 7. The price buyers pay rises to $700, the price sellers receive falls to $400, and the quantity sold falls to 40 units.
   b. See Exhibit 8. The price buyers pay rises to $700, the price sellers receive falls to $400, and the quantity sold falls to 40 units.

EXHIBIT 8

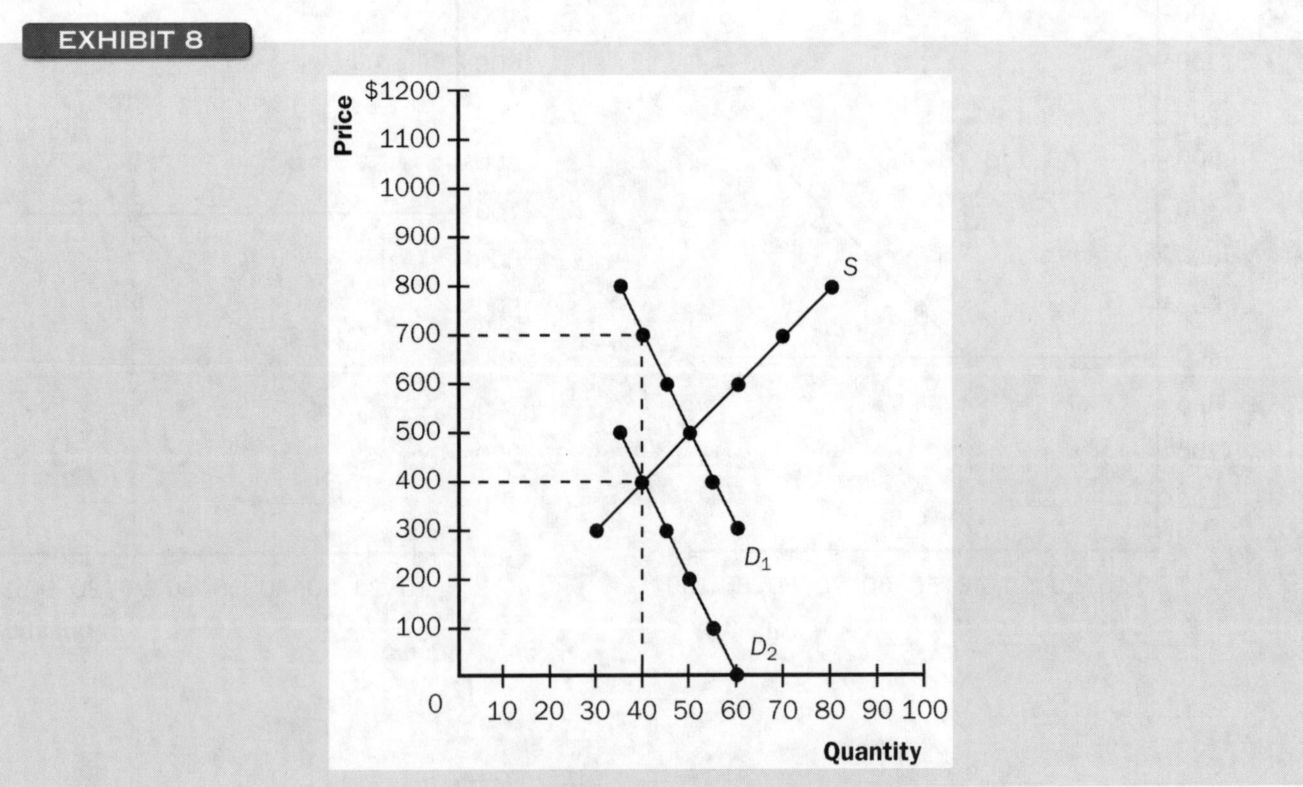

c. The impact of a tax collected from sellers is equivalent to the impact of a tax collected from buyers.
d. The greater burden of the tax has fallen on the buyers. The free market equilibrium price was $500. After the tax, the price the buyers pay has risen $200 while the price the sellers receive has fallen $100. This is because demand is less elastic than supply.

Short-Answer Questions

1. There is no impact because the price can move to equilibrium without restriction. That is, the price ceiling is not a binding constraint.

2. The quantity supplied decreases and the quantity demanded increases, causing a shortage.

3. There will be a shortage, buyers may wait in lines, sellers may be able to discriminate among buyers, the quality of the product may be reduced, and bribes may be paid to sellers.

4. The impact is greater in the long run because both supply and demand tend to be more elastic in the long run. As a result, the shortage becomes more severe in the long run.

5. There is no impact because the price can move to equilibrium without restriction. That is, the price floor is not a binding constraint.

6. The quantity supplied increases and the quantity demanded decreases, causing a surplus.

7. The demand curve is shifted downward by the size of the tax because the amount the buyer is willing to offer the seller has been reduced precisely by the size of the tax.

8. The supply curve is shifted upward by the size of the tax because the amount the seller requires from the buyer has been increased by precisely the size of the tax.

9. A tax places a wedge between what the buyer pays and the seller receives. Whether the buyer or the seller actually hands the tax to the government makes no difference whatsoever.

10. The sellers will bear the greater burden because the demand for luxuries tends to be highly elastic. That is, when the price buyers pay rises due to the tax, wealthy buyers can easily shift their purchases toward alternative items while producers cannot quickly reduce production when the price they receive falls. The burden falls on side of the market that is less elastic.

True/False Questions

1. F; a price ceiling set above the equilibrium price is not binding.

2. F; it causes a shortage.

3. T

4. T

5. F; some may be helped but others become unemployed and still others quit school to earn what appears to a teenager to be a good wage.

6. F; it causes a 1 to 3 percent reduction in employment.

7. T

8. F; it creates a surplus only if the floor is set above the equilibrium price.

9. F; the difference between what the sellers receive and the buyers pay will be $10 but the price received by the sellers usually will fall some so the price paid by the buyers will rise by less than $10.

10. T

11. T

12. F; we shift the demand curve downward by the size of the tax.

13. T

14. T

15. F; the burden of a tax is determined by the relative elasticities of supply and demand.

Multiple-Choice Questions

1. b	5. d	9. d	13. a	17. a
2. a	6. c	10. c	14. c	18. a
3. d	7. a	11. b	15. d	19. d
4. b	8. c	12. c	16. b	20. b

Advanced Critical Thinking

1. No. The tax burden is determined by the elasticity of supply and demand. The burden of a tax falls most heavily on the side of the market that is less elastic. That is, the burden is on the side of the market least willing to leave the market when the price moves unfavorably.

2. The burden will fall most heavily on the buyers of food regardless of whether the tax is collected from the buyers or the sellers. Food is a necessity and therefore the demand for food is relatively inelastic. When the price rises due to the tax, people still must eat. Grocery chains can sell another product line when the price they receive for food falls due to the tax.

7

CONSUMERS, PRODUCERS, AND THE EFFICIENCY OF MARKETS

GOALS

In this chapter you will

- Examine the link between buyers' willingness to pay for a good and the demand curve
- Learn how to define and measure consumer surplus
- Examine the link between sellers' costs of producing a good and the supply curve
- Learn how to define and measure producer surplus
- See that the equilibrium of supply and demand maximizes total surplus in a market

OUTCOMES

After accomplishing these goals, you should be able to

- Derive a demand curve from a group of individual buyers' willingness to pay schedules
- Locate consumer surplus on a supply and demand graph
- Derive a supply curve from a group of individual sellers' cost of production schedules
- Locate producer surplus on a supply and demand graph
- Demonstrate why all other quantities other than the equilibrium quantity fail to maximize total surplus in a market

CHAPTER OVERVIEW

Context and Purpose

Chapter 7 is the first chapter in a three-chapter sequence on welfare economics and market efficiency. Chapter 7 employs the supply and demand model to develop consumer surplus and producer surplus as a measure of welfare and market efficiency. These concepts are then utilized in Chapters 8 and 9 to determine the winners and losers from taxation and restrictions on international trade.

The purpose of Chapter 7 is to develop *welfare economics*—the study of how the allocation of resources affects economic well-being. Chapters 4 through 6 employed supply and demand in a positive framework when we asked the question, "What is the equilibrium price and quantity in a market?" We now address the normative question, "Is the equilibrium price and quantity in a market the best possible solution to the resource allocation problem or is it simply the price and quantity that balance supply and demand?" We will discover that under most circumstances the equilibrium price and quantity is also the one that maximizes welfare.

CHAPTER REVIEW

Introduction

In this chapter we address **welfare economics**—the study of how the allocation of resources affects economic well-being. We measure the benefits that buyers and sellers receive from taking part in a market and we discover that the equilibrium price and quantity in a market maximizes the total benefits received by buyers and sellers.

Consumer Surplus

Consumer surplus measures the benefits received by buyers from participating in a market. Each potential buyer in a market has some **willingness to pay** for a good. This willingness to pay is the maximum amount that a buyer will pay for the good. If we plot the value of the greatest willingness to pay for the first unit followed by the next greatest willingness to pay for the second unit and so on (on a price and quantity graph) we have plotted the market demand curve for the good. That is, the height of the demand curve is the marginal buyers' willingness to pay. Since some buyers value a good more than other buyers, the demand curve is downward sloping.

Consumer surplus is a buyer's willingness to pay minus the amount the buyer actually pays. For example, if you are willing to pay $20 for a new CD by your favorite music artist and you are able to purchase it for $15, you receive consumer surplus on that CD of $5. In general, since the height of the demand curve measures the value buyers place on a good measured by the buyer's willingness to pay, *consumer surplus is the area below the demand curve and above the price.*

When the price of a good falls, consumer surplus increases for two reasons. First, existing buyers receive greater surplus because they are allowed to pay less for the quantities they were already going to purchase and, second, new buyers are brought into the market because the price is now lower than their willingness to pay.

Note that since the height of the demand curve is the value buyers place on a good measured by their willingness to pay, consumer surplus measures the benefits received by buyers *as the buyers themselves perceive it*. Therefore, consumer surplus is an appropriate measure of buyers' benefits if policymakers respect the preferences of buyers. Economists generally believe that buyers are rational and that buyer preferences should be respected except possibly in cases of drug addiction, and so on.

Producer Surplus

Producer surplus measures the benefits received by sellers from participating in a market. Each potential seller in a market has some *cost* of production. This **cost** is the value of everything a seller must give up to produce a good and it should be interpreted as the producers' opportunity cost of production—actual out-of-pocket expenses plus the value of the producers' time. The cost of production is the minimum amount a seller is willing to accept in order to produce the good. If we plot the cost of the least cost producer of the first unit, then the next least cost producer of the second unit, and so on (on a price and quantity graph), we have plotted the market supply curve for the good. That is, the height of the supply curve is the marginal sellers' cost of production. Since some sellers have a lower cost than other sellers, the supply curve is upward sloping.

Producer surplus is the amount a seller is paid for a good minus the seller's cost. For example, if a musician can produce a CD for a cost of $10 and sell it for

$15, the musician receives a producer surplus of $5 on that CD. In general, since the height of the supply curve measures the sellers' costs, *producer surplus is the area below the price and above the supply curve.*

When the price of a good rises, producer surplus increases for two reasons. First, existing sellers receive greater surplus because they receive more for the quantities they were already going to sell and, second, new sellers are brought into the market because the price is now higher than their cost.

Market Efficiency

We measure economic well-being with *total surplus*—the sum of consumer and producer surplus.

Total surplus = (value to buyers – amount paid by buyers) +
(amount received by sellers – cost to sellers)

Total surplus = value to buyers – cost to sellers.

Graphically, total surplus is the area below the demand curve and above the supply curve. Resource allocation is said to exhibit **efficiency** if it maximizes the total surplus received by all members of society. Free market equilibrium is efficient because it maximizes total surplus. This efficiency is demonstrated by the following observations:

- Free markets allocate output to the buyers who value it the most—those with a willingness to pay greater than or equal to the equilibrium price. Therefore consumer surplus cannot be increased by moving consumption from a current buyer to any other non-buyer.

- Free markets allocate buyers for goods to the sellers who can produce at least cost—those with a cost of production less than or equal to the equilibrium price. Therefore producer surplus cannot be increased by moving production from a current seller to any other non-seller.

- Free markets produce the quantity of goods that maximizes the sum of consumer and producer surplus or total surplus. If we produce less than the equilibrium quantity, we fail to produce units where the value to buyers exceeds the cost to producers. If we produce more than the equilibrium quantity, we produce units where the cost to producers exceeds the value to buyers.

Economists generally advocate free markets because they are efficient. Since markets are efficient, many believe that government policy should be *laissez-faire* which means "allow them to do." Adam Smith's "invisible hand" of the marketplace guides buyers and sellers to an allocation of resources that maximizes total surplus. Many economists argue that free markets for scalped tickets (and possibly even markets for organs for transplant) maximize total surplus. The recognition that free markets are efficient is not new. Prior to Adam Smith, the Pilgrims discovered that when they practiced "farming in common" (socialized farming) there was famine, but when they allowed each to till their own soil and trade, there was plenty.

In addition to efficiency, policymakers may also be concerned with **equity**—the fairness of the distribution of well-being among the members of society. The issue of equity involves normative judgements that go beyond the realm of economics.

Conclusion: Market Efficiency and Market Failure

There are two main reasons a free market may not be efficient:

- A market may not be perfectly competitive. If individual buyers or sellers (or small groups of them) can influence the price, they have *market power* and they may be able to keep the price and quantity away from equilibrium.

- A market may generate side effects, or *externalities*, which affect people who are not participants in the market at all. These side effects, such as pollution, are not taken into account by buyers and sellers in a market so the market equilibrium may not be efficient for society as a whole.

Market power and externalities are the two main types of *market failure*—the inability of some unregulated markets to allocate resources efficiently.

HELPFUL HINTS

1. To better understand "willingness to pay" for the buyer and "cost" to seller, read both demand and supply "backward." That is, read both demand and supply from the quantity axis to the price or dollar axis. When we read demand from quantity to price, we find that the potential buyer for the first unit has a very high willingness to pay because that buyer places a great value on the good. As we move farther out along the quantity axis, the buyers for those quantities have a somewhat lower willingness to pay and, thus, the demand curve slopes negatively. When we read supply from quantity to price, we find that the potential seller for the first unit is extremely efficient and, accordingly, has a very low cost of production. As we move farther out along the quantity axis, the sellers for those quantities have somewhat higher costs and, thus, the supply curve slopes upward. At equilibrium between supply and demand, only those units are produced which generate a value to buyers that exceeds the cost to the sellers.

2. Consumer surplus exists, in part, because in a competitive market there is one price and all participants are price takers. With a single market price determined by the interactions of many buyers and sellers, individual buyers may have a willingness to pay that exceeds the price and, as a result, some buyers receive consumer surplus. If, however, sellers are aware of the buyers' willingness to pay and the sellers engage in price discrimination, that is, charge each buyer their willingness to pay, there would be no consumer surplus. Each buyer would be forced to pay their individual willingness to pay. This issue will be addressed in later chapters.

TERMS AND DEFINITIONS

Choose a definition for each key term.

Key terms:

_____ Welfare economics

_____ Willingness to pay

_____ Consumer surplus

_____ Cost

_____ Producer surplus

_____ Efficiency

_____ Equity

_____ Market failure

Definitions:

1. A buyer's willingness to pay minus the amount the buyer actually pays
2. The property of a resource allocation of maximizing the total surplus received by all members of society
3. The study of how the allocation of resources affects economic well-being
4. The inability of some unregulated markets to allocate resources efficiently
5. The fairness of the distribution of well-being among the members of society
6. The amount a seller is paid for a good minus the seller's cost
7. The maximum amount that a buyer will pay for a good
8. The value of everything a seller must give up to produce a good

PROBLEMS AND SHORT-ANSWER QUESTIONS

Practice Problems

1. The following information describes the value Lori Landlord places on having her five apartment houses repainted. She values the repainting of each apartment house at a different amount depending on how badly it needs repainting.

Value of new paint on first apartment house	$5,000
Value of new paint on second apartment house	4,000
Value of new paint on third apartment house	3,000
Value of new paint on fourth apartment house	2,000
Value of new paint on fifth apartment house	1,000

a. Plot Lori Landlord's willingness to pay in Exhibit 1.

b. If the price to repaint her apartments is $5,000 each, how many will she repaint? What is the value of her consumer surplus?

____

____

____

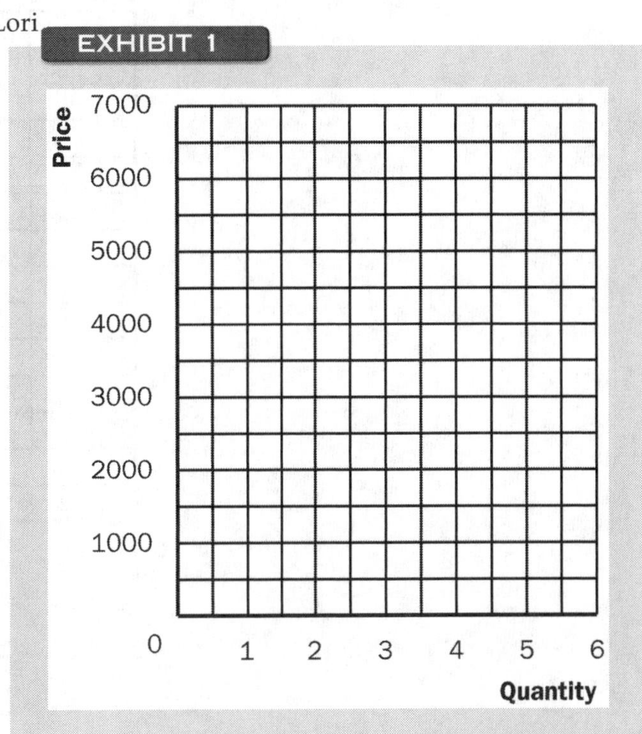

____

c. Suppose the price to repaint her apartments falls to $2,000 each. How many apartments will Lori choose to have repainted? What is the value of her consumer surplus?

____

____

d. What happened to Ms. Landlord's consumer surplus when the price of having her apartments repainted fell? Why?

____

____

____

2. The following information shows the costs incurred by Peter Painter when he paints apartments. Because painting is backbreaking work, the more he paints, the higher the costs he incurs in both pain and chiropractic bills.

Cost of painting first apartment house	$1,000
Cost of painting second apartment house	2,000
Cost of painting third apartment house	3,000
Cost of painting fourth apartment house	4,000
Cost of painting fifth apartment house	5,000

EXHIBIT 2

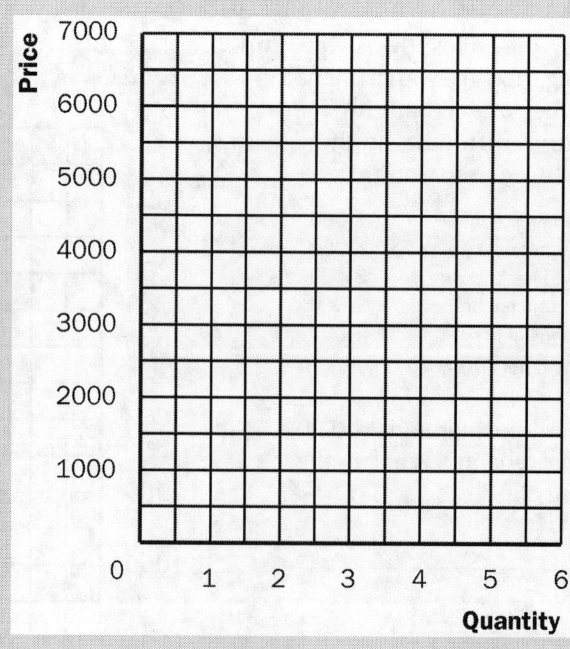

a. Plot Peter Painter's cost in Exhibit 2.
b. If the price of painting apartment houses is $2000 each, how many will he paint? What is the value of his producer surplus?

____

____

c. Suppose the price to paint apartments rises to $4000 each. How many apartments will Peter choose to repaint? What is the value of his producer surplus?

____

____

d. What happened to Mr. Painter's producer surplus when the price to paint apartments rose? Why?

____

____

____

3. Use the information about willingness to pay and cost from (1) and (2) above to answer the following questions.
   a. If a benevolent social planner sets the price for painting apartment houses at $5,000, what is the value of consumer surplus? Producer surplus? Total surplus?

____

____

   b. If a benevolent social planner sets the price for painting apartment houses at $1,000, what is the value of consumer surplus? Producer surplus? Total surplus?

____

____

c. If the price for painting apartment houses is allowed to move to its free market equilibrium price of $3,000, what is the value of consumer surplus, producer surplus, and total surplus in the market? How does total surplus in the free market compare to the total surplus generated by the social planner?

EXHIBIT 3

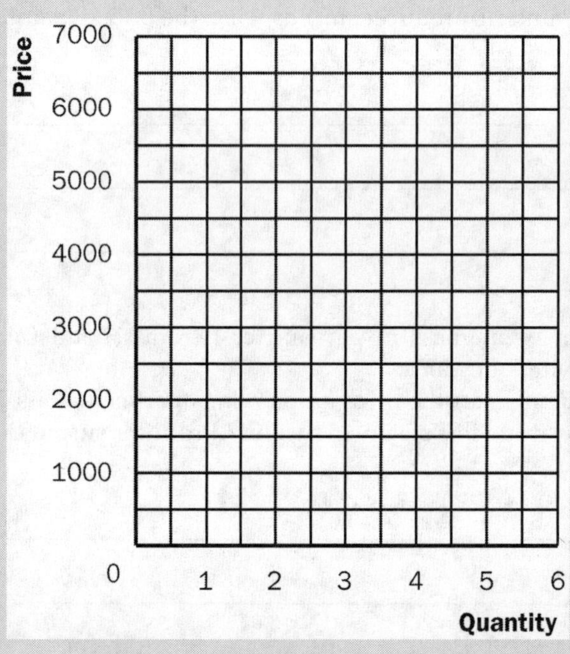

4. In Exhibit 3, plot the linear supply and demand curves for painting apartments implied by the information in questions (1) and (2) above (draw them so that they contact the vertical axis). Show consumer and producer surplus for the free market equilibrium price and quantity. Is this allocation of resources efficient? Why?

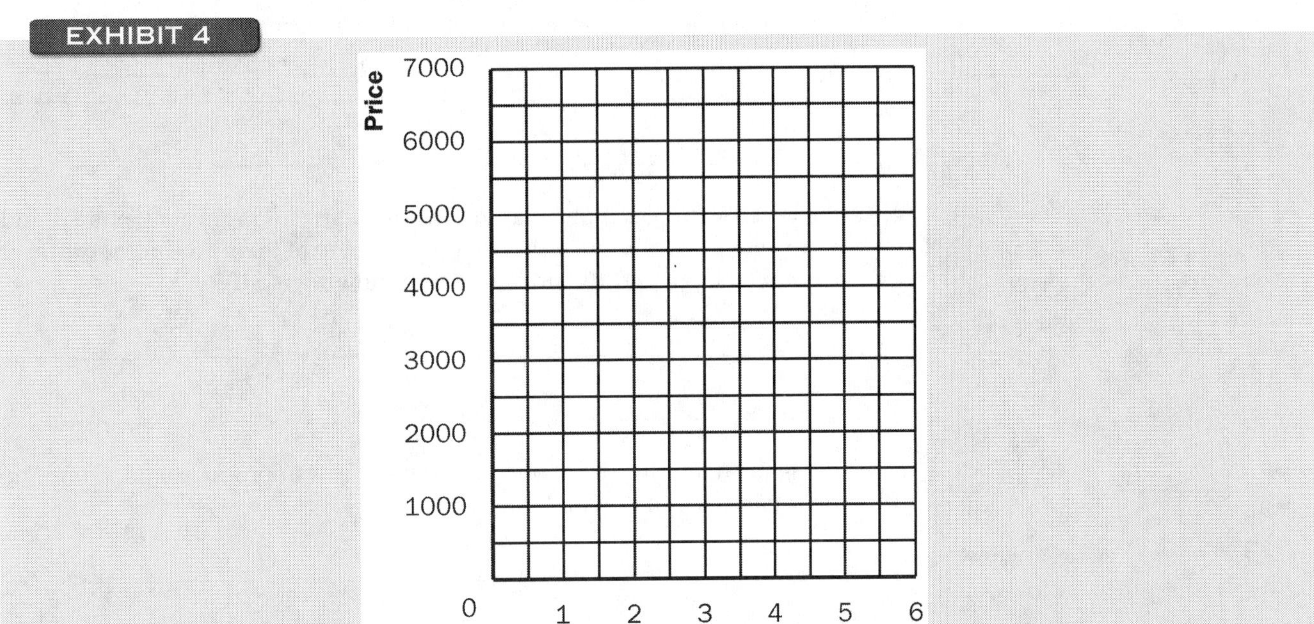

5. Suppose Lori Landlord has difficulty renting her dilapidated apartments so she increases her willingness to pay for painting by $2,000 per apartment. Plot Lori's new willingness to pay along with Peter's cost in Exhibit 4. If the equilibrium price rises to $4,000, what is the value of consumer surplus, producer surplus, and total surplus? Show consumer and producer surplus on the graph. Compare your answer to the answer you found in 3 (c) above.

____

____

____

____

____

Short-Answer Questions

1. What is the relationship between the buyers' willingness to pay for a good and the demand curve for that good?

____

____

2. What is consumer surplus and how is it measured?

____

____

3. What is the value of consumer surplus for the marginal buyer? Why?

____

____

4. If the cost for Moe to mow a lawn is $5, for Larry to mow a lawn is $7, and for Curly to mow a lawn is $9, what is the value of their producer surplus if each mow a lawn and the price for lawn mowing is $10?

____

____

5. What is the relationship between the sellers' cost to produce a good and the supply curve for that good?

____

____

6. What is producer surplus and how is it measured?

____

____

7. When the price of a good rises, what happens to producer surplus? Why?

____

____

____

8. Can a benevolent social planner choose a quantity that provides greater economic welfare than the equilibrium quantity generated in a competitive market? Why?

____

____

____

9. What does an economist mean by "efficiency?"

____

____

10. Is a competitive market efficient? Why?

____

____

11. How does a competitive market choose which producers will produce and sell a product?

____

____

____

SELF-TEST

True/False Questions

_____ 1. Consumer surplus is the buyer's willingness to pay minus the seller's cost.

_____ 2. If the demand curve in a market is stationary, consumer surplus decreases when the price in that market increases.

_____ 3. If your willingness to pay for a hamburger is $3.00 and the price is $2.00, your consumer surplus is $5.00.

_____ 4. Producer surplus is a measure of the unsold inventories of suppliers in a market.

_____ 5. Consumer surplus is a good measure of buyers' benefits if buyers are rational.

_____ 6. Cost to the seller includes the opportunity cost of the seller's time.

_____ 7. The height of the supply curve is the marginal seller's cost.

_____ 8. Total surplus is the seller's cost minus the buyer's willingness to pay.

_____ 9. Free markets are efficient because they allocate output to buyers who have a willingness to pay that is below the price.

_____10. Producer surplus is the area above the supply curve and below the price.

_____11. The major advantage of allowing free markets to allocate resources is that the outcome of the allocation is efficient.

_____12. Equilibrium in a competitive market maximizes total surplus.

_____13. The two main types of market failure are market power and externalities.

____ 14. Externalities are side effects, such as pollution, that are not taken into account by the buyers and sellers in a market.

____ 15. Producing more of a product always adds to total surplus.

Multiple-Choice Questions

1. Consumer surplus is the area
   a. above the supply curve and below the price.
   b. below the supply curve and above the price.
   c. above the demand curve and below the price.
   d. below the demand curve and above the price.
   e. below the demand curve and above the supply curve.

2. A buyer's willingness to pay is that buyer's
   a. consumer surplus.
   b. producer surplus.
   c. maximum amount they are willing to pay for a good.
   d. minimum amount they are willing to pay for a good.
   e. none of the above.

3. If a buyer's willingness to pay for a new Honda is $20,000 and she is able to actually buy it for $18,000, her consumer surplus is
   a. $0.
   b. $2,000.
   c. $18,000.
   d. $20,000.
   e. $38,000.

4. An increase in the price of a good along a stationary demand curve
   a. increases consumer surplus.
   b. decreases consumer surplus.
   c. improves the material welfare of the buyers.
   d. improves market efficiency.

5. Suppose there are three identical vases available to be purchased. Buyer 1 is willing to pay $30 for one, buyer 2 is willing to pay $25 for one, and buyer 3 is willing to pay $20 for one. If the price is $25, how many vases will be sold and what is the value of consumer surplus in this market?
   a. One vase will be sold and consumer surplus is $30.
   b. One vase will be sold and consumer surplus is $5.
   c. Two vases will be sold and consumer surplus is $5.
   d. Three vases will be sold and consumer surplus is $0.
   e. Three vases will be sold and consumer surplus is $80.

6. Producer surplus is the area
   a. above the supply curve and below the price.
   b. below the supply curve and above the price.
   c. above the demand curve and below the price.
   d. below the demand curve and above the price.
   e. below the demand curve and above the supply curve.

7. If a benevolent social planner chooses to produce less than the equilibrium quantity of a good, then
   a. producer surplus is maximized.
   b. consumer surplus is maximized.
   c. total surplus is maximized.
   d. the value placed on the last unit of production by buyers exceeds the cost of production.
   e. the cost of production on the last unit produced exceeds the value placed on it by buyers.

8. If a benevolent social planner chooses to produce more than the equilibrium quantity of a good, then
   a. producer surplus is maximized.
   b. consumer surplus is maximized.
   c. total surplus is maximized.
   d. the value placed on the last unit of production by buyers exceeds the cost of production.
   e. the cost of production on the last unit produced exceeds the value placed on it by buyers.

9. The seller's cost of production is
   a. the seller's consumer surplus.
   b. the seller's producer surplus.
   c. the maximum amount the seller is willing to accept for a good.
   d. the minimum amount the seller is willing to accept for a good.
   e. none of the above.

10. Total surplus is the area
    a. above the supply curve and below the price.
    b. below the supply curve and above the price.
    c. above the demand curve and below the price.
    d. below the demand curve and above the price.
    e. below the demand curve and above the supply curve.

11. An increase in the price of a good along a stationary supply curve
    a. increases producer surplus.
    b. decreases producer surplus.
    c. improves market equity.
    d. does all of the above.

12. Adam Smith's "invisible hand" concept suggests that a competitive market outcome
    a. minimizes total surplus.
    b. maximizes total surplus.
    c. generates equality among the members of society.
    d. both (b) and (c).

13. In general, if a benevolent social planner wanted to maximize the total benefits received by buyers and sellers in a market, the planner should
    a. choose a price above the market equilibrium price.
    b. choose a price below the market equilibrium price.
    c. allow the market to seek equilibrium on its own.
    d. choose any price the planner wants because the losses to the sellers (buyers) from any change in price are exactly offset by the gains to the buyers (sellers).

14. If buyers are rational and there is no market failure,
    a. free market solutions are efficient.
    b. free market solutions are equitable.
    c. free market solutions maximize total surplus.
    d. all of the above.
    e. (a) and (c) are correct.

15. If a producer has market power (can influence the price of the product in the market) then free market solutions
    a. are equitable.
    b. are efficient.
    c. are inefficient.
    d. maximize consumer surplus.

16. If a market is efficient, then
    a. the market allocates output to the buyers that value it the most.
    b. the market allocates buyers to the sellers who can produce the good at least cost.
    c. the quantity produced in the market maximizes the sum of consumer and producer surplus.
    d. all of the above.
    e. none of the above.

17. If a market generates a side effect or externality, then free market solutions
    a. are equitable.
    b. are efficient.
    c. are inefficient.
    d. maximize producer surplus.

18. Medical care clearly enhances peoples lives. Therefore, we should consume medical care until
    a. everyone has as much as they would like.
    b. the benefit buyers place on medical care is equal to the cost of producing it.
    c. buyers receive no benefit from another unit of medical care.
    d. we must cut back on the consumption of other goods.

19. Joe has ten baseball gloves and Sue has none. A baseball glove costs $50 to produce. If Joe values an additional baseball glove at $100 and Sue values a baseball glove at $40, then to maximize
    a. efficiency Joe should receive the glove.
    b. efficiency Sue should receive the glove.
    c. consumer surplus both should receive a glove.
    d. equity, Joe should receive the glove.

20. Suppose that the price of a new bicycle is $300. Sue values a new bicycle at $400. It costs $200 for the seller to produce the new bicycle. What is the value of total surplus if Sue buys a new bike?
    a. $100
    b. $200
    c. $300
    d. $400
    e. $500

ADVANCED CRITICAL THINKING

Suppose you are having an argument with your roommate about whether the Federal Government should subsidize the production of food. Your roommate argues that since food is something that is unambiguously good (unlike liquor, guns, and drugs which may be considered inherently evil by some members of society) we simply cannot have too much of it. That is, since food is clearly good, having more of it must always improve our economic well-being.

1. Is it true that you cannot have too much of a good thing? Conversely, is it possible to overproduce unambiguously good things such as food, clothing, and shelter? Why?

   ____

   ____

   ____

   ____

   ____

2. In Exhibit 5, demonstrate your answer to question (1) above with a supply and demand graph for food by showing the impact on economic well-being of producing quantities in excess of the equilibrium quantity.

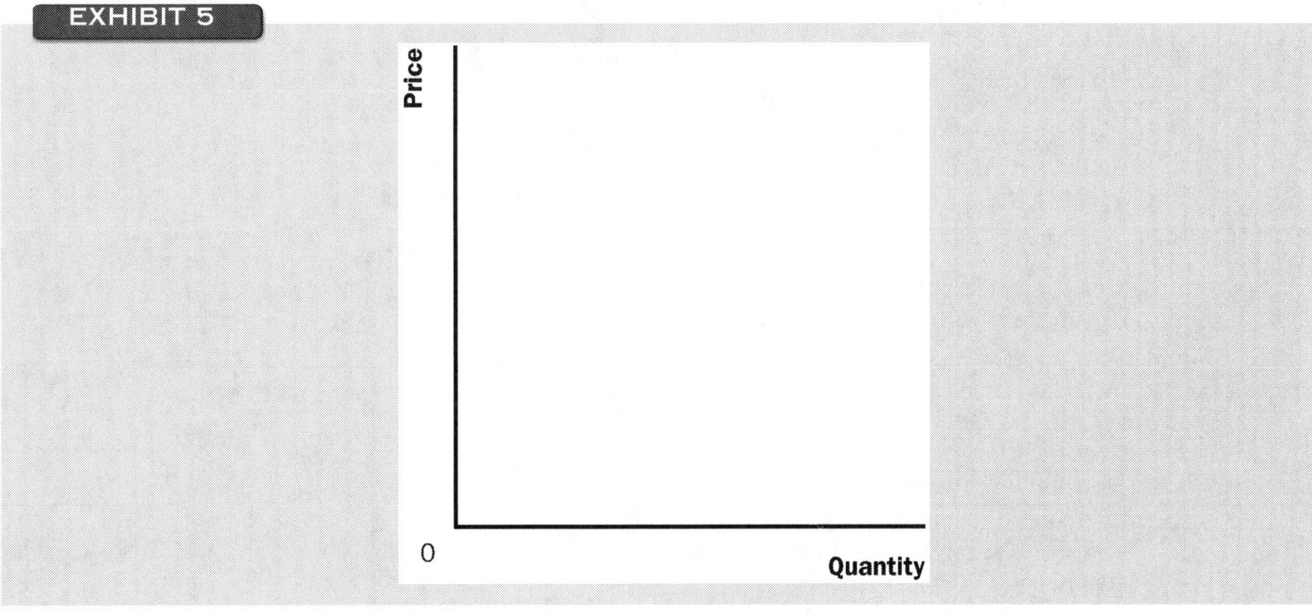

SOLUTIONS

Terms and Definitions

3 Welfare economics

7 Willingness to pay

1 Consumer surplus

8 Cost

6 Producer surplus

2 Efficiency

5 Equity

4 Market failure

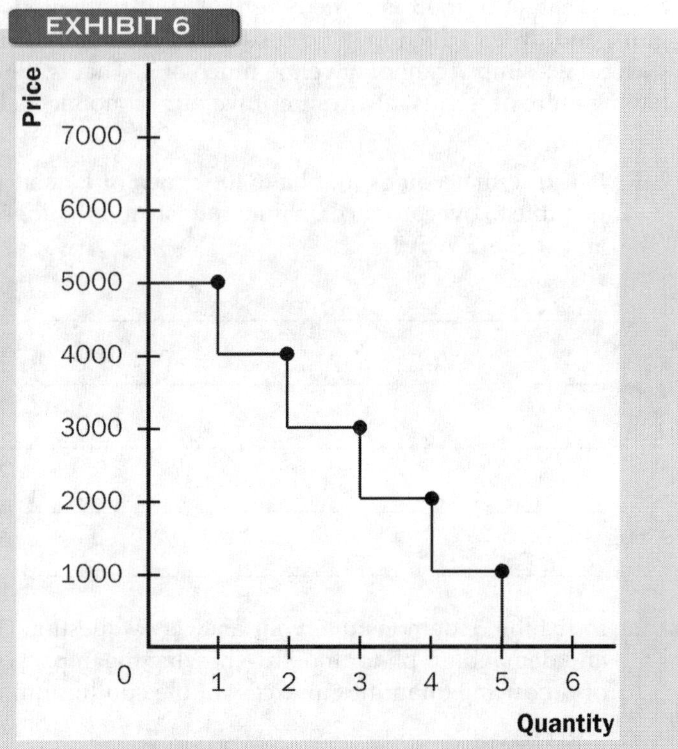

Practice Problems

1. a. See Exhibit 6.
   b. One apartment painted. $5000 – $5000 = 0, therefore she has no consumer surplus.
   c. Four apartments painted. ($5000 – $2000) + ($4000 – $2000) + ($3000 – $2000) + ($2000 – $2000) = $6000 of consumer surplus.
   d. Her consumer surplus rose because she gains surplus on the unit she would have already purchased at the old price plus she gains surplus on the new units she now purchases due to the lower price.

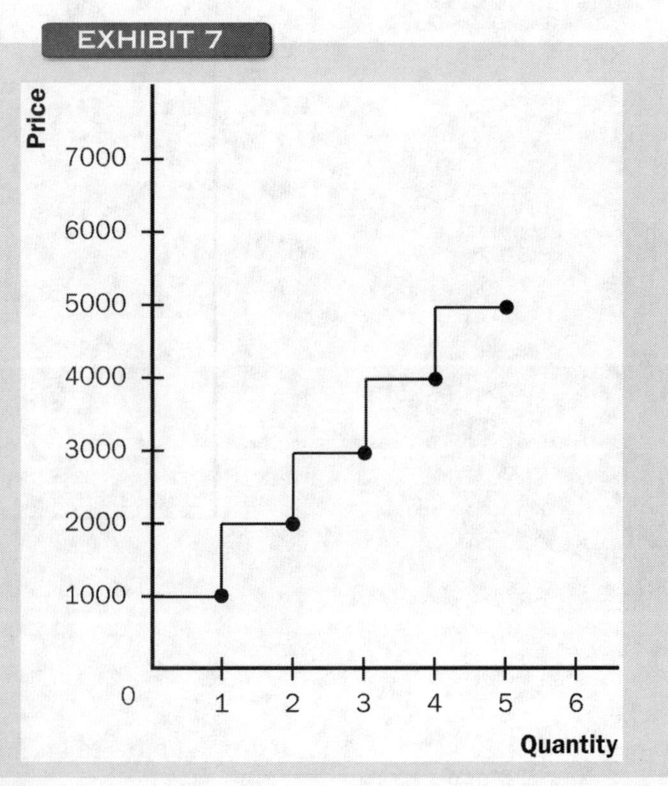

2. a. See Exhibit 7.
   b. Two. ($2000 – $1000) + ($2000 – $2000) = $1000 of producer surplus.
   c. Four apartments. ($4000 – $1000) + ($4000 – $2000) + ($4000 – $3000) + ($4000 – $4000) = $6000 of producer surplus.
   d. He received greater producer surplus on the unit he would have produced anyway plus additional surplus on the units he now chooses to produce due to the increase in price.

3. a. Only one unit will be purchased so consumer surplus = ($5000 – $5000)

= $0, producer surplus = ($5000 – $1000) = $4000, and total surplus = $0 + $4000 = $4000.

b. Only one unit will be produced so consumer surplus = ($5000 – $1000) = $4000, producer surplus = ($1000 – $1000) = $0, and total surplus = $4000 + $0 = $4000.

c. Consumer surplus = ($5000 – $3000) + ($4000 – $3000) + ($3000 – $3000) = $3000. Producer surplus = ($3000 – $1000) + ($3000 – $2000) + ($3000 – $3000) = $3000. Total surplus = $3000 + $3000 = $6000. Free market total surplus is greater than social planner total surplus.

4. See Exhibit 8. Yes, it is efficient because at a quantity that is less than the equilibrium quantity we fail to produce units that buyers value more than their cost. At a quantity above the equilibrium quantity, we produce units that cost more than the buyers value them. At equilibrium we produce all possible units that are valued in excess of what they cost, which maximizes total surplus.

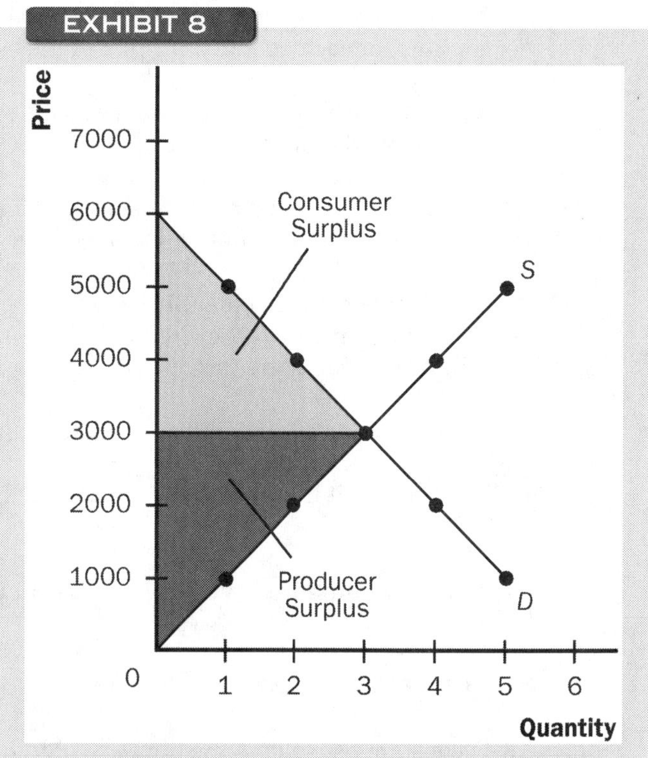

5. See Exhibit 9. Consumer surplus = $3000 + $2000 + $1000 + $0 = $6000.

Producer surplus = $3000 + $2000 + $1000 + $0 = $6000.

Total surplus = $6000 + $6000 = $12000.

Consumer surplus, producer surplus, and total surplus have all increased.

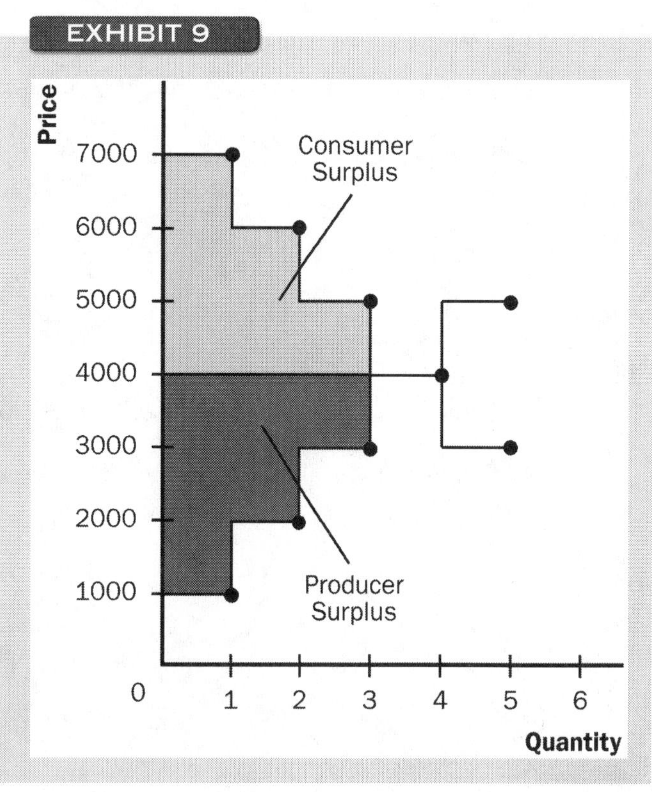

Short-Answer Questions

1. The height of the demand curve at any quantity is the marginal buyer's willingness to pay. Therefore, a plot of buyers' willingness to pay for each quantity is a plot of the demand curve.

2. Consumer surplus is a buyer's willingness to pay minus the amount the buyer actually pays. It is measured as the area below the demand curve and above the price.

3. Zero, because the marginal buyer is the buyer who would leave the market if the price were any higher. Therefore, they are paying their willingness to pay and are receiving no surplus.

4. ($10 – $5) + ($10 – $7) + ($10 – $9) = $9

5. The height of the supply curve at any quantity is the marginal seller's cost. Therefore, a plot of the sellers' cost for each quantity is a plot of the supply curve.

6. Producer surplus is the amount a seller is paid for a good minus the seller's cost. It is measured as the area below the price and above the supply curve.

7. Producer surplus increases because existing sellers receive a greater surplus on the units they were already going to sell and new sellers enter the market because the price is now above their cost.

8. Generally, no. At any quantity below the equilibrium quantity, the market fails to produce units where the value to the buyers exceeds the cost. At any quantity above the equilibrium quantity, the market produces units where the cost exceeds the value to the buyers.

9. It is a resource allocation that maximizes the total surplus received by all members of society.

10. Yes, because it maximizes the area below the demand curve and above the supply curve, or total surplus.

11. Only those producers who have costs at or below the market price will be able to produce and sell that good.

True/False Questions

1. F; consumer surplus is the buyer's willingness to pay minus the amount the buyer actually pays.

2. T

3. F; $3.00 – $2.00 = $1.00.

4. F; it is a measure of the benefits of market participation to the sellers in a market.

5. T

6. T

7. T

8. F; total surplus is the buyer's willingness to pay minus the seller's cost.

9. F; free markets allocate output to buyers who have a willingness to pay that is above the price.

10. T

11. T

12. T

13. T

14. T

15. F; producing above the equilibrium quantity reduces total surplus because units are produced for which cost exceeds the value to buyers.

Multiple-Choice Questions

1. d	5. c	9. d	13. c	17. c
2. c	6. a	10. e	14. e	18. b
3. b	7. d	11. a	15. c	19. a
4. b	8. e	12. b	16. d	20. b

Advanced Critical Thinking

1. You can have too much of a good thing. Yes, any good with a positive cost and a declining willingness to pay from the consumer can be overproduced. This is because at some point of production, the cost per unit will exceed the value to the buyer and there will be a loss to total surplus associated with additional production.

2. See Exhibit 10.

EXHIBIT 10

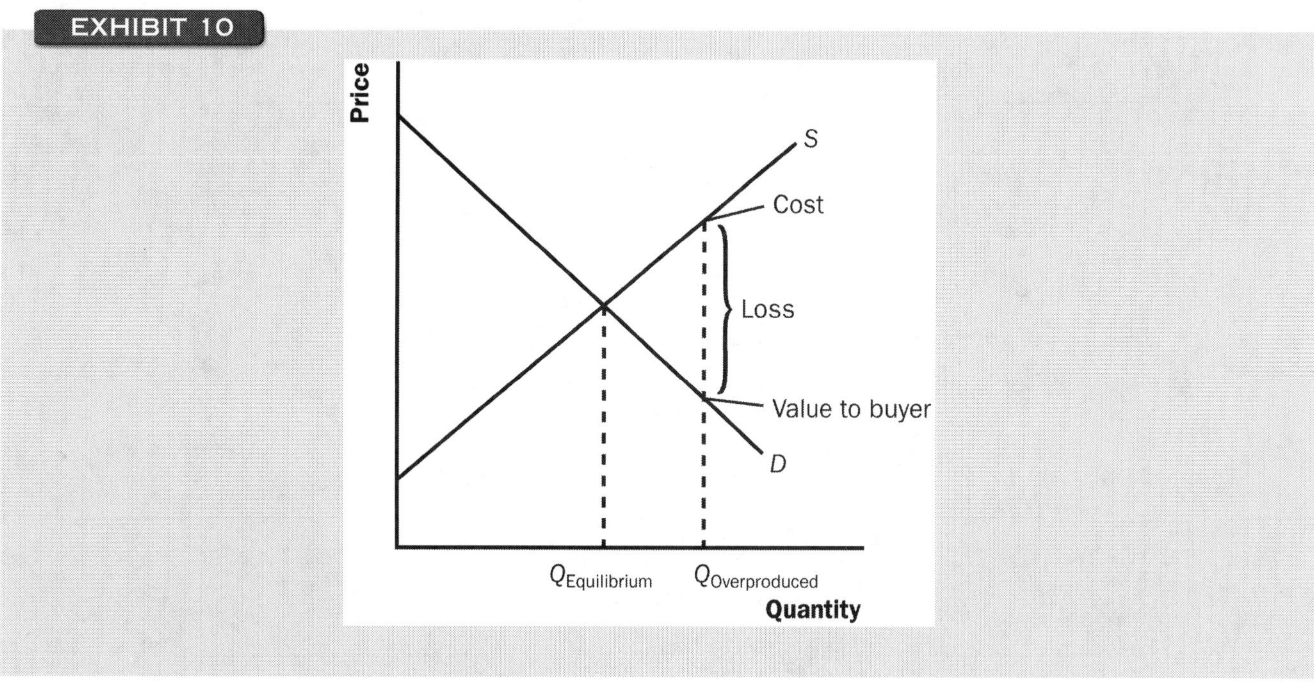

8

GOALS

In this chapter you will

- Examine how taxes reduce consumer and producer surplus
- Learn the meaning and causes of the deadweight loss of a tax
- Consider why some taxes have larger deadweight losses than others
- Examine how tax revenue and deadweight loss vary with the size of a tax

OUTCOMES

After accomplishing these goals, you should be able to

- Place a tax wedge in a supply and demand graph and determine the tax revenue and the levels of consumer and producer surplus
- Place a tax wedge in a supply and demand graph and determine the value of the deadweight loss
- Show why a given tax will generate a greater deadweight loss if supply and demand are elastic than if they are inelastic
- Demonstrate why some very large taxes generate little tax revenue but a great deal of deadweight loss

APPLICATION: THE COSTS OF TAXATION

CHAPTER OVERVIEW

Context and Purpose

Chapter 8 is the second chapter in a three-chapter sequence dealing with welfare economics. In the previous section on supply and demand, Chapter 6 introduced taxes and demonstrated how a tax affects the price and quantity sold in a market. Chapter 6 also described the factors that determine how the burden of the tax is divided between the buyers and sellers in a market. Chapter 7 developed welfare economics—the study of how the allocation of resources affects economic well-being. Chapter 8 combines the lessons learned in Chapters 6 and 7 and addresses the effects of taxation on welfare. Chapter 9 will address the effects of trade restrictions on welfare.

The purpose of Chapter 8 is to apply the lessons learned about welfare economics in Chapter 7 to the issue of taxation which we addressed in Chapter 6. We will learn that the cost of a tax to buyers and sellers in a market exceeds the revenue collected by the government. We will also learn about the factors that determine the degree by which the cost of a tax exceeds the revenue collected by the government.

CHAPTER REVIEW

Introduction

Taxes raise the price buyers pay, reduce the price sellers receive, and reduce the quantity exchanged. Clearly, the welfare of the buyers and sellers is reduced and the welfare of the government is increased. However, overall welfare is reduced because the cost of a tax to buyers and sellers exceeds the revenue raised by the government.

The Deadweight Loss of Taxation

Recall from Chapter 6 that a tax places a wedge between what a buyer pays and a seller receives and reduces the quantity sold regardless of whether the tax is collected from the buyer or the seller. With regard to welfare, recall from Chapter 7 that consumer surplus is the amount buyers are willing to pay minus the price they actually pay, while producer surplus is the price sellers actually receive minus their costs. The welfare or benefit to the government from a tax is the revenue it collects from the tax, which is the quantity of the good sold *after the tax is placed on the good* multiplied by the tax per unit. This benefit actually accrues to those on whom the tax revenue is spent.

Referring to Exhibit 1, without a tax the price is P_0 and the quantity is Q_0. Thus, consumer surplus is the area A + B + C and producer surplus is D + E + F. Tax revenue is zero. Total surplus is A + B + C + D + E + F.

With a tax, the price to buyers rises to P_B, the price to sellers falls to P_S, and the quantity falls to Q_1. Consumer surplus is now A, producer surplus is now F, and tax revenue is B + D. Total surplus is now A + B + D + F. Consumer surplus and producer surplus have both been reduced and tax revenue has been increased. However, consumer and producer surplus have been reduced by B + C + D + E and government revenue has been increased by only B + D. Therefore, losses to buyers and sellers from a tax exceed the revenue raised by the government. The

EXHIBIT 1

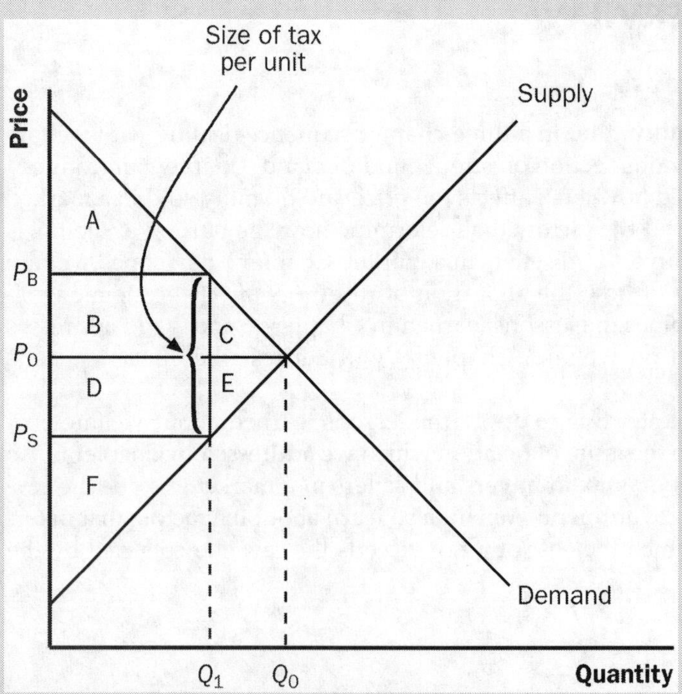

reduction in total surplus that results from a tax is known as **deadweight loss** and is equal to C + E.

Taxes cause deadweight losses because taxes prevent buyers and sellers from realizing some of the gains from trade. That is, taxes distort incentives because taxes raise the price paid by buyers, which reduces the quantity demanded, and lowers the price received by sellers, which reduces the quantity supplied. The size of the market is reduced below its optimum and sellers fail to produce and sell goods for which the benefits to buyers exceed the costs of the producers. Deadweight loss is a loss of potential gains from trade.

The Determinants of the Deadweight Loss

The size of the deadweight loss from a tax depends on the elasticities of supply and demand. Deadweight loss from a tax is caused by the distortion in the price faced by buyers and sellers. The more sensitive buyers are to an increase in the price of the good (more elastic demand), the more they reduce their quantity demanded when a tax is placed on a good. The more sensitive sellers are to a decrease in the price of a good (more elastic supply), the more they reduce their quantity supplied when a tax is placed on a good. A greater reduction in the quantity exchanged in the market causes a greater deadweight loss. As a result, *the greater the elasticities of supply and demand, the greater the deadweight loss of a tax.*

The most important tax in the U.S. economy is the tax on labor—federal and state income taxes and Social Security taxes. Taxes on labor encourage workers to work fewer hours, second earners to stay home, the elderly to retire early, and the unscrupulous to enter the underground economy. The more elastic the supply of labor, the greater the deadweight loss of taxation and, thus, the greater the cost of any government program that relies on income tax revenue for funding. Economists and politicians argue about how elastic the supply of labor is and, thus, how large these effects are.

Henry George, a 19th century economist, suggested that there should be a single tax on land because the supply of land is inelastic. Therefore, the burden of the tax would be entirely on the owners of land and the tax would have no deadweight loss. Few modern economists support a single tax on land because it would not raise enough revenue and because it would need to be a tax on unimproved land (which would be difficult to implement). A tax on improved land would cause landowners to devote fewer resources toward improving their land and would create a deadweight loss.

Deadweight Loss and Tax Revenue as Taxes Vary

Deadweight loss increases as a tax increases. Indeed, deadweight loss increases at an increasing rate as a tax increases. It increases as the square of the factor of increase in the tax. For example, if a tax is doubled, the deadweight loss rises by a factor of 4. If a tax is tripled, the deadweight loss rises by a factor of 9, and so on.

Tax revenue first increases and then decreases as a tax increases. This is because, at first, an increase in a tax increases the taxes collected per unit more than it reduces the units sold. At some point, however, an ever increasing tax reduces the size of the market (the quantity sold and taxed) to such a degree that the government begins to collect a large tax on such a small quantity that tax revenue begins to fall.

The idea that a high tax rate could so shrink the market that it reduces tax revenue was expressed by Arthur Laffer in 1974. The *Laffer curve* is a diagram that shows that as the size of a tax on a good is increased, revenue first rises and then falls. The implication is that if tax rates are already extremely high, a reduction in tax rates could increase tax revenue. This is a part of what has come to be called supply-side economics. Evidence has shown that this may be true for individuals who are taxed at extremely high rates, but it is unlikely to be true for an entire economy. A possible exception is Sweden in the 1980s because its tax rates were about 80 percent for the typical worker.

Conclusion

Taxes place a cost on market participants in two ways:

- Resources are diverted from buyers and sellers to the government.
- Taxes distort incentives so fewer goods are produced and sold than otherwise. That is, taxes cause society to lose some of the benefits of efficient markets.

HELPFUL HINTS

1. As a tax increases, it reduces the size of the market more and more. At some point, the tax is so high that it is greater than or equal to the potential surplus even from the first unit. At that point, the tax has become a *prohibitive tax* because it eliminates the market altogether. Note that when a tax is prohibitive, the government collects no revenue at all from the tax because no units are sold. The market has reached the far side of the Laffer curve.

2. As a tax increases, the deadweight loss increases *at an increasing rate* because there are two sources to the deadweight loss and both sources are generating an increase in deadweight loss as a tax increases. First, an increase in a tax reduces the quantity exchanged and that increases deadweight loss. Second, as quantity exchanged decreases due to the tax, each successive unit that is not produced and sold *has a higher total surplus associated with it*. This further increases the deadweight loss from a tax.

TERMS AND DEFINITIONS

Choose a definition for each key term.

Key terms:

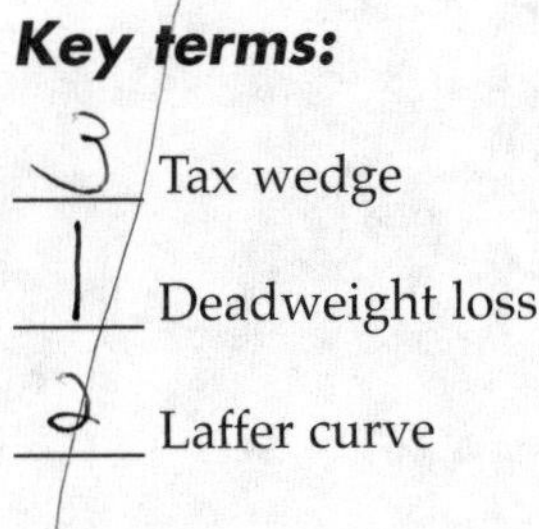

____ Tax wedge

____ Deadweight loss

____ Laffer curve

Definitions:

1. The reduction in total surplus that results from a tax
2. A graph showing the relationship between the size of a tax and the tax revenue collected
3. The difference between what the buyer pays and the seller receives when a tax is placed in a market

PROBLEMS AND SHORT-ANSWER QUESTIONS

Practice Problems

1. Exhibit 2 shows the market for tires. Suppose that a $12 road-use tax is placed on each tire sold.
   a. In Exhibit 2, locate consumer surplus, producer surplus, tax revenue, and the deadweight loss.

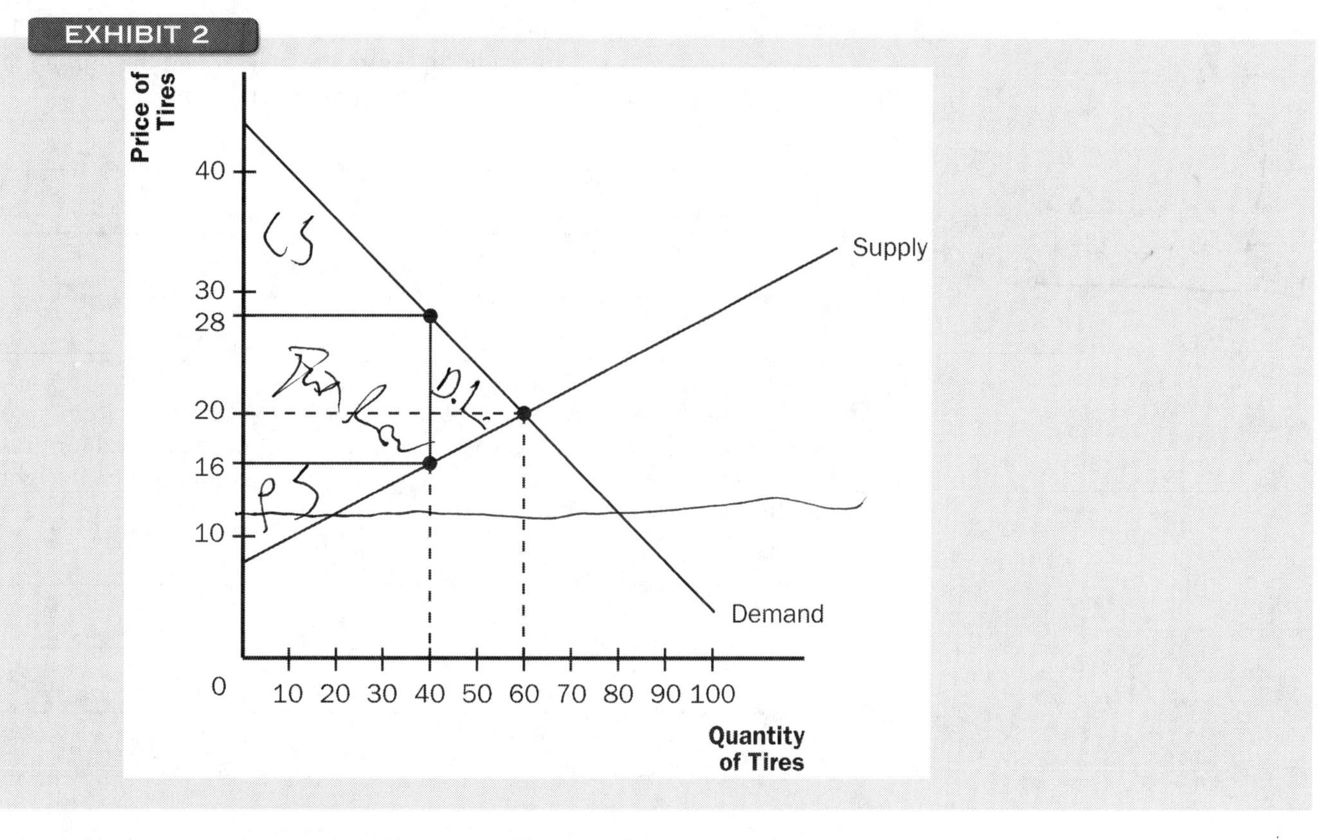

b. Why is there a deadweight loss in the market for tires after the tax is imposed?

c. What is the value of the tax revenue collected by the government? Why wasn't the government able to collect $12 per tire on 60 tires sold (the original equilibrium quantity)?

d. What is the value of the tax revenue collected from the buyers? What is the value of the tax revenue collected from the sellers? Did the burden of the tax fall more heavily on the buyers or the sellers? Why?

e. Suppose over time, buyers of tires are able to substitute away from auto tires (they walk and ride bicycles). Because of this, their demand for tires becomes more elastic. What will happen to the size of the deadweight loss in the market for tires? Why?

2. Use Exhibit 3, which shows the market for music CDs, to answer the following questions.

a. Complete the table. (Note: to calculate deadweight loss, the area of a triangle is 1/2 base × height).

Tax per unit	Tax revenue collected	Deadweight loss
$ 0		
3		
6		
9		
12		
15		
18		

EXHIBIT 3

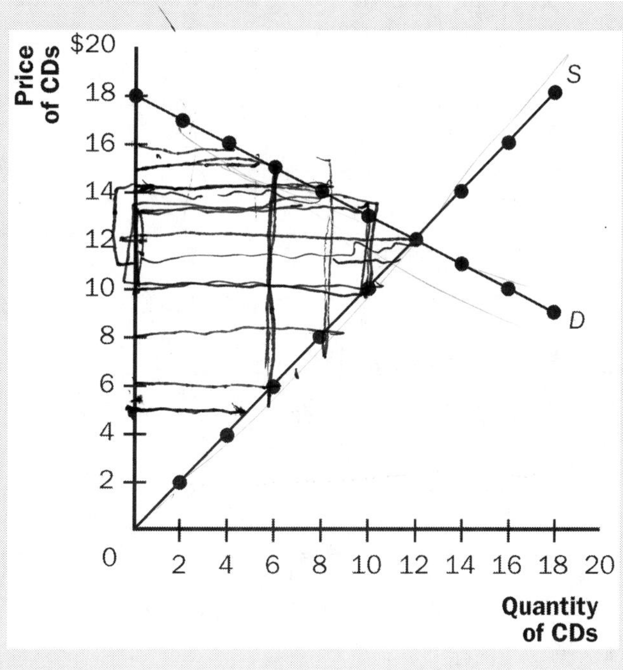

b. As the tax is increased, what happens to the amount of tax revenue collected? Why?

____

____

____

____

c. At a tax of $18 per CD, how much tax revenue is collected? Why?

____

____

____

d. If the government wanted to maximize tax revenue, what tax per unit should it impose?

____

____

e. If the government wanted to maximize efficiency (total surplus) what tax per unit should it impose?

____

f. What happens to the deadweight loss due to the tax as the tax is increased? Why?

Short-Answer Questions

1. Why does a tax reduce consumer surplus?

2. Why does a tax reduce producer surplus?

3. Why does a tax generally produce a deadweight loss?

4. Under what conditions would a tax fail to produce a deadweight loss?

5. When a tax is placed on a good, does the government collect revenue equal to the loss in total surplus due to the tax? Why?

6. Suppose Rachel values having her house painted at $1,000. The cost for Paul to paint her house is $700. What is the value of the total surplus or the gains from trade on this transaction? What is the size of the tax that would eliminate this trade? What is the deadweight loss from this tax? What generalization can you make from this exercise?

7. Would you expect a tax on gasoline to have a greater deadweight loss in the short run or the long run? Why?

8. Would a tax on unimproved land generate a large deadweight loss? Why? Who would bear the burden of the tax, the renter or the landlord? Why?

9. As a tax on a good increases, what happens to tax revenue? Why?

10. As a tax on a good increases, what happens to the deadweight loss from the tax? Why?

SELF-TEST

True/False Questions

______1. In general, a tax raises the price the buyers pay, lowers the price the sellers receive, and reduces the quantity sold.

______2. If a tax is placed on a good and it reduces the quantity sold, there must be a deadweight loss from the tax.

______3. Deadweight loss is the reduction in consumer surplus that results from a tax.

______4. When a tax is placed on a good, the revenue the government collects is exactly equal to the loss of consumer and producer surplus from the tax.

______5. If John values having his hair cut at $20 and Mary's cost of providing the hair cut is $10, any tax on hair cuts larger than $10 will eliminate the gains from trade and cause a $20 loss of total surplus.

______6. If a tax is placed on a good in a market where supply is perfectly inelastic, there is no deadweight loss and the sellers bear the entire burden of the tax.

______7. A tax on cigarettes would likely generate a larger deadweight loss than a tax on luxury boats.

______8. A tax will generate a greater deadweight loss if supply and demand are inelastic.

______9. A tax causes a deadweight loss because it eliminates some of the potential gains from trade.

______10. A larger tax always generates more tax revenue.

______11. A larger tax always generates a larger deadweight loss.

______12. If an income tax rate is high enough, a reduction in the tax rate could increase tax revenue.

______13. A tax collected from buyers generates a smaller deadweight loss than a tax collected from sellers.

______14. If a tax is doubled, the deadweight loss from the tax more than doubles.

______15. A deadweight loss results when a tax causes market participants to fail to produce and consume units on which the benefits to the buyers exceeded the costs to the sellers.

Multiple-Choice Questions

Use Exhibit 4 for questions 1 through10.

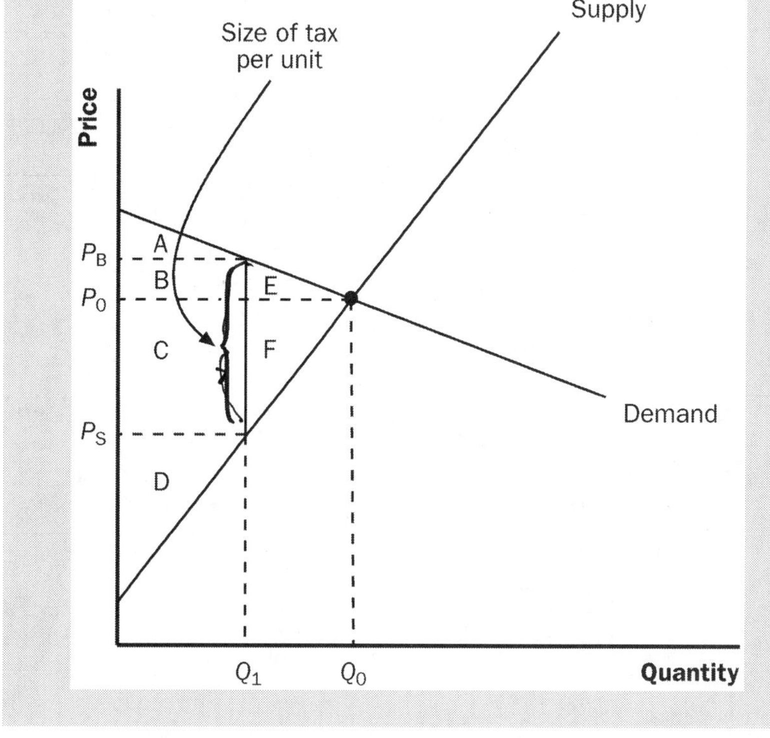

1. If there is no tax placed on the product in this market, consumer surplus is the area
   a. A + B + C.
   b. D + C + B.
   c. A + B + E.
   d. C + D + F.
   e. A.

2. If there is no tax placed on the product in this market, producer surplus is the area
   a. A + B + C + D.
   b. C + D + F.
   c. D.
   d. C + F.
   e. A + B + E.

3. If a tax is placed on the product in this market, consumer surplus is the area
   a. A.
   b. A + B.
   c. A + B + E.
   d. A + B + C + D.
   e. D.

4. If a tax is placed on the product in this market, producer surplus is the area
   a. A.
   b. A + B + E.
   c. C + D + F.
   d. D.
   e. A + B + C + D.

5. If a tax is placed on the product in this market, tax revenue paid by the buyers is the area
   a. A.
   b. B.
   c. C.
   d. B + C.
   e. B + C + E + F.

6. If a tax is placed on the product in this market, tax revenue paid by the sellers is the area
   a. A.
   b. B.
   c. C.
   d. C + F.
   e. B + C + E + F.

7. If there is no tax placed on the product in this market, total surplus is the area
   a. A + B + C + D.
   b. A + B + C + D + E + F.
   c. B + C + E + F.
   d. E + F.
   e. A + D + E + F.

8. If a tax is placed on the product in this market, total surplus is the area
   a. A + B + C + D.
   b. A + B + C + D + E + F.
   c. B + C + E + F.
   d. E + F.
   e. A + D.

9. If a tax is placed on the product in this market, deadweight loss is the area
   a. B + C.
   b. B + C + E + F.
   c. A + B + C + D.
   d. E + F.
   e. A + D.

10. Which of the following is true with regard to the burden of the tax in Exhibit 4?
    a. The buyers pay a larger portion of the tax because demand is more inelastic than supply.
    b. The buyers pay a larger portion of the tax because demand is more elastic than supply.
    c. The sellers pay a larger portion of the tax because supply is more elastic than demand.
    d. The sellers pay a larger portion of the tax because supply is more inelastic than demand.

11. Which of the following would likely cause the greatest deadweight loss?
    a. a tax on cigarettes
    b. a tax on salt
    c. a tax on cruise line tickets
    d. a tax on gasoline

12. A tax on gasoline is likely to
    a. cause a greater deadweight loss in the long run when compared to the short run.
    b. cause a greater deadweight loss in the short run when compared to the long run.
    c. generate a deadweight loss that is unaffected by the time period over which it is measured.
    d. none of the above

13. Deadweight loss is greatest when
    a. both supply and demand are relatively inelastic.
    b. both supply and demand are relatively elastic.
    e. supply is elastic and demand is perfectly inelastic.
    d. demand is elastic and supply is perfectly inelastic.

14. Since the supply of unimproved land is relatively inelastic, a tax on unimproved land would generate
    a. a large deadweight loss and the burden of the tax would fall on the renter.
    b. a small deadweight loss and the burden of the tax would fall on the renter.
    c. a large deadweight loss and the burden of the tax would fall on the landlord.
    d. a small deadweight loss and the burden of the tax would fall on the landlord.

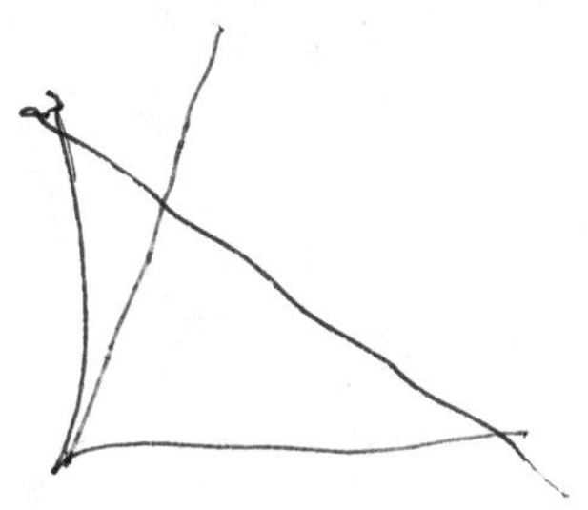

15. Which of the following is true with regard to a tax on labor income? Taxes on labor income tend to encourage
    a. workers to work fewer hours.
    b. second earners to stay home.
    c. the elderly to retire early.
    d. the unscrupulous to enter the underground economy.
    e. all of the above.

16. When a tax on a good starts small and is gradually increased, tax revenue
    a. will rise.
    b. will fall.
    c. will first rise and then fall.
    d. will first fall and then rise.
    e. none of the above

17. The graph that shows the relationship between the size of a tax and the tax revenue collected by the government is known as a
    a. Keynesian curve.
    b. Henry George curve.
    c. Laffer curve.
    d. Reagan curve.
    e. none of the above

18. If a tax on a good is doubled, the deadweight loss from the tax
    a. stays the same.
    b. doubles.
    c. increases by a factor of four.
    d. could rise or fall.

19. The reduction of a tax
    a. could increase tax revenue if the tax had been extremely high.
    b. will always reduce tax revenue regardless of the prior size of the tax.
    c. will have no impact on tax revenue.
    d. causes a market to become less efficient.

20. When a tax distorts incentives to buyers and sellers so that fewer goods are produced and sold than otherwise, the tax has
    a. increased efficiency.
    b. decreased equity.
    c. generated no tax revenue.
    d. caused a deadweight loss.

ADVANCED CRITICAL THINKING

You are watching the local news report on television with your roommate. The news anchor reports that the state budget has a deficit of $100 million. Since the state currently collects exactly $100 million from its 5 percent sales tax, your roommate says, "I can tell them how to fix their deficit. They should simply double the sales tax to 10 percent. That will double their tax revenue from $100 million to $200 million and provide the needed $100 million."

1. Is it true that doubling a tax will always double tax revenue? Why?

____

____

____

____

____

____

2. Will doubling the sales tax affect the tax revenue and the deadweight loss in all markets to the same degree? Explain?

____

____

____

____

____

____

____

SOLUTIONS

Terms and Definitions

3 Tax wedge

1 Deadweight loss

2 Laffer curve

Practice Problems

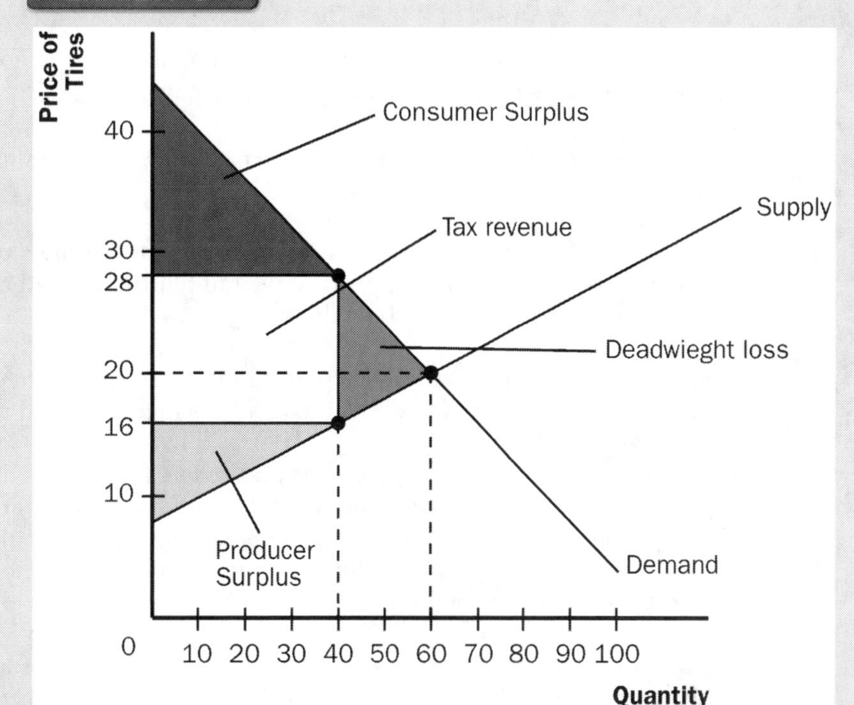

1. a. See Exhibit 5.
   b. The tax raises the price paid by buyers and lowers the price received by sellers causing them to reduce their quantities demanded and supplied. Therefore, they fail to produce and exchange units where the value to buyers exceeds the cost to sellers.
   c. $12 × 40 = $480. The tax distorted prices to the buyers and sellers so that the quantity supplied and demanded with the tax is reduced to 40 units from 60 units.
   d. $8 × 40 = $320 from buyers. $4 × 40 = $160 from sellers. The burden fell more heavily on the buyers because the demand for tires was less elastic than the supply of tires.
   e. Deadweight loss will increase because when buyers are more sensitive to an increase in price (due to the tax) they will reduce their quantity demanded even more and shrink the market more. Thus, even fewer units that are valued by buyers in excess of their cost will be sold.

2. a.

Tax per unit	Tax revenue collected	Deadweight loss
$0	$0	$0
3	30	($3 × 2)/2 = $3
6	48	($6 × 4)/2 = $12
9	54	($9 × 6)/2 = $27
12	48	($12 × 8)/2 = $48
15	30	($15 × 10)/2 = $75
18	0	($18 × 12)/2 = $108

   b. It first rises, then falls. At first, as the tax is increased tax revenue rises. At some point, the tax reduces the size of the market to such a degree that the government is collecting a large tax on such a small quantity that tax revenue begins to fall.
   c. No tax revenue is collected because the tax is as large as the total surplus on the first unit. Therefore, there is no incentive to produce and consume even one unit and the entire market is eliminated.
   d. $9 per unit.
   e. $0 per unit which causes the market to return to its free market equilibrium.
   f. It increases. Indeed, it increases at an increasing rate. This is because as the tax increases it causes the quantity exchanged to be reduced on units that have an ever larger potential surplus attached to them.

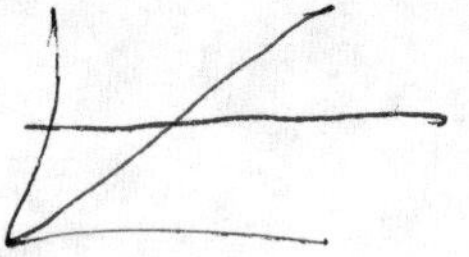

Short-Answer Questions

1. Consumer surplus is what the buyer is willing to pay for a good minus what the buyer actually pays and a tax raises the price the buyer actually pays.

2. Producer surplus is the amount the seller receives for a good minus the seller's cost and a tax reduces what the seller receives for a good.

3. A tax raises the price buyers pay and lowers the price sellers receive. This price distortion reduces the quantity demanded and supplied so we fail to produce and consume units where the benefits to the buyers exceeds the cost to the sellers.

4. If either supply or demand were perfectly inelastic (insensitive to a change in price), then a tax would fail to reduce the quantity exchanged and the market would not shrink.

5. No. The tax distorts prices to buyers and sellers and causes them to reduce their quantities demanded and supplied. Taxes are collected only on the units sold after the tax is imposed. Those units that are no longer produced and sold generate no tax revenue but those units would have added to total surplus because they were valued by buyers in excess of their cost to sellers. The reduction in total surplus is the deadweight loss.

6. Total surplus = \$300. Any tax larger than \$300. Deadweight loss would be \$300. A tax that is greater than the potential gains from trade will eliminate trade and create a deadweight loss equal to the lost gains from trade.

7. There would be a greater deadweight loss in the long run. This is because both demand and supply tend to be more elastic in the long run as consumers and producers are able to substitute away from this market when prices move in an adverse direction. The more a market shrinks from a tax the greater the deadweight loss.

8. No, because the supply of unimproved land is highly inelastic so the quantity supplied is not responsive to a decrease in the price received by the seller. The landlord would bear the burden of the tax for the same reason—supply of unimproved land is highly inelastic.

9. First tax revenue increases. At some point tax revenue decreases as the distortion in prices to buyers and sellers causes the market to shrink and large taxes are collected on a small number of units exchanged.

10. Deadweight loss increases continuously because as a tax increases the distortion in prices caused by the tax causes the market to shrink continuously. Thus, we fail to produce more and more units where the benefits to buyers exceeded the costs to sellers.

True/False Questions

1. T

2. T

3. F; deadweight loss is the reduction in *total surplus* that results from a tax.

4. F; the loss of producer and consumer surplus exceeds the revenue from the tax. The difference is deadweight loss.

5. F; the loss in total surplus is the buyer's value minus the seller's cost or \$20 – \$10 = \$10.

6. T

7. F; the more elastic the demand curve the greater the deadweight loss and the demand for cigarettes (a necessity) should be more inelastic than the demand for luxury boats (a luxury).

8. F; a tax generates a greater deadweight loss when supply and demand are more elastic.

9. T

10. F; as a tax increases, revenue first rises and then falls as the tax shrinks the market to a point where all trades are eliminated and tax revenue is zero.

11. T

12. T

13. F; taxes collected from the either the buyers or the sellers are equivalent. That is why economists simply use a tax wedge when analyzing a tax and avoid the issue altogether.

14. T

15. T

Multiple-Choice Questions

1. c	5. b	9. d	13. b	17. c
2. b	6. c	10. d	14. d	18. c
3. a	7. b	11. c	15. e	19. a
4. d	8. a	12. a	16. c	20. d

Advanced Critical Thinking

1. No. Usually an increase in a tax will reduce the size of the market because the tax will increase the price to buyers causing them to reduce their quantity demanded and decrease the price to sellers causing them to reduce their quantity supplied. Therefore, when taxes double, the government collects twice as mucsh per unit on many fewer units so tax revenue will increase by less than double and tax revenue could, in some extreme cases, even go down.

2. No. Some markets may have extremely elastic supply and demand curves. In these markets, an increase in a tax causes market participants to leave the market and little revenue is generated from the tax increase but deadweight loss increases a great deal. Other markets may have inelastic supply and demand curves. In these markets, an increase in a tax fails to cause market participants to leave the market and a great deal of additional tax revenue is generated with little increase in deadweight loss.

9

APPLICATION: INTERNATIONAL TRADE

GOALS

In this chapter you will

Consider what determines whether a country imports or exports a good

Examine who wins and who loses from international trade

Learn that the gains to winners from international trade exceed the losses to losers

Analyze the welfare effects of tariffs and import quotas

Examine the arguments people use to advocate trade restrictions

OUTCOMES

After accomplishing these goals, you should be able to

Determine whether a country imports or exports a good if the world price is greater than the before-trade domestic price

Show that the consumer wins and the producer loses when a country imports a good

Use consumer and producer surplus to show that the gains of the consumer exceed the losses of the producer when a country imports a good

Show the deadweight loss associated with a tariff or a quota

Defeat the arguments made in support of trade restrictions

CHAPTER OVERVIEW

Context and Purpose

Chapter 9 is the third chapter in a three-chapter sequence dealing with welfare economics. Chapter 7 introduced welfare economics—the study of how the allocation of resources affects economic well-being. Chapter 8 applied the lessons of welfare economics to taxation. Chapter 9 applies the tools of welfare economics from Chapter 7 to the study of international trade, a topic that was first introduced in Chapter 3.

The purpose of Chapter 9 is to use our knowledge of welfare economics to address the gains from trade more precisely than we did in Chapter 3 when we studied comparative advantage and the gains from trade. We will develop the conditions that determine whether a country imports or exports a good and discover who wins and who loses when a country imports or exports a good. We will find that when free trade is allowed, the gains of the winners exceed the losses of the losers. Since there are gains from trade, we will see that restrictions on free trade reduce the gains from trade and cause deadweight losses similar to those generated by a tax.

CHAPTER REVIEW

Introduction

This chapter employs welfare economics to address the following questions:

- How does international trade affect economic well-being?
- Who gains and who loses from free international trade?
- How do the gains from trade compare to the losses from trade?

The Determinants of Trade

In the absence of international trade, a market generates a domestic price that equates the domestic quantity supplied and domestic quantity demanded in that market. The **world price** is the price of the good that prevails in the world market for that good. Prices represent opportunity costs. Therefore, comparing the world price and the domestic price of a good before trade indicates whether a country has the lower opportunity cost of production and, thus, a comparative advantage in the production of a good, or if other countries have a comparative advantage in the production of the good.

- If the world price is above the domestic price for a good, the country has a comparative advantage in the production of that good and that good should be exported if trade is allowed.
- If the world price is below the domestic price for a good, foreign countries have a comparative advantage in the production of that good and that good should be imported if trade is allowed.

The Winners and Losers from Trade

Assume that the country being analyzed is a small country and is therefore a *price taker* on world markets. This means that the country takes the world price as given and cannot influence the world price.

Exhibit 1 depicts a situation where the world price is higher than the before-trade domestic price. This country has a comparative advantage in the production of this good. If free trade is allowed, the domestic price will rise to the world price and it will export the difference between the domestic quantity supplied and the domestic quantity demanded.

With regard to gains and losses to an exporting country from trade, before trade consumer surplus was A + B and producer surplus was C so total surplus was A + B + C. After trade, consumer surplus is A and producer surplus is B + C + D (the area below the price and above the supply curve). Total surplus is now A + B + C + D for a gain of area D. This analysis generates two conclusions:

- When a country allows trade and becomes an exporter of a good, domestic producers are better off and domestic consumers are worse off.
- Trade increases the economic well-being of a nation because the gains of the winners exceed the losses of the losers.

Exhibit 2 depicts a situation where the world price is lower than the before-trade domestic price. Other countries have a comparative advantage in the production of this good. If free trade is allowed, the domestic price will fall to the

EXHIBIT 1

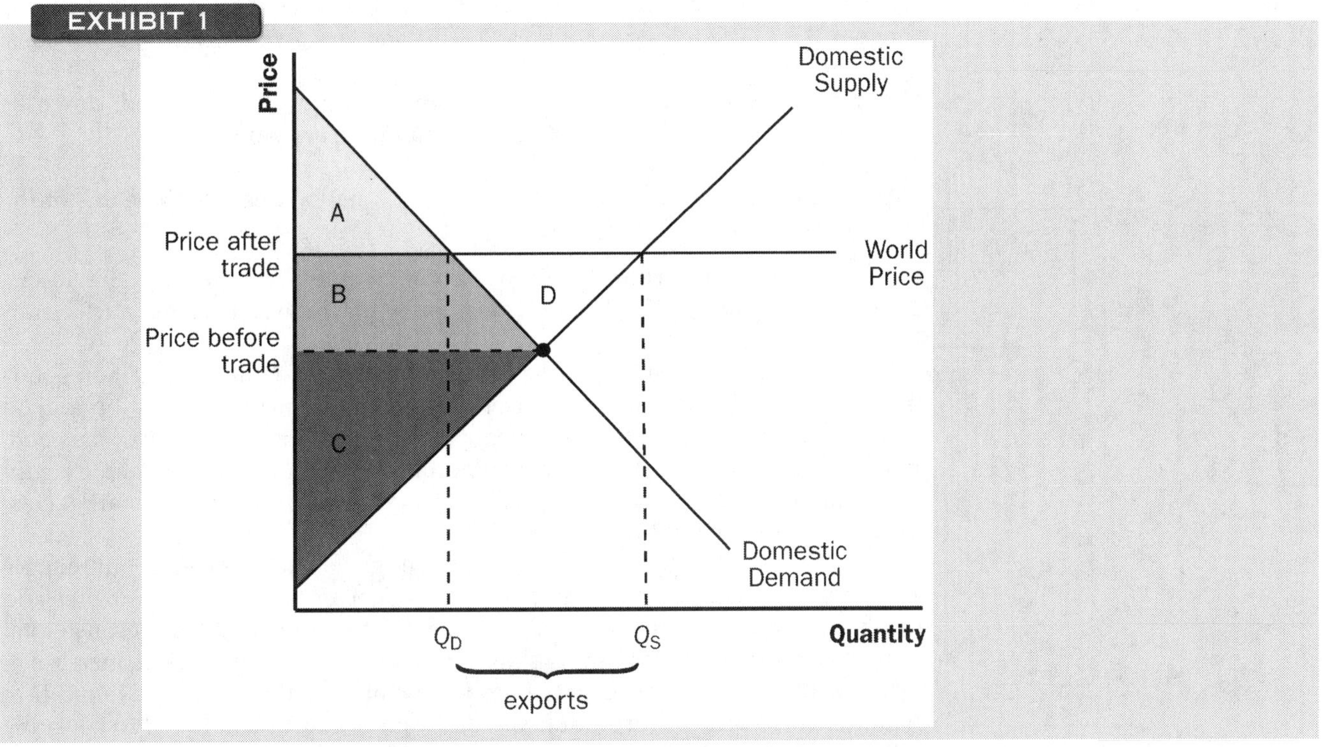

world price and it will import the difference between the domestic quantity supplied and the domestic quantity demanded.

With regard to gains and losses to an importing country from trade, before trade consumer surplus was A and producer surplus was B + C so total surplus was A + B + C. After trade, consumer surplus is A + B + D (the area below the

EXHIBIT 2

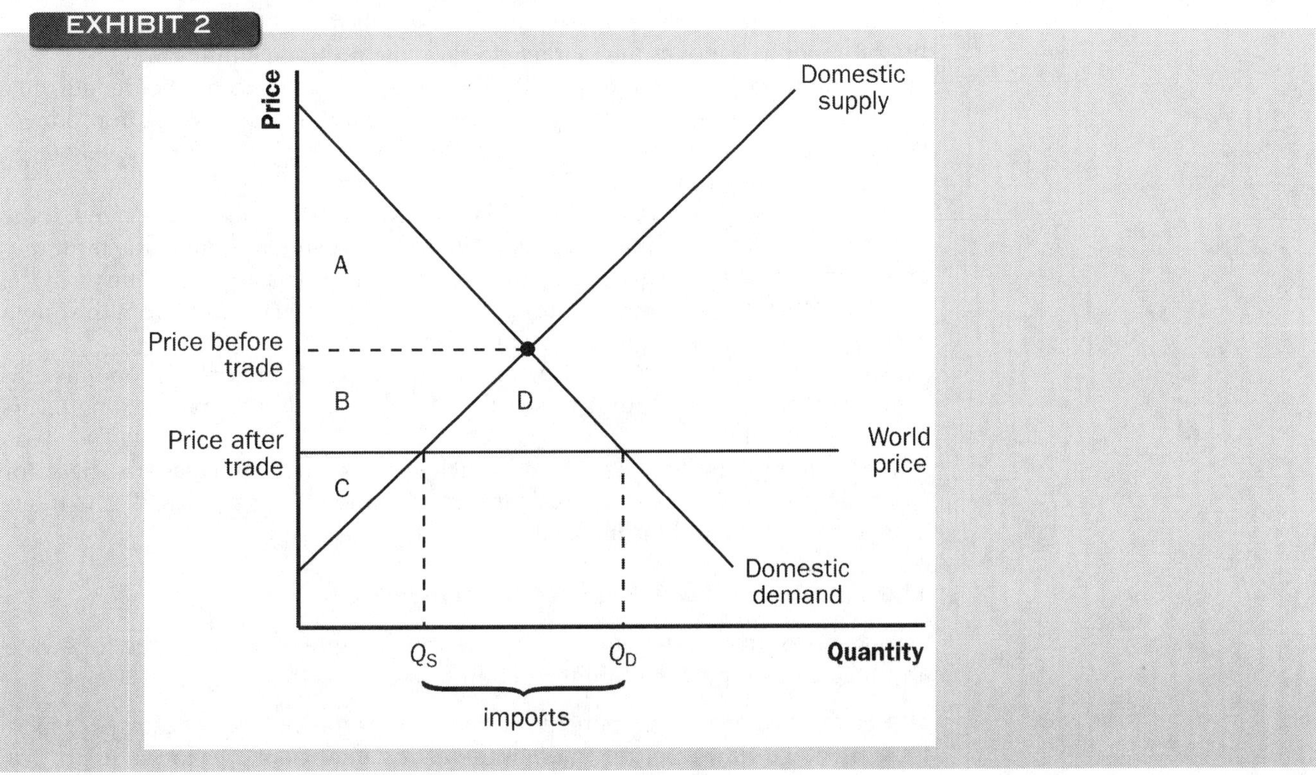

demand curve and above the price) and producer surplus is C. Total surplus is now A + B + C + D for a gain of area D. This analysis generates two conclusions:

- When a country allows trade and becomes an importer of a good, domestic consumers are better off and domestic producers are worse off.

- Trade increases the economic well-being of a nation because the gains of the winners exceed the losses of the losers.

Trade can make everyone better off if the winners compensate the losers. Compensation is rarely paid so the losers lobby for trade restrictions, such as tariffs and import quotas.

Tariffs and import quotas restrict international trade. A **tariff** is a tax on goods produced abroad and sold domestically. Therefore, a tariff is placed on a good only if the country is an importer of that good. A tariff raises the price of the good, reduces the domestic quantity demanded, increases the domestic quantity supplied, and, thus, reduces the quantity of imports. A tariff moves the market closer to the no-trade equilibrium.

A tariff increases producer surplus, increases government revenue, but reduces consumer surplus by a greater amount than the increase in producer surplus and government revenue. Therefore, a tariff creates a deadweight loss because total surplus is reduced. The deadweight loss comes from two sources. The increase in the price due to the tariff causes the production of units that cost more to produce than the world price (overproduction) and causes consumers to fail to consume units where the value to the consumer is greater than world price (underconsumption).

An **import quota** sets a limit on the quantity of a good that can be produced abroad and sold domestically. To accomplish this, a government can distribute a limited number of import licenses. An import quota shifts the portion of the domestic supply curve above the world price to the right by the size of the quota. An import quota raises the price of the good, reduces the domestic quantity demanded, increases the domestic quantity supplied, and, thus reduces the quantity of imports. It moves the market closer to the no-trade equilibrium.

An import quota increases producer surplus, increases license holder surplus, but reduces consumer surplus by a greater amount than the increase in producer and license holder surplus. Therefore, an import quota also creates a deadweight loss in a manner similar to a tariff.

Note that the results of a tariff and an import quota are nearly the same. If the government sells the import licenses, it will collect revenue equal to the tariff revenue and a tariff and a quota become identical. If quotas are "voluntary" in the sense that they are imposed by the exporting country, the revenue from the quota accrues to the foreign firms or governments.

Tariffs and import quotas cause deadweight losses. Therefore, if economic efficiency is a policy goal, countries should allow free trade and avoid using tariffs and import quotas.

Free trade offers benefits beyond efficiency. Free trade increases variety for consumers, allows firms to take advantage of economies of scale, makes markets more competitive, and facilitates the spread of technology.

The Arguments for Restricting Trade

Opponents of free trade (often producers hurt by free trade) offer the following arguments in support of trade restrictions:

The jobs argument Opponents of free trade argue that trade destroys domestic jobs. However, while free trade does destroy inefficient jobs in the importing sector, it creates more efficient jobs in the export sector, industries where the country has a comparative advantage. This is always true because each country has a comparative advantage in the production of something.

The national-security argument Some industries argue that their product is vital for national security so it should be protected from international competition. The danger of this argument is that it runs the risk of being overused.

The infant-industry argument New industries argue that they need temporary protection from international competition until they become mature enough to compete. However, there is a problem choosing which new industries to protect and, once protected, temporary protection often becomes permanent. In addition, industries truly expected to be competitive in the future don't need protection because the owners will accept short-term losses.

The unfair-competition argument Opponents of free trade argue that other countries provide their industries with unfair advantages such as subsidies, tax breaks, and lower environmental restrictions. However, the gains of consumers in the importing country will exceed the losses of the producers in that country, and the country will gain when importing subsidized production.

The protection-as-a-bargaining-chip argument Opponents of free trade argue that the threat of trade restrictions may result in other countries lowering their trade restrictions. However, if this does not work, the threatening country must back down or reduce trade—neither of which is desirable.

When countries choose to reduce trade restrictions, they can take a *unilateral* approach and remove trade restrictions on their own. Alternatively, they can take a *multilateral* approach and reduce trade restrictions along with other countries. Examples of the multilateral approach are NAFTA and GATT. The rules of GATT are enforced by the WTO. The multilateral approach has advantages in that it provides freer overall trade because many countries do it together and thus it is sometimes more easily accomplished politically. However, it may fail if negotiations between countries break down. Many economists suggest a unilateral approach because there will be gains to the domestic economy and this will cause other countries to emulate it.

Globalization is blamed by the uninformed for low wages and poor working conditions in less-developed countries. Economists argue, however, that low wages in poor countries are due to such things as low productivity. Attempts to increase wages in poor countries by restricting trade causes workers in poor countries to lose their jobs, which makes the poor even poorer.

Conclusion

Economists overwhelmingly support free trade. Free trade between states in the United States improves welfare by allowing each area of the country to specialize in the production of goods for which they have a comparative advantage. In the same manner, free trade between countries allows each country to enjoy the benefits of comparative advantage and the gains from trade.

HELPFUL HINTS

1. Countries that restrict trade usually restrict imports rather than exports. This is because producers lose from imports and gain from exports and producers are better organized to lobby the government to protect their interests. For example, when a country imports a product, consumers win and producers lose. Consumers are less likely to be able to organize and lobby

the government than the affected producers so imports may be restricted. When a country exports a product, producers win and consumers lose. But again, consumers are less likely to organize and lobby the government to restrict exports so exports are rarely restricted.

2. The overwhelming majority of economists find no sound *economic* argument in opposition to free trade. The only argument against free trade that may not be defeated on economic grounds is the "national-security argument." This is because it is the only argument against free trade that is not based on economics but rather is based on other strategic objectives.

3. A *prohibitive* tariff or import quota is one that is so restrictive that it returns the market to its original no-trade equilibrium. This occurs if the tariff is greater than or equal to the difference between the world price and the no-trade domestic price or if the import quota is set at zero.

TERMS AND DEFINITIONS

Choose a definition for each key term.

Key terms:

3 World price

2 Price takers

4 Tariff

1 Import quota

Definitions:

1. A limit on the quantity of a good that can be produced abroad and sold domestically
2. Market participants that cannot influence the price so they view the price as given
3. The price of a good that prevails in the world market for that good
4. A tax on goods produced abroad and sold domestically

PROBLEMS AND SHORT-ANSWER QUESTIONS

Practice Problems

1. Use Exhibit 3 to answer the following questions.
   a. If trade is not allowed, what is the equilibrium price and quantity in this market?

   ____

   ____

   b. If trade is allowed, will this country import or export this commodity? Why?

   ____

   ____

EXHIBIT 3

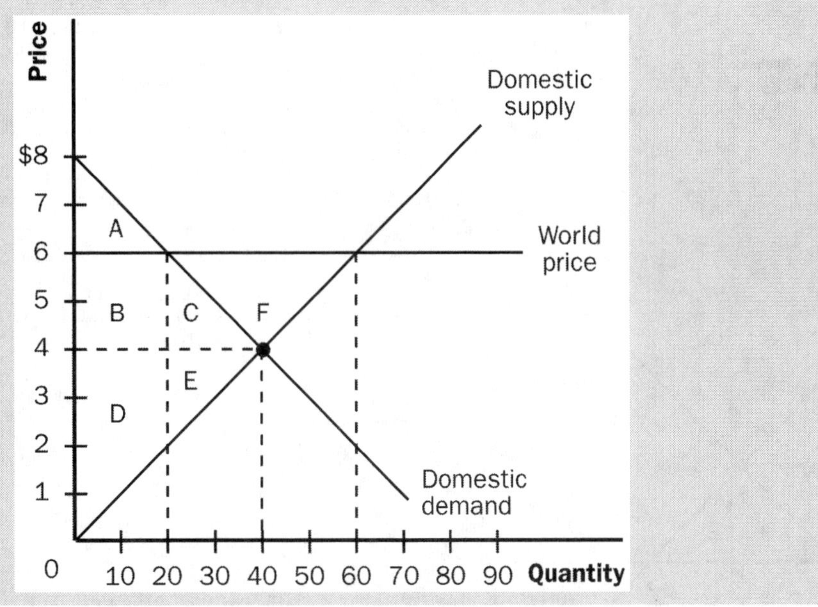

c. If trade is allowed, what is the price at which the good is sold, the domestic quantity supplied and demanded, and the quantity imported or exported?

____

____

d. What area corresponds to consumer surplus if no trade is allowed?

____

e. What area corresponds to consumer surplus if trade is allowed?

____

f. What area corresponds to producer surplus if no trade is allowed?

____

g. What area corresponds to producer surplus if trade is allowed?

____

h. If free trade is allowed, who gains and who loses, the consumers or the producers, and what area corresponds to their gain or loss?

____

____

i. What area corresponds to the gains from trade?

____

2. Use Exhibit 4 to answer the following questions.
   a. If trade is not allowed, what is the equilibrium price and quantity in this market?

   b. If trade is allowed, will this country import or export this commodity? Why?

   c. If trade is allowed, what is the price at which the good is sold, the domestic quantity supplied and demanded, and the quantity imported or exported?

   d. What area corresponds to consumer surplus if no trade is allowed?

   e. What area corresponds to consumer surplus if trade is allowed?

   f. What area corresponds to producer surplus if no trade is allowed?

   g. What area corresponds to producer surplus if trade is allowed?

   h. If free trade is allowed, who gains and who loses, the consumers or the producers, and what area corresponds to their gain or loss?

EXHIBIT 4

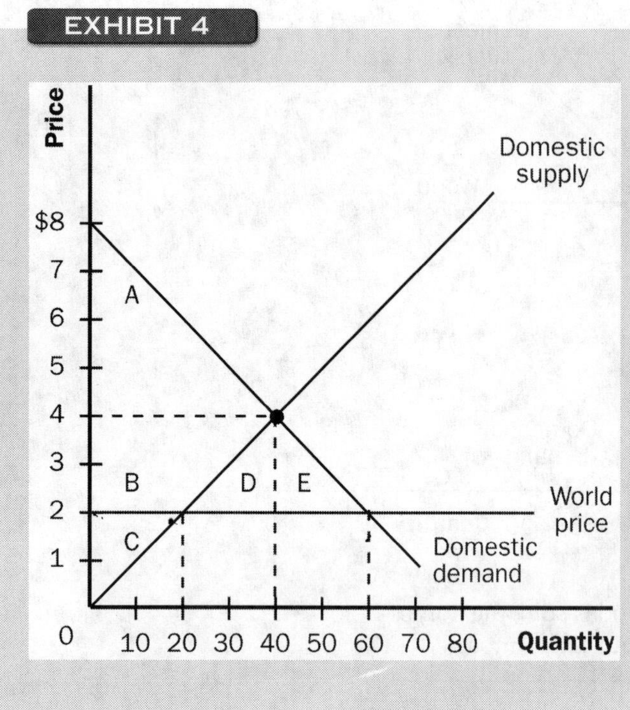

i. What area corresponds to the gains from trade?

____

EXHIBIT 5

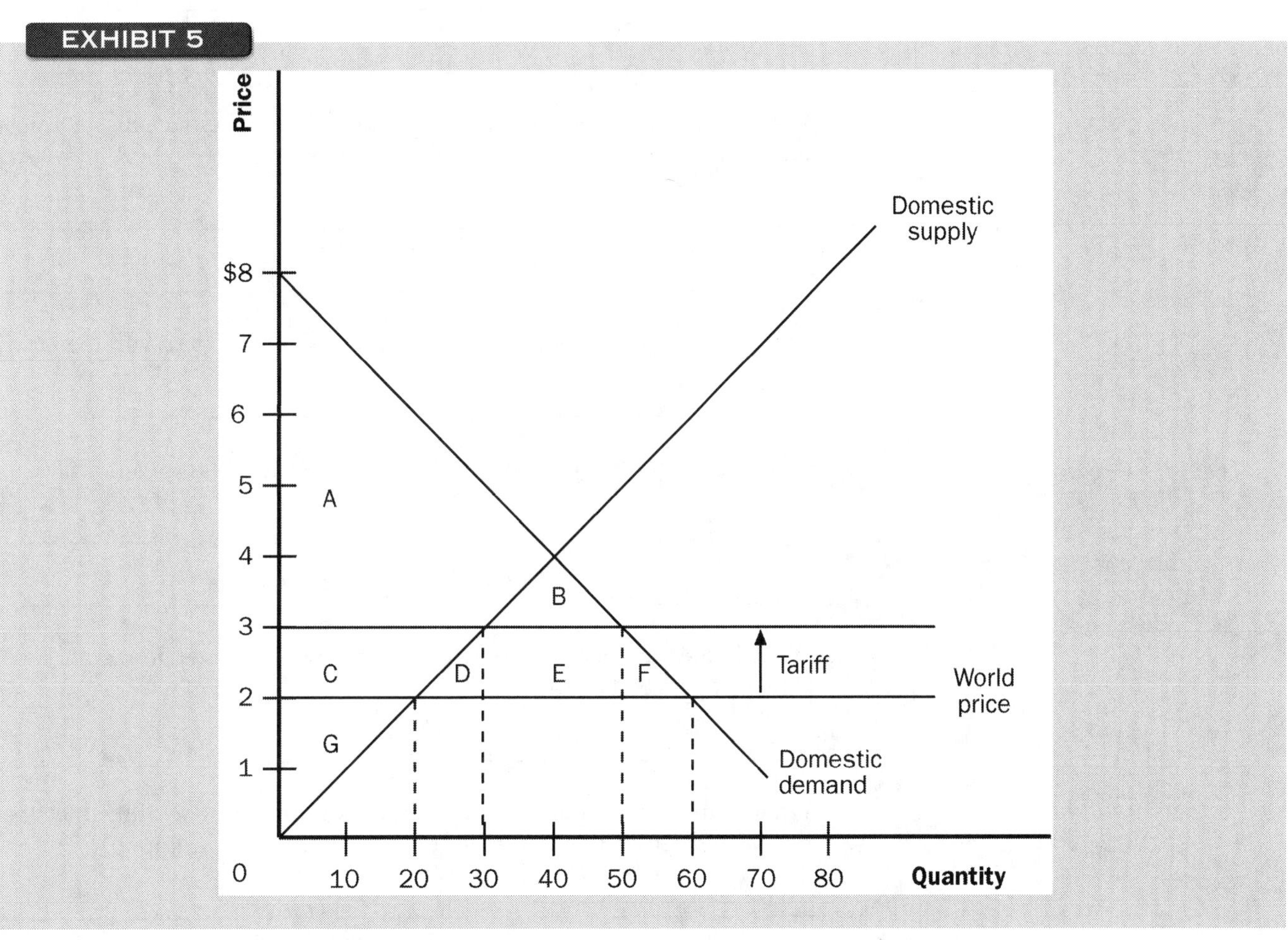

3. Use Exhibit 5 to answer the following questions.
   a. If free trade is allowed, what is the domestic quantity supplied, domestic quantity demanded, and the quantity imported?

   ____

   ____

   b. If a $1 tariff is placed on this good, what is the domestic quantity supplied, domestic quantity demanded, and the quantity imported?

   ____

   ____

c. What area corresponds to consumer and producer surplus before the tariff is applied?

d. What area corresponds to consumer surplus, producer surplus, and government revenue after the tariff is applied?

e. What area corresponds to the deadweight loss associated with the tariff?

f. Describe in words the sources of the deadweight loss from a tariff.

g. What is the size of the import quota that would generate results most similar to this $1 tariff?

h. What is the size of the tariff that would eliminate trade altogether (i.e. that would return the market to its no-trade domestic solution)?

Short-Answer Questions

The following table shows the amount of output a worker can produce per hour in Partyland and Laborland.

	Beer	Pizza
Partyland	2	4
Laborland	4	12

1. If free trade is allowed, which good will each country export to the other? Why? (Explain in terms of each country's opportunity cost of production.)

2. If the world price for a good is above a country's before-trade domestic price, will this country import or export this good? Why?

___

___

3. If residents of a country are allowed to import a good, who gains and who loses when compared to the before-trade equilibrium, the producers or the consumers? Why?

___

___

4. Describe in words the source of the gains from trade (the additional total surplus) received by an exporting country.

___

___

5. Describe in words the source of the gains from trade (the additional total surplus) received by an importing country.

___

___

6. Describe in words the source of the deadweight loss from restricting trade.

___

___

___

7. For every tariff there is an import quota that will generate a similar result. What are the short-comings of using an import quota to restrict trade versus using a tariff?

___

___

___

___

8. What arguments are made to support trade restrictions?

____

____

____

____

9. Present the free-trade response to the argument that imports should be restricted on goods that a country needs for national security.

____

____

10. If tariffs and quotas reduce total surplus and, therefore, total economic well-being, why do governments employ them?

____

____

____

11. List other benefits of free trade beyond those suggested by our standard analysis.

____

____

____

SELF-TEST

True/False Questions

______1. If the world price for a good exceeds a country's before-trade domestic price for that good, the country should import that good.

______2. Countries should import products for which they have a comparative advantage in production.

______3. If a worker in Brazil can produce 6 oranges or 2 apples in an hour while a worker in Mexico can produce 2 oranges or 1 apple in an hour, then Brazil should export oranges and Mexico should export apples.

______4. If free trade is allowed and a country imports wheat, domestic buyers of bread are better off and domestic farmers are worse off when compared to the before-trade domestic equilibrium.

______5. If free trade is allowed and a country exports a good, domestic producers of the good are worse off and domestic consumers of the good are better off when compared to the before-trade domestic equilibrium.

______6. If free trade is allowed and a country exports a good, the gains of domestic producers exceed the losses of domestic consumers and total surplus rises.

______7. Trade makes everyone better off.

______8. Trade can make everyone better off if the winners from trade compensate the losers from trade.

______9. Trade increases the economic well-being of a nation because the gains of the winners exceed the losses of the losers.

______10. Tariffs tend to benefit consumers.

______11. A tariff raises the price of a good, reduces the domestic quantity demanded, increases the domestic quantity supplied, and increases the quantity imported.

______12. An import quota that restricts imports to the same degree as a tariff raises more government revenue than the equivalent tariff.

______13. Opponents of free trade often argue that free trade destroys domestic jobs.

______14. If a foreign country subsidizes its export industries, its tax payers are paying to improve the welfare of consumers in the importing countries.

______15. Tariffs and quotas cause deadweight losses because they raise the price of the imported good and cause overproduction and underconsumption of the good in the importing country.

Multiple-Choice Questions

1. If free trade is allowed, a country will export a good if the world price is
   a. below the before-trade domestic price of the good.
   b. above the before-trade domestic price of the good.
   c. equal to the before-trade domestic price of the good.
   d. none of the above

2. Suppose the world price is below the before-trade domestic price for a good. If a country allows free trade in this good,
   a. consumers will gain and producers will lose.
   b. producers will gain and consumers will lose.
   c. both producers and consumers will gain.
   d. both producers and consumers will lose.

The following table shows the amount of output a worker can produce per hour in the United States and Canada.

	Pens	Pencils
United States	8	4
Canada	8	2

3. Which of the following statements about free trade between the United States and Canada is true?
   a. The United States will export pencils but there will be no trade in pens because neither country has a comparative advantage in the production of pens.
   b. The United States will export pens and Canada will export pencils.
   c. The United States will export pencils and Canada will export pens.
   d. The United States will export both pens and pencils.

4. If the world price for a good exceeds the before-trade domestic price for a good, then that country must have
   a. an absolute advantage in the production of the good.
   b. an absolute disadvantage in the production of the good.
   c. a comparative advantage in the production of the good.
   d. a comparative disadvantage in the production of the good.

EXHIBIT 6

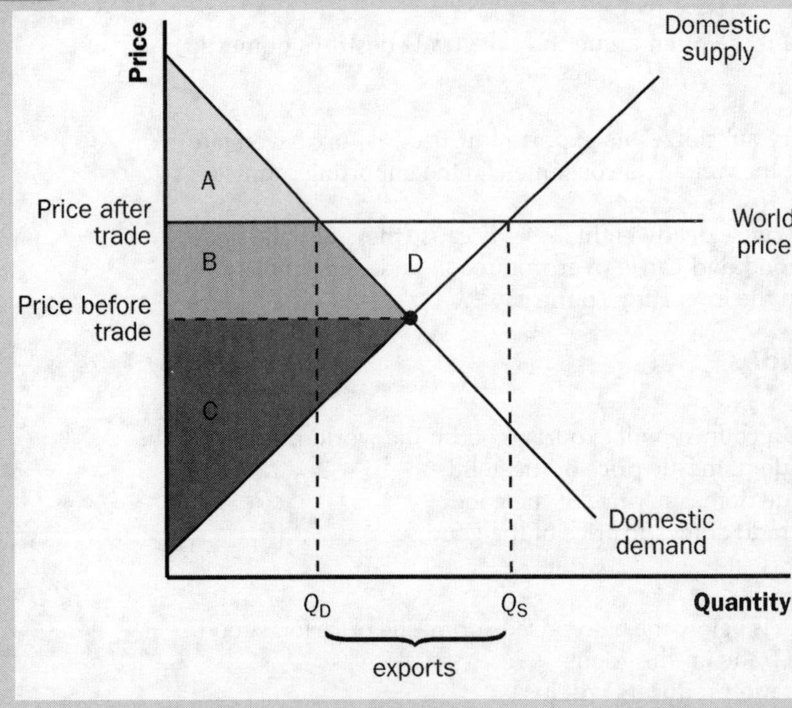

Use Exhibit 6 for questions 5 through 9.

5. If trade is not allowed, consumer surplus is the area
   a. A.
   b. A + B.
   c. A + B + C.
   d. A + B + D.
   e. A + B + C + D.

6. If free trade is allowed, consumer surplus is the area
   a. A.
   b. A + B.
   c. A + B + C.
   d. A + B + D.
   e. A + B + C + D.

7. If trade is not allowed, producer surplus is the area
   a. C.
   b. B + C.
   c. B + C + D.
   d. A + B + C.
   e. A + B + C + D.

8. If free trade is allowed, producer surplus is the area
   a. C.
   b. B + C.
   c. B + C + D.
   d. A + B + C.
   e. A + B + C + D.

9. The gains from trade correspond to the area
   a. A.
   b. B.
   c. C.
   d. D.
   e. B + D.

10. When a country allows trade and exports a good,
    a. domestic consumers are better off, domestic producers are worse off, and the nation is worse off because the losses of the losers exceed the gains of the winners.
    b. domestic consumers are better off, domestic producers are worse off, and the nation is better off because the gains of the winners exceed the losses of the losers.
    c. domestic producers are better off, domestic consumers are worse off, and the nation is worse off because the losses of the losers exceed the gains of the winners.
    d. domestic producers are better off, domestic consumers are worse off, and the nation is better off because the gains of the winners exceed the losses of the losers.

EXHIBIT 7

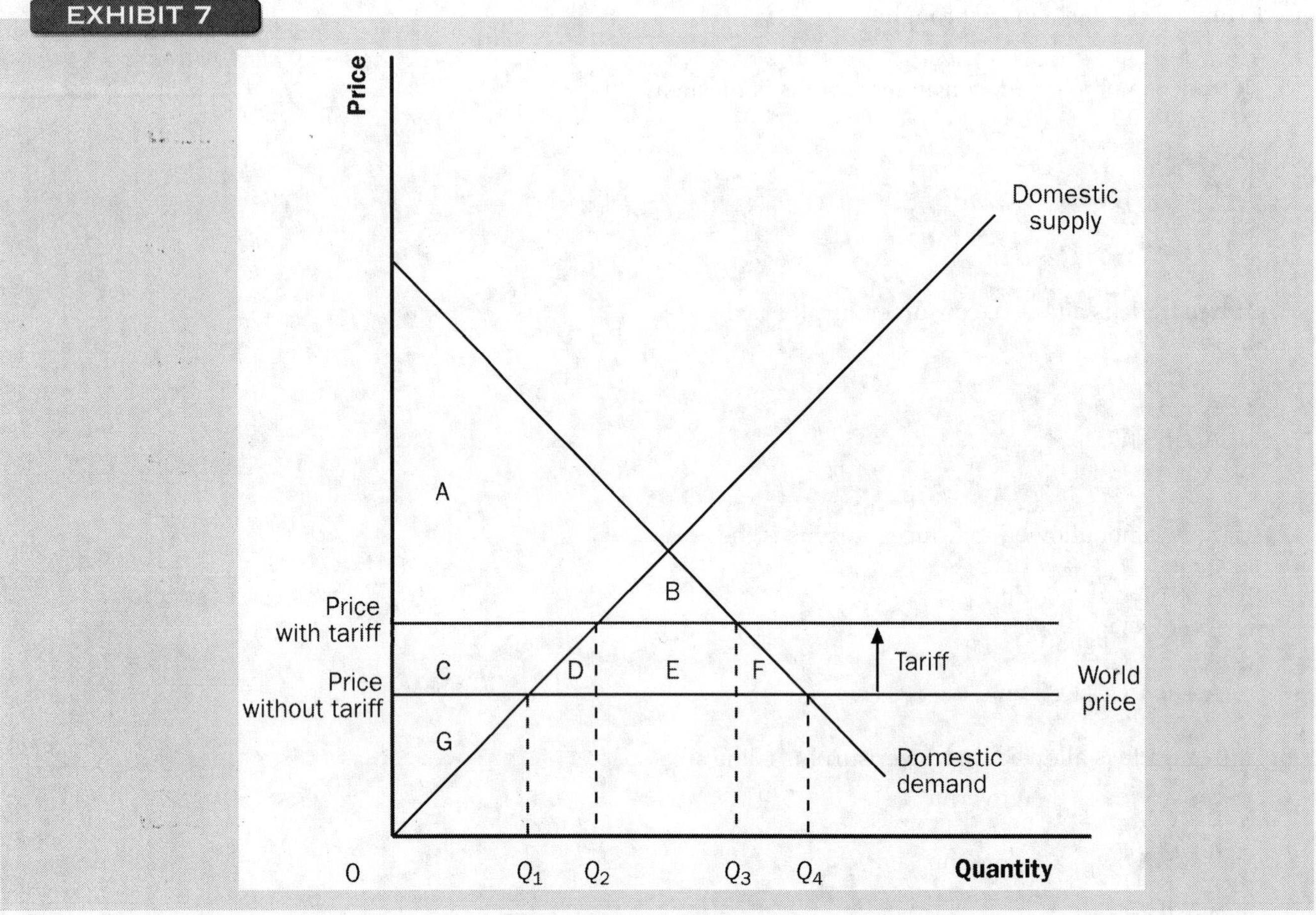

Use Exhibit 7 for questions 11 through 16.

11. If free trade is allowed, consumer surplus is the area
    a. A.
    b. A + B.
    c. A + B + C.
    d. A + B + C + D + E + F.
    e. A + B + C + D + E + F + G.

12. If a tariff is placed on this good, consumer surplus is the area
    a. A.
    b. A + B.
    c. A + B + C.
    d. A + B + C + D + E + F.
    e. A + B + C + D + E + F + G.

13. Government revenue from the tariff is the area
    a. C + D + E + F.
    b. D + E + F.
    c. D + F.
    d. G.
    e. E.

14. If a tariff is placed on this good, producer surplus is the area
    a. G.
    b. G + C.
    c. G + C + D + E + F.
    d. G + C + D + E + F + B.
    e. G + C + E.

15. The deadweight loss from the tariff is the area
    a. B + D + E + F.
    b. B.
    c. D + E + F.
    d. D + F.
    e. E.

16. What is the size of the import quota that would have the same impact on trade as the tariff?
    a. $Q_2 - Q_1$
    b. $Q_3 - Q_2$
    c. $Q_4 - Q_3$
    d. $Q_4 - Q_1$
    e. none of the above

17. Which of the following statements about a tariff is true?
    a. A tariff increases producer surplus, decreases consumer surplus, increases revenue to the government, and reduces total surplus.
    b. A tariff increases consumer surplus, decreases producer surplus, increases revenue to the government, and reduces total surplus.
    c. A tariff increases producer surplus, decreases consumer surplus, increases revenue to the government, and increases total surplus.
    d. A tariff increases consumer surplus, decreases producer surplus, increases revenue to the government, and increases total surplus.

18. Which of the following statements about import quotas is true?
    a. Import quotas are preferred to tariffs because they raise more revenue for the imposing government.
    b. Voluntary quotas established by the exporting country reduce the importing country's deadweight loss from the trade restriction.
    c. For every tariff, there is an import quota that could have generated a similar result.
    d. An import quota reduces the price to the domestic consumers.

19. Which of the following is not employed as an argument in support of trade restrictions?
    a. Free trade destroys domestic jobs.
    b. Free trade harms the national security if vital products are imported.
    c. Free trade is harmful to importing countries if foreign countries subsidize their exporting industries.
    d. Free trade harms both domestic producers and domestic consumers and therefore reduces total surplus.
    e. Free trade harms infant industries in an importing country.

20. Because producers are better able to organize than consumers, we would expect there to be political pressure to create
    a. free trade.
    b. import restrictions.
    c. export restrictions.
    d. none of the above.

ADVANCED CRITICAL THINKING

You are watching the nightly news. A political candidate being interviewed says, "I'm for free trade, but it must be fair trade. If our foreign competitors will not raise their environmental regulations, reduce subsidies to their export industries, and lower tariffs on their imports of our goods, we should retaliate with tariffs and import quotas on their goods to show them that we won't be played for fools!"

1. If a foreign country artificially lowers the cost of production for its producers with lax environmental regulations and direct subsidies and then exports the products to us, who gains and who loses in our country, producers or consumers?

____

____

2. Continuing from question 1 above, does our country gain or lose? Why?

____

____

3. If a foreign country subsidizes the production of a good exported to the United States, who bears the burden of their mistaken policy?

____

4. What happens to our overall economic well-being if we restrict trade with a country that subsidizes its export industries? Explain.

____

____

____

5. Is there any difference in the analysis of our importation of a good sold at the cost of production or sold at a subsidized price? Why?

____

____

____

____

6. Is it a good policy to threaten trade restrictions in the hope that foreign governments will reduce their trade restrictions? Explain.

____

____

____

SOLUTIONS

Terms and Definitions

3 World price

2 Price takers

4 Tariff

1 Import quota

Practice Problems

1. a. Price = $4, quantity = 40 units.
   b. Export because the world price is above the domestic price which implies that this country has a comparative advantage in the production of this good.
   c. Price = $6, quantity supplied = 60 units, quantity demanded = 20 units, quantity exported = 40 units.
   d. A + B + C
   e. A
   f. D + E
   g. B + C + D + E + F
   h. Consumers lose B + C, producers gain B + C + F
   i. F

2. a. Price = $4, quantity = 40 units.
   b. Import because the world price is below the domestic price, which implies that other countries have a comparative advantage in the production of this good.
   c. Price = $2, quantity supplied = 20 units, quantity demanded = 60 units, quantity imported = 40 units.
   d. A
   e. A + B + D + E
   f. B + C
   g. C
   h. Consumers gain B + D + E, producers lose B
   i. D + E

3. a. Quantity supplied = 20 units, quantity demanded = 60 units, quantity imported = 40 units.
   b. Quantity supplied = 30 units, quantity demanded = 50 units, quantity imported = 20 units.
   c. Consumer surplus = A + B + C + D + E + F, producer surplus = G
   d. Consumer surplus = A + B, producer surplus = C + G, government revenue = E
   e. D + F
   f. First, the rise in the price due to the tariff causes *overproduction* because units are produced that cost more than the world price. Second, the rise in price causes *underconsumption* because consumers fail to consume units where the value to consumers is greater than the world price.
   g. Import quota of 20 units—the same number of units imported with the $1 tariff.
   h. A $2 tariff would raise the price to $4 (the no-trade domestic price) and eliminate trade.

Short-Answer Questions

1. In Partyland, the opportunity cost of 1 beer is 2 pizzas. In Laborland, the opportunity cost of 1 beer is 3 pizzas. Partyland has the lower opportunity cost of beer and, thus, a comparative advantage in beer

production, and it will export beer. In Laborland, the opportunity cost of 1 pizza is 1/3 of a beer. In Partyland, the opportunity cost of 1 pizza is 1/2 of a beer. Laborland has the lower opportunity cost of pizza and, thus, a comparative advantage in pizza production, and it will export pizza. The fact that Laborland is more efficient at both is irrelevant.

2. Export, because the domestic opportunity cost of production is lower than the opportunity cost of production in other countries.

3. Consumers gain and producers lose because, if trade is allowed, the domestic price falls to the world price.

4. The gains are the additional value placed on the exported units by buyers in the rest of the world in excess of the domestic cost of production.

5. The gains are the additional value placed by domestic buyers on the imported units in excess of their cost of production in the rest of the world.

6. The rise in price from restricting trade causes overproduction of the good (production of units that cost more than the world price) and underconsumption of the good (failure to consume units valued more than the world price).

7. The revenue from an import quota will accrue to the license holders or foreign firms and governments unless the domestic government sells the import licenses for the maximum possible amount. In addition, expenditures incurred while lobbying the government to obtain import licenses add to the deadweight loss from the import quota.

8. Free trade will destroy domestic jobs, reduce national security, harm infant industries, force domestic producers to compete with foreign companies that have unfair advantages, and allow other countries to have trade restrictions while our country does not.

9. The danger is that nearly any good (far beyond standard military items) can be argued to be necessary for national security, including watches, clothing, shoes . . .

10. Tariffs and quotas harm domestic consumers while helping domestic producers. Producers are better able to organize than are consumers and, thus, they are better able to lobby the government on their behalf.

11. Free trade increases the variety of goods for consumers, allows firms to take advantage of economies of scale, makes markets more competitive, and facilitates the spread of technology.

True/False Questions

1. F; the country should export that good.

2. F; countries should export goods for which they have a comparative advantage in production.

3. T

4. T

5. F; producers gain, consumers lose.

6. T

7. F; Some gain and some lose but the gains of the winners outweigh the losses of the losers.
8. T
9. T
10. F; tariffs benefit producers.
11. F; tariffs decrease imports.
12. F; at most, a quota can raise the same revenue if the government sells the import licenses for the maximum amount possible.
13. T
14. T
15. T

Multiple-Choice Questions

1. b	5. b	9. d	13. e	17. a
2. a	6. a	10. d	14. b	18. c
3. c	7. a	11. d	15. d	19. d
4. c	8. c	12. b	16. b	20. b

Advanced Critical Thinking

1. Consumers gain, producers lose.
2. Our country gains because the gains of the consumers exceed the losses of the producers.
3. The taxpayers of the foreign country.
4. Producers gain, consumers lose, but consumers lose more than producers gain so total surplus is reduced and there is a deadweight loss. The result is no different than restricting trade when the foreign producer has no unfair advantage.
5. No. In either case, the world price is lower than the before-trade domestic price, causing consumers to gain and producers to lose from trade. Also, restrictions on trade cause consumers to lose more than producers gain whether the production of the good was subsidized or not.
6. Usually not. If the other country fails to give in to the threat, the threatening country has to choose between backing down and reducing trade—neither of which is desirable.

10

EXTERNALITIES

GOALS

In this chapter you will

- Learn what an externality is
- See why externalities can make market outcomes inefficient
- Examine how people can sometimes solve the problem of externalities on their own
- Consider why private solutions to externalities sometimes do not work
- Examine the various government policies aimed at solving the problem of externalities

OUTCOMES

After accomplishing these goals, you should be able to

- Distinguish between a positive and a negative externality
- Demonstrate why the optimal quantity and the market quantity differ in the presence of an externality
- Define the Coase theorem
- Explain how transaction costs may impede a private solution to an externality
- Demonstrate the potential equality of a Pigovian tax and pollution permits

CHAPTER OVERVIEW

Context and Purpose

Chapter 10 is the first chapter in the microeconomic section of the text. It is the first chapter in a three-chapter sequence on the economics of the public sector. Chapter 10 addresses externalities—the uncompensated impact of one person's actions on the well-being of a bystander. Chapter 11 will address public goods and common resources (goods that will be defined in Chapter 11) and Chapter 12 will address the tax system.

In Chapter 10, we address different sources of externalities and a variety of potential cures for externalities. Markets maximize total surplus to buyers and sellers in a market. However, if a market generates an externality (a cost or benefit to someone external to the market) the market equilibrium may not maximize the total benefit to society. Thus, in Chapter 10 we will see that while markets are usually a good way to organize economic activity, governments can sometimes improve market outcomes.

CHAPTER REVIEW

Introduction

An **externality** is the uncompensated impact of one person's actions on the well-being of a bystander. If the effect is beneficial, it is called a *positive externality*. If the effect is adverse, it is called a *negative externality*. Markets maximize total surplus to buyers and sellers in a market and this is usually efficient. However, if a market generates an externality, the market equilibrium may not maximize the total benefit to society as a whole and, thus, the market is inefficient. Government policy may be needed to improve efficiency.

Examples of negative externalities are pollution from exhaust and noise. Examples of positive externalities are historic building restorations and research into new technologies.

Externalities and Market Inefficiency

The height of the demand curve measures the value of the good to the marginal consumer. The height of the supply curve measures the cost to the marginal producer. If there is no government intervention, the price adjusts to balance supply and demand. The quantity produced maximizes consumer and producer surplus. If there is no externality, the market solution is efficient because it maximizes the well-being of buyers and sellers in the market and their well-being is all that matters. However, if there is an externality and bystanders are affected by this market, the market does not maximize the total benefit to society as a whole because others beyond just the buyers and sellers in the market are affected.

There are two types of externalities:

- *Negative externality:* When the production of a good generates pollution, costs accrue to society beyond those that accrue to the producing firm. Thus, the social cost exceeds the private cost of production and, graphically, the social cost curve is above the supply curve (private cost curve). Total surplus is the value to the consumers minus the true social cost of production. Therefore, the optimal quantity that maximizes total surplus is less than the equilibrium quantity generated by the market.

- *Positive externality:* A good such as education generates benefits to people beyond just the buyers of education. As a result, the social value of education exceeds the private value. Graphically, the social value curve is above the demand curve (private value curve). Total surplus is the true social value minus the cost to producers. Therefore, the optimal quantity that maximizes total surplus is greater than the equilibrium quantity generated by the market.

Internalizing an externality is the altering of incentives so that people take account of the external effects of their actions. To internalize externalities, the government can create taxes and subsidies to shift the supply and demand curves until they are the same as the true social cost and social value curves. This will make the equilibrium quantity and the optimal quantity the same and the market becomes efficient. Negative externalities can be internalized with taxes while positive externalities can be internalized with subsidies.

High technology production (robotics, etc.) generates a positive externality for other producers known as a *technology spillover*. Some economists consider this spillover effect to be so pervasive that they believe that the government should have a *technology policy*—government intervention to promote technology-enhancing industries. Other economists are skeptical. At present, the government provides a *property right* for new ideas in the form of patent protection.

Private Solutions to Externalities

Government action is not always needed to solve the externality problem. Some private solutions to the externality problem are:

- *Moral codes and social sanctions*. People "do the right thing" and do not litter.

- *Charities*. People give money to environmental groups and private colleges and universities.

- *Private markets that harness self-interest and cause efficient mergers*. The bee keeper merges with the apple orchard and the resulting firm produces more apples and more honey.

- *Private markets that harness self-interest and create contracts among affected parties.* The apple orchard and the bee keeper can agree to produce the optimal combined quantity of apples and honey.

The **Coase theorem** is the proposition that if private parties can bargain without cost over the allocation of resources, they can solve the problem of externalities on their own. In other words, regardless of the initial distribution of rights, the interested parties can always reach a bargain in which everyone is better off and the outcome is efficient. For example, if the value of peace and quiet exceeds the value of owning a barking dog, the party desiring quiet will buy the right to quiet from the dog owner and remove the dog or the dog owner will fail to buy the right to own a barking dog from the owner of quiet space. Regardless of whether one has the property right to peace and quiet or the other has the right to make noise, there is no barking dog, which, in this case, is efficient. The result is the opposite and is also efficient if the value of owning a dog exceeds the value of peace and quiet.

Private parties often fail to reach efficient agreements, however, due to **transaction costs.** Transaction costs are the costs that parties incur in the process of agreeing and following through on a bargain. If transaction costs exceed the potential gains from the agreement, no private solution will occur. Some sources of high transaction costs are:

- lawyers' fees to write the agreement.

- costs of enforcing the agreement.

- a breakdown in bargaining when there is a range of prices that would create efficiency.

- a large number of interested parties.

Public Policies toward Externalities

When private bargaining does not work, the government can sometimes improve the outcome by responding in one of two ways: *command-and-control* policies or *market-based* policies.

- Command-and-control policies are regulations that require or prohibit (or limit) certain behaviors. The problem here is that the regulator must know all of the details of an industry and alternative technologies in order to create the efficient rules. Prohibiting a behavior altogether can be best if the cost of a particular type of pollution is enormous.

- Market-based policies align private incentives with social efficiency. Taxes and subsidies can be used by the government to internalize externalities.

A tax enacted to correct the effects of a negative externality is known as a **Pigovian tax.** Pigovian taxes can reduce negative externalities at a lower cost than regulations because the tax essentially places a price on a negative externality, say pollution. Those firms that can reduce their pollution at least cost reduce their pollution a great deal while other firms that have higher costs of reducing their pollution reduce their pollution very little. The same amount of total reduction in pollution can be achieved with the tax as with regulation, but at lower cost. In addition, with the tax firms have incentive to develop cleaner technologies and reduce pollution even further than the regulation would have required. Unlike other taxes, Pigovian taxes enhance efficiency rather than reduce efficiency. For example, the tax on gasoline is a Pigovian tax because, rather than causing a deadweight loss, it causes there to be less traffic congestion, safer roads, and a cleaner environment.

Tradable pollution permits allow the holder of the permit to pollute a certain amount. Those firms that have a high cost of reducing their pollution will be willing to pay a high price for the permits and those firms that can reduce pollution at a low cost will sell their permits and will instead reduce their pollution. The initial allocation of the permits among industries does not affect the efficient outcome. This method is similar to a Pigovian tax. While a Pigovian tax sets the price of pollution (the tax), tradable pollution permits set the quantity of pollution permitted. In the market for pollution, either method can reach the efficient solution. Tradable pollution permits may be superior because the regulator does not need to know the demand to pollute in order to restrict pollution to a particular quantity. The EPA is increasingly using pollution permits to reduce pollution.

Some people object to an economic analysis of pollution. They feel that any pollution is too much and that putting a price on pollution is immoral. Since all economic activity creates pollution to some degree and all activities involve tradeoffs, economists have little sympathy for this argument. Rich productive countries demand a cleaner environment and market-based policies reduce pollution at a lower cost than alternatives, further increasing the demand for a clean environment.

Conclusion

Markets maximize total surplus to buyers and sellers in a market and this is usually efficient. However, if a market generates an externality, the market equilibrium may not maximize the total benefit to society as a whole and, thus, the market is inefficient. The Coase theorem says that people can bargain among themselves and reach an efficient solution. If transaction costs are high, however, government policy may be needed to improve efficiency. Pigovian taxes and pollution permits are preferred to command-and-control polices because they reduce pollution at a lower cost and, therefore, increase the quantity demanded of a clean environment.

HELPFUL HINTS

1. Why do we use the word "externality" to refer to the uncompensated impact of one person's actions on the well-being of a bystander? An easy way to remember is to know that the word externality refers to the "external effects" of a market transaction or to costs and benefits that land on a bystander who is "external to the market."

2. Negative externalities cause the socially optimal quantity of a good to be less than the quantity produced by the market. Positive externalities cause the socially optimal quantity of a good to be greater than the quantity produced by the market. To remedy the problem, the government can tax goods that have negative externalities and subsidize goods that have positive externalities.

TERMS AND DEFINITIONS

Choose a definition for each key term.

Key terms:

_____ Externality

_____ Positive externality

_____ Negative externality

_____ Social cost

_____ Internalizing an externality

_____ Coase theorem

_____ Transaction costs

_____ Pigovian tax

Definitions:

1. The proposition that if private parties can bargain without cost over the allocation of resources, they can solve the problem of externalities on their own
2. The costs that parties incur in the process of agreeing and following through on a bargain
3. A situation when a person's actions have an adverse impact on a bystander
4. A tax enacted to correct the effects of a negative externality
5. The uncompensated impact of one person's actions on the well-being of a bystander
6. Altering incentives so that people take account of the external effects of their actions
7. The sum of private costs and external costs
8. A situation when a person's actions have a beneficial impact on a bystander

PROBLEMS AND SHORT-ANSWER QUESTIONS

Practice Problems

1. The information below provides the prices and quantities in a hypothetical market for automobile antifreeze.

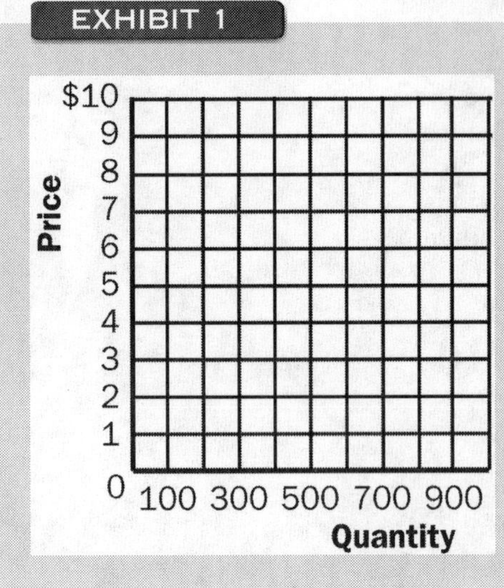

Price per Gallon	Quantity Demanded	Quantity Supplied
$1	700	300
2	600	400
3	500	500
4	400	600
5	300	700
6	200	800
7	100	900
8	0	1,000

a. Plot the supply and demand curves for antifreeze in Exhibit 1.
b. What is the equilibrium price and quantity generated by buyers and sellers in the market?

____

____

c. Suppose that the production of antifreeze generates pollution in the form of chemical runoff and that the pollution imposes a $2 cost on society for each gallon of antifreeze produced. Plot the social cost curve in Exhibit 1.
d. What is the optimal quantity of antifreeze production? Does the market overproduce or underproduce antifreeze?

____

____

e. If the government were to intervene to make this market efficient, should it impose a Pigovian tax or a subsidy? What is the value of the appropriate tax or subsidy?

____

____

2. Suppose citizens living around Metropolitan Airport value peace and quiet at a value of $3 billion.
a. If it costs the airlines $4 billion to make their planes quieter (the airlines value noise at $4 billion), is it efficient for the government to require that the planes be muffled? Why?

____

____

____

b. If it costs the airlines $2 billion to make their planes quieter, is it efficient for the government to require that the planes be muffled? Why?

____

____

c. Suppose there are no transaction costs and suppose that *people have the right to peace and quiet*. If it costs the airlines $2 billion to make their planes quieter, what is the private solution to the problem?

____

____

d. Suppose there are no transaction costs and suppose that *airlines have the right to make as much noise as they please*. If it costs the airlines $2 billion to make their planes quieter, what is the private solution to the problem?

____

____

e. Compare your answers to (c) and (d) above. What are the similarities and what are the differences? What general rule can you make from the comparison?

____

____

____

____

f. Suppose it costs the airlines $2 billion to make their planes quieter. If a private solution to the noise problem requires an additional $2 billion of transaction costs (due to legal fees, the large number of affected parties, and enforcement costs) can there be a private solution to the problem? Why?

____

____

3. Suppose there are four firms that each wish to dump one barrel of waste chemicals into the river. Firm 1 produces a product that is so valued by society and sells for such a high price that it is willing to pay $8 million to dump a barrel. Firm 2 produces a somewhat less valuable product and is only will-

ing to pay $6 million to dump a barrel. In similar fashion, suppose firm 3 is willing to pay $4 million to dump a barrel and firm 4 will pay $2 million.

a. Draw the demand for the right to pollute in Exhibit 2.

b. Suppose the EPA estimates that the safe level of pollutants in the river is 3 barrels. At what value should they set a Pigovian tax?

EXHIBIT 2

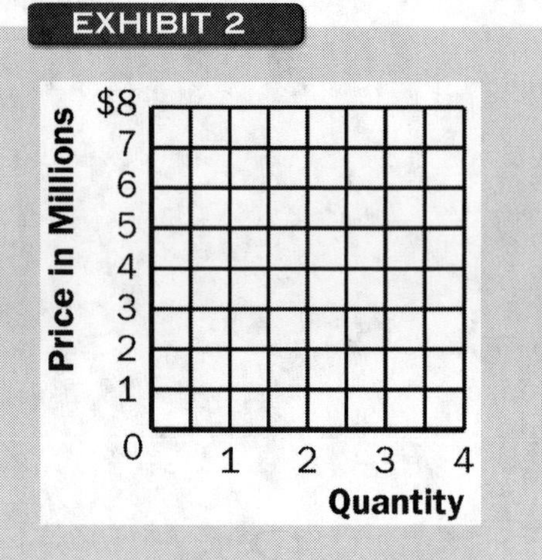

c. Suppose the EPA estimates that the safe level of pollutants in the river is 3 barrels. How many tradable pollution permits should they allocate? At what price will the permits trade?

d. Compare part (b) and (c) above. How many barrels are dumped in each case? What is the price paid to pollute in each case? Is there an advantage to one method of internalizing the externality compared to the other?

SHORT-ANSWER QUESTIONS

Use the following information for questions 1 through 3.

Suppose that a commercial apple orchard uses pesticides in the production of apples. In the process, dangerous fumes drift across a nearby neighborhood.

1. Is this an example of a positive or a negative externality? Explain.

2. If this externality is not internalized, does the market overproduce or underproduce apples? What does it mean to overproduce or underproduce a product?

3. To internalize this externality, should the government tax or subsidize apples? Why?

4. Suppose an individual enjoys lawn care and gardening a great deal. He uses pesticides to control insects and the harmful residue drifts across the neighborhood. He values the use of the pesticides at $10,000 and the neighborhood values clean air at $15,000. What does the Coase theorem suggest will take place?

5. In question 4 above, how large would the transactions costs need to be in order to ensure that no private solution to the problem can be found?

6. What are the sources of transaction costs when affected parties try to eliminate an externality?

7. What are some types of private solutions to externalities?

8. What are the two types of public policies toward externalities? Describe them. Which one do economists prefer? Why?

9. Does a Pigovian tax reduce or increase efficiency? Why?

____

____

10. Why are tradable pollution permits considered superior to Pigovian taxes at reducing pollution?

____

____

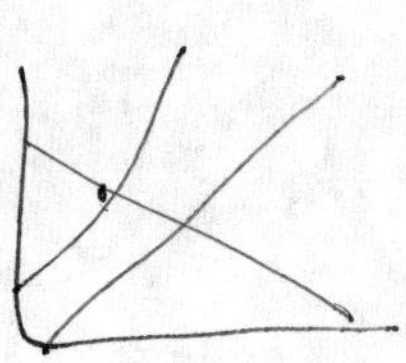

SELF-TEST

True/False Questions

F 1. A positive externality is an external benefit that accrues to the buyers in a market while a negative externality is an external cost that accrues to the sellers in a market.

T 2. If a market generates a negative externality, the social cost curve is above the supply curve (private cost curve).

T 3. If a market generates a positive externality, the social value curve is above the demand curve (private value curve).

F 4. A market that generates a negative externality that has not been internalized generates an equilibrium quantity that is less than the optimal quantity.

_____5. If a market generates a negative externality, a Pigovian tax will move the market toward a more efficient outcome.

_____6. According to the Coase theorem, an externality always requires government intervention in order to internalize the externality.

_____7. To reduce pollution by some targeted amount, it is most efficient if each firm that pollutes reduces its pollution by an equal amount.

_____8. When Smokey the Bear says, "Only you can prevent forest fires," society is attempting to use moral codes and social sanctions to internalize the externality associated with using fire while camping.

_____9. A tax always makes a market less efficient.

_____10. If Bob values smoking in a restaurant at $10 and Sue values clean air while she eats at $15, according to the Coase theorem, Bob will not smoke in the restaurant only if Sue owns the right to clean air.

_____11. If transactions costs exceed the potential gains from an agreement between affected parties to an externality, there will be no private solution to the externality.

______12. A Pigovian tax sets the price of pollution while tradable pollution permits sets the quantity of pollution.

______13. An advantage of using tradable pollution permits to reduce pollution is that the regulator need not know anything about the demand for pollution rights.

______14. The majority of economists do not like the idea of putting a price on polluting the environment.

______15. For any given demand curve for pollution, a regulator can achieve the same level of pollution with either a Pigovian tax or by allocating tradable pollution permits.

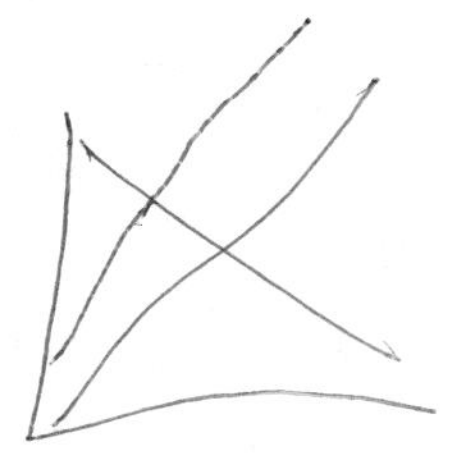

Multiple-Choice Questions

1. An externality is
   a. the benefit that accrues to the buyer in a market.
   b. the cost that accrues to the seller in a market.
   c. the uncompensated impact of one person's actions on the well-being of a bystander.
   d. the compensation paid to a firm's external consultants.
   e. none of the above.

2. A negative externality generates
   a. a social cost curve that is above the supply curve (private cost curve) for a good.
   b. a social cost curve that is below the supply curve (private cost curve) for a good.
   c. a social value curve that is above the demand curve (private value curve) for a good.
   d. none of the above.

3. A positive externality generates
   a. a social cost curve that is above the supply curve (private cost curve) for a good.
   b. a social value curve that is above the demand curve (private value curve) for a good.
   c. a social value curve that is below the demand curve (private value curve) for a good.
   d. none of the above.

4. A negative externality (that has not been internalized) causes the
   a. optimal quantity to exceed the equilibrium quantity.
   b. equilibrium quantity to exceed the optimal quantity.
   c. equilibrium quantity to equal the optimal quantity.
   d. equilibrium quantity to be either above or below the optimal quantity.

5. A positive externality (that has not been internalized) causes the
   a. optimal quantity to exceed the equilibrium quantity.
   b. equilibrium quantity to exceed the optimal quantity.
   c. equilibrium quantity to equal the optimal quantity.
   d. equilibrium quantity to be either above or below the optimal quantity.

6. To internalize a negative externality, an appropriate public policy response would be to
   a. ban the production of all goods creating negative externalities.
   b. have the government take over the production of the good causing the externality.
   c. subsidize the good.
   d. tax the good.

7. The government engages in a *technology policy*
   a. to internalize the negative externality associated with industrial pollution.
   b. to internalize the positive externality associated with technology-enhancing industries.
   c. to help stimulate private solutions to the technology externality.
   d. by allocating tradable technology permits to high technology industry.

8. When an individual buys a car in a congested urban area, it generates
   a. an efficient market outcome.
   b. a technology spillover.
   c. a positive externality.
   d. a negative externality.

9. The most efficient pollution control system would ensure that
   a. each polluter reduce its pollution an equal amount.
   b. the polluters with the lowest cost of reducing pollution reduce their pollution the greatest amount.
   c. no pollution of the environment is tolerated.
   d. the regulators decide how much each polluter should reduce its pollution.

10. According to the Coase theorem, private parties can solve the problem of externalities if
    a. each affected party has equal power in the negotiations.
    b. the party affected by the externality has the initial property right to be left alone.
    c. there are no transaction costs.
    d. the government requires them to negotiate with each other.
    e. there are a large number of affected parties.

11. To internalize a positive externality, an appropriate public policy response would be to
    a. ban the good creating the externality.
    b. have the government produce the good until the value of an additional unit is zero.
    c. subsidize the good.
    d. tax the good.

12. Which of the following is *not* considered a transaction cost incurred by parties in the process of contracting to eliminate a pollution externality?
    a. costs incurred to reduce the pollution
    b. costs incurred due to lawyers fees
    c. costs incurred to enforce the agreement
    d. costs incurred due to a large number of parties affected by the externality
    e. All of the above are considered transaction costs.

13. Bob and Tom live in a university dorm. Bob values playing loud music at a value of $100. Tom values peace and quiet at a value of $150. Which of the following statements is true?
    a. It is efficient for Bob to continue to play loud music.
    b. It is efficient for Bob to stop playing loud music only if Tom has the property right to peace and quiet.
    c. It is efficient for Bob to stop playing loud music only if Bob has the property right to play loud music.
    d. It is efficient for Bob to stop playing loud music regardless of who has the property right to the level of sound.

14. Bob and Tom live in a university dorm. Bob values playing loud music at a value of $100. Tom values peace and quiet at a value of $150. Which of the following statements is true about an efficient solution to this externality problem if Bob has the right to play loud music and if there are no transaction costs?
    a. Bob will pay Tom $100 and Bob will stop playing loud music.
    b. Tom will pay Bob between $100 and $150 and Bob will stop playing loud music.
    c. Bob will pay Tom $150 and Bob will continue to play loud music.
    d. Tom will pay Bob between $100 and $150 and Bob will continue to play loud music.

15. Which of the following is true regarding tradable pollution permits and Pigovian taxes?
    a. Pigovian taxes are more likely to reduce pollution to a targeted amount than tradable pollution permits.
    b. Tradable pollution permits efficiently reduce pollution only if they are initially distributed to the firms that can reduce pollution at the lowest cost.
    c. To set the quantity of pollution with tradable pollution permits, the regulator must know everything about the demand for pollution rights.
    d. Pigovian taxes and tradable pollution permits create an efficient market for pollution.
    e. All of the above are true.

16. The gas-guzzler tax that is placed on new vehicles that get very poor mileage is an example of
    a. a tradable pollution permit.
    b. an application of the Coase theorem.
    c. an attempt to internalize a positive externality.
    d. an attempt to internalize a negative externality.

17. A Pigovian tax on pollution
    a. sets the price of pollution.
    b. sets the quantity of pollution.
    c. determines the demand for pollution rights.
    d. reduces the incentive for technological innovations to further reduce pollution.

18. Tradable pollution permits
   a. set the price of pollution.
   b. set the quantity of pollution.
   c. determine the demand for pollution rights.
   d. reduce the incentive for technological innovations to further reduce pollution.

19. When wealthy alumni provide charitable contributions to their alma mater to reduce the tuition payments of current students, it is an example of
   a. an attempt to internalize a positive externality.
   b. an attempt to internalize a negative externality.
   c. a Pigovian tax.
   d. a command-and-control policy.

20. Suppose an industry emits a negative externality such as pollution and the possible methods to internalize the externality are command-and-control policies, Pigovian taxes, and tradable pollution permits. If economists were to rank these methods for internalizing a negative externality based on efficiency, ease of implementation, and the incentive for the industry to further reduce pollution in the future, they would likely rank them in the following order (from most favored to least favored):
   a. Pigovian taxes, command-and-control policies, tradable pollution permits.
   b. command-and-control policies, tradable pollution permits, Pigovian taxes.
   c. tradable pollution permits, Pigovian taxes, command-and-control policies.
   d. tradable pollution permits, command-and-control policies, Pigovian taxes.
   e. They would all rank equally high because the same result can be obtained from any one of the policies.

ADVANCED CRITICAL THINKING

You are home for semester break. Your father opens the mail. One of the letters is your parent's property tax bill. On the property tax bill, there is a deduction if the property owner has done anything to beautify his/her property. The property owner can deduct 50 percent of any expenditure on things such as landscaping from his/her property taxes. For example, if your parents spent $2000 on landscaping, they can reduce their tax bill by 0.50 × $2000 = $1000 so that the true cost of the landscaping was only $1000. Your father announces, "This an outrage. If someone wants to improve their house, it is no one's business but their own. I remember some of my college economics and I know that taxes and subsidies are *always* inefficient."

1. What is the city government trying to subsidize with this tax break?

____

____

2. What is the externality that this subsidy is trying to internalize?

____

____

____

3. While taxes and subsidies usually create inefficiencies, are taxes and subsidies always inefficient? Why?

____

____

____

SOLUTIONS

Terms and Definitions

5 Externality

8 Positive externality

3 Negative externality

7 Social cost

6 Internalizing an externality

1 Coase theorem

2 Transactions costs

4 Pigovian tax

Practice Problems

1. a. See Exhibit 3.
   b. Price = $3, quantity = 500 units.
   c. See Exhibit 4.
   d. 400 units. The market overproduces because the market quantity is 500 while the optimal quantity is 400 units.
   e. The government should impose a Pigovian tax of $2 per unit.

EXHIBIT 3

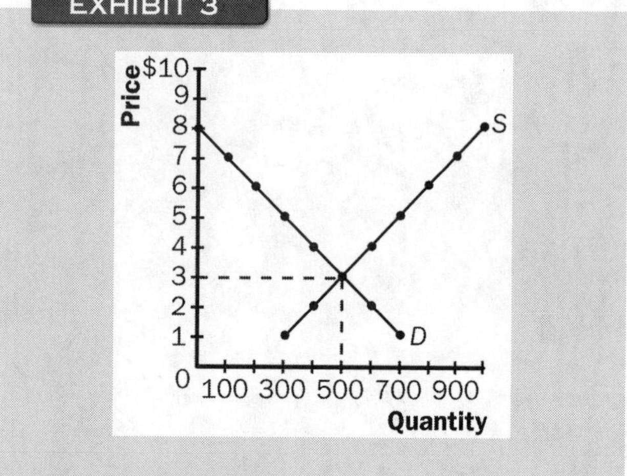

2. a. No, because the cost of correcting the externality exceeds the value placed on it by the affected parties.
   b. Yes, because the value placed on peace and quiet exceeds the cost of muffling the planes.
   c. The airlines could spend $2 billion and make their planes quieter or buy the right to make noise for $3 billion, so they will choose to make the planes quieter for $2 billion.
   d. The affected citizens must pay at least $2 billion and are willing to pay up to $3 billion to the airlines to have the planes made quieter.
   e. Similarities: the planes will be made quieter regardless of the original property rights because it is efficient. Differences: if the citizens have the right to quiet, citizens gain and airlines lose. If the airlines have the right to make noise, airlines gain and citizens lose.
   f. No, because the transaction costs exceed the potential gains from trade. (The potential gains are the $3 billion value of quiet minus the $2 billion cost to quiet the planes, or $1 billion.)

EXHIBIT 4

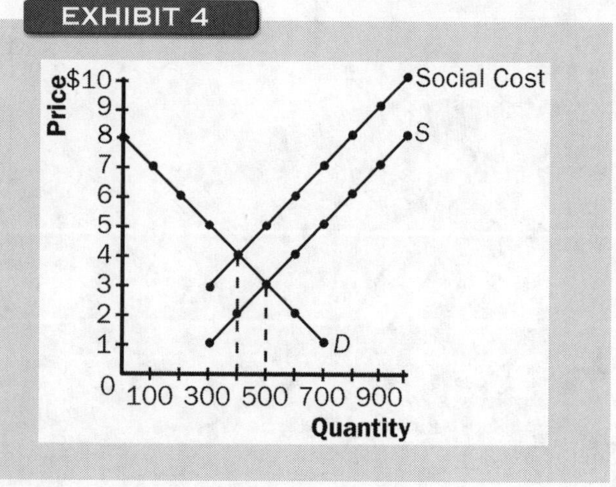

3. a. See Exhibit 5.
   b. $4 million per barrel.
   c. 3 permits should be sold. They will trade at a price of $4 million per permit.
   d. 3 barrels. $4 million per barrel. Yes, with the tradable pollution permits the regulator does not need to know anything about the demand for pollution in this market in order to target pollution at 3 barrels and the initial allocation of pollution permits will not have an impact on the efficient solution.

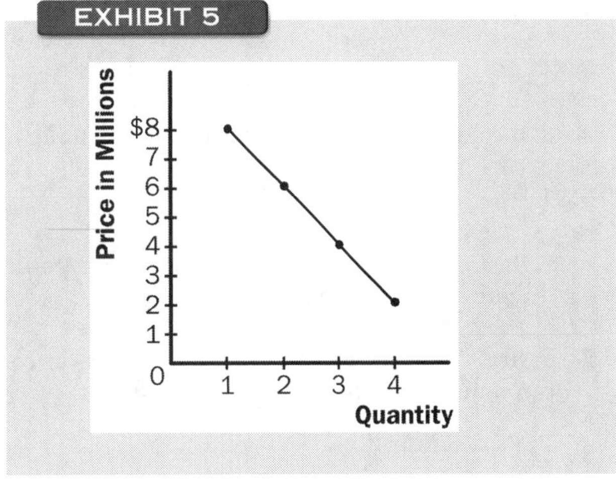

Short-Answer Questions

1. Negative externality because the social cost of producing apples exceeds the private cost of producing apples.

2. Overproduce. To overproduce is to produce units where the true cost exceeds the true value. To underproduce is to fail to produce units where the true value exceeds the true cost.

3. Tax apples because to internalize this externality, it requires that the supply curve for apples be shifted upward until it equals the true social cost curve.

4. No pesticides will be used and the air will be clean, regardless of whether the individual owns the right to use pesticides or the neighborhood residents own the right to clean air. Either the individual will fail to buy the right to pollute or the neighborhood residents will pay the individual not to pollute.

5. There are $15,000 – $10,000 = $5,000 of potential benefits. If transaction costs exceed this amount, there will be no private solution.

6. Lawyers fees, costs of enforcement, a breakdown in bargaining when there is a range of prices that would create efficiency, and a large number of interested parties.

7. Moral codes and social sanctions, charities, mergers between affected firms, contracts between affected firms.

8. Command-and-control policies are regulations that prohibit certain behaviors. Market-based policies align private incentives with social efficiency. Economists prefer market-based policies because they are more efficient and they provide incentives for even further reduction in, say, pollution through advances in technology.

9. It increases efficiency by shifting the supply or demand curve toward the true social cost or value curve, thereby making the market solution equal to the optimal or efficient solution.

10. The regulator doesn't need to know anything about the demand to pollute in order to arrive at the targeted amount of pollution.

True/False Questions

1. F; a positive externality is a benefit that accrues to a *bystander* and a negative externality is a cost that accrues to a *bystander*.

2. T
3. T
4. F; the equilibrium quantity is greater than the optimal quantity.
5. T
6. F; the Coase theorem suggests that private parties can solve the problem of an externality on their own if there are no transaction costs.
7. F; firms that can reduce pollution at a lower cost should reduce their pollution more than firms that can reduce pollution at a greater cost.
8. T
9. F; Pigovian taxes can make a market more efficient.
10. F; the original distribution of property rights to the air will not affect the efficient solution.
11. T
12. T
13. T
14. F; economists generally think that a market for pollution will reduce pollution most efficiently.
15. T

Multiple-Choice Questions

1. c	5. a	9. b	13. d	17. a
2. a	6. d	10. c	14. b	18. b
3. b	7. b	11. c	15. d	19. a
4. b	8. d	12. a	16. d	20. c

Advanced Critical Thinking

1. Expenditures on home improvement.
2. When a house is well maintained, it raises the value (or fails to reduce the value) of the nearby property. Individual buyers and sellers in the market for home repair do not take this into account when choosing the quantity of home repair and, thus, the optimal quantity exceeds the equilibrium quantity.
3. No. Appropriate Pigovian taxes and subsidies move a market closer to efficiency because the market equilibrium is inefficient to begin with.

11

PUBLIC GOODS AND COMMON RESOURCES

CHAPTER OVERVIEW

Context and Purpose

Chapter 11 is the second chapter in a three-chapter sequence on the economics of the public sector. Chapter 10 addressed externalities. Chapter 11 addresses public goods and common resources—goods for which it is difficult to charge prices to users. Chapter 12 will address the tax system.

The purpose of Chapter 11 is to address a group of goods that are free to the consumer. When goods are free, market forces that normally allocate resources are absent. Therefore, free goods, such as playgrounds and public parks, may not be produced and consumed in the proper amounts. Government can potentially remedy this market failure and improve economic well-being.

CHAPTER REVIEW

Introduction

Some goods are free to the consumer—beaches, lakes, playgrounds. When goods are free, market forces that normally allocate resources are absent. Therefore, free goods, such as playgrounds and public parks, may not be produced and con-

GOALS

In this chapter you will

Learn the defining characteristics of public goods and common resources

Examine why private markets fail to provide public goods

Consider some of the important public goods in our economy

See why the cost-benefit analysis of public goods is both necessary and difficult

Examine why people tend to use common resources too much

Consider some of the important common resources in our economy

OUTCOMES

After accomplishing these goals, you should be able to

Classify goods into the categories of public goods, private goods, common resources, or goods produced by a natural monopoly

Explain why production of public goods is unprofitable to private industry

Explain the public good nature of national defense

Explain why surveys to determine the benefits of public goods are a less precise valuation of benefits than prices of private goods

Tell the story of the "tragedy of the commons"

Explain why fish and wildlife are common resources

sumed in the proper amounts. Government can potentially remedy this market failure and improve economic well-being.

The Different Kinds of Goods

There are two characteristics of goods that are useful when defining types of goods:

- **Excludability:** the property of a good whereby a person can be prevented from using it. A good is excludable if a seller can exclude non-payers from using it (food in the grocery store) and not excludable if a seller cannot exclude non-payers from using it (broadcast television or radio signal).

- **Rivalness:** the property of a good whereby one person's use of a good diminishes other people's use. A good is rival if only one person can consume the good (food) and not rival if the good can be consumed by more than one at the same time (streetlight).

With these characteristics, goods can be divided into four categories:

1. **Private goods:** Goods that are both excludable and rival. Most goods like bread and blue jeans are private goods and are allocated efficiently by supply and demand in markets.

2. **Public goods:** Goods that are neither excludable nor rival, such as national defense and streetlights.

3. **Common resources:** Goods that are rival but not excludable, such as fish in the ocean.

4. Goods produced by a *natural monopoly:* Goods that are excludable but not rival, such as fire protection and cable TV. Natural monopolies will be addressed in Chapter 15.

This chapter examines the two types of goods that are not excludable and, thus, are free: public goods and common resources.

Public Goods

Public goods are difficult for a private market to provide because of the *free-rider problem*. A **free rider** is a person who receives the benefit of a good but avoids paying for it. Since public goods are not excludable, firms cannot prevent non-payers from consuming the good and, thus, there is no incentive for a firm to produce a public good.

For example, a streetlight may be valued by each of ten homeowners in a neighborhood at $1000. If the cost is $5000, no individual will buy a streetlight because no one can sell the right to use the light to their neighbors for $1000 each. This is because after the streetlight is in place, their neighbors can consume the light whether they pay or not. Even though the neighborhood values the streetlight at a total value of $10,000 and the cost of a streetlight is only $5000, the private market will not be able to provide it. Public goods are related to positive externalities in that each neighbor ignores the external benefit provided to others when deciding whether to buy a streetlight. Often government steps in and provides goods, such as streetlights, where benefits exceed the costs and pays for them with tax revenue. In this case, the government could provide the streetlight and tax each resident $500 and everyone would be better off.

Some important public goods are national defense, basic research, and possibly, programs to fight poverty.

Some goods can switch between being public goods and private goods depending on the circumstances. A lighthouse is a public good if the owner cannot charge each ship as it passes the light. A lighthouse becomes a private good if the owner can charge the port to which the ships are traveling.

When a private market cannot produce a public good, governments must decide whether to produce the good. Their decision tool is often **cost-benefit analysis:** a study that compares the costs and benefits to society of providing a public good. There are two problems with cost-benefit analysis:

- quantifying benefits is difficult using the results of a questionnaire
- respondents have little incentive to tell the truth

When governments decide whether to spend money on additional safety measures such as stoplights and stop signs, they must consider the value of a human life because the benefit of such an expenditure is the probability of saving a life times the value of a life. Studies suggest that the value of a human life is about $10 million.

Common Resources

Common resources are not excludable but are rival (fish in the ocean). Therefore, common resources are free but when one person uses it, it diminishes other people's enjoyment of it. This is similar to a negative externality because consumers of a good do not take into account the negative impact on others from their consumption. The result is that common resources are used excessively.

The **Tragedy of the Commons** is a parable that illustrates why common resources get used more than is desirable from the standpoint of society as a whole. The town common (open land to be grazed) will be overgrazed to the point where it becomes barren because, since it is free, private incentives suggest that each individual should graze as many sheep as possible, yet this is overgrazing from a social perspective. Possible solutions are to regulate the number of sheep grazed, tax sheep, auction off sheep-grazing permits, or divide the land and sell it to individual sheep herders making grazing land a private good.

Some important common resources are clean air and water, congested nontoll roads, fish, whales, and other wildlife. Private decision makers use a common resource too much so governments regulate behavior or impose fees to reduce the problem of overuse.

Conclusion: The Importance of Property Rights

In the case of public goods and common resources, markets fail to allocate resources efficiently because property rights are not clearly established. With private markets, no one owns the clean air so no one can charge people when they pollute. The result is that people pollute too much or use too much clean air (common resource example). Further, no one can charge those who are protected by national defense for the benefit they receive so people produce too little national defense (public good example).

The government can potentially solve these problems by selling pollution permits, regulating private behavior, or providing the public good.

HELPFUL HINTS

1. In general, public goods are underproduced and common resources are overconsumed. This is because they are free. Since public goods are free, it is not profitable to produce them (streetlights and national defense). Since common resources are free, people overconsume them (clean air and fish in the ocean.)

2. Public goods are defined by their characteristics, not by who provides them. A streetlight is a public good because it is not excludable and not rival. This is true even if, as an individual, I choose to buy one and put it in my front yard. Once in my front yard, I cannot charge you for standing near it, and when you do, it does not reduce my benefits from using it. Therefore, a streetlight is a public good whether I buy it or the city government buys it. Further, if the city government sets up a food stand and sells hot dogs, the hot dogs are private goods even though they are provided by the government because the hot dogs are both excludable and rival.

3. When governments use cost-benefit analysis as a tool to help them decide whether to produce a public good, we noted that it is difficult to collect data on the true benefits that people would receive from a public good. This is because they have an incentive to exaggerate their benefit if they would use the public good and underreport their benefit if they don't plan to use the public good very much. This is sometimes called the *liars problem*.

TERMS AND DEFINITIONS

Choose a definition for each key term.

Key terms:

_____ Excludability
_____ Rivalry
_____ Private goods
_____ Public goods
_____ Common resources
_____ Natural monopoly
_____ Free rider
_____ Cost-benefit analysis
_____ Tragedy of the Commons

Definitions:

1. Goods that are both excludable and rival
2. The property of a good whereby one person's use diminishes other people's use
3. A person who receives the benefit of a good but avoids paying for it
4. A study that compares the costs and benefits to society of providing a public good
5. Goods that are rival but not excludable
6. The property of a good whereby a person can be prevented from using it
7. A parable that illustrates why common resources get used more than is desirable from the standpoint of society as a whole
8. Goods that are neither excludable nor rival
9. Firm that produces goods that are excludable but not rival

PROBLEMS AND SHORT-ANSWER QUESTIONS

Practice Problems

1. Consider the rivalry and excludability of each of the following goods. Use this information to determine whether the goods are public goods, private goods, common resources, or produced by a natural monopoly. Explain.
   a. Fish in a private pond

   b. Fish in the ocean

   c. Broadcast television signals

   d. Cable television signals

   e. Basic research on lifestyle and cholesterol levels

   f. Specific research on a cholesterol lowering drug for which a patent can be obtained

   g. An uncongested highway (no tolls)

h. A congested highway (no tolls)

i. An uncongested toll road

j. A hot dog served at a private party

k. A hot dog sold at a stand owned by the city government

2. Suppose the city of Roadville is debating whether to build a new highway from its airport to the downtown area. The city surveys its citizens and finds that, on average, each of the one million residents values the new highway at a value of $50 and the highway costs $40 million to construct.
   a. Assuming the survey was accurate, is building a new highway efficient? Why?

   b. Under what conditions would private industry build the road?

   c. Is it likely that private industry will build the road? Why?

   d. Should the city build the road? On average, how much should it increase each resident's tax bill to pay for the road?

e. Is it certain that building the highway is efficient? That is, what are the problems associated with using cost-benefit analysis as a tool for deciding whether to provide a public good?

Short-Answer Questions

1. What does it mean to say that a good is excludable?

2. Why is it difficult for private industry to provide public goods?

3. How is a streetlight (a public good) related to a positive externality?

4. Suppose the value of a human life is $10 million. Suppose the use of airbags in cars reduces the probability of dying in a car accident over one's lifetime from 0.2 percent to 0.1 percent. Further, suppose that a lifetime supply of airbags will cost the average consumer $12,000. If these numbers were accurate, would it be efficient for the government to require airbags in cars? Why?

5. What type of problem are hunting and fishing licenses intended to relieve? Explain.

6. How are fish in the ocean (a common resource) related to a negative externality?

7. How can the establishment of individual property rights eliminate the problems associated with a common resource?

8. Food is more important than roads to the public, yet the government provides roads for the public and rarely provides food. Why?

9. Why did buffalo almost become extinct while cows (a similar animal) are unlikely to ever become extinct?

10. Were the buffalo hunters that almost made the buffalo extinct behaving irrationally? Explain.

SELF-TEST

True/False Questions

____ 1. A public good is both rival and excludable.

____ 2. A common resource is neither rival nor excludable.

____ 3. An apple sold in a grocery store is a private good.

____ 4. Goods produced by a natural monopoly are free to the consumer of the good.

____ 5. Private markets have difficulty providing public goods due to the free-rider problem.

____ 6. If the city government sells apples at a roadside stand, the apples are public goods because they are provided by the government.

____ 7. Public goods are related to positive externalities because the potential buyers of public goods ignore the external benefits those goods provide to other consumers when they make their decision about whether to purchase public goods.

____ 8. Common resources are overused because common resources are free to the consumer.

____ 9. The socially optimal price for a fishing license is zero.

____ 10. The government should continue to spend to improve the safety of our highways until there are no deaths from auto accidents.

____ 11. Common resources are related to negative externalities because consumers of common resources ignore the negative impact of their consumption on other consumers of the common resource.

____ 12. If someone owned the property rights to clean air, that person could charge for the use of the clean air in a market for clean air and, thus, air pollution could be reduced to the optimal level.

____ 13. A fireworks display at a private amusement park is a good provided by natural monopoly.

____ 14. When the government uses cost-benefit analysis to decide whether to provide a public good, the potential benefit of the public good can easily be established by surveying the potential consumers of the public good.

____ 15. National defense is a classic example of a common resource.

Multiple-Choice Questions

1. If one person's consumption of a good diminishes other people's use of the good, the good is said to be
   a. a common resource.
   b. a good produced by a natural monopoly.
   c. rival.
   d. excludable.

2. A public good is
   a. both rival and excludable.
   b. neither rival nor excludable.
   c. rival but not excludable.
   d. not rival but excludable.

3. A private good is
   a. both rival and excludable.
   b. neither rival nor excludable.
   c. rival but not excludable.
   d. not rival but excludable.

4. A good produced by a natural monopoly is
   a. both rival and excludable.
   b. neither rival nor excludable.
   c. rival but not excludable.
   d. not rival but excludable.

5. A common resource is
   a. both rival and excludable.
   b. neither rival nor excludable.
   c. rival but not excludable.
   d. not rival but excludable.

6. Public goods are difficult for a private market to provide due to
   a. the public goods problem.
   b. the rivalness problem.
   c. the Tragedy of the Commons.
   d. the free-rider problem.

7. Suppose each of 20 neighbors on a street values street repairs at $3,000. The cost of the street repair is $40,000. Which of the following statements is true?
   a. It is not efficient to have the street repaired.
   b. It is efficient for each neighbor to pay $3,000 to repair the section of street in front of his/her home.
   c. It is efficient for the government to tax the residents $2,000 each and repair the road.
   d. None of the above are true.

8. A free rider is a person who
   a. receives the benefit of a good but avoids paying for it.
   b. produces a good but fails to receive payment for the good.
   c. pays for a good but fails to receive any benefit from the good.
   d. fails to produce goods but is allowed to consume goods.

9. Which of the following is an example of a public good?
   a. whales in the ocean
   b. apples on a tree in a public park
   c. hot dogs at a picnic
   d. national defense

10. A positive externality affects market efficiency in a manner similar to a
    a. private good.
    b. public good.
    c. common resource.
    d. rival good.

11. Suppose that requiring motorcycle riders to wear helmets reduces the probability of a motorcycle fatality from 0.3 percent to 0.2 percent over the lifetime of a motorcycle rider and that the cost of a lifetime supply of helmets is $500. It is efficient for the government to require riders to wear helmets if human life is valued at
   a. $100 or more.
   b. $150 or more.
   c. $500 or more.
   d. $50,000 or more.
   e. $500,000 or more.

12. A negative externality affects market efficiency in a manner similar to
   a. a private good.
   b. a public good.
   c. a common resource.
   d. an excludable good.

13. When governments employ cost-benefit analysis to help them decide whether to provide a public good, measuring benefits is difficult because
   a. one can never place a value on human life or the environment.
   b. respondents to questionnaires have little incentive to tell the truth.
   c. there are no benefits to the public since a public good is not excludable.
   d. the benefits are infinite because a public good is not rival and an infinite amount of people can consume it at the same time.

14. Which of the following is an example of a common resource?
   a. a national park
   b. a fireworks display
   c. national defense
   d. iron ore

15. The Tragedy of the Commons is a parable that illustrates why
   a. public goods are underproduced.
   b. private goods are underconsumed.
   c. common resources are overconsumed.
   d. natural monopolies overproduce goods.

16. Which of the following are potential solutions to the problem of air pollution?
   a. Auction off pollution permits.
   b. Grant rights of the clean air to citizens so that firms must purchase the right to pollute.
   c. Regulate the amount of pollutants that firms can put in the air.
   d. all of the above

17. When markets fail to allocate resources efficiently, the ultimate source of the problem is usually
   a. that prices are not high enough so people overconsume.
   b. that prices are not low enough so firms overproduce.
   c. that property rights have not been well established.
   d. government regulation.

18. If a person can be prevented from using a good, the good is said to be
    a. a common resource.
    b. a public good.
    c. rival.
    d. excludable.

19. A congested toll road is
    a. a private good.
    b. a public good.
    c. a common resource.
    d. a good produced by a natural monopoly.

20. A person who regularly watches public television but fails to contribute to public television's fund-raising drives is known as
    a. a common resource.
    b. a costly rider.
    c. a free rider.
    d. an unwelcome rider.
    e. excess baggage.

ADVANCED CRITICAL THINKING

Broadcast television and broadcast radio send out signals that can be received by an infinite number of receivers without reducing the quality of the reception of other consumers of the signal and it is not possible to charge any of the consumers of the signal.

1. What type of good (private, public, common resource, produced by a natural monopoly) is a broadcast television or broadcast radio signal? Explain.

____

____

2. Is this type of good normally provided by private industry? Why?

____

____

3. Private companies have been providing broadcast radio television and radio since the invention of the medium. How do they make it profitable if they cannot charge the recipient of the signal?

____

____

____

____

4. What are the "recent" alternatives to traditional commercial television and commercial radio?

____

____

5. What type of good (private, public, common resource, produced by a natural monopoly) is this newer type of television and music provision?

____

____

SOLUTIONS

Terms and Definitions

6 Excludability

2 Rivalry

1 Private goods

8 Public goods

5 Common resources

9 Natural monopoly

3 Free rider

4 Cost–benefit analysis

7 Tragedy of the Commons

Practice Problems

1. a. Rival and excludable, private good. Only one can eat a fish. Since it is private, non-payers can be excluded from fishing.
   b. Rival but not excludable, common resource. Only one can eat a fish but the ocean is not privately owned so non-payers cannot be excluded.
   c. Not rival and not excludable, public good. Additional viewers can turn on their TV without reducing the benefits to other consumers and non-payers cannot be excluded.
   d. Not rival but excludable, produced by a natural monopoly. More houses can be wired without reducing the benefit to other consumers and the cable company can exclude non-payers.
   e. Not rival and not excludable, public good. Once discovered, additional people can benefit from the knowledge without reducing the benefit to other consumers of the knowledge and once in the public domain, non-payers cannot be excluded.
   f. Not rival but excludable, produced by a natural monopoly. Additional users of the knowledge could use it without reducing the benefit to other consumers therefore it is not rival. If a patent can be obtained, no one else can produce the anti-cholesterol pill so it is excludable.
   g. Not rival and not excludable, public good. Additional cars can travel the road without reducing the benefit to other consumers and the additional cars cannot be forced to pay for the road.
   h. Rival but not excludable, common resource. Additional cars reduce the benefits of current users but they cannot be forced to pay for the use of the highway.
   i. Not rival but excludable, produced by a natural monopoly. Additional cars do not reduce the benefits to current users but they can be excluded if they don't pay the toll.
   j. Rival but not excludable, common resource. If one eats the hot dog, another cannot. However, once provided, party-goers cannot be charged for eating the hot dogs.
   k. Rival and excludable, private good. If one eats the hot dog, another cannot. Even though it is supplied by the government, it is being sold so non-payers can be excluded.

2. a. Yes, because the total benefit is $50 × 1,000,000 = $50 million while the cost is $40 million.
   b. If the road could be built as a toll road, then private industry could make the road excludable and the project could be profitable.

c. No. Toll roads are usually in rural areas where they can be made as limited-access roads and therefore excludable. It would be very difficult to make a downtown urban road limited-access or excludable.
d. Yes. $40.
e. No. Quantifying benefits is difficult using the results from a questionnaire and respondents have little incentive to tell the truth. Therefore, those who would use the road exaggerate their benefit and those that would rarely use it understate their benefit.

Short-Answer Questions

1. It means that those who do not pay for the good can be excluded from consuming it.

2. Because public goods are not excludable, the free-rider problem makes it unprofitable for private industry to produce public goods.

3. When people consider buying a street light, they fail to consider the external benefit it would provide to others and only consider their personal benefit. Thus, there is an underproduction and consumption of both public goods and goods that generate positive externalities.

4. No, because the expected benefit from airbags is (0.002 – 0.001) × $10,000,000 = $10,000 while the cost is $12,000.

5. The overconsumption of common resources. Since common resources are free, people use them excessively. Selling a limited number of hunting or fishing licenses restricts the number of users.

6. A common resource is free so it is overconsumed. Each consumer of fish fails to take into account the negative impact on others of their consumption causing overuse of the resource from a social perspective.

7. People overuse common resources because their benefit is positive and their cost is zero. If ownership over the resource exists, the cost of using the resource is realized and a socially optimal price is generated.

8. Food is both rival and excludable so it can be efficiently provided by the private market. Roads are often neither rival nor excludable so they will not be provided by private markets and may be most efficiently provided by government.

9. Buffalo were a common resource and overconsumed. Cows are private goods and are produced and sold at the socially efficient price and quantity.

10. No. Because the buffalo were a common property resource, the buffalo were free. Each hunter pursued his own best interest but failed to take into account the impact of his actions on other people.

True/False Questions

1. F; it is neither rival nor excludable.

2. F; it is rival but not excludable.

3. T

4. F; they are excludable so a price must be paid to receive them but they are not rival so they can be enjoyed by many at the same time.

5. T

6. F; goods are categorized as public or private based on their characteristics, not who provided them, so an apple sold to a consumer is private regardless who provided the apple.

7. T

8. T

9. F; a positive price is optimal so that the price reduces the quantity demanded of fish to the socially optimal level.

10. F; at some point, the cost of increasing safety (reducing highway deaths) exceeds the value of a life.

11. T

12. T

13. T

14. F; quantifying benefits is difficult and respondents have little incentive to tell the truth.

15. F; national defense is an example of a public good.

Multiple-Choice Questions

1. c
2. b
3. a
4. d
5. c
6. d
7. c
8. a
9. d
10. b
11. e
12. c
13. b
14. a
15. c
16. d
17. c
18. d
19. a
20. c

Advanced Critical Thinking

1. Public good. A broadcast signal is not rival and not excludable.

2. No, because it is not profitable to produce a good for which non-payers cannot be excluded from consuming it.

3. Broadcasters charge advertisers for the commercials they show during the broadcasters' programming. That is why it is called commercial television or commercial radio.

4. Cable television, pay-per-view television, and cable music included with cable television.

5. Produced by a natural monopoly because it is not rival but it is excludable.

12

THE DESIGN OF THE TAX SYSTEM

GOALS

In this chapter you will

Get an overview of how the U.S. government raises and spends money

Examine the efficiency costs of taxes

Learn alternative ways to judge the equity of a tax system

See why studying tax incidence is crucial for evaluating tax equity

Consider the tradeoff between efficiency and equity in the design of a tax system

OUTCOMES

After accomplishing these goals, you should be able to

List the four largest sources of tax revenue to the U.S. government from the largest to the smallest source

Describe the administrative burdens of a tax

Compare the benefits principle to the ability-to-pay principle of allocating a tax burden

Explain why the burden of a tax often lands on someone other than the person from whom the tax is collected

Discuss the efficiency and equity of a flat tax

CHAPTER OVERVIEW

Context and Purpose

Chapter 12 is the third chapter in a three-chapter sequence on the economics of the public sector. Chapter 10 addressed externalities. Chapter 11 addressed public goods and common resources. Chapter 12 addresses the tax system. Taxes are inevitable because when the government remedies an externality, provides a public good, or regulates the use of a common resource, it needs tax revenue to perform these functions.

The purpose of Chapter 12 is to build on the lessons learned about taxes in previous chapters. We have seen that a tax reduces the quantity sold in a market, that the distribution of the burden of a tax depends on the relative elasticities of supply and demand, and that taxes cause deadweight losses. We expand our study of taxes in Chapter 12 by addressing how the U.S. government raises and spends money. We then address the difficulty of making a tax system both efficient and equitable.

CHAPTER REVIEW

Introduction

Taxes are inevitable because when the government remedies an externality, provides a public good, or regulates the use of a common resource it needs tax revenue to perform these functions. In previous chapters that dealt with taxation, we learned that a tax reduces the quantity sold in a market, that the distribution of the burden of a tax depends on the relative elasticities of supply and demand, and that taxes cause deadweight losses. We now address how the U.S. government raises and spends money and how difficult it is to make a tax system both efficient and equitable.

A Financial Overview of the U.S. Government

The government is composed of federal, state, and local governments. Over time, the government has taken a larger share of total income in taxes—from 7 percent in 1902 to 31 percent in 2000. The tax burden in the U.S. as measured by the central government's tax revenue as a percent of GDP is 19.3 percent. The U.S. tax burden is about average when compared to other countries. European countries have a higher tax burden and less-developed countries have a lower tax burden than the United States. As countries become wealthier, the tax burden tends to increase.

The U.S. federal government collects about two-thirds of the taxes in our economy. In 2001, the average American paid $6,986 in taxes to the federal government. The largest source of tax revenue for the federal government is individual income taxes (50 percent), followed by social insurance taxes or payroll taxes (35 percent), corporate income taxes (8 percent), and all other taxes (8 percent). A family's tax liability is a percentage of income after deductions (mortgage interest payments and charitable giving) and is based on the number of dependents. Corporate profits are taxed twice—once as corporate income and once as individual income when profits are paid out as dividends. The category of "other taxes" includes excise taxes (taxes on specific goods), estate taxes, and customs duties.

In 2001, the federal government's greatest spending was on Social Security (23 percent) followed by national defense (17 percent), income security or welfare (14 percent), Medicare (12 percent), net interest (11 percent), health (mostly Medicaid, 9 percent), and all others that included federal court system, space program, farm-support programs, and Congressional salaries (14 percent). Social Security and income security are *transfer payments*—payments for which the government does not receive a good or service in return.

A **budget surplus** is an excess of government receipts over government spending. A **budget deficit** is an excess of government spending over government receipts.

State and local governments collect about 40 percent of all taxes paid. Their greatest source of revenue is sales taxes (20 percent), followed by property taxes (17 percent), individual income taxes (13 percent), corporate income taxes (2 percent), from the federal government (19 percent), and all others that include license fees, tolls, and fares for public transportation (29 percent).

State and local governments spend the greatest share of their funds on education (34 percent), public welfare (16 percent), highways (7 percent), and all others that include libraries, police, trash and snow removal, fire protection, and park maintenance (43 percent).

Taxes and Efficiency

A tax system should be both *efficient* and *equitable*. Here we address efficiency. A tax is more efficient than another if it raises the same amount of revenue at a smaller cost to taxpayers. The cost of a tax includes the actual tax payment itself plus

- the deadweight loss that results when taxes distort private decisions,
- the administrative burden taxpayers bear when they comply with the tax laws.

Recall from Chapter 8 that the deadweight loss from a tax is the reduction in economic well-being of taxpayers in excess of the amount of revenue raised by the government. The loss is generated when buyers and sellers allocate resources according to the prices they face after the tax rather than the true costs and benefits of the goods. As a result of a tax, we fail to produce and consume goods on which the benefits exceed the cost of production.

Income taxes place a tax on interest income and therefore discourage saving. A consumption tax would not distort people's saving decisions.

The administrative burden of a tax includes the time spent filling out tax forms, the time spent throughout the year keeping records for tax purposes, and the resources the government uses to enforce the tax laws. Simplifying the tax laws would reduce the administrative burden but it would require the elimination of many favorite loopholes of taxpayers.

The **average tax rate** is total taxes paid divided by total income. The **marginal tax rate** is the extra taxes paid on an additional dollar of income. The average tax rate is most appropriate for gauging the sacrifice made by a taxpayer. The marginal tax rate, however, is most appropriate for gauging how much the tax system distorts incentives and, thus, how inefficient the tax is. Since people think at the margin, a high marginal tax rate discourages hard work and causes a large deadweight loss.

Rational people think at the margin and respond to incentives. In Iceland, when the government moved from collecting taxes based on the previous year's income to collecting taxes on the current year's income, a year of income had a zero marginal tax rate. As expected, hours worked and production rose during the year with the zero marginal tax rate. As an additional example, when marginal tax rates were reduced in the United States, there was an increase in the percent of married women who chose to work and the number of hours worked increased for those women who already had jobs.

A **lump-sum tax** is a tax that is the same amount for every person, regardless of income. A lump-sum tax is the most efficient tax because a lump-sum tax:

- generates a marginal tax rate of zero so it does not distort decision making and thus creates no deadweight loss,
- imposes the minimum administrative burden.

We rarely see lump-sum taxes, however, because many perceive them as unfair or not equitable since rich and poor pay the same amount.

Taxes and Equity

There are different principles on which taxes can be based to generate fairness or equity. The **benefits principle** states that people should pay taxes based on the benefits they receive from government services. This principle can be used to justify gasoline taxes to pay for roads, to justify that the rich should pay more taxes than the poor because the rich benefit more from fire and police protection, national defense, and the court system. This principle can also be used to justify antipoverty programs paid for by the rich because the rich may benefit more than the middle class from not living is a society with poverty.

The **ability-to-pay principle** states that taxes should be levied on a person according to how well that person can shoulder the burden. This principle suggests that all taxpayers should make an "equal sacrifice" to support the government. The concept of "equal sacrifice" leads to two notions of equity: vertical equity and horizontal equity. **Vertical equity** states that taxpayers with a greater ability to pay taxes should pay larger amounts and **horizontal equity** states that taxpayers with similar abilities to pay taxes should pay the same amount.

A **proportional tax** is a tax for which high-income and low-income taxpayers pay the same fraction of income. A **regressive tax** is a tax for which high-income taxpayers pay a smaller fraction of their income than do low-income taxpayers. A **progressive tax** is a tax for which high-income taxpayers pay a larger fraction of their income than do low-income taxpayers. If taxes are based on the ability-to-pay principle, then vertical equity requires that the rich pay more taxes than the poor and, thus, taxes should be progressive. The U.S. tax system is progressive because the highest income quintile of American families pays 27.4 percent of their income in taxes while the lowest income quintile pays 5.3 percent. After taking account of government transfers, the poorest quintile pays a negative 30 percent in taxes (they receive more than they pay).

Horizontal equity is difficult to accomplish because it is difficult to determine when two families truly have similar abilities to pay. For example, married couples are taxed as if they were a single taxpayer. Since they get only one exclusion (income that is not taxed), a greater amount of a married couple's combined income is taxed than when each member of the couple was single. This is the so-called "marriage tax."

It is necessary to address tax incidence in order to evaluate tax equity. This is because the person from whom the tax is collected often is not the person that bears the burden of the tax. The *flypaper theory* of tax incidence ignores the true burden of the tax and mistakenly assumes that the person from whom the tax is collected is also the one that bears the burden of the tax. For example, the corporate income tax is collected from corporations but it is actually paid by the owners, customers, and workers of the corporation.

Conclusion: The Tradeoff between Equity and Efficiency

The goals of equity and efficiency for the tax system often conflict and people attach different weights to these two goals. President Reagan was concerned with the efficiency of the tax system so he proposed lowering marginal tax rates. President Clinton was more concerned with equity of the tax system so he proposed raising marginal tax rates. George W. Bush plans to reduce the highest rate to 35 percent.

HELPFUL HINTS

1. The benefits principle of taxation suggests that people should pay taxes based on the benefits they receive from government services. This is similar to having the government utilize a *user fee* (a price charged by the government for using a public good) when it supplies a public good. For example, the government can charge people a direct user fee when they use a government-owned toll road. Alternatively, the government can utilize a gaso-

line tax as an indirect user fee to pay for the entire road system. Either way, the people who benefit from the road pay for the road.

2. Remember, only people pay taxes. When we tax a business such as a corporation, the corporation is a tax collector, not a taxpayer. The burden of the tax will be shifted to the owners, customers, and workers of the corporation based on the elasticities of supply and demand in the relevant markets for the corporation's labor, capital, and products.

TERMS AND DEFINITIONS

Choose a definition for each key term.

Key terms:

____ Budget deficit

____ Budget surplus

____ Average tax rate

____ Marginal tax rate

____ Lump-sum tax

____ Benefits principle

____ Ability-to-pay principle

____ Vertical equity

____ Horizontal equity

____ Proportional tax

____ Regressive tax

____ Progressive tax

Definitions:

1. A tax for which high-income and low-income taxpayers pay the same fraction of income
2. The idea that taxes should be levied on a person according to how well that person can shoulder the burden
3. The extra taxes paid on an additional dollar of income
4. A tax that is the same amount for every person
5. An excess of government receipts over government spending
6. The idea that taxpayers with a greater ability to pay taxes should pay larger amounts
7. A tax for which high-income taxpayers pay a larger fraction of their income than do low-income taxpayers
8. An excess of government spending over government receipts
9. The idea that taxpayers with similar abilities to pay taxes should pay the same amount
10. The idea that people should pay taxes based on the benefits they receive from government services
11. Total taxes paid divided by total income
12. A tax for which high-income taxpayers pay a smaller fraction of their income than do low-income taxpayers

PROBLEMS AND SHORT-ANSWER QUESTIONS

Practice Problems

1. a. Fill out the table below assuming that the government taxes 20 percent of the first $30,000 of income and 50 percent of all income above $30,000.

Income	Taxes Paid	Average Tax Rate	Marginal Tax Rate
$10,000	_____	_____	_____
20,000	_____	_____	_____
30,000	_____	_____	_____
40,000	_____	_____	_____
50,000	_____	_____	_____

b. Compare the taxes for someone making $10,000 to those of someone making $50,000 in part (a) above. Is this tax system progressive, regressive, or proportional? Explain.

____

____

____

____

2. a. Fill out the table below assuming that the government imposes a lump-sum tax of $6,000 on all individuals.

Income	Taxes Paid	Average Tax Rate	Marginal Tax Rate
$10,000	_____	_____	_____
20,000	_____	_____	_____
30,000	_____	_____	_____
40,000	_____	_____	_____
50,000	_____	_____	_____

b. Compare the taxes for someone making $10,000 to those of someone making $50,000 in part (a) above. Is this tax system progressive, regressive, or proportional? Explain

____

____

____

____

3. a. Fill out the table below assuming that the government taxes 20 percent of all income.

Income	Taxes Paid	Average Tax Rate	Marginal Tax Rate
$10,000	______	______	______
20,000	______	______	______
30,000	______	______	______
40,000	______	______	______
50,000	______	______	______

b. Compare the taxes for someone making $10,000 to those of someone making $50,000 in part (a) above. Is this tax system progressive, regressive, or proportional? Explain.

____

____

____

4. a. Fill out the table below assuming that the government taxes 40 percent of the first $10,000 of income and 10 percent of all income above $10,000.

Income	Taxes Paid	Average Tax Rate	Marginal Tax Rate
$10,000	______	______	______
20,000	______	______	______
30,000	______	______	______
40,000	______	______	______
50,000	______	______	______

b. Compare the taxes for someone making $10,000 to those of someone making $50,000 in part (a) above. Is this tax system progressive, regressive, or proportional? Explain.

5. a. Suppose the only objective of the tax system is to collect $6,000 from people who make $30,000. Which of the tax systems described in questions 1 through 4 is best? Why?

b. Suppose the only objective of the tax system is to be efficient. Which of the tax systems described in questions 1 through 4 is best? Why?

c. Suppose the only objective of the tax system is to be vertically equitable based on the ability-to-pay principle. Which of the tax systems described in questions 1 though 4 is best? Why?

Short-Answer Questions

1. List the sources of revenue for the federal government from the largest source to the smallest.

2. List the categories of spending by the federal government from the largest to the smallest.

3. List the sources of revenue for state and local governments from the largest source to the smallest.

4. List the categories of spending by state and local governments from the largest to the smallest.

5. What does it mean to say that a tax is *efficient*? What makes a tax efficient?

6. Is a consumption tax efficient? Explain.

7. Is a lump-sum tax efficient? Explain. Why do we rarely see lump-sum taxes in the real world?

8. Explain the difference between the benefits principle and the ability-to-pay principle of taxation. Which principle of taxation stresses vertical equity? Explain.

____

____

____

____

9. Are corporate income taxes truly paid by the corporation? That is, is the burden of the tax on the corporation? Explain.

____

____

____

SELF-TEST

True/False Questions

_____ 1. The largest source of revenue for the federal government is the individual income tax.

_____ 2. An excise tax is a tax on income.

_____ 3. Expenditures on national defense are an example of a government transfer payment.

_____ 4. To judge the vertical equity of a tax system, one should look at the average tax rate of taxpayers of differing income levels.

_____ 5. The marginal tax rate is the appropriate tax rate to judge how much a particular tax system distorts economic decision making.

_____ 6. A lump-sum tax is a progressive tax.

_____ 7. Lump-sum taxes are equitable but not efficient.

_____ 8. More taxes are collected by state and local governments than by the federal government.

_____ 9. An efficient tax is one that generates minimal deadweight losses and minimal administrative burdens.

_____ 10. The federal income tax system in the United States is regressive.

______11. The horizontal inequity of the federal income tax system is demonstrated by the fact that when two individuals marry, their combined income tax bill will increase.

______12. Corporations bear the burden of the corporate income tax.

______13. A tax system with a low marginal tax rate generates less deadweight loss and is more efficient than a similar tax system with a higher marginal tax rate.

______14. If the government runs a budget deficit, it means that there is an excess of government spending over government receipts.

______15. The marginal tax rate is total taxes paid divided by total income.

Multiple-Choice Questions

1. Which of the following lists the sources of tax revenue to the federal government from the largest source to the smallest source?
   a. individual income taxes, corporate income taxes, social insurance taxes.
   b. corporate income taxes, individual income taxes, social insurance taxes.
   c. individual income taxes, social insurance taxes, corporate income taxes.
   d. social insurance taxes, individual income taxes, corporate income taxes.
   e. none of the above

2. In the United States, the tax system is
   a. progressive.
   b. regressive.
   c. proportional.
   d. lump sum.

3. In 2001, the average American paid federal taxes of about
   a. $4000.
   b. $5000.
   c. $6000.
   d. $7000.
   e. $8000.

4. Which of the following lists the spending by the federal government from the largest category to the smallest category?
   a. Social Security, national defense, income security, Medicare, net interest, health
   b. national defense, net interest, Social Security, income security, health, Medicare
   c. health, national defense, net interest, Social Security, income security, Medicare
   d. net interest, Social Security, national defense, health, Medicare, income security
   e. none of the above

5. Which one of the following statements regarding the taxes and spending of state and local governments is true?
   a. State and local governments collect more tax revenue than the federal government.
   b. The greatest expenditure of state and local governments is on education.
   c. Corporate income taxes are a greater source of tax revenue to state and local governments than individual income taxes.
   d. The greatest source of tax revenue to state and local governments is property taxes.

6. If the federal government runs a budget surplus, there is a(n)
   a. excess of government spending over government receipts.
   b. excess of government receipts over government spending.
   c. equality of government spending and receipts.
   d. surplus of government workers.

7. Susan values a pair of blue jeans at $40. If the price is $35, Susan buys the jeans and generates consumer surplus of $5. Suppose a tax is placed on blue jeans that causes the price of blue jeans to rise to $45. Now Susan fails to buy a pair of jeans. This example has demonstrated
   a. the administrative burden of a tax.
   b. horizontal equity.
   c. the ability-to-pay principle.
   d. the benefits principle.
   e. the deadweight loss from a tax.

8. A tax for which high income taxpayers pay a smaller fraction of their income than do low-income taxpayers is known as a(n)
   a. proportional tax.
   b. progressive tax.
   c. regressive tax.
   d. equitable tax.

9. An efficient tax
   a. raises revenue at the smallest possible cost to taxpayers.
   b. minimizes the deadweight loss from the tax.
   c. minimizes the administrative burden from the tax.
   d. does all of the above.

10. The marginal tax rate is
    a. total taxes paid divided by total income.
    b. the taxes paid by the marginal worker.
    c. the extra taxes paid on an additional dollar of income.
    d. total income divided by total taxes paid.

11. The appropriate tax rate to employ to judge the vertical equity of a tax system is the
    a. marginal tax rate.
    b. average tax rate.
    c. proportional tax rate.
    d. horizontal tax rate.

12. The average tax rate is
    a. total taxes paid divided by total income.
    b. the taxes paid by the marginal worker.
    c. the extra taxes paid on an additional dollar of income.
    d. total income divided by total taxes paid.

13. Which of the following taxes is the most efficient tax?
    a. a proportional income tax
    b. a progressive income tax
    c. a consumption tax
    d. a lump-sum tax

14. A progressive tax system is one where
    a. marginal tax rates are low.
    b. marginal tax rates are high.
    c. higher income taxpayers pay more taxes than do lower income taxpayers.
    d. higher income taxpayers pay a greater percentage of their income in taxes than do lower income taxpayers.

Use the following information about a tax system to answer questions 15 through 17.

Income	Amount of Tax
$10,000	$1,000
20,000	2,000
30,000	5,000
40,000	15,000

15. The average tax rate for a taxpayer earning $20,000 is
    a. 0 percent.
    b. 5 percent.
    c. 10 percent.
    d. 20 percent.
    e. none of the above.

16. This tax system is
    a. progressive
    b. lump-sum.
    c. regressive.
    d. proportional.

17. The marginal tax rate for a taxpayer whose earnings rises from $30,000 to $40,000 is
    a. 0 percent.
    b. 16.7 percent.
    c. 37.5 percent.
    d. 100 percent.
    e. none of the above.

18. The ability-to-pay principle of taxation suggests that if a tax system is to be vertically equitable, it should be
    a. regressive.
    b. proportional.
    c. progressive.
    d. efficient.
    e. lump-sum.

19. Which of the following taxes can be supported by the benefits principle of taxation?
    a. gasoline taxes used to pay for roads
    b. progressive income taxes used to pay for national defense
    c. property taxes used to pay for police and the court system
    d. progressive income taxes used to pay for antipoverty programs
    e. All of the above can be supported by the benefits principle of taxation.

20. The appropriate tax rate to employ to gauge how much the tax system distorts incentives and decision making is the
    a. marginal tax rate.
    b. average tax rate.
    c. proportional tax rate.
    d. horizontal tax rate.
    e. vertical tax rate.

ADVANCED CRITICAL THINKING

You are having a political debate with a friend. The discussion centers on taxation. You show your friend some data from your economics textbook that suggests that the average American paid about $7,000 in federal income tax in 2001. Your friend says, "If $7,000 per person is what it takes to run this country, then I think that it would be much simpler if we just billed each American $7,000 and eliminated the complex tax code."

1. What type of tax is your friend suggesting? What is its appeal?

    ____

    ____

2. Is this type of tax supported by the "benefits principle" of tax equity? Explain.

    ____

    ____

3. Is this type of tax supported by the "ability-to-pay" principle of tax equity? Is it vertically equitable? Is it horizontally equitable?

    ____

    ____

    ____

    ____

4. Since your friend agrees that the tax she suggested is not equitable, she now suggests that we simply tax rich corporations since they can clearly afford it and then people wouldn't have to pay any taxes. Is she correct? Who

would actually pay the taxes? Explain how she mistakenly employed the *flypaper theory* of taxation.

____

____

____

____

SOLUTIONS

Terms and Definitions

8 Budget deficit

5 Budget surplus

11 Average tax rate

3 Marginal tax rate

4 Lump-sum tax

10 Benefits principle

2 Ability-to-pay principle

6 Vertical equity

9 Horizontal equity

1 Proportional tax

12 Regressive tax

7 Progressive tax

Practice Problems

1. a.

Income	Taxes Paid	Average Tax Rate	Marginal Tax Rate
$10,000	$2,000	20%	20%
20,000	4,000	20	20
30,000	6,000	20	20
40,000	11,000	27.5	50
50,000	16,000	32	50

b. Progressive because the average tax rate for a person making $50,000 exceeds the average tax rate for a person making $10,000. That is, the rich pay a larger fraction of their income than do poor people.

2. a.

Income	Taxes Paid	Average Tax Rate	Marginal Tax Rate
$10,000	$6,000	60%	0%
20,000	6,000	30	0
30,000	6,000	20	0
40,000	6,000	15	0
50,000	6,000	12	0

b. Regressive because the average tax rate for a person making $10,000 exceeds the average tax rate for a person making $50,000. That is, the poor pay a larger fraction of their income than do rich people.

3. a.

Income	Taxes Paid	Average Tax Rate	Marginal Tax Rate
$10,000	$2,000	20%	20%
20,000	4,000	20	20
30,000	6,000	20	20
40,000	8,000	20	20
50,000	10,000	20	20

b. Proportional because the average tax rate for a person making $10,000 is equal to that of a person making $50,000.

4. a.

Income	Taxes Paid	Average Tax Rate	Marginal Tax Rate
$10,000	$4,000	40%	10%
20,000	5,000	25	10
30,000	6,000	20	10
40,000	7,000	17.5	10
50,000	8,000	16	10

b. Regressive because the average tax rate for a person making $10,000 is greater than that of a person making $50,000.

5. a. They are all equally suitable because each system generates $6,000 tax revenue from people making $30,000.
b. Taxes are more efficient if they generate smaller deadweight losses and smaller administrative burdens. The lump-sum tax in question 2 has a zero marginal rate so it does not distort economic decision making (no deadweight loss) and it is simple (small administrative burden), therefore it is most efficient. However, it is regressive.
c. The tax system in question 1 because it is the only one that is progressive.

Short-Answer Questions

1. Individual income taxes, social insurance taxes, corporate income taxes, and other taxes.

2. Social Security, national defense, income security, Medicare, net interest, health, and other spending.

3. Sales taxes, property taxes, individual income taxes, corporate income taxes. They also receive money from the federal government and other fees (license fees, tolls, fares, etc.).

4. Education, public welfare, highways, and other spending (libraries, police, trash and snow removal, fire protection, park maintenance).

5. A tax is efficient if it raises the same amount of revenue at a smaller cost to taxpayers. It should generate a small deadweight loss and a small administrative burden.

6. Yes. It is more efficient than an income tax because a consumption tax does not tax saving and, thus, it does not distort the saving decision. An income tax does tax saving so it does distort the saving decision and causes a deadweight loss.

7. Yes. The marginal tax rate associated with a lump-sum tax is zero so a lump-sum tax does not distort decision making at the margin and, thus, it generates no deadweight loss. It is rarely used because it is regressive.

8. The benefits principle argues that people should pay taxes based on the benefits they receive while the ability-to-pay principle argues that taxes should be based on how well a person can shoulder the burden. The ability-to-pay principle stresses vertical equity because vertical equity requires that taxpayers with a greater ability-to-pay should pay larger taxes.

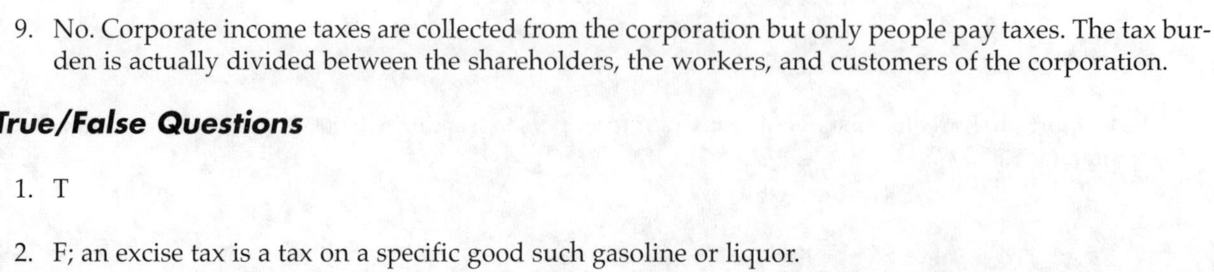

9. No. Corporate income taxes are collected from the corporation but only people pay taxes. The tax burden is actually divided between the shareholders, the workers, and customers of the corporation.

True/False Questions

1. T
2. F; an excise tax is a tax on a specific good such gasoline or liquor.
3. F; a transfer payment is an expenditure for which no good or service is received in return.
4. T
5. T
6. F; a lump-sum tax is regressive.
7. F; lump-sum taxes are efficient but not equitable.
8. F; state and local governments collect about 40 percent of the taxes.
9. T
10. F; it is progressive because higher income people pay a larger percentage of their income in taxes.
11. T
12. F; the corporation's shareholders, workers, and purchasers of the corporation's products bear the burden of the corporate income tax.
13. T
14. T
15. F; the marginal tax rate is the extra taxes paid on an additional dollar of income.

Multiple-Choice Questions

1. c	5. b	9. d	13. d	17. d
2. a	6. b	10. c	14. d	18. c
3. d	7. e	11. b	15. c	19. e
4. a	8. c	12. a	16. a	20. a

Advanced Critical Thinking

1. Lump-sum tax. It is the most efficient tax—its marginal rate is zero so it does not distort incentives, and it imposes the minimum administrative burden.

2. No, if wealthy people benefit more from public services such as police and national defense, they should pay more in taxes.

3. No, wealthy people have a greater ability to pay. Therefore, it is not vertically equitable. However, it is horizontally equitable in that people with the same ability to pay are paying the same amount because all pay the same amount.

4. No, only people pay taxes—corporations collect taxes. The taxes are paid by the owners, workers, and customers of the corporations. The flypaper theory of taxation mistakenly says that burden of a tax is on the person or company from whom the taxes are collected.

13

THE COSTS OF PRODUCTION

GOALS

In this chapter you will

Examine what items are included in a firm's costs of production

Analyze the link between a firm's production process and its total costs

Learn the meaning of average total cost and marginal cost and how they are related

Consider the shape of a typical firm's cost curves

Examine the relationship between short-run and long-run costs

OUTCOMES

After accomplishing these goals, you should be able to

Explain the difference between economic profit and accounting profit

Utilize a production function to derive a total cost curve

Explain why the marginal cost curve must intersect the average total cost curve at the minimum point of the average total cost curve

Explain why a production function might exhibit increasing marginal product at low levels of output and decreasing marginal product at high levels of output

Explain why, as a firm expands its scale of operation, it tends to first exhibit economies of scale, then constant returns to scale, then diseconomies of scale

CHAPTER OVERVIEW

Context and Purpose

Chapter 13 is the first chapter in a five-chapter sequence dealing with firm behavior and the organization of industry. It is important that you become comfortable with the material in Chapter 13 because chapters 14 through 17 are based on the concepts developed in Chapter 13. To be more specific, Chapter 13 develops the cost curves on which firm behavior is based. The remaining chapters in this section (Chapters 14 through 17) utilize these cost curves to develop the behavior of firms in a variety of different market structures—competitive, monopolistic, oligopolistic, and monopolistically competitive.

The purpose of Chapter 13 is to address the costs of production and develop the firm's cost curves. These cost curves underlie the firm's supply curve. In previous chapters, we summarized the firm's production decisions by starting with the supply curve. While this is suitable for answering many questions, it is now necessary to address the costs that underlie the supply curve in order to address the part of economics known as *industrial organization*—the study of how firms' decisions about prices and quantities depend on the market conditions they face.

CHAPTER REVIEW

Introduction

In previous chapters, we summarized the firm's production decisions by starting with the supply curve. While this is suitable for answering many questions, it is now necessary to address the costs that underlie the supply curve in order to address the part of economics known as *industrial organization*—the study of how firms' decisions about prices and quantities depend on the market conditions they face.

What Are Costs?

Economists generally assume that the goal of a firm is to maximize **profits.**

Profit = total revenue – total cost.

Total revenue is the quantity of output the firm produces times the price at which it sells the output. **Total cost** is more complex. An economist considers the firm's cost of production to include all of the *opportunity costs* of producing its output. The total opportunity cost of production is the sum of the *explicit* and *implicit* costs of production. **Explicit costs** are input costs that require an outlay of money by the firm, such as when money flows out of a firm to pay for raw materials, workers' wages, rent, and so on. **Implicit costs** are input costs that do not require an outlay of money by the firm. Implicit costs include the value of the income forgone by the owner of the firm had the owner worked for someone else plus the forgone interest on the financial capital that the owner invested in the firm.

Accountants are only concerned with the firm's flow of money so they record only explicit costs. Economists are concerned with the firm's decision making so they are concerned with total opportunity costs, which are the sum of explicit costs and implicit costs. Since accountants and economists view costs differently, they view profits differently:

- **Economic profit** = total revenue – (explicit costs + implicit costs),
- **Accounting profit** = total revenue – explicit costs.

Because an accountant ignores implicit costs, accounting profit is greater than economic profit.

The big business scandals of 2001 and 2002 begin with the fraudulent measurement of revenue, costs, and therefore profit. The result was inflated stock prices and inflated values of stock options owned by corporate executives.

Production and Costs

For the following discussion, we assume that the size of the production facility (factory) is fixed in the short run. Therefore, this analysis describes production decisions in the short run.

A firm's costs reflect its production process. A **production function** shows the relationship between the quantity of inputs used to make a good (horizontal axis) and the quantity of output of that good (vertical axis). The **marginal product** of any input is the increase in output that arises from an additional unit of that input. The marginal product of an input can be measured as the slope of the production function or "rise over run." Production functions exhibit **diminishing marginal product**—the property whereby the marginal product of an input declines as the quantity of the input increases. Hence, the slope of a production function gets flatter as more and more inputs are added to the production process.

The *total cost curve* shows the relationship between the quantity of output produced and the total cost of production. Since the production process exhibits diminishing marginal product, the quantity of inputs necessary to produce equal increments of output rises as we produce more output and, thus, the total cost curve rises at an increasing rate or gets steeper as the amount produced increases.

The Various Measures of Cost

Several measures of cost can be derived from data on the firm's total cost. Costs can be divided into fixed costs and variable costs. **Fixed costs** are costs that do not vary with the quantity of output produced—for example, rent. **Variable costs** are costs that do vary with the quantity of output produced—for example, expenditures on raw materials and temporary workers. The sum of fixed and variable cost equals total costs.

In order to choose the optimal amount of output to produce, the producer needs to know the cost of the typical unit of output and the cost of producing one additional unit. The cost of the typical unit of output is measured by **average total cost** which is total cost divided by the quantity of output. Average total cost is the sum of **average fixed cost** (fixed costs divided by the quantity of output) and **average variable cost** (variable costs divided by the quantity of output). **Marginal cost** is the cost of producing one additional unit. It is measured as the increase in total costs that arises from an extra unit of production. In symbols, if Q = quantity, TC = total cost, ATC = average total cost, FC = fixed costs, AFC = average fixed costs, VC = variable costs, AVC = average variable costs, and MC = marginal cost, then:

$$ATC = TC/Q,$$

$$AVC = VC/Q,$$

$$AFC = FC/Q,$$

$$MC = \Delta TC/\Delta Q.$$

When these cost curves are plotted on a graph with cost on the vertical axis and quantity produced on the horizontal axis, these cost curves will have predictable shapes. At low levels of production, the marginal product of an extra worker is large so the marginal cost of another unit of output is small. At high levels of production, the marginal product of a worker is small so the marginal cost of another unit is large. Therefore, because of diminishing marginal product, the marginal-cost curve is increasing or upward sloping. The average-total-cost curve is U-shaped because at low levels of output, average costs are high due to high fixed costs. As output increases, average costs fall because fixed costs are spread across additional units of output. However, at some point, diminishing returns begin to increase average costs again. The **efficient scale** of the firm is the quantity of output that minimizes average total cost. Whenever marginal cost is less than average total cost, average total cost is falling. Whenever marginal cost is greater than average total cost, average total cost is rising. Therefore, the marginal-cost curve crosses the average-total-cost curve at the efficient scale.

To this point, we have assumed that the production function exhibits diminishing marginal product at all levels of output and, therefore, there are rising marginal costs at all levels of output. Often, however, production first exhibits increasing marginal product and decreasing marginal costs at very low levels of output as the addition of workers allows for specialization of skills. At higher levels of output, diminishing returns eventually set in and marginal costs begin to rise, causing all cost-curve relationships previously described to continue to hold. In particular:

- Marginal cost eventually rises with the quantity of output.
- The average-total-cost curve is U-shaped.
- The marginal-cost curve crosses the average-total-cost curve at the minimum of average total cost.

Costs in the Short Run and in the Long Run

The division of costs between fixed and variable depends on the time horizon. In the short run, the size of the factory is fixed and, for many firms, the only way to vary output is hiring or firing workers. In the long run, the firm can change the size of the factory and all costs are variable. The long-run average-total-cost curve, although flatter than the short-run average-total-cost curves, is still U-shaped. For each particular factory size, there is a short-run average-total-cost curve that lies on or above the long-run average-total-cost curve. In the long run, the firm gets to choose on which short-run curve it wants to operate. In the short run, it must operate on the short-run curve it chose in the past. Some firms reach the long run faster than do others because some firms can change the size of their factory relatively easily.

At low levels of output, firms tend to have **economies of scale**—the property whereby long-run average total cost falls as the quantity of output increases. At high levels of output, firms tend to have **diseconomies of scale**—the property whereby long-run average total cost rises as the quantity of output increases. At intermediate levels of output, firms tend to have **constant returns to scale**—the property whereby long-run average total cost stays the same as the quantity of output changes. Economies of scale may be caused by increased *specialization* among workers as the factory gets larger while diseconomies of scale may be caused by coordination problems inherent in extremely large organizations. Adam Smith, 200 years ago, recognized the efficiencies captured by large factories that allowed workers to specialize in particular jobs.

Conclusion

This chapter developed a typical firm's cost curves. These cost curves will be used in the following chapters to see how firms make production and pricing decisions.

HELPFUL HINTS

1. Since accountants and economists view costs and, thus, profits differently, it is possible for a firm that appears profitable according to an accountant to be unprofitable according to an economist. For example, suppose a firm incurs $20,000 in explicit costs to produce output that is sold for total revenue of $30,000. According to the accountant, the firm's profit is $10,000. However, suppose that the owner/manager of the firm could have worked for another firm and earned $15,000 during this period. While the account-

ant would still record the firm's profits at $30,000 – $20,000 = $10,000 the economist would argue that the firm is not profitable because the total explicit and implicit costs are $20,000 + $15,000 = $35,000 which exceeds the $30,000 of total revenue.

2. In the case of discrete numerical examples, marginal values are determined over a range of a variable rather than at a point. Therefore, when we plot a marginal value, we plot it halfway between the two end points of the range of the variable of concern. For example, if we are plotting the marginal cost of production as we move from the fifth unit to the sixth unit of production, we calculate the change in cost as we move from producing five units to producing six units and then we plot this marginal cost as if it is for the fifth and a half unit. Notice the marginal cost curves in your text. Although it is not discussed explicitly in your text, each marginal cost curve is plotted in this manner. In like manner, if we were plotting the marginal cost of production as we move from producing 50 units to producing 60 units, we would plot the marginal cost of that change in production as if it were for the 55th unit.

3. The long run is usually defined as the period of time necessary for all inputs to become variable. That is, the long run is the period of time necessary for the firm to be able to change the size of the production facility or factory. Note that this period of time differs across industries. For example, it may take many years for all of the inputs of a railroad to become variable because the railroad tracks are quite permanent and the right-of-way for new track is difficult to obtain. However, an ice cream shop could add on to its production facility in just a matter of months. Thus, its takes longer for a railroad to reach the long run than it does for an ice cream shop.

TERMS AND DEFINITIONS

Choose a definition for each key term.

Key terms:

_____ Total revenue
_____ Total cost
_____ Profit
_____ Explicit costs
_____ Implicit costs
_____ Economic profit
_____ Accounting profit
_____ Production function
_____ Marginal product
_____ Diminishing marginal product
_____ Fixed costs
_____ Variable costs
_____ Average total cost
_____ Average fixed cost
_____ Average variable cost
_____ Marginal cost
_____ Efficient scale
_____ Economies of scale
_____ Diseconomies of scale
_____ Constant returns to scale

Definitions:

1. Costs that do not vary with the quantity of output produced
2. Total revenue minus total cost
3. The increase in total cost that arises from an extra unit of production
4. The property whereby long-run average total cost falls as the quantity of output increases
5. The property whereby long-run average total cost stays the same as the quantity of output changes
6. Input costs that do not require an outlay of money by the firm
7. The increase in output that arises from an additional unit of input
8. The market value of the inputs a firm uses in production
9. The property whereby long-run average total cost rises as the quantity of output increases
10. Fixed costs divided by the quantity of output
11. Costs that vary with the quantity of output produced
12. The quantity of output that minimizes average total cost
13. The amount a firm receives for the sale of its output
14. The relationship between quantity of inputs used to make a good and the quantity of output of that good
15. Variable costs divided by the quantity of output
16. Total cost divided by the quantity of output
17. The property whereby the marginal product of an input declines as the quantity of the input increases
18. Total revenue minus total cost, including both explicit and implicit costs
19. Total revenue minus total explicit cost
20. Input costs that require an outlay of money by the firm

PROBLEMS AND SHORT-ANSWER QUESTIONS

Practice Problems

1. Joe runs a small boat factory. He can make ten boats per year and sell them for $25,000 each. It costs Joe $150,000 for the raw materials (fiberglass, wood, paint, and so on) to build the ten boats. Joe has invested $400,000 in the factory and equipment needed to produce the boats: $200,000 from his own savings and $200,000 borrowed at 10 percent interest (assume that Joe could have loaned his money out at 10 percent, too). Joe can work at a competing boat factory for $70,000 per year.
   a. What is the total revenue Joe can earn in a year?

   ____

   b. What are the explicit costs Joe incurs while producing ten boats?

   ____

   c. What are the total opportunity costs of producing ten boats (explicit and implicit)?

   ____

   ____

   d. What is the value of Joe's accounting profit?

   ____

   e. What is the value of Joe's economic profit?

   ____

   f. Is it truly profitable for Joe to operate his boat factory? Explain.

   ____

   ____

   ____

   ____

2. a. Complete the following table. It describes the production and cost of hamburgers at a roadside stand. All figures are measured per hour.

Number of Workers	Output	Marginal Product of Labor	Cost of Factory	Cost of Workers	Total Cost
0	0		$25	$0	______
		______			
1	6		25	5	______
		______			
2	11		25	10	______
		______			
3	15		25	15	______
		______			
4	18		25	20	______
		______			
5	20		25	25	______

b. Plot the production function in Exhibit 1.

c. What happens to the marginal product of labor as more workers are added to the production facility? Why? Use this information about the marginal product of labor to explain the slope of the production function you plotted above.

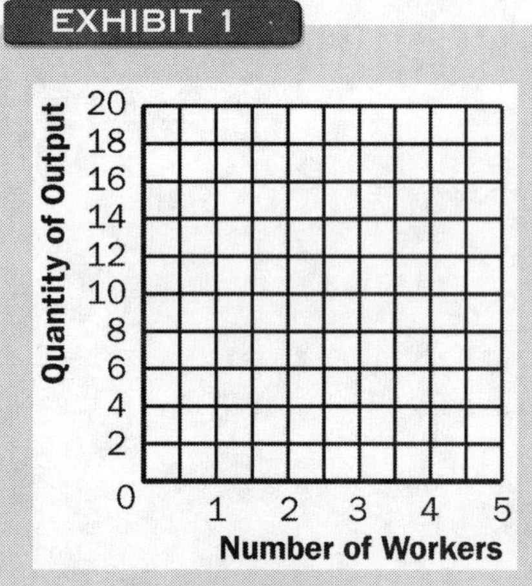

EXHIBIT 2

Total Cost: $50, 40, 30, 20, 10, 0

Quantity of Output: 4, 8, 12, 16, 20

d. Plot the total-cost curve in Exhibit 2.

e. Explain the shape of the total-cost curve.

3. a. The information below is for Bob's blue jeans manufacturing plant. All data is per hour. Complete the table. Note the following abbreviations: *FC* (fixed cost), *VC* (variable cost), *TC* (total cost), *AFC* (average fixed cost), *AVC* (average variable cost), *ATC* (average total cost), *MC* (marginal cost).

Quantity	FC	VC	TC	AFC	AVC	ATC	MC
0	$16	$0	_____	_____	_____	_____	
							_____
1	16	18	_____	_____	_____	_____	
							_____
2	16	31	_____	_____	_____	_____	
							_____
3	16	41	_____	_____	_____	_____	
							_____
4	16	49	_____	_____	_____	_____	
							_____
5	16	59	_____	_____	_____	_____	
							_____
6	16	72	_____	_____	_____	_____	
							_____
7	16	90	_____	_____	_____	_____	
							_____
8	16	114	_____	_____	_____	_____	
							_____
9	16	145	_____	_____	_____	_____	
							_____
10	16	184	_____	_____	_____	_____	

b. Plot *AFC, AVC, ATC,* and *MC* in Exhibit 3. (Note: read Helpful Hint 2 above before plotting *MC*).

EXHIBIT 3

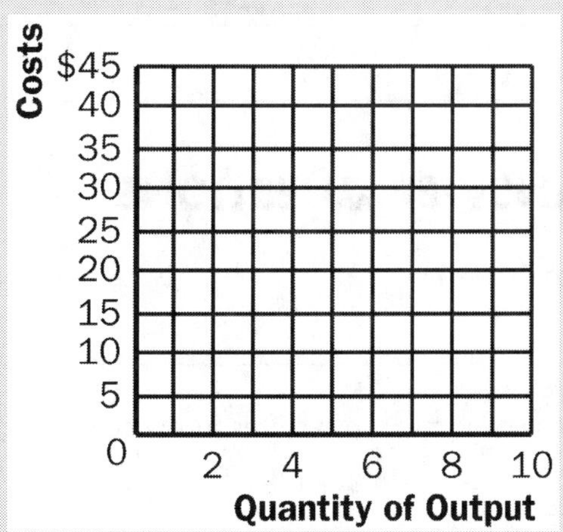

c. Explain the shape of each of the curves you plotted in part (b) above.

____

____

____

____

____

____

d. Explain the relationship between *ATC* and *MC*.

e. Explain the relationship between *ATC*, *AFC*, and *AVC*.

f. What is Bob's efficient scale? How do you find the efficient scale? Explain.

SHORT-ANSWER QUESTIONS

1. What is profit?

2. How does economic profit differ from accounting profit?

3. Suppose you own and operate your own business. Further, suppose that interest rates rise and another firm offers you a job paying twice what you thought you were worth in the labor market. What has happened to your accounting profit? What has happened to your economic profit? Are you more or less likely to continue to operate your own firm?

4. Explain the relationship between the production function and the total-cost curve.

5. Is the salary of management in a firm a fixed cost or a variable cost? Why?

6. What is the efficient scale of a firm?

7. Explain the relationship between marginal cost and average total cost.

8. What is the shape of the marginal cost curve in the typical firm? Why is it shaped this way?

9. If a firm is operating in the area of constant returns to scale, what will happen to average total costs in the short run if the firm expands production? Why? What will happen to average total costs in the long run? Why?

10. When a small firm expands the scale of its operation, why does it usually first experience increasing returns to scale? When the same firm grows to be extremely large, why might a further expansion of the scale of operation generate decreasing returns to scale?

SELF-TEST

True/False Questions

_____ 1. Total revenue equals the quantity of output the firm produces times the price at which it sells its output.

_____ 2. Wages and salaries paid to workers are an example of implicit costs of production.

_____ 3. If total revenue is $100, explicit costs are $50, and implicit costs are $30, then accounting profit equals $50.

_____ 4. If there are implicit costs of production, accounting profits will exceed economic profits.

______5. When a production function gets flatter, the marginal product is increasing.

______6. If a firm continues to employ more workers within the same size factory, it will eventually experience diminishing marginal product.

______7. If the production function for a firm exhibits diminishing marginal product, the corresponding total-cost curve for the firm will become flatter as the quantity of output expands.

______8. Fixed costs plus variable costs equal total costs.

______9. Average total costs are total costs divided by marginal costs.

______10. When marginal costs are below average total costs, average total costs must be falling.

______11. If, as the quantity produced increases, a production function first exhibits increasing marginal product and later diminishing marginal product, the corresponding marginal-cost curve will be U-shaped.

______12. The average-total-cost curve crosses the marginal-cost curve at the minimum of the marginal-cost curve.

______13. The average-total-cost curve in the long run is flatter than the average-total-cost curve in the short run.

______14. The efficient scale for a firm is the quantity of output that minimizes marginal cost.

______15. In the long run, as a firm expands its production facilities, it generally first experiences diseconomies of scale, then constant returns to scale, and finally economies of scale.

Multiple-Choice Questions

1. Accounting profit is equal to total revenue minus
   a. implicit costs.
   b. explicit costs.
   c. the sum of implicit and explicit costs.
   d. marginal costs.
   e. variable costs.

2. Economic profit is equal to total revenue minus
   a. implicit costs.
   b. explicit costs.
   c. the sum of implicit and explicit costs.
   d. marginal costs.
   e. variable costs.

Use the following information for the next two questions. Madelyn owns a small pottery factory. She can make 1,000 pieces of pottery per year and sell them for $100 each. It costs Madelyn $20,000 for the raw materials to produce the 1,000 pieces of pottery. She has invested $100,000 in her factory and equipment: $50,000 from her savings and $50,000 borrowed at 10 percent (assume that she could have loaned her money out at 10 percent, too). Madelyn can work at a competing pottery factory for $40,000 per year.

3. The accounting profit at Madelyn's pottery factory is
   a. $30,000.
   b. $35,000.
   e. $70,000.
   d. $75,000.
   e. $80,000.

4. The economic profit at Madelyn's pottery factory is
   a. $30,000.
   b. $35,000.
   e. $70,000.
   d. $75,000.
   e. $80,000.

5. If there are implicit costs of production,
   a. economic profit will exceed accounting profit.
   b. accounting profit will exceed economic profit.
   c. economic profit and accounting profit will be equal.
   d. economic profit will always be zero.
   e. accounting profit will always be zero.

6. If a production function exhibits diminishing marginal product, its slope
   a. becomes flatter as the quantity of the input increases.
   b. becomes steeper as the quantity of the input increases.
   c. is linear (a straight line).
   d. could be any of the above.

7. If a production function exhibits diminishing marginal product, the slope of the corresponding total-cost curve
   a. becomes flatter as the quantity of output increases.
   b. becomes steeper as the quantity of output increases.
   c. is linear (a straight line).
   d. could be any of the above.

Use the following information for the next two questions.

Number of Workers	Output
0	0
1	23
2	40
3	50

8. The marginal product of labor as production moves from employing one worker to employing two workers is
   a. 0.
   b. 10.
   c. 17.
   d. 23.
   e. 40.

9. The production process described above exhibits
   a. constant marginal product of labor.
   b. increasing marginal product of labor.
   c. diminishing marginal product of labor.
   d. increasing returns to scale.
   e. decreasing returns to scale.

10. Which of the following is a variable cost in the short run?
   a. wages paid to factory labor
   b. payment on the lease for factory equipment
   c. rent on the factory
   d. interest payments on borrowed financial capital
   e. salaries paid to upper management

Use the following information to answer the following four questions.

Quantity of Output	Fixed Costs	Variable Costs	Total Costs	Marginal Costs
0	$10	$0		
1	10	5		
2	10	11		
3	10	18		
4	10	26		
5	10	36		

11. The average fixed cost of producing four units is
   a. $26.
   b. $10.
   c. $5.
   d. $2.50.
   e. none of the above.

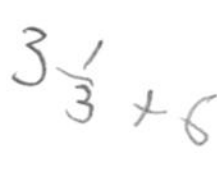

12. The average total cost of producing three units is
   a. $3.33.
   b. $6.
   c. $9.33.
   d. $18.
   e. $28.

13. The marginal cost of changing production from three units to four units is
    a. $5.
    b. $6.
    c. $7.
    d. $8.
    e. $9.

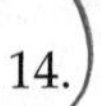

14. The efficient scale of production is
    a. one unit.
    b. two units.
    c. three units.
    d. four units.
    e. five units.

15. When marginal costs are below average total costs,
    a. average fixed costs are rising.
    b. average total costs are falling.
    c. average total costs are rising.
    d. average total costs are minimized.

16. If marginal costs equal average total costs,
    a. average total costs are rising.
    b. average total costs are falling.
    c. average total costs are minimized.
    d. average total cost are maximized.

17. If, as the quantity produced increases, a production function first exhibits increasing marginal product and later diminishing marginal product, the corresponding marginal-cost curve will
    a. slope upward.
    b. be U-shaped.
    c. slope downward.
    d. be flat (horizontal).

18. In the long run, if a very small factory were to expand its scale of operations, it is likely that it would initially experience
    a. economies of scale.
    b. constant returns to scale.
    c. diseconomies of scale.
    d. an increase in average total costs.

19. The efficient scale of production is the quantity of output that minimizes
    a. average total cost.
    b. marginal cost.
    c. average fixed cost.
    d. average variable cost.

20. Which of the following statements is true?
    a. All costs are fixed in the long run.
    b. All costs are variable in the long run.
    c. All costs are fixed in the short run.
    d. All costs are variable in the short run.

ADVANCED CRITICAL THINKING

Your friend has a large garden and grows fresh fruit and vegetables to be sold at a local "farmer's market." Your friend comments, "I hired a college student who was on summer vacation to help me this summer and my production more than doubled. Next summer, I think I'll hire two or maybe three helpers and my output should go up more than three- or fourfold."

1. If all production processes eventually exhibit diminishing marginal product of the variable inputs, could it be true that your friend hired a helper (doubled the labor) and more than doubled his production? Why?

___

___

___

___

2. Is it likely that he could hire more workers and continue to reap greater than proportional increases in production? Why?

___

___

___

3. In the long run, what must your friend do to the scale of his operation if he wants to continue to hire workers and have those workers generate proportional increases in production? Explain. Even in the long run, could your friend expand his scale of operation forever and continue to keep average total costs at a minimum? Explain.

___

___

___

___

___

SOLUTIONS

Terms and Definitions

13 Total revenue

8 Total cost

2 Profit

20 Explicit costs

6 Implicit costs

18 Economic profit

19 Accounting profit

14 Production function

7 Marginal product

17 Diminishing marginal product

1 Fixed costs

11 Variable costs

16 Average total cost

10 Average fixed cost

15 Average variable cost

3 Marginal cost

12 Efficient scale

4 Economies of scale

9 Diseconomies of scale

5 Constant returns to scale

Practice Problems

1. a. 10 × $25,000 = $250,000
   b. $150,000 + ($200,000 × 0.10) = $170,000
   c. $150,000 + ($400,000 × 0.10) + $70,000 = $260,000
   d. $250,000 – $170,000 = $80,000
   e. $250,000 – $260,000 = –$10,000
   f. No. Joe could make $70,000 plus 10 percent interest on his $200,000 financial capital for a total of $90,000 if he worked for the competition instead of running his own factory. His factory makes an accounting profit of only $80,000 per year so it costs him $10,000 to run his own factory (the size of the economic loss).

2. a.

Number of Workers	Output	Marginal Product of Labor	Cost of Factory	Cost of Workers	Total Cost
0	0		$25	$0	$25
		6			
1	6		25	5	30
		5			
2	11		25	10	35
		4			
3	15		25	15	40
		3			
4	18		25	20	45
		2			
5	20		25	25	50

b. See Exhibit 4.

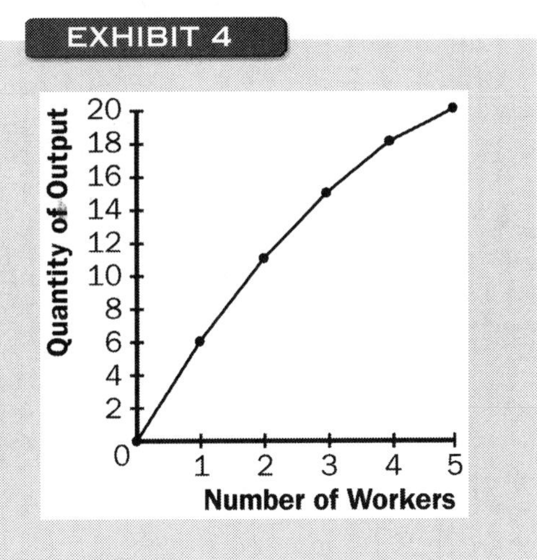

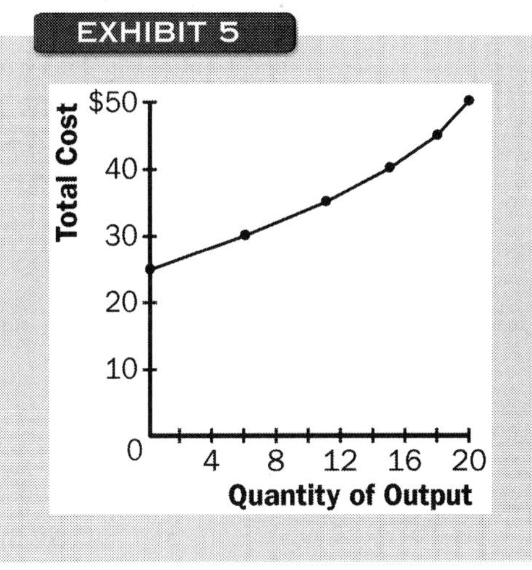

c. It diminishes because additional workers have to share the production equipment and the work area becomes more crowded. The slope of the production function is the change in output from a change in a unit of input, which is the marginal product of labor. Since it is diminishing, the slope of the production function gets flatter as a greater number of inputs are used.

d. See Exhibit 5.

e. The total-cost curve gets steeper as the quantity produced rises due to the diminishing marginal product of labor. That is, in order to produce additional equal increments of output the firm must employ ever greater amounts of inputs and costs rise at an increasing rate.

3. a.

Quantity	***FC***	***VC***	***TC***	***AFC***	***AVC***	***ATC***	***MC***
0	$16	$0	$16	—	—	—	
							$18
1	16	18	34	$16.00	$18.00	$34.00	
							13
2	16	31	47	8.00	15.50	23.50	
							10
3	16	41	57	5.33	13.67	19.00	
							8
4	16	49	65	4.00	12.25	16.25	
							10
5	16	59	75	3.20	11.80	15.00	
							13
6	16	72	88	2.67	12.00	14.67	
							18
7	16	90	106	2.29	12.86	15.14	
							24
8	16	114	130	2.00	14.25	16.25	
							31
9	16	145	161	1.78	16.11	17.88	
							39
10	16	184	200	1.60	18.40	20.00	

b. See Exhibit 6.
c. *AFC* declines as the quantity goes up because a fixed cost is spread across a greater number of units. *MC* declines for the first four units due to an increasing marginal product of the variable input. *MC* rises thereafter due to decreasing marginal product. *AVC* is U-shaped for the same reason as *MC*. *ATC* declines due to falling *AFC* and increasing marginal product. *ATC* rises at higher levels of production due to decreasing marginal product.
d. When *MC* is below *ATC, ATC* must be declining. When *MC* is above *ATC, ATC* must be rising. Therefore, *MC* crosses *ATC* at the minimum of *ATC*.
e. *AFC* plus *AVC* equals *ATC*.
f. Six pairs of blue jeans. Efficient scale is the output that minimizes *ATC*. It is also the place where *MC* crosses the average-total-cost curve.

EXHIBIT 6

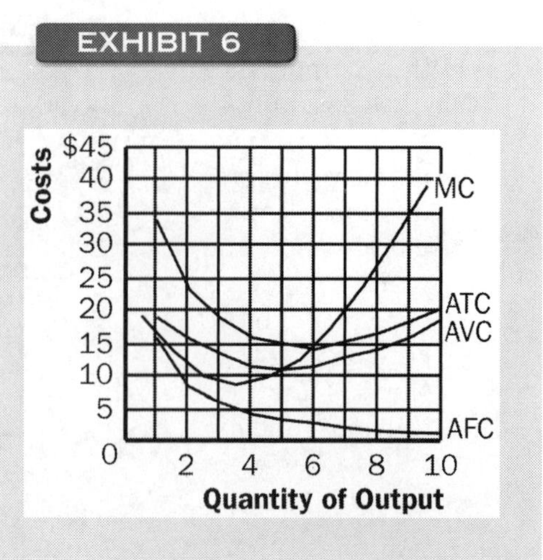

Short-Answer Questions

1. Profit = total revenue – total cost.

2. Economic profit is total revenue minus explicit costs and *implicit costs*. Accounting profit is total revenue minus explicit costs.

3. Accounting profit is unchanged. Economic profit is reduced because implicit costs have risen—the opportunity cost of your invested money and of your time both went up. You are less likely to continue to operate your own firm because it is less profitable.

4. The total-cost curve reflects the production function. When an input exhibits diminishing marginal product, the production function gets flatter because additional increments of inputs increase output by ever smaller amounts. Correspondingly, the total-cost curve gets steeper as the amount produced rises.

5. It is a fixed cost because the salary paid to management doesn't vary with the quantity produced.

6. It is the quantity of production that minimizes average total cost.

7. When marginal cost is below average total cost, the average-total-cost curve must be falling. When marginal cost is above average total cost, the average-total-cost curve must be rising. Thus, the marginal-cost curve crosses the average-total-cost curve at the minimum of average total cost.

8. Typically, the marginal cost curve is U-shaped. The firm often experiences increasing marginal product at very small levels of output as workers are allowed to specialize in their activities. Thus, marginal cost falls. At some point, the firm will experience diminishing marginal product and the marginal cost curve will begin to rise.

9. In the short run, the size of the production facility is fixed so the firm will experience diminishing returns and increasing average total costs when adding additional workers. In the long run, the firm will expand the size of the factory and the number of workers together and, if the firm experiences constant returns to scale, average total costs will remain fixed at the minimum.

10. As a small firm expands the scale of operation, the higher production level allows for greater specialization of the workers and long-run average total costs fall. As an enormous firm continues to expand, it will likely develop coordination problems and long-run average total costs begin to increase.

True/False Questions

1. T
2. F; wages and salaries are explicit costs of production because dollars flow out of the firm.
3. T
4. T
5. F; marginal product is the slope of the production function so marginal product is decreasing when the production function gets flatter.
6. T
7. F; diminishing marginal product means that it requires ever greater amounts of an input to produce equal increments of output so total costs rise at an increasing rate.
8. T
9. F; average total costs are total costs divided by the quantity of output.
10. T
11. T
12. F; the marginal-cost curve crosses the average-total-cost curve at the minimum of the average-total-cost curve.
13. T
14. F; efficient scale minimizes average total costs.
15. F; a firm generally experiences economies of scale, constant returns to scale, and diseconomies of scale as the scale of production expands.

Multiple-Choice Questions

1. b	5. b	9. c	13. d	17. b
2. c	6. a	10. a	14. d	18. a
3. d	7. b	11. d	15. b	19. a
4. a	8. c	12. c	16. c	20. b

Advanced Critical Thinking

1. Yes. Many production processes first exhibit increasing marginal product of the variable inputs (in this case, workers). This result may occur due to specialization of labor. After the second worker is hired, one worker specializes in weeding while the other specializes in watering.

2. No. At some point, if any input is fixed (say the size of the garden) the firm will experience diminishing marginal product of the variable inputs. That is, at some point, the garden will become crowded and additional workers will add smaller and smaller amounts to output.

3. It is likely that the garden is small enough that the firm would experience economies of scale if it increased its scale of operation by expanding the size of the garden and hiring more workers. No, your friend cannot expand his scale of operation forever because, at some point, the firm becomes so large that it develops coordination problems and the firm experiences diseconomies of scale.

14

FIRMS IN COMPETITIVE MARKETS

GOALS

In this chapter you will

Learn what characteristics make a market competitive

Examine how competitive firms decide how much output to produce

Examine how competitive firms decide when to shut down production temporarily

Examine how competitive firms decide whether to exit or enter a market

See how firm behavior determines a market's short-run and long-run supply curves

OUTCOMES

After accomplishing these goals, you should be able to

List up to three conditions that characterize a competitive market

Locate the supply curve for a competitive firm on a graph of its cost curves

Demonstrate why firms temporarily shut down if the price they receive for their output is less than average variable cost

Demonstrate why firms exit a market permanently if the price they receive for their output is less than average total cost

Show why the long-run supply curve in a competitive market is more elastic than the short-run supply curve

CHAPTER OVERVIEW

Context and Purpose

Chapter 14 is the second chapter in a five-chapter sequence dealing with firm behavior and the organization of industry. Chapter 13 developed the cost curves on which firm behavior is based. These cost curves are employed in Chapter 14 to show how a competitive firm responds to changes in market conditions. Chapters 15 through 17 will employ these cost curves to see how firms with market power (monopolistic, oligopolistic, and monopolistically competitive firms) respond to changes in market conditions.

The purpose of Chapter 14 is to examine the behavior of competitive firms—firms that do not have market power. The cost curves developed in the previous chapter shed light on the decisions that lie behind the supply curve in a competitive market.

CHAPTER REVIEW

Introduction

In this chapter, we examine the behavior of competitive firms—firms that do not have *market power*. Firms that have market power can influence the market price of the goods they sell. The cost curves developed in the previous chapter shed light on the decisions that lie behind the supply curve in a competitive market.

What is a Competitive Market?

A **competitive market** has two main characteristics:

- There are many buyers and sellers in the market.
- The goods offered for sale are largely the same.

The result of these two conditions is that each buyer and seller is a *price taker*. A third condition sometimes thought to characterize competitive markets is:

- Firms can freely enter or exit the market.

Firms in competitive markets try to maximize profits, which equals total revenue minus total cost. Total revenue (TR) is $P \times Q$. Since a competitive firm is small compared to the market, it takes the price as given. Thus, total revenue is proportional to the amount of output sold—doubling output sold doubles total revenue.

Average revenue (AR) equals total revenue (TR) divided by the quantity of output (Q) or $AR = TR/Q$. Since $TR = P \times Q$, then $AR = (P \times Q)/Q = P$. That is, for all firms, *average revenue equals the price of the good.*

Marginal revenue (MR) equals the change in total revenue from the sale of an additional unit of output or $MR = \Delta TR/\Delta Q$. When Q rises by one unit, total revenue rises by P dollars. Therefore, for competitive firms, *marginal revenue equals the price of the good.*

Profit Maximization and the Competitive Firm's Supply Curve

Firms maximize profit by comparing marginal revenue and marginal cost. For the competitive firm, marginal revenue is fixed at the price of the good and marginal cost is increasing as output rises. As long as marginal revenue exceeds marginal cost, increasing the quantity produced raises profit. *Profit is maximized when firms produce output up to the point where marginal cost equals marginal revenue.*

Assume that we have a firm with typical cost curves. Graphically, marginal cost (MC) is upward sloping, average total cost (ATC) is U-shaped, and MC crosses ATC at the minimum of ATC. If we draw $P = AR = MR$ on this graph, we can see that the firm will choose to produce a quantity that will maximize profit based on the intersection of MR and MC. That is, the firm will choose to produce the quantity where $MR = MC$. At any quantity lower than the optimal quantity, $MR > MC$ and profit is increased if output is increased. At any quantity above the optimal quantity, $MC > MR$ and profit is increased if output is reduced.

If the price were to increase, the firm would respond by increasing production to the point where the new higher $P = AR = MR$ is equal to MC. That is, the firm moves up its MC curve until $MR = MC$ again. Therefore, *because the firm's marginal-cost curve determines how much the firm is willing to supply at any price, it is the competitive firm's supply curve.*

A firm will temporarily *shut down* (produce nothing) *if the revenue that it would get from producing is less than the variable costs (VC) of production*. Examples of temporary shut downs are farmers leaving land idle for a season and restaurants closing for lunch. For the temporary shut-down decision, the firm ignores fixed costs because these are considered to be **sunk costs** or costs that are not recoverable because the firm must pay them whether they produce output or not. Mathematically, the firm should temporarily shut down if $TR < VC$. Divide by Q

and get $TR/Q < VC/Q$ which is $AR = MR = P < AVC$. That is, the firm should shut down if $P < AVC$. Therefore, *the competitive firm's short-run supply curve is the portion of its marginal-cost curve that lies above the average-variable-cost curve.*

In general, beyond the example of a competitive firm, all rational decision-makers think at the margin and ignore sunk costs when making economics decisions. Rational decision-makers undertake activities where the marginal benefit exceeds the marginal cost.

In the long run, a firm will *exit the market* (permanently cease operations) *if the revenue it would get from producing is less than its total costs.* If the firm exits the industry, it saves on both the fixed and variable costs or total costs. Mathematically, the firm should exit if $TR < TC$. Divide by Q and get $TR/Q = TC/Q$ which is $AR = MR = P < ATC$. That is, the firm should exit if $P <$ ATC. Therefore, *the competitive firm's long-run supply curve is the portion of its marginal-cost curve that lies above the average-total-cost curve.*

A competitive firm's profit = $TR - TC$. Divide and multiply by Q and get Profit $= (TR/Q - TC/Q) \times Q$ or Profit $= (P - ATC) \times Q$. If price is above ATC, the firm is profitable. If price is below ATC, the firm generates losses and would eventually choose to exit the market.

The Supply Curve in a Competitive Market

In the short run, the number of firms in the market is fixed because firms cannot quickly enter or exit the market. Therefore, in the short run, the market supply curve is the horizontal sum of the portion of the individual firm's marginal-cost curves that lie above their average-variable-cost curves. That is, the market supply curve is simply the sum of the quantities supplied by each firm in the market at each price. Since the individual marginal-cost curves are upward sloping, *the short-run market supply curve is also upward sloping.*

In the long run, firms are able to enter and exit the market. Suppose all firms have the same cost curves. If firms in the market are making profits, new firms will enter the market increasing the quantity supplied and causing the price to fall until economic profits are zero. If firms in the market are making losses, some existing firms will exit the market decreasing the quantity supplied and causing the price to rise until economic profits are zero. In the long run, *firms that remain in the market must be making zero economic profit.* Since profit $= (P - ATC) \times Q$, *profit equals zero only when $P = ATC$.* Since for the competitive firm, $P = MC$ and MC intersects ATC at the minimum of ATC, *the long-run equilibrium of a competitive market with free entry and exit must have firms operating at their efficient scale.* Also, since firms enter or exit the market if the price is above or below minimum ATC, the price always returns to the minimum of ATC for each firm but the total quantity supplied in the market rises and falls with the number of firms. Thus, there is only one price consistent with zero profits and *the long-run market supply curve must be horizontal* (perfectly elastic) at that price.

Competitive firms stay in business even though they are making zero economic profits in the long run. Recall that economists define total costs to include all the opportunity costs of the firm, so the zero-profit equilibrium is compensating the owners of the firm for their time and their money invested.

In the short run, an increase in demand increases the price of a good and existing firms make economic profits. In the long run, this attracts new firms to enter the market causing a corresponding increase in the market supply. This increase in supply reduces the price to its original level consistent with zero profits but the quantity sold in the market is now higher. Thus, if at present firms are earning high profits in a competitive industry, they can expect new firms to enter the market and prices and profits to fall in the future.

While the standard case is one where the long-run market supply curve is perfectly elastic, the long-run market supply curve might be upward sloping for two reasons:

- If an input necessary for production is in limited supply, an expansion of firms in that industry will raise the costs for all existing firms and increase the price as output supplied increases.

- If firms have different costs (some are more efficient than others) in order to induce new less efficient firms to enter the market, the price must increase to cover the less efficient firm's costs. In this case, only the *marginal firm* earns zero economic profits while more efficient firms earn profits in the long run.

Regardless, because firms can enter and exit more easily in the long run than in the short run, *the long-run market supply curve is more elastic than the short-run market supply curve.*

Conclusion: Behind the Supply Curve

The supply decision is based on marginal analysis. In competitive markets, firms produce where marginal cost equals price equals minimum average total cost.

HELPFUL HINTS

1. We have determined that, in the short run, the firm will produce the quantity of output where $P = MC$ as long as the price equals or exceeds average variable cost. An additional way to see the logic of this behavior is to recognize that since fixed costs must be paid regardless of the level of production, any time the firm can at least cover its variable costs, any additional revenue beyond its variable costs can be applied to its fixed costs. Therefore, in the short run, the firm loses less money than it would if it shut down if the price exceeds its average variable costs. As a result, the short-run supply curve for the firm is the portion of marginal cost curve that is above the average-variable-cost curve.

2. Recall that rational decision-makers think at the margin. The decision rule for any action is that we should do things for which the marginal benefit exceeds the marginal cost and continue to do that thing until the marginal benefit equals the marginal cost. This decision rule translates directly to the firm's production decision in that the firm should continue to produce additional output until marginal revenue (the marginal benefit to the firm) equals marginal cost.

3. In this chapter, we derived the equation for profit as Profit = $(P - ATC) \times Q$. It helps to remember that, in words, this formula says that profit simply equals the average profit per unit times the number of units sold. This holds true even in the case of losses. If the price is less than average total cost, then we have the average loss per unit times the number of units sold.

TERMS AND DEFINITIONS

Choose a definition for each key term.

Key terms:

6 Price takers

2 Competitive market

3 Average revenue

5 Marginal revenue

1 Shut down

7 Exit

4 Sunk cost

Definitions:

1. A short-run decision to temporarily cease production during a specific period of time due to current market conditions
2. A market with many buyers and sellers trading identical products so that each buyer and seller is a price taker
3. Total revenue divided by the quantity sold

4. A cost to which one is already committed and is not recoverable
5. The change in total revenue from an additional unit sold

6. Buyers and sellers in a competitive market that must accept the price that the market determines
7. A long-run decision to permanently cease production and leave the market

PROBLEMS AND SHORT-ANSWER QUESTIONS

Practice Problems

1. Are the following markets likely to be perfectly competitive? Explain.
   a. The market for gasoline

   Yes

b. The market for blue jeans

No

c. The market for agricultural products such as corn and beans

d. The market for the common stock of IBM

e. The market for electricity

No

f. The market for cable television

No

2. a. The following table contains information about the revenues and costs for Barry's Baseball Manufacturing. All data are per hour. Complete the first group of columns which correspond to Barry's production if $P = \$3$. ($TR$ = total revenue, TC = total cost, MR = marginal revenue, MC = marginal cost)

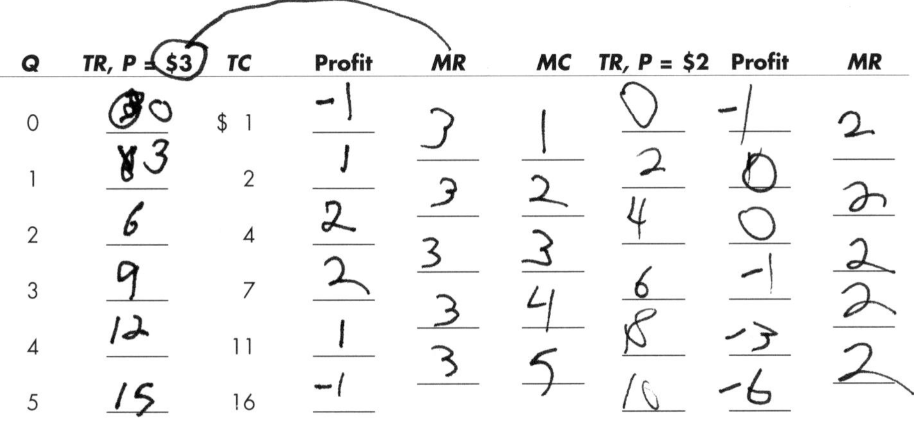

Q	TR, P = $3	TC	Profit	MR	MC	TR, P = $2	Profit	MR
0		$ 1						
1		2						
2		4						
3		7						
4		11						
5		16						

b. If the price is $3 per baseball, what is Barry's optimal level of production? What criteria did you use to determine the optimal level of production?

c. Is $3 per baseball a long-run equilibrium price in the market for baseballs? Explain. What adjustment will take place in the market for baseballs and what will happen to the price in the long run?

d. Suppose the price of baseballs falls to $2. Fill out the remaining three columns of the table above. What is the profit-maximizing level of output when the price is $2 per baseball? How much profit does Barry's Baseball Manufacturing earn when the price of baseballs is $2?

e. Is $2 per baseball a long-run equilibrium price in the market for baseballs? Explain. Why would Barry continue to produce at this level of profit?

f. Describe the slope of the short-run supply curve for the market for baseballs. Describe the slope of the long-run supply curve in the market for baseballs.

____

____

____

3. a. In Exhibit 1, show the cost curves of a representative firm in long-run equilibrium along side the corresponding market equilibrium.

EXHIBIT 1

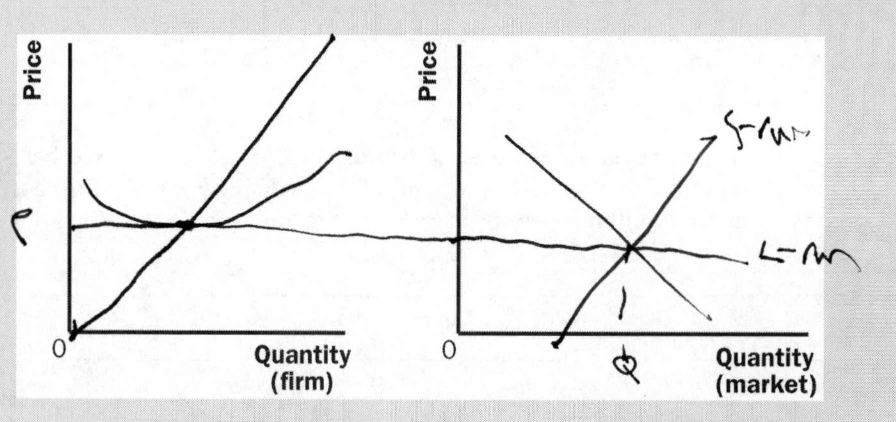

b. Suppose there is a *decrease* in the demand for this product. In Exhibit 2, show the shift in demand in the market for this product and the corresponding profit or loss on the cost curves of the representative firm.

EXHIBIT 2

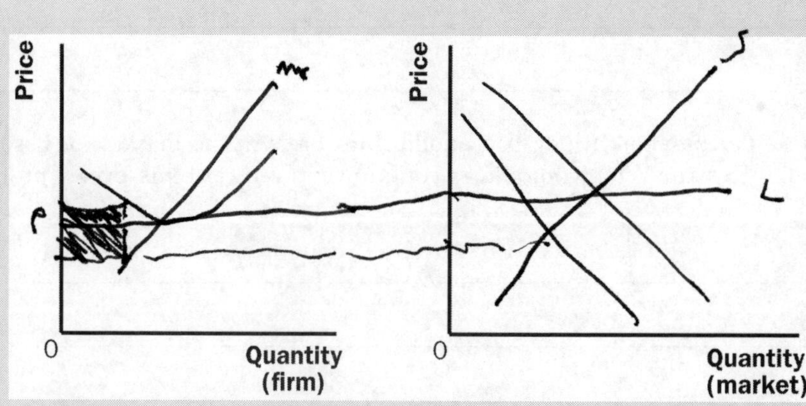

c. In Exhibit 3, show the adjustment that takes place in order to return the market and firm to long-run equilibrium.

EXHIBIT 3

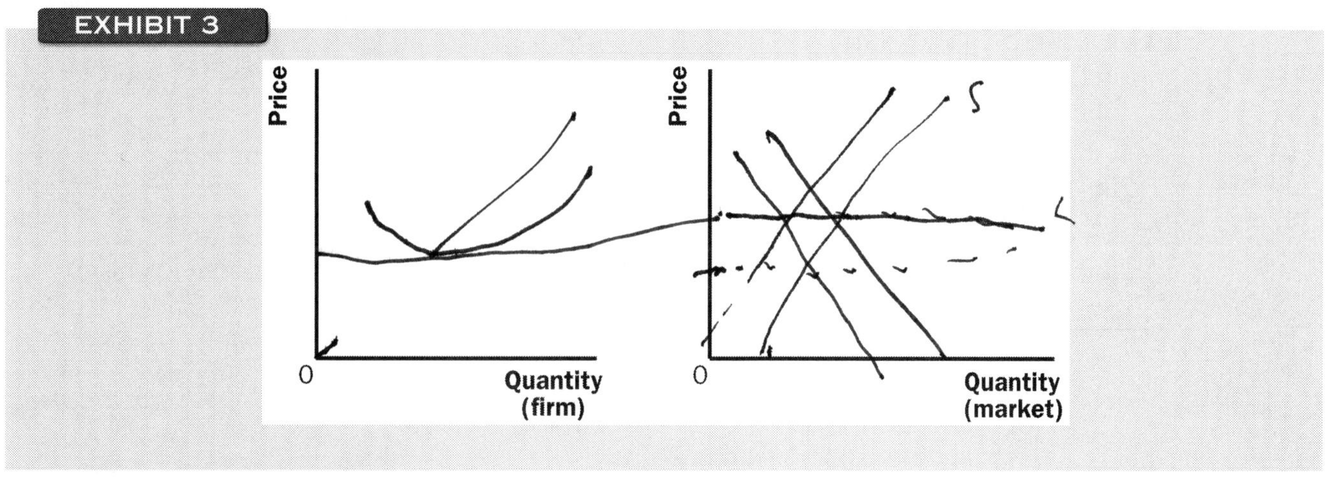

d. After the market has returned to long-run equilibrium, is the price higher, lower, or the same as the initial price? Are there more, fewer, or the same number of firms producing in the market?

Short-Answer Questions

1. What are the three conditions that characterize a competitive market?

2. If a firm is in a competitive market, what happens to its total revenue if it doubles its output? Why?

3. If a firm is producing a level of output where marginal revenue exceeds marginal cost, would it improve profits by increasing output, decreasing output, or keeping output unchanged? Why?

4. What constitutes a competitive firm's short-run supply curve? Explain.

5. What constitutes a competitive firm's long-run supply curve? Explain.

6. You go to your campus bookstore and see a coffee mug emblazoned with your university's shield. It costs $5 and you value it at $8, so you buy it. On the way to your car, you drop it and it breaks into pieces. Should you buy another one or should you go home because the total expenditure of $10 now exceeds the $8 value that you place on it? Why?

7. Suppose the price for a firm's output is above the average variable cost of production but below the average total cost of production. Will the firm shut down in the short run? Explain. Will the firm exit the market in the long run? Explain.

8. Why must the long-run equilibrium in a competitive market (with free entry and exit) have all firms operating at their efficient scale?

9. Why is the short-run market supply curve upward sloping while the standard long-run market supply curve is perfectly elastic?

____

____

____

____

____

10. Under what conditions would the long-run market supply curve be upward sloping?

____

____

SELF-TEST

True/False Questions

______1. The only requirement for a market to be perfectly competitive is for the market to have many buyers and sellers.

______2. For a competitive firm, marginal revenue equals the price of the good it sells.

______3. If a competitive firm sells three times the amount of output, its total revenue also increases by a factor of three.

______4. A firm maximizes profit when it produces output up to the point where marginal cost equals marginal revenue.

______5. If marginal cost exceeds marginal revenue at a firm's current level of output, the firm can increase profit if it increases its level of output.

______6. A competitive firm's short-run supply curve is the portion of its marginal cost curve that lies above its average-total-cost curve.

______7. A competitive firm's long-run supply curve is the portion of its marginal cost curve that lies above its average-variable-cost curve.

______8. In the short run, if the price a firm receives for a good is above its average variable costs but below its average total costs of production, the firm will temporarily shut down.

______9. In a competitive market, both buyers and sellers are price takers.

______10. In the long run, if the price firms receive for their output is below their average total costs of production, some firms will exit the market.

______11. In the short run, the market supply curve for a good is the sum of the quantities supplied by each firm at each price.

______12. The short-run market supply curve is more elastic than the long-run market supply curve.

______13. In the long run, perfectly competitive firms earn small but positive economic profits.

______14. In the long run, if firms are identical and there is free entry and exit in the market, all firms in the market operate at their efficient scale.

______15. If the price of a good rises above the minimum average total cost of production, positive economic profits will cause new firms to enter the market, which drives the price back down to the minimum average total cost of production.

Multiple-Choice Questions

1. Which of the following is *not* a characteristic of a competitive market?
   a. There are many buyers and sellers in the market.
   b. The goods offered for sale are largely the same.
   c. Firms can freely enter or exit the market.
   d. Firms generate small but positive economic profits in the long run.
   e. All of the above are characteristics of a competitive market.

2. Which of the following markets would most closely satisfy the requirements for a competitive market?
   a. gold bullion
   b. electricity
   c. cable television
   d. soda
   e. All of the above represent competitive markets.

3. If a competitive firm doubles its output, its total revenue
   a. more than doubles.
   b. doubles.
   c. less than doubles.
   d. cannot be determined because the price of the good may rise or fall.

4. For a competitive firm, marginal revenue is
   a. equal to the price of the good sold.
   b. average revenue divided by the quantity sold.
   c. total revenue divided by the quantity sold.
   d. equal to the quantity of the good sold.

5. The competitive firm maximizes profit when it produces output up to the point where
   a. marginal cost equals total revenue.
   b. marginal revenue equals average revenue.
   c. marginal cost equals marginal revenue.
   d. price equals average variable cost.

6. If a competitive firm is producing a level of output where marginal revenue exceeds marginal cost, the firm could increase profits if it
   a. increased production.
   b. decreased production.
   c. maintained production at the current level.
   d. temporarily shut down.

Use Exhibit 4 for problems 7 through 11.

7. If the price is P_4, a competitive firm will maximize profits if it produces
   a. Q_1.
   b. Q_2.
   c. Q_3.
   d. Q_4.
   e. Q_5.

8. If the price is P_4, the firm will earn profits equal to the area
   a. $(P_2 - P_1) \times Q_2$.
   b. $(P_3 - P_2) \times Q_3$.
   c. $(P_4 - P_2) \times Q_4$.
   d. $(P_4 - P_3) \times Q_3$.
   e. none of the above

EXHIBIT 4

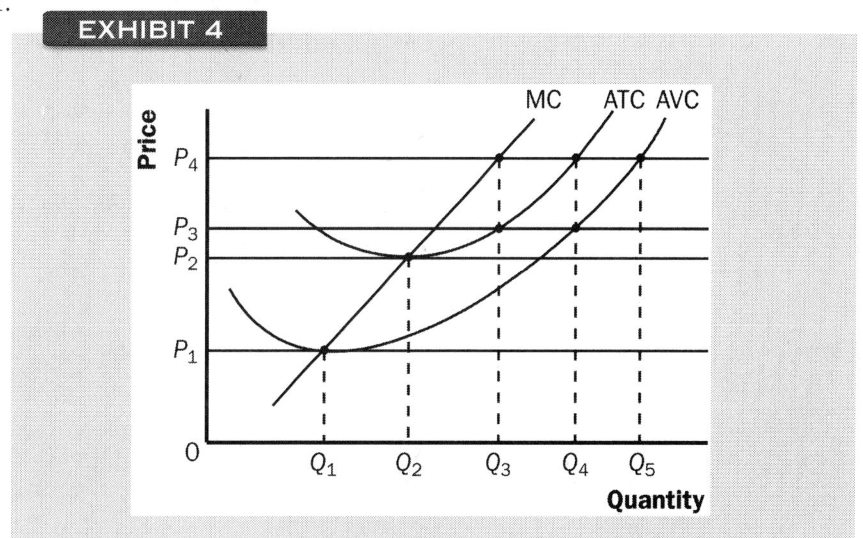

9. In the short run, competitive firms will temporarily shut down production if the price falls below
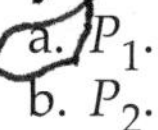
   a. P_1.
   b. P_2.
   c. P_3.
   d. P_4.

10. In the long run, some competitive firms will exit the market if the price is below
   a. P_1.
   b. P_2.
   c. P_3.
   d. P_4.

11. In the long run, the competitive equilibrium is
   a. P_1, Q_1.
   b. P_2, Q_2.
   c. P_4, Q_3.
   d. P_4, Q_4.
   e. P_4, Q_5.

12. In the short run, the competitive firm's supply curve is the
    a. entire marginal cost curve.
    b. portion of the marginal-cost curve that lies above the average-total-cost curve.
    c. portion of the marginal-cost curve that lies above the average-variable-cost curve.
    d. upward-sloping portion of the average-total-cost curve.
    e. upward-sloping portion of the average-variable-cost curve.

13. In the long run, the competitive firm's supply curve is the
    a. entire marginal cost curve.
    b. portion of the marginal-cost curve that lies above the average-total-cost curve.
    c. portion of the marginal-cost curve that lies above the average-variable-cost curve.
    d. upward-sloping portion of the average-total-cost curve.
    e. upward-sloping portion of the average-variable-cost curve.

14. A grocery store should close at night if the
    a. total costs of staying open are greater than the total revenue due to staying open.
    b. total costs of staying open are less than the total revenue due to staying open.
    c. variable costs of staying open are greater than the total revenue due to staying open.
    d. variable costs of staying open are less than the total revenue due to staying open.

15. The long-run market supply curve
    a. is always more elastic than the short-run market supply curve.
    b. is always less elastic than the short-run market supply curve.
    c. has the same elasticity as the short-run market supply curve.
    d. is always perfectly elastic.

16. In the long-run, some firms will exit the market if the price of the good offered for sale is less than
    a. marginal revenue.
    b. marginal cost.
    c. average revenue.
    d. average total cost.

17. If all firms in a market have identical cost structures and if inputs used in the production of the good in that market are readily available, then the long-run market supply curve for that good should be
    a. perfectly elastic.
    b. downward sloping.
    c. upward sloping.
    d. perfectly inelastic.

18. If an input necessary for production is in limited supply so that an expansion of the industry raises costs for all existing firms in the market, then the long-run market supply curve for a good could be
    a. perfectly elastic.
    b. downward sloping.
    c. upward sloping.
    d. perfectly inelastic.

19. If the long-run market supply curve for a good is perfectly elastic, an increase in the demand for that good will, in the long run, cause
    a. an increase the price of the good and an increase in the number of firms in the market.
    b. an increase the price of the good but no increase in the number of firms in the market.
    c. an increase in the number of firms in the market but no increase in the price of the good.
    d. no impact on either the price of the good or the number of firms in the market.

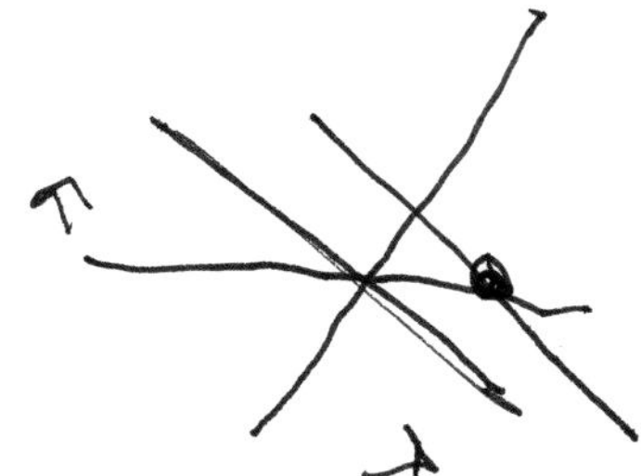

20. In long-run equilibrium in a competitive market, firms are operating at
    a. the minimum of their average-total-cost curves.
    b. the intersection of marginal cost and marginal revenue.
    c. their efficient scale.
    b. zero economic profit.
    e. all of the above.

ADVANCED CRITICAL THINKING

In some regions of the country it is common for Wal-Mart stores and large supermarkets to stay open 24 hours a day, 365 days a year.

1. You walk into a Wal-Mart store at 2:00 a.m. with a friend to buy some VCR tapes. Your friend says, "I can't believe that these stores stay open all night. Only one out of fifteen checkout lines is open. There can't be more than ten shoppers in this store. It just doesn't make any sense for this store to be open all night." Explain to your friend what conditions must be true for it to be to the advantage of Wal-Mart to stay open all night.

____

____

____

____

2. Are the costs of rent, equipment, fixtures, salaries of management, and so on, relevant when Wal-Mart makes the decision whether to stay open at night? Why?

____

____

3. If Wal-Mart had the same number of customers during its day-time hours as you observed during its night-time hours, do you think it would continue to operate? Explain.

____

____

____

____

____

SOLUTIONS

Terms and Definitions

6 Price takers

2 Competitive market

3 Average revenue

5 Marginal revenue

1 Shutdown

7 Exit

4 Sunk cost

Practice Problems

1. a. Yes, many buyers and sellers and the product of different sellers is nearly identical.
   b. Probably not, many buyers and sellers but the product is not identical (Levi vs. Lee) so each seller is not a price taker.
   c. Yes, many buyers and sellers and the product of different sellers is identical.
   d. Yes, many buyers and sellers and the product of different sellers is identical.
   e. No, few sellers (often only one). If there were multiple sellers, the product would be identical.
   f. No, few sellers (often only one). If there were multiple sellers, the product would be nearly identical.

2. a.

Q	TR, P = $3	TC	Profit	MR	MC	TR, P = $2	Profit	MR
0	$0	$1	–$1			$0	–$1	
				$3	$1			$2
1	3	2	1			2	0	
				3	2			2
2	6	4	2			4	0	
				3	3			2
3	9	7	2			6	–1	
				3	4			2
4	12	11	1			8	–3	
				3	5			2
5	15	16	–1			10	–6	

   b. Optimal production is either two or three baseballs per hour. This level of production maximizes profit (at $2) and it is the level of output where $MC = MR$ (at $3).
   c. No, because Barry is earning positive economic profits of $2. These profits will attract new firms to enter the market for baseballs, the market supply will increase, and the price will fall until economic profits are zero.
   d. See answers for the table in part (a) above. Optimal production is either one or two baseballs per hour. Zero economic profit is earned by Barry.
   e. Yes. Economic profits are zero and firms neither enter nor exit the industry. Zero economic profits means that Barry doesn't earn anything beyond his opportunity costs of production but his revenues do cover the cost of his inputs and the value of his time and money.
   f. The slope of the short-run supply curve is positive because when $P = \$2$, quantity supplied is one or two units per firm and when $P = \$3$, quantity supplied is two or three units per firm. In the long

run, supply is horizontal (perfectly elastic) at $P = \$2$ because any price above \$2 causes firms to enter and drives the price back to \$2.

3. a. See Exhibit 5.
   b. See Exhibit 6.
   c. See Exhibit 7.
   d. The price has returned to its initial level. There are fewer firms producing in this market.

EXHIBIT 5

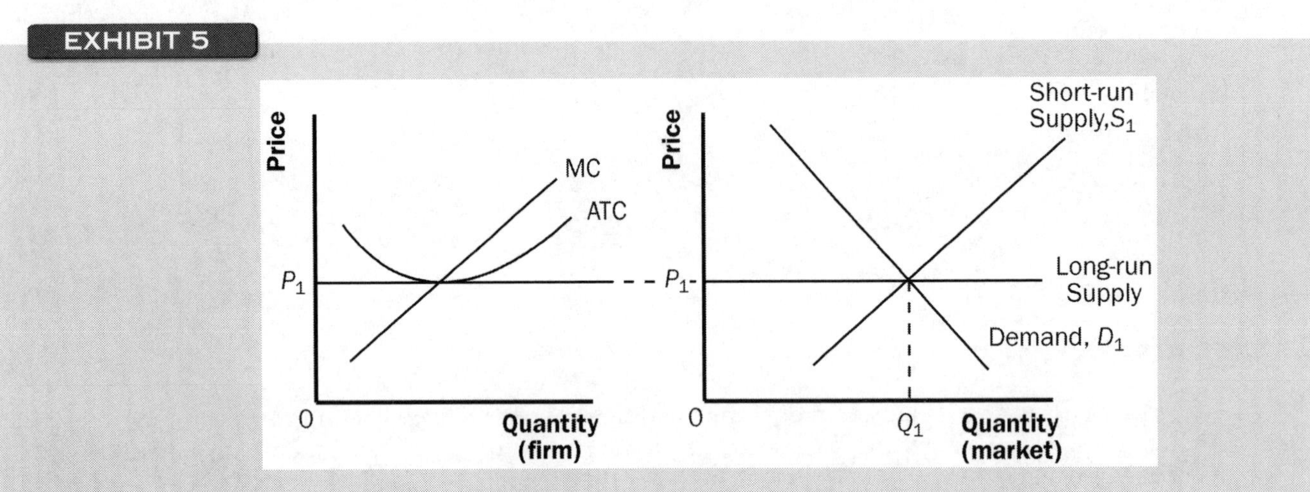

EXHIBIT 6

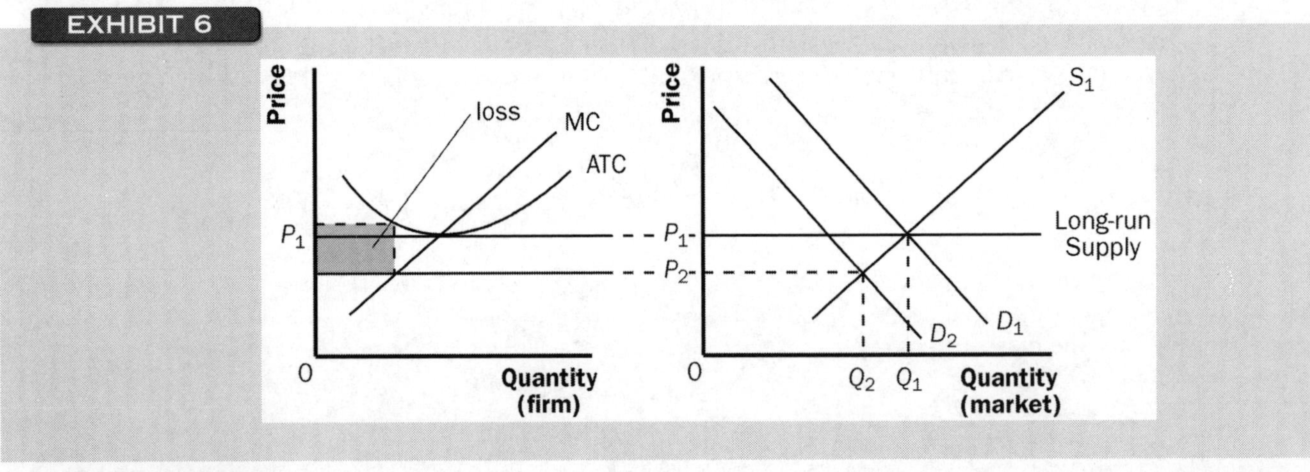

EXHIBIT 7

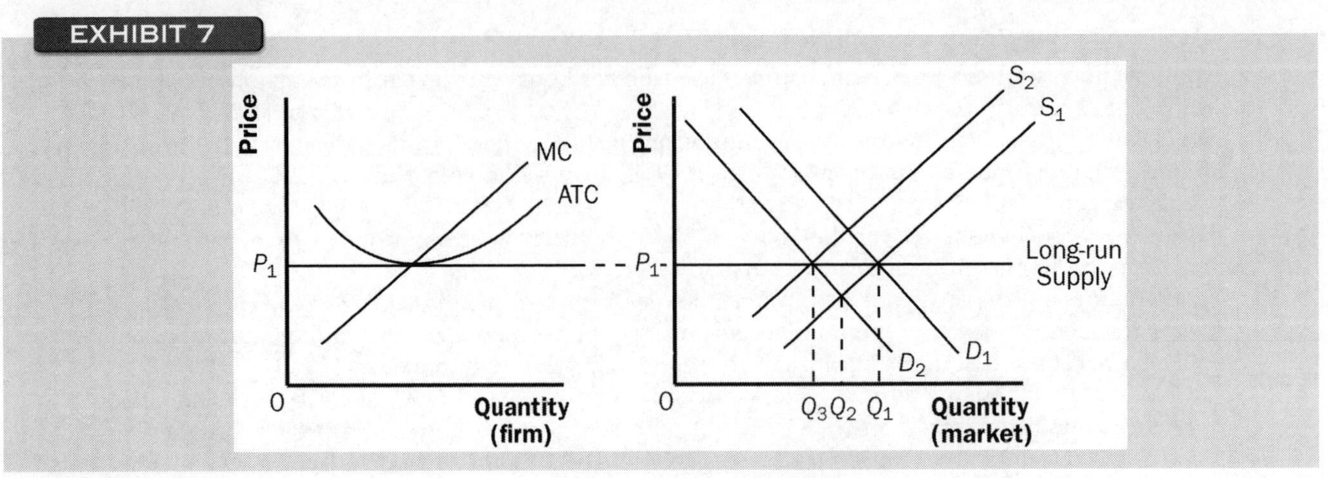

Short-Answer Questions

1. There are many buyers and sellers, the goods offered for sale are largely the same, and firms can freely enter or exit the market.

2. Total revenue doubles. This is because, in a competitive market, the price is unaffected by the amount sold by any individual firm.

3. If $MR > MC$, increasing output will increase profits because an additional unit of production increases revenue more than it increases costs.

4. It is the portion of the firm's marginal-cost curve that lies above its average-variable-cost curve because the firm maximizes profit where $P = MC$ and, in the short run, fixed or sunk costs are irrelevant and the firm must only cover its variable costs.

5. It is the portion of the firm's marginal-cost curve that lies above its average-total-cost curve because the firm maximizes profit where $P = MC$ and, in the long run, the firm must cover its total costs or it should exit the market.

6. You should buy another mug because the marginal benefit ($8) still exceeds the marginal cost ($5). The broken mug is a sunk cost and is not recoverable. Therefore, it is irrelevant.

7. No. In the short run, the firm's fixed costs are sunk costs so the firm will not shut down because it only needs to cover its variable costs. Yes. In the long run, the firm must cover total costs and if $P < ATC$ the firm generates losses in the long run and it will exit the market.

8. In the long-run equilibrium, firms must be making zero economic profits so that firms are not entering or exiting the industry. Zero profits occur when $P = ATC$ and for the competitive firm $P = MC$ determines the production level. $P = ATC = MC$ only at the minimum of ATC.

9. In the short run, firms cannot exit or enter the market so the market supply curve is the horizontal sum of the upward-sloping MC curves of the existing firms. However, in the long run, if the price is above or below minimum ATC, firms will enter or exit the market causing the price to always return to minimum ATC for each firm but the total quantity supplied in the market rises and falls with the number of firms. Thus, the market supply curve is horizontal.

10. If an input necessary for production is in limited supply or if firms have different costs.

True/False Questions

1. F; the goods offered for sale are largely the same and (possibly) firms can freely enter or exit the market.

2. T

3. T

4. T

5. F; the firm increases profits if it reduces output.

6. F; it is the portion of the MC curve that lies above its average-variable-cost curve.

7. F; it is the portion of the MC curve that lies above its average-total-cost curve.

8. F; the firm will continue to operate in the short run as long as price exceeds average variable costs.

9. T

10. T

11. T

12. F; the long-run market supply curve is more elastic than the short-run market supply curve.

13. F; they earn zero economic profits in the long run.

14. T

15. T

Multiple-Choice Questions

1. d	5. c	9. a	13. b	17. a
2. a	6. a	10. b	14. c	18. c
3. b	7. c	11. b	15. a	19. c
4. a	8. d	12. c	16. d	20. e

Advanced Critical Thinking

1. For Wal-Mart to stay open all night (and not undertake a temporary shut down) it must be true that its total revenue at night must equal or exceed its *variable costs* incurred from staying open the additional hours (electricity, wages of night shift workers, . . .).

2. No. These costs are fixed costs or sunk costs—costs that cannot be recovered even if Wal-Mart chooses not to operate at night.

3. It is unlikely. This is because the temporary shut-down decision (staying open additional hours at night) depends on whether total revenue equals or exceeds *variable costs*, but the decision to remain in the market in the long-run depends on whether total revenue equals or exceeds *total costs*. It is unlikely that the revenue earned at night covers total costs (both fixed and variable costs).

15

MONOPOLY

GOALS

In this chapter you will

Learn why some markets have only one seller

Analyze how a monopoly determines the quantity to produce and the price to charge

See how the monopoly's decisions affect economic well-being

Consider the various public policies aimed at solving the problem of monopoly

See why monopolies try to charge different prices to different customers

OUTCOMES

After accomplishing these goals, you should be able to

List three reasons why a monopoly can remain the sole seller of a product in a market

Use a monopolist's cost curves and the demand curve it faces to show the profit earned by a monopolist

Show the deadweight loss from a monopolist's production decision

Show why forcing a natural monopoly to charge its marginal cost of production creates losses for the monopolist

Demonstrate the surprising result that price discrimination by a monopolist can raise economic welfare above that generated by standard monopoly pricing

CHAPTER OVERVIEW

Context and Purpose

Chapter 15 is the third chapter in a five-chapter sequence dealing with firm behavior and the organization of industry. Chapter 13 developed the cost curves on which firm behavior is based. These cost curves were employed in Chapter 14 to show how a competitive firm responds to changes in market conditions. In Chapter 15, these cost curves are again employed, this time to show how a monopolistic firm chooses the quantity to produce and the price to charge. Chapters 16 and 17 will address the decisions made by oligopolistic and monopolistically competitive firms.

A monopolist is the sole seller of a product without close substitutes. As such, it has market power because it can influence the price of its output. That is, a monopolist is a price maker as opposed to a price taker. The purpose of Chapter 15 is to examine the production and pricing decisions of monopolists, the social implications of their market power, and the ways in which governments might respond to the problems caused by monopolists.

CHAPTER REVIEW

Introduction

Monopolists have market power because they can influence the price of their output. That is, monopolists are *price makers* as opposed to *price takers*. While competitive firms choose to produce a quantity of output such that the given market price equals the marginal cost of production, monopolists charge prices that exceed marginal cost. In this chapter we examine the production and pricing decisions of monopolists, the social implications of their market power, and the ways in which governments might respond to the problems caused by monopolists.

Why Monopolies Arise

A **monopoly** is a firm that is the sole seller of a product without close substitutes. A monopoly is able to remain the only seller in a market only if there are *barriers to entry*. That is, other firms are unable to enter the market and compete with it. There are three sources of barriers to entry:

- *A key resource is owned by a single firm.* For example, if a firm owns the only well in town, it has a monopoly for the sale of water. DeBeers essentially has a monopoly in the market for diamonds because it controls 80 percent of the world's production of diamonds. This source of monopoly is somewhat rare.

- *The government gives a single firm the exclusive right to produce some good.* When the government grants patents (which last for 20 years) to inventors and copyrights to authors, it is giving someone the right to be the sole producer of that good. The benefit is that it increases incentives for creative activity. The costs will be discussed later in the chapter.

- *The costs of production make a single producer more efficient than a large number of producers.* A **natural monopoly** arises when a single firm can supply a good to an entire market at an smaller cost than could two or more firms. This happens when there are economies of scale over the relevant range of output. That is, the average-total-cost curve for an individual firm continually declines at least to the quantity that could supply the entire market. This cost advantage is a natural barrier to entry because firms with higher costs find it undesirable to enter the market. Common examples are utilities such as water and electricity distribution.

How Monopolies Make Production and Pricing Decisions

A competitive firm is small relative to the market so it takes the price of the good it produces as given. Since it can sell as much as it chooses at the given market price, the competitive firm faces a demand curve that is perfectly elastic at the market price. A monopoly is the sole producer in its market so it faces the entire downward-sloping market demand curve. The monopolist can choose any price/quantity combination on the demand curve by choosing the quantity and seeing what price buyers will pay. As with competitive firms, monopolies choose a quantity of output that maximizes profit (total revenue minus total cost).

Since the monopolist faces a downward-sloping demand curve, it must lower the price of the good if it wishes to sell a greater quantity. Therefore, when it sells an additional unit, the sale of the additional unit has two effects on total revenue ($P \times Q$):

- *The output effect*: Q is higher.

- *The price effect*: P is lower (on the marginal unit *and on the units it was already selling.*)

Since the monopolist must reduce the price on every unit it sells when it expands output by one unit, marginal revenue ($\Delta TR/\Delta Q$) for the monopolist declines as Q increases and *marginal revenue is always less than the price of the good.*

As with a competitive firm, the monopolist maximizes profit at the level of output where marginal revenue (*MR*) equals marginal cost (*MC*). As *Q* increases, *MR* decreases and *MC* increases. Therefore, at low levels of output, $MR > MC$ and an increase in *Q* increases profit. At high levels of output, $MC > MR$ and a decrease in output increases profit. The monopolist, therefore, should produce up to the point where $MR = MC$. That is, the profit-maximizing level of output is determined by the intersection of the marginal-revenue and marginal-cost curves. Since the *MR* curve lies below the demand curve, the price the monopolist charges is found by reading up to the demand curve from the $MR = MC$ intersection.

Recall that for the competitive firm, since the demand curve facing the firm is perfectly elastic so that $P = MR$, the profit-maximizing equilibrium requires that $P = MR = MC$. However, for the monopoly firm, $MR < P$ so the profit maximizing equilibrium requires that $P > MR = MC$. As a result, *in competitive markets, price equals marginal cost while in monopolized markets, price exceeds marginal cost.*

Evidence from the pharmaceutical drug market is consistent with our theory. While the patent is enforced, the price of a drug is high. When the patent expires and generic drugs become available, the price falls substantially.

As with the competitive firm, Profit = $(P - ATC) \times Q$, or profit equals the average profit per unit times the number of units sold.

The Welfare Cost of Monopoly

Does a monopoly market maximize economic well-being as measured by total surplus? Recall that total surplus is the sum of consumer surplus and producer surplus. Equilibrium of supply and demand in a competitive market naturally maximizes total surplus because all units are produced where the value to buyers are greater than or equal to the cost of production to the sellers.

For a monopolist to produce the socially efficient quantity (maximize total surplus by producing all units where the value to buyers exceeds or equals the cost of production) it would have to produce the level of output where the marginal-cost curve intersects the demand curve. However, the monopolist chooses to produce the level of output where the marginal-revenue curve intersects the marginal cost curve. Since for the monopolist the marginal-revenue curve is always below the demand curve, *the monopolist produces less than the socially efficient quantity of output.*

The small quantity produced by the monopolist allows the monopolist to charge a price that exceeds the marginal cost of production. Therefore, the monopolist generates a *deadweight loss* because, at the high monopoly price, consumers fail to buy units of output where the value to them exceeds the cost to the monopolist.

The deadweight loss from a monopoly is similar to the deadweight loss from a tax and the monopolist's profit is similar to tax revenue except that the revenue is received by a private firm. Since the profit earned by a monopolist is simply a transfer of consumer surplus to producer surplus, a monopoly's profit is not a social cost. The social cost of a monopoly is the deadweight loss generated when the monopolist produces a quantity of output below that which is efficient.

Public Policy toward Monopolies

Monopolies fail to allocate resources efficiently because they produce less than the socially optimal quantity of output and charge prices that exceed marginal cost. Policymakers can respond to the problem of monopoly in one of four ways:

- *By trying to make monopolized industries more competitive.* The Justice Department can employ antitrust laws (statutes aimed at reducing monopoly power) to prevent mergers that reduce competition, break up extremely large companies to increase competition, and prevent companies from colluding. However, some mergers result in synergies that reduce costs and raise efficiency. Therefore, it is difficult for government to know which mergers to block and which ones to allow.

- *By regulating the behavior of the monopolies.* The prices charged by natural monopolies such as utilities are often regulated by government. If a natural monopoly is required to set its price equal to its marginal cost, the efficient quantity will be consumed but the monopoly will lose money because marginal cost must be below average variable cost if average variable cost is declining. Thus, the monopolist will exit the industry. In response, regulators can subsidize a natural monopoly with tax revenue (which creates its own deadweight loss) or allow average-total-cost pricing which is an improvement over monopoly pricing but it is not as efficient as marginal-cost pricing. Another problem with regulating prices is that monopolists have no incentive to reduce costs because their prices are reduced when their costs are reduced.

- *By turning some private monopolies into public enterprises.* Instead of regulating the prices charged by a natural monopoly, the government can run the monopoly itself. The Postal Service is an example. Economists generally prefer private ownership to government ownership because private owners have a greater incentive to minimize costs.

- *By doing nothing at all.* Since each of the solutions above has its own shortcomings, some economists urge that monopolies be left alone. They believe that the "political failure" in the real world is more costly than the "market failure" caused by monopoly pricing.

Price Discrimination

Price discrimination is the business practice of selling the same good at different prices to different customers. Price discrimination can only be practiced by a firm with market power such as a monopolist. There are three lessons to note about price discrimination:

- Price discrimination is a rational strategy for a profit-maximizing monopolist because a monopolist's profits are increased when it charges each customer a price closer to his or her individual willingness to pay.

- Price discrimination is only possible if the monopolist is able to separate customers according to their willingness to pay—by age, income, location, etc. If there is *arbitrage*—the process of buying a good in one market at a low price and selling it in another market at a higher price—price discrimination is not possible.

- Price discrimination can raise economic welfare because output increases beyond that which would result under monopoly pricing. However, the additional surplus (reduced deadweight loss) is received by the producer, not the consumer.

Perfect price discrimination occurs when a monopolist charges each customer his or her exact willingness to pay. In this case, the efficient quantity is produced and consumed and there is no deadweight loss. However, total surplus goes to the monopolist in the form of profit. In reality, perfect price discrimination cannot be accomplished. Imperfect price discrimination may raise, lower, or leave unchanged total surplus in a market.

Examples of price discrimination include movie tickets, airline tickets, discount coupons, financial aid for college tuition, and quantity discounts. Prescription drug manufacturers charge different prices for the same drug when selling to people versus pets, and when selling to people from different countries. Sometimes price discrimination allows a manufacturer to sell drugs to the residents of poor countries at a discounted price so that more people receive the drug than would under a single-price policy. Sometimes differential pricing just raises prices.

Conclusion: The Prevalence of Monopoly

In one sense, monopolies are common because most firms have some control over the prices they charge. On the other hand, firms with substantial monopoly power are rare. Monopoly power is a matter of degree.

HELPFUL HINTS

1. A monopolist can choose the quantity and see what price buyers will pay or a monopolist can choose the price and see what quantity buyers will purchase. That is, a monopolist is still subject to the demand curve for its product. The monopolist cannot choose both a high price and a large quantity if that combination does not lie on the demand curve facing the monopolist.

2. A monopolist is not guaranteed to earn profits. Any one of us can be the monopolist in the production of gold-plated textbook covers (since there is currently no producer of such a product) but the demand for such a product is likely to be too low to cover the costs of production. In like manner, gaining a patent on a product does not guarantee the holder of the patent future profits.

TERMS AND DEFINITIONS

Choose a definition for each key term.

Key terms:

_____ Monopoly

_____ Natural monopoly

_____ Price discrimination

_____ Arbitrage

_____ Perfect price discrimination

Definitions:

1. A monopoly that arises because a single firm can supply a good or service to an entire market at a smaller cost than could two or more firms
2. A firm that is the sole seller of a product without close substitutes
3. A situation in which the monopolist is able to charge each customer precisely his or her willingness to pay
4. The business practice of selling the same good at different prices to different customers
5. The process of buying a good in one market at a low price and selling it in another market at a higher price

PROBLEMS AND SHORT-ANSWER QUESTIONS

Practice Problems

1. a. What are the three sources of the barriers to entry that allow a monopoly to remain the sole seller of a product?

____

____

b. What is the entry barrier that is the source of the monopoly power for the following products or producers? List some competitors that keep these products or producers from having absolute monopoly power.

1. United States Postal Service

____

____

2. Perrier Spring Water

____

____

3. Prozac (a brand-name drug)

____

____

4. DeBeers Diamonds

____

____

5. *Principles of Economics,* by N. Gregory Mankiw (your textbook)

____

____

6. Edison Power Company

____

____

2. Suppose a firm has a patent on a special process to make a unique smoked salmon. The following table provides information about the demand facing this firm for this unique product.

Pounds of Salmon	Price	($P \times Q$) Total Revenue	($\Delta TR/\Delta Q$) Marginal Revenue
0	$20		
1	18		
2	16		
3	14		
4	12		
5	10		
6	8		
7	6		

a. Complete the table above.

b. Plot the demand curve and the marginal revenue curve in Exhibit 1. (Read Helpful Hint 2 in Chapter 13 of this study guide for a reminder on how to plot marginal values.)

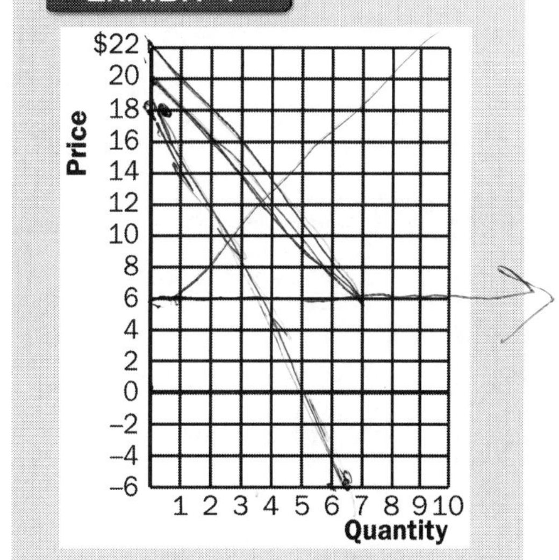

c. Suppose that there are no fixed costs and that the marginal cost of production of smoked salmon is constant at $6 per pound. (Thus, the average total cost is also constant at $6 per pound.) What is the quantity and price chosen by the monopolist? What is the profit earned by the monopolist? Show your solution on the graph you created in part (b) above.

____

____

____

d. What is the price and quantity that maximizes total surplus?

____

e. Compare the monopoly solution and the efficient solution. That is, is the monopolist's price too high or too low? Is the monopolist's quantity too high or too low? Why?

____

____

____

____

f. Is there a deadweight loss in this market if the monopolist charges the monopoly price? Explain.

g. If the monopolist is able to costlessly and perfectly price discriminate, is the outcome efficient? Explain. What is the value of consumer surplus, producer surplus, and total surplus? Explain.

3. a. What type of market is represented in Exhibit 2: perfect competition, monopoly, or natural monopoly? Explain.

EXHIBIT 2

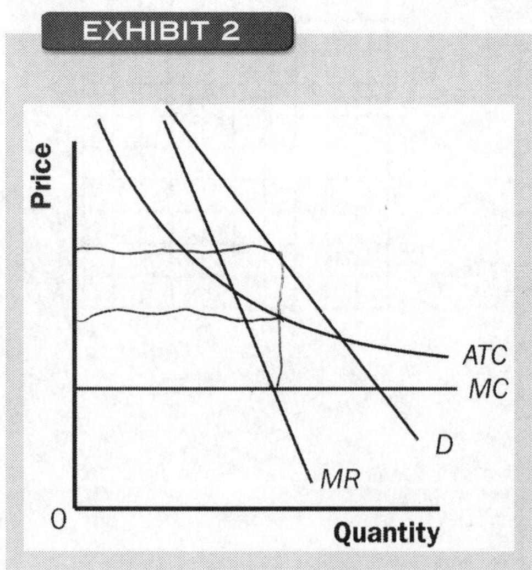

b. Show the profit or loss generated by this firm in Exhibit 2 assuming that the firm maximizes profit.

c. Suppose government regulators force this firm to set the price equal to its marginal cost in order to improve efficiency in this market. In Exhibit 3 show the profit or loss generated by this firm.

EXHIBIT 3

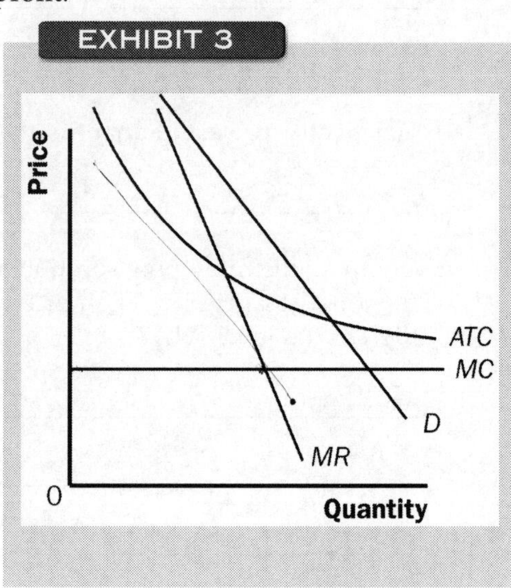

d. In the long run, will forcing this firm to charge a price equal to its marginal cost improve efficiency? Explain.

Short-Answer Questions

1. What is a *barrier to entry*? What are the three sources of barriers to entry that allow a monopoly to remain the sole seller in a market?

2. If a natural monopoly is forced through regulation to charge a price equal to its marginal cost, will the outcome be efficient? Why?

3. Does a monopolist charge the highest possible price for its output? Why? How does a monopolist choose the price it will charge for its product?

4. Why does a monopolist produce less than the socially efficient quantity of output?

5. Are the monopolist's profits part of the social cost of monopoly? Explain.

6. What are the four ways that policymakers can respond to the problem of monopoly?

7. Should antitrust laws be utilized to stop all mergers? Why?

8. What are some of the problems associated with regulating the price charged by a natural monopoly?

9. Is perfect price discrimination efficient? Explain. Who receives the surplus?

10. What is the necessary condition for a monopolist to be able to price discriminate?

SELF-TEST

True/False Questions

_____ 1. Monopolists are price takers.

_____ 2. The most common source of a barrier to entry into a monopolist's market is that the monopolist owns a key resource necessary for production of that good.

_____ 3. A monopoly is the sole seller of a product with no close substitutes.

_____ 4. A natural monopoly is a monopoly that uses its ownership of natural resources as a barrier to entry into its market.

_____ 5. The demand curve facing a monopolist is the market demand curve for its product.

_____ 6. For the monopolist, marginal revenue is always less than the price of the good.

_____ 7. The monopolist chooses the quantity of output at which marginal revenue equals marginal cost and then uses the demand curve to find the price that will induce consumers to buy that quantity.

_____ 8. The supply curve for a monopolist is always positively sloped.

_____ 9. A monopolist produces an efficient quantity of output but it is still inefficient because it charges a price that exceeds marginal cost and the resulting profit is a social cost.

_____10. Using regulations to force a natural monopoly to charge a price equal to its marginal cost of production will cause the monopoly to lose money and exit the industry.

_____11. Most economists argue that the most efficient solution to the problem of monopoly is that the monopoly should be publicly owned.

_____12. Price discrimination is only possible if there is no arbitrage.

_____13. Price discrimination can raise economic welfare because output increases beyond that which would result under monopoly pricing.

_____14. Perfect price discrimination is efficient but all of the surplus is received by the consumer.

_____15. Universities are engaging in price discrimination when they charge different levels of tuition to poor and wealthy students.

Multiple-Choice Questions

1. Which of the following is *not* a barrier to entry in a monopolized market?
   a. The government gives a single firm the exclusive right to produce some good.
   b. The costs of production make a single producer more efficient than a large number of producers.
   c. A key resource is owned by a single firm.
   d. A single firm is very large.

2. A firm whose average total cost continually declines at least to the quantity that could supply the entire market is known as a
   a. perfect competitor.
   b. natural monopoly.
   c. government monopoly.
   d. regulated monopoly.

3. When a monopolist produces an additional unit, the marginal revenue generated by that unit must be
   a. above the price because the output effect outweighs the price effect.
   b. above the price because the price effect outweighs the output effect.
   c. below the price because the output effect outweighs the price effect.
   d. below the price because the price effect outweighs the output effect.

4. A monopolist maximizes profit by producing the quantity at which
   a. marginal revenue equals marginal cost.
   b. marginal revenue equals price.
   c. marginal cost equals price.
   d. marginal cost equals demand.
   e. none of the above.

5. Which of the following statements about price and marginal cost in competitive and monopolized markets is true?
   a. In competitive markets, price equals marginal cost; in monopolized markets, price equals marginal cost.
   b. In competitive markets, price exceeds marginal cost; in monopolized markets, price exceeds marginal cost.
   c. In competitive markets, price equals marginal cost; in monopolized markets, price exceeds marginal cost.
   d. In competitive markets, price exceeds marginal cost; in monopolized markets, price equals marginal cost.

6. South-Western is a monopolist in the production of your textbook because
   a. South-Western owns a key resource in the production of textbooks.
   b. South-Western is a natural monopoly.
   c. the government has granted South-Western exclusive rights to produce this textbook.
   d. South-Western is a very large company.

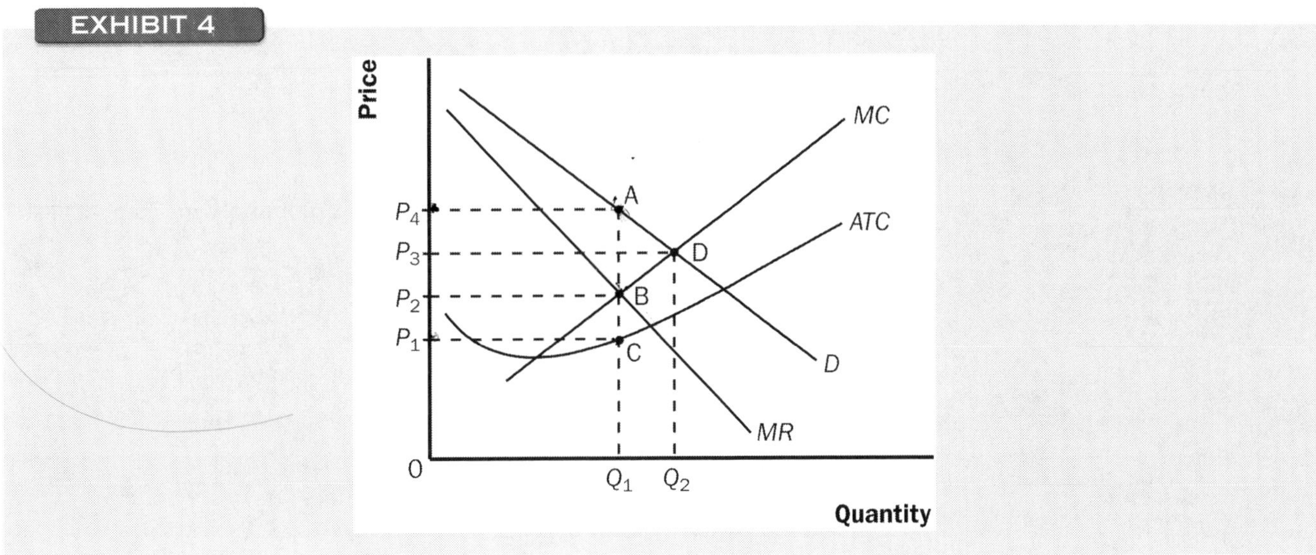

Use Exhibit 4 for the following four questions.

7. The profit-maximizing monopolist will choose the price and quantity represented by point
   a. A.
   b. B.
   c. C.
   d. D.
   e. none of the above.

8. The profit earned by the profit-maximizing monopolist is represented by the area
   a. P_4ABP_2.
   b. P_4ACP_1.
   c. P_4AQ_10.
   d. P_3DQ_20.
   e. none of the above.

9. The deadweight loss associated with monopoly pricing is represented by the area
   a. P_4ABP_2.
   b. P_4ACP_1.
   c. ABD.
   d. P_2BCP_1.
   e. none of the above

10. The efficient price and quantity are represented by point
    a. A.
    b. B.
    c. C.
    d. D.
    e. none of the above

11. The inefficiency associated with monopoly is due to
    a. the monopoly's profits.
    b. the monopoly's losses.
    c. overproduction of the good.
    d. underproduction of the good.

12. Compared to a perfectly competitive market, a monopoly market will usually generate
    a. higher prices and higher output.
    b. higher prices and lower output.
    c. lower prices and lower output.
    d. lower prices and higher output.

13. The monopolist's supply curve
    a. is the marginal cost curve above average variable cost.
    b. is the marginal cost curve above average total cost.
    c. is the upward-sloping portion of the average total cost curve.
    d. is the upward-sloping portion of the average variable cost.
    e. does not exist.

14. Using government regulations to force a natural monopoly to charge a price equal to its marginal cost will
    a. improve efficiency.
    b. raise the price of good.
    c. attract additional firms to enter the market.
    d. cause the monopolist to exit the market.

15. The purpose of antitrust laws is to
    a. regulate the prices charged by a monopoly.
    b. increase competition in an industry by preventing mergers and breaking up large firms.
    c. increase merger activity to help generate synergies that reduce costs and raise efficiency.
    d. create public ownership of natural monopolies.
    e. do all of the above.

16. Public ownership of natural monopolies
    a. tends to be inefficient.
    b. usually lowers the cost of production dramatically.
    c. creates synergies between the newly acquired firm and other government-owned companies.
    d. does none of the above.

17. Which of the follow statements about price discrimination is *not* true?
    a. Price discrimination can raise economic welfare.
    b. Price discrimination requires that the seller be able to separate buyers according to their willingness to pay.
    c. Perfect price discrimination generates a deadweight loss.
    d. Price discrimination increases a monopolist's profits.
    e. For a monopolist to engage in price discrimination, buyers must be unable to engage in arbitrage.

18. If regulators break up a natural monopoly into many smaller firms, the cost of production
    a. will fall.
    b. will rise.
    c. will remain the same.
    d. could either rise or fall depending on the elasticity of the monopolist's supply curve.

19. A monopoly is able to continue to generate economic profits in the long run because
    a. potential competitors sometimes don't notice the profits.
    b. there is some barrier to entry to that market.
    c. the monopolist is financially powerful.
    d. antitrust laws eliminate competitors for a specified number of years.
    e. all of the above

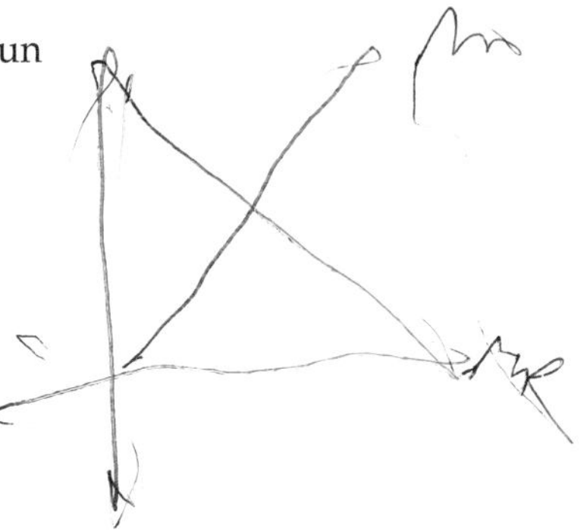

20. If marginal revenue exceeds marginal cost, a monopolists should
    a. increase output.
    b. decrease output.
    c. keep output the same because profits are maximized when marginal revenue exceeds marginal cost.
    d. raise the price.

ADVANCED CRITICAL THINKING

You are watching a television news show. A consumer advocate is discussing the airline industry. He says, "There are so many rates offered by airlines that it is technically possible for a 747 to be carrying a full load of passengers where no two of them paid the same price for their tickets. This is clearly unfair and inefficient." He continues, "In addition, the profits of the airlines have doubled in the last few years since they began this practice and these additional profits are clearly a social burden. We need legislation that requires airlines to charge all passengers on an airplane the same price for their travel."

1. List some of the ways airlines divide their customers according to their willingness to pay.

____

____

____

____

2. Is it necessarily inefficient for airlines to charge different prices to different customers? Why?

____

____

____

____

3. Is the increase in profits generated by this type of price discrimination a social cost? Explain.

____

____

____

____

SOLUTIONS

Terms and Definitions

2 Monopoly

1 Natural monopoly

4 Price discrimination

5 Arbitrage

3 Perfect price discrimination

Practice Problems

1. a. A key resource is owned by a single firm (monopoly resource), the government gives a single firm the exclusive right to produce a good (government created monopoly), the costs of production make a single producer more efficient (natural monopoly).
   b. 1. Natural monopoly. E-mail, Fax machines, telephone, private delivery such as Federal Express.
      2. Monopoly resource. Other bottled water, soft drinks.
      3. Government created monopoly due to a patent. Other drugs for depression, generic drugs when the patent expires.
      4. Monopoly resource. Other gems such as emeralds, rubies, sapphires.
      5. Government created monopoly due to copyright. Other principles of economics texts.
      6. Natural monopoly. Wood burning stoves, gas lanterns, home generators.

2. a.

Pounds of Salmon	Price	($P \times Q$) Total Revenue	($\Delta TR/\Delta Q$) Marginal Revenue
0	$20	0	
			18
1	18	18	
			14
2	16	32	
			10
3	14	42	
			6
4	12	48	
			2
5	10	50	
			–2
6	8	48	
			–6
7	6	42	

EXHIBIT 5

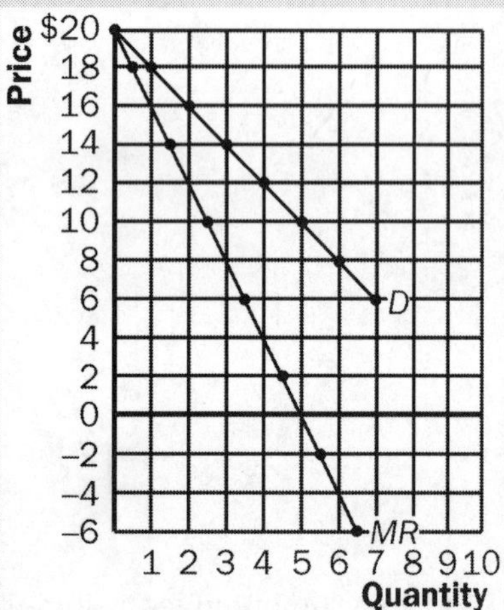

EXHIBIT 6

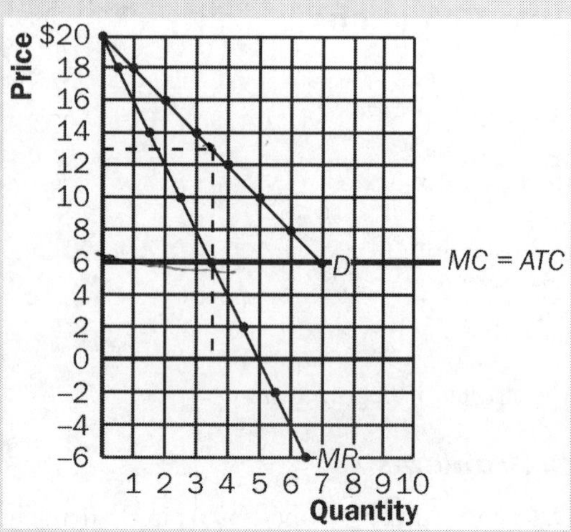

b. See Exhibit 5.

c. Q = between 3 and 4 units (say 3.5), P = between \$12 and \$14, (say \$13). Profit = $TR - TC$ or profit = (3.5 × \$13) – (3.5 × \$6) = \$45.50 – \$21.00 = \$24.50. (Or profit = $(P - ATC) \times Q$ = (\$13 – \$6) × 3.5 = \$24.50.) See Exhibit 6.

d. 7 units at \$6 each. (The efficient solution is where the market produces all units where benefits exceed or equal costs of production which is where demand intersects *MC*.)

e. The monopolist's price is too high and quantity produced too low because the monopolist faces a downward-sloping demand curve that makes $MR < P$. Therefore, when the profit-maximizing monopolist sets $MR = MC$ and the *MR* curve is below the demand curve, the quantity is less than optimal and the price charged exceeds the *MC* of production.

f. Yes. Units from 3.5 to 7, or an additional 3.5 pounds of salmon are valued by the consumer at values in excess of the \$6 per pound *MC* of production and these units are not produced and consumed when the price is \$13. (Deadweight loss = the deadweight loss triangle = 1/2 (7 – 3.5) × (\$13 – \$6) = \$12.25.)

g. Yes, all units are produced where the value to buyers is greater than or is equal to the cost of production (7 units). Total surplus is now producer surplus and there is no consumer surplus. Total surplus and producer surplus is the area under the demand curve and above the price or 1/2 (\$20 – \$6) × 7 = \$49. Consumer surplus = \$0.

EXHIBIT 7

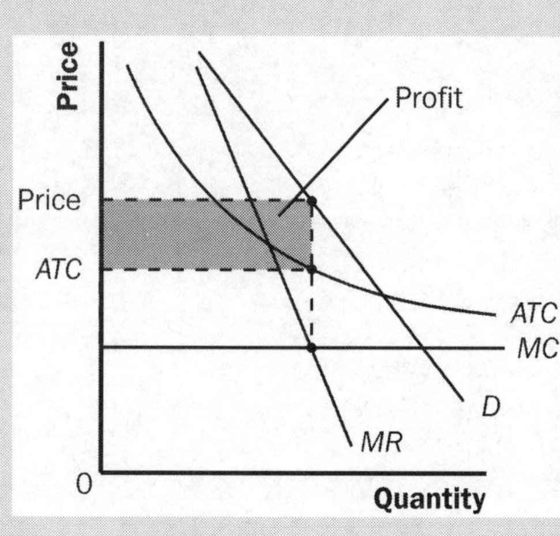

3. a. Natural monopoly because *ATC* is still declining at the quantity that could satisfy the entire market.

   b. See Exhibit 7.

c. See Exhibit 8.

d. No. Since marginal cost must be below average total cost if average total cost is declining, this firm will generate losses if forced to charge a price equal to marginal cost. It will simply exit the market, which eliminates all surplus associated with this market.

EXHIBIT 8

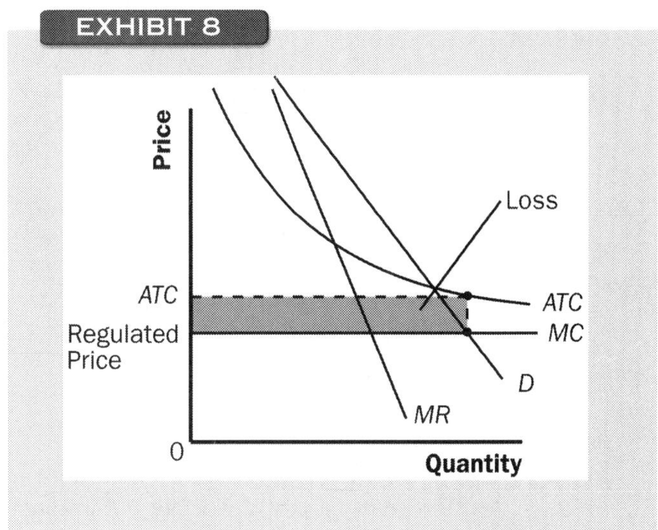

Short-Answer Questions

1. Anything that restricts new firms from entering a market. A key resource is owned by a single firm, the government gives a single firm the exclusive right to produce a good, or the costs of production make a single producer more efficient than a large number of producers.

2. No. The monopolist will generate losses and will exit the market.

3. No. Even a monopolist is subject to the demand for its product so a high price would cause buyers to buy very little of the good. The monopolist chooses its price by first choosing the optimal quantity based on the intersection of *MR* and *MC* and then charging the price consistent with that quantity.

4. For a monopolist, $P > MR$ because for a monopolist to sell another unit, it must reduce the price on the marginal unit *and all of its previous units*. Therefore, while a monopolist equates *MR* and *MC*, it charges a price that is greater than *MC*, which causes consumers to buy less than the efficient amount of the good.

5. No. The monopolist's profits are a redistribution of consumer surplus to producer surplus. The social cost of monopoly is the deadweight loss associated with the reduced production of output.

6. Try to make monopolized industries more competitive, regulate the behavior of the monopolies, turn private monopolies into public enterprises, or do nothing at all.

7. No, many mergers capture synergies between the merging firms that reduce costs and increase efficiency.

8. The monopolist may lose money and exit the market. Subsidies to prevent this require taxes that also generate deadweight losses. Regulated monopolists have little incentive to reduce costs.

9. Yes, because every unit is produced where the value to buyers is greater than or equal to the cost to the producer. However, the entire total surplus is received by the producer (the monopolist).

10. The monopolist must be able to separate buyers according to their willingness to pay.

True/False Questions

1. F; monopolists are price makers.

2. F; owning a key resource is the rarest source of barriers to entry.

3. T

4. F; a natural monopoly is a firm with an average total cost curve that continually declines at least to the quantity that satisfies the entire market.

5. T

6. T

7. T

8. F; monopolists have no supply curve.

9. F; the inefficiency generated by a monopoly results from the failure of the monopolist to produce units of output where the value to consumers equals or exceeds the cost of production. The monopolist's profits are not a cost to society but are just a redistribution from consumer surplus to producer surplus.

10. T

11. F; economists usually prefer private ownership to public ownership because private owners have a greater incentive to reduce costs.

12. T

13. T

14. F; all of the surplus is received by the producer.

15. T

Multiple-Choice Questions

1. d	5. c	9. c	13. e	17. c
2. b	6. c	10. d	14. d	18. b
3. d	7. a	11. d	15. b	19. b
4. a	8. b	12. b	16. a	20. a

Advanced Critical Thinking

1. Airlines segment people by age (young and old fly cheaper), by location (more competitive routes are cheaper), by length of time between leaving and returning (tourists fly cheaper than business travelers), by length of time of advance booking (later bookings can be more expensive until the very last minute when it may become cheaper again) and so on.

2. No. Price discrimination can improve efficiency. By charging buyers their willingness to pay, the monopolist increases production to the point where all units are produced where the value to buyers is greater than or equal to the cost of production.

3. No. Some of the additional profits are from the creation of additional surplus that accrues entirely to the producer and some of the profits are a redistribution of surplus from consumer surplus to producer surplus.

16

OLIGOPOLY

GOALS

In this chapter you will

See what market structures lie between monopoly and competition

Examine what outcomes are possible when a market is an oligopoly

Learn about the prisoners' dilemma and how it applies to oligopoly and other issues

Consider how the antitrust laws try to foster competition in oligopolistic markets

OUTCOMES

After accomplishing these goals, you should be able to

Describe the characteristics of oligopoly and monopolistic competition

Describe the conditions under which an oligopolistic market generates the same outcome as a monopolistic market

Show why the outcome of the prisoners' dilemma may change if the game is repeated

Show why some business practices that appear to reduce competition may have a legitimate business purpose

CHAPTER OVERVIEW

Context and Purpose

Chapter 16 is the fourth chapter in a five-chapter sequence dealing with firm behavior and the organization of industry. The previous two chapters discussed the two extreme forms of market structure—competition and monopoly. The market structure that lies between competition and monopoly is known as *imperfect competition*. There are two types of imperfect competition—oligopoly and monopolistic competition. Chapter 16 addresses oligopoly while the final chapter in this sequence, Chapter 17, addresses monopolistic competition.

The purpose of Chapter 16 is to discuss *oligopoly*—a market structure in which only a few sellers offer similar or identical products. Since there are only a few sellers in an oligopolistic market, oligopolistic firms are interdependent while competitive firms are not. That is, in a competitive market, the decisions of one firm have no impact on the other firms in the market while in an oligopolistic market, the decisions of any one firm may affect the pricing and production decisions of the other firms in the market.

CHAPTER REVIEW

Introduction

The market structure that lies between competition and monopoly is known as *imperfect competition*. One type of imperfectly competitive market is **oligopoly**—a market structure in which only a few sellers offer similar or identical products. Oligopoly differs from competition because in a competitive market the decisions of one firm have no impact on the other firms in the market while in an oligopolistic market, the decisions of any one firm may affect the pricing and production decisions of other firms in the market. Oligopolistic firms are interdependent.

Between Monopoly and Perfect Competition

Competitive firms charge a price equal to marginal cost and, in the long run, this is equal to average total cost, causing each firm to earn no economic profits. A monopolist charges a price that exceeds marginal cost. This reduces output and causes a deadweight loss. The market structure that lies between the extremes of competition and monopoly and contains elements of both is known as imperfect competition. There are two types of imperfect competition—oligopoly and monopolistic competition. *Oligopoly* is a market structure in which only a few sellers offer similar or identical products. **Monopolistic competition** is a market structure in which many firms sell products that are similar but not identical. To summarize the distinguishing characteristics of the various market structures:

- Monopoly has only one firm,
- Oligopoly has a few firms selling similar or identical products,
- Perfect competition has many firms selling identical products,
- Monopolistic competition has many firms selling differentiated products.

It is often difficult to decide which structure best describes a particular market.

Markets with Only a Few Sellers

A *duopoly* is an oligopoly with only two firms. If a market were perfectly competitive, the price of output would equal marginal cost. If a market were monopolistic, the profit-maximizing price would exceed marginal cost and the result would be inefficient.

Collusion is an agreement among firms in a market about quantities to produce or prices to charge. A **cartel** is a group of firms acting in unison. If duopolists collude and form a cartel, the market solution is the same as if it were served by a monopolist and the two firms divide the monopoly profits.

Oligopolists may fail to cooperate because antitrust laws prohibit collusion or because self-interest makes it difficult to agree on how to divide the profits. Without a binding agreement, each oligopolist will maximize its profit given the production levels of the other firms. A **Nash equilibrium** is a situation in which economic actors interacting with one another each choose their best strategy given the strategies that all the other actors have chosen. A Nash equilibrium is a type of oligopolistic equilibrium. When oligopolists individually choose production levels to maximize individual profits, they produce a quantity that is greater than the level produced by monopoly but less than that produced by competition and they will charge a price that is less than the monopoly price but greater than the competitive price.

The larger the oligopoly (more firms) the more difficult it is for them to form a cartel and behave as a monopolist. If they each choose their own level of production to maximize individual profits, they will make the marginal decision of whether to produce an additional unit based on the following:

- *The output effect*: Because price is above marginal cost, selling one more unit at the going price will raise profit.

- *The price effect*: Raising production one unit will increase the total sold but it will lower the price and the profit on all of the other units sold.

If the output effect exceeds the price effect, the oligopolist will produce another unit and it will continue to expand output until these two effects balance. The greater the number of sellers in an oligopoly, the smaller the price effect because each individual firm's impact on the price is small. Thus, the level of output increases. As the number of sellers in an oligopoly grows larger, the price approaches marginal cost and the quantity approaches the socially efficient level. When there are a large number of firms, the price effect disappears altogether and the market becomes competitive.

Unrestricted international trade increases the number of firms in domestic oligopolies and moves the outcome of the market closer to the competitive solution where prices are equal to marginal cost.

Two examples of cartels are the Atlantic shipping cartels that set the prices for cargo shipping across the Atlantic and OPEC (Organization of Petroleum Exporting Countries) which limits the production of oil. Oligopolies may become a larger portion of the economy because high tech industries have high fixed costs and small marginal costs, so mergers are particularly attractive. We observe this effect in cable television, publishing, and Web site providers.

Game Theory and the Economics of Cooperation

Game theory is the study of how people behave in strategic situations. Strategic situations are when decision makers must consider how others might respond to their actions. The **prisoners' dilemma** is a particular "game" between two captured prisoners that illustrates why cooperation is difficult to maintain even when it is mutually beneficial. The game applies to oligopoly because oligopolistic firms would always be better off to cooperate yet they often do not.

An example of a prisoners' dilemma is the following: Two criminals are captured. If one confesses and the other does not, the confessor goes free while the other receives a long sentence. If both confess they each receive an intermediate term. If neither confess, they each receive a very short term. If the two could cooperate, the best strategy is for each to keep quiet. However, since they cannot guarantee cooperation after they are caught, the best strategy for each is to confess. That is, confessing is a **dominant strategy**—a strategy that is best for a player in a game regardless of the strategies chosen by the other players.

The prisoners' dilemma applies to oligopoly in the following manner: Two oligopolists are better off if they cooperate by keeping production low and sharing the monopoly profits. However, after the agreement is made, the dominant strategy for each is to cheat and produce more than they agreed to produce to enhance their individual profits. The result is that profits fall for both. Self-interest makes it difficult to maintain cooperation.

The prisoners' dilemma applies to:

- *Arms races:* Each country prefers to live in a safe world but the dominant strategy is to increase armaments and the world is less safe.

- *Advertising:* Each firm prefers to not advertise and simply divide the market and the large profits but the dominant strategy is to advertise and joint profits fall.

- *Common resources:* Users of a common resource would find it more profitable to jointly limit their use of the resource but the dominant strategy is to overuse the resource and joint profits fall.

Lack of cooperation in the cases above is harmful to society. However, lack of cooperation between oligopolists regarding the level of production may be bad for the oligopolists but it is good from the standpoint of society as a whole.

While cooperation is difficult to maintain, it is not impossible. If the game is repeated, the prisoners' dilemma can be solved and agreements can be maintained. For example, oligopolies may include a penalty for violation of the agreement. If the penalty is that they all maintain high production forever if someone cheats, then all should maintain low production levels and share monopoly profits. If the game is played on a periodic basis (each week, month, or year new production levels are chosen) then a simple strategy of tit-for-tat generates the greatest likelihood of cooperation. *Tit-for-tat* is when a player in a game starts by cooperating and then does whatever the other player did last period. If the other player cooperated, then cooperate the next period. If the other player defected (cheated), then cheat the next period, and so on.

Public Policy toward Oligopolies

Since cooperating oligopolists reduce output and raise prices, policymakers try to induce firms in an oligopoly market to compete rather than cooperate. The Sherman Antitrust Act of 1890 makes agreements to not compete (to reduce quantities or raise prices) a criminal conspiracy. The Clayton Act of 1914 allows individuals harmed by such agreements the right to sue for triple damages. Price fixing clearly reduces economic welfare and is illegal.

There is some disagreement over the use of antitrust laws against some business practices that appear like price fixing. For example:

- *Resale price maintenance* or *fair trade* is when a manufacturer requires retailers to charge a certain price. This appears to prevent retailers from competing on price. However, some economists defend the practice as legitimate because (1) if the manufacturer has market power, it is at wholesale not retail, and the manufacturer would not gain from eliminating competition at the retail level, and (2) resale price maintenance stops discount retailers from free riding on the services provided by full service retailers.

- *Predatory pricing* occurs when a firm cuts prices with the intention of driving competitors out of the market so that the firm can become a monopolist and later raise prices. Some economists think that this behavior is unlikely because it hurts the firm that is engaged in predatory pricing the most.

- *Tying* occurs when a manufacturer bundles two products together and sells them for one price. Courts argue that tying gives the firm more market power by connecting a weak product with a strong product. Some economists disagree. They suggest that it allows the firm to price discriminate, which may actually increase efficiency. Tying remains controversial.

An antitrust case has been brought against Microsoft for tying its browser to its operating system. Some economists argue that future antitrust suits should take into account that the new high tech industries may be natural monopolies – firms whose costs continue to decline at least to the quantity that satisfies the entire market.

Conclusion

Oligopolies will look more like a competitive market if there are a large number of firms and more like a monopoly if there are a small number of firms. The prisoners' dilemma shows why cooperation is difficult to maintain even when it is in the best interest of the oligopolists. The use of antitrust laws against price fixing improves economic efficiency but their use in other areas is more controversial.

HELPFUL HINTS

1. Oligopoly lies between monopoly and perfect competition. If oligopolists are able to collude and form a cartel, the market solution is the same as that for a monopoly. If oligopolists are unable to collude and form a cartel, the production and pricing in the market depends on the number of firms. The fewer the number of firms, the more the result appears like monopoly where the price exceeds marginal cost and the quantity is below the efficient level. The greater the number of firms, the more the result appears like competition where the price equals marginal cost and the quantity is efficient.

TERMS AND DEFINITIONS

Choose a definition for each key term.

Key terms:

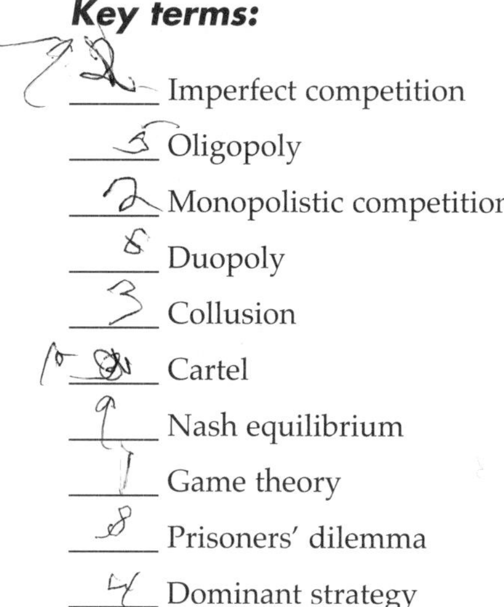

_____ Imperfect competition
_____ Oligopoly
_____ Monopolistic competition
_____ Duopoly
_____ Collusion
_____ Cartel
_____ Nash equilibrium
_____ Game theory
_____ Prisoners' dilemma
_____ Dominant strategy

Definitions:

1. The study of how people behave in strategic situations
2. A market structure in which many firms sell products that are similar but not identical
3. An agreement among firms in a market about quantities to produce or prices to charge
4. A strategy that is best for a player in a game regardless of the strategies chosen by the other players
5. The market structure that lies between competition and monopoly
6. An oligopoly with only two firms
7. A market structure in which only a few sellers offer similar or identical products
8. A particular "game" between two captured prisoners that illustrates why cooperation is difficult to maintain even when it is mutually beneficial
9. A situation in which economic actors interacting with one another each choose their best strategy given the strategies that all the other actors have chosen
10. A group of firms acting in unison

PROBLEMS AND SHORT-ANSWER QUESTIONS

Practice Problems

1. In which market structure would you place each of the following products—monopoly, oligopoly, monopolistic competition, or perfect competition? Why?
   a. Retail market for electricity

   ____

   b. Principles of economics textbooks

   ____

   c. *Principles of Economics,* by N. Gregory Mankiw

   ____

   d. Photographic film

   ____

   e. Retail market for gasoline

   ____

   f. Restaurants in a large city

   ____

   g. Auto tires

   ____

   h. Trash collection

   ____

   i. Legal services in a metropolitan area

   ____

   j. Breakfast cereal

   ____

   k. Gold bullion

   ____

   l. Air travel from any one airport

   ____

2. The following information describes the demand schedule for a unique type of apple. This type of apple can only be produced by two firms because they own the land on which these unique trees spontaneously grow. As a result, the marginal cost of production is zero for these duopolists, causing total revenue to equal profit.
   a. Complete the following table.

Price per bushel	Quantity (in bushels)	Total revenue (profit)
$12	0	0
11	5	55
10	10	100
9	15	______
8	20	______
7	25	______
6	30	______
5	35	______
4	40	______
3	45	______
2	50	100
1	55	55
0	60	0

   b. If the market were perfectly competitive, what price and quantity would be generated by this market? Explain.

____

____

   c. If these two firms colluded and formed a cartel, what price and quantity would be generated by this market, what is the level of profit generated by the market, and what is the level of profit generated by each firm?

____

____

____

____

d. If one firm cheats and produces one additional increment (five units) of production, what is the level of profit generated by each firm?

____

e. If both firms cheat and each produces one additional increment (five units) of production (compared to the cooperative solution), what is the level of profit generated by each firm?

____

f. If both firms are cheating and producing one additional increment of output (five additional units compared to the cooperative solution), will either firm choose to produce an additional increment (five more units)? Why? What is the value of the Nash equilibrium in this duopoly market?

____

____

____

g. Compare the competitive equilibrium to the Nash equilibrium. In which situation is society better off? Explain.

____

____

h. What would happen to the price and quantity in this market (qualitatively) if an additional firm were able to grow these unique apples?

____

____

EXHIBIT 1

		Firm 1 Decision	
		Sell 15	**Sell 20**
Firm 2 Decision	**Sell 15**		
	Sell 20		

Use the data from the duopoly example above to fill in the boxes of the prisoners' dilemma. Place the value of the profits earned by each duopolist in the appropriate box in Exhibit 1.

j. What is the solution to this prisoners' dilemma? Explain.

k. What might the solution be if the participants were able to repeat the "game?" Why? What simple strategy might they use to maintain their cartel?

Short-Answer Questions

1. What are the two types of imperfect competition? Describe them.

2. The market for vitamins and dietary supplements is dominated by five firms. What type of market structure does it represent? Explain.

3. What is the outcome in an oligopolistic market if the oligopolists collude and form a cartel? Explain.

4. Suppose a group of oligopolists do not collude but instead reach a Nash equilibrium. What price and quantity will result in this oligopolist market when compared to the monopolistic or competitive result?

5. Referring to question 4 above, what would happen to the price and quantity in the Nash equilibrium if an additional firm were to join the oligopoly? Why?

6. If oligopolists would be better off if they collude, why do they so often fail to cooperate?

7. Is it better for society as a whole if oligopolists cooperate? Explain. What measures do we take to try to prevent cooperation between oligopolists?

8. Suppose High-Tech Software sells two products—a word processing package and a spreadsheet package. Suppose that the business community values the word processing package at $100 per unit and the spreadsheet package at $250 per unit while the university community values the word processing package at $125 and the spreadsheet at $200. (Assume that the marginal cost of each unit is zero). What are the profit-maximizing prices that High-Tech should charge if they sell each product separately and what is the total price of the two goods? If High-Tech is able to engage in tying, what is the profit-maximizing price for the two products as a bundle? Should this be legal?

SELF-TEST

True/False Questions

______1. An oligopoly is a market structure in which many firms sell products that are similar but not identical.

______2. The market for crude oil is an example of an oligopolistic market.

______3. The unique feature of an oligopoly market is that the actions of one seller have a significant impact on the profits of all of the other sellers in the market.

______4. When firms cooperate with one another, it is generally good for society as a whole.

______5. When firms cooperate with one another, it is generally good for the cooperating firms.

______6. When oligopolists collude and form a cartel, the outcome in the market is similar to that generated by a perfectly competitive market.

______7. The price and quantity generated by a Nash equilibrium is closer to the competitive solution than the price and quantity generated by a cartel.

______8. The greater the number of firms in the oligopoly, the more the outcome of the market looks like that generated by a monopoly.

______9. Cooperation is easily maintained in an oligopoly because cooperation maximizes each individual firm's profits.

______10. The prisoners' dilemma demonstrates why it is difficult to maintain cooperation even when cooperation is mutually beneficial.

______11. There is a constant tension in an oligopoly between cooperation and self-interest because after an agreement to reduce production is reached, it is profitable for each individual firm to cheat and produce more.

______12. The dominant strategy for an oligopolist is to cooperate with the group and maintain low production regardless of what the other oligopolists do.

______13. Antitrust laws require manufacturers to engage in *resale price maintenance* or *fair trade.*

______14. Predatory pricing occurs when a firm cuts prices with the intention of driving competitors out of the market so that the firm can become a monopolist and later raise prices.

______15. If a prisoners' dilemma game is repeated, the participants are more likely to independently maximize their profits and reach a Nash equilibrium.

Multiple-Choice Questions

1. The market for hand tools (such as hammers and screwdrivers) is dominantd by Black & Decker, Stanley, and Craftsman. This market is best described as
   a. competitive.
   b. a monopoly.
   c. an oligopoly.
   d. monopolistically competitive.

2. A market structure in which many firms sell products that are similar but not identical is known as
   a. perfect competition.
   b. monopoly.
   c. oligopoly.
   d. monopolistic competition.

3. If oligopolists engage in collusion and successfully form a cartel, the market outcome is
   a. the same as if it were served by a monopoly.
   b. the same as if it were served by competitive firms.
   c. efficient because cooperation improves efficiency.
   d. known as a Nash equilibrium.

4. Suppose an oligopolist individually maximizes its profits. When calculating profits, if the output effect exceeds the price effect on the marginal unit of production, then the oligopolist
   a. has maximized profits.
   b. should produce more units.
   c. should produce fewer units.
   d. should exit the industry.
   e. is in a Nash equilibrium.

5. As the number of sellers in an oligopoly grow larger, an oligopolistic market looks more like
   a. monopoly.
   b. monopolistic competition.
   c. a competitive market.
   d. a collusion solution.

6. When an oligopolist individually chooses its level of production to maximize its profits, it produces an output that is
   a. more than the level produced by a monopoly and less than the level produced by a competitive market.
   b. less than the level produced by a monopoly and more than the level produced by a competitive market.
   c. more than the level produced by either monopoly or a competitive market.
   d. less than the level produce by either monopoly or a competitive market.

7. When an oligopolist individually chooses its level of production to maximize its profits, it charges a price that is
   a. more than the price charged by a monopoly and less than the price charged by a competitive market.
   b. less than the price charged by a monopoly and more than the price charged by a competitive market.
   c. more than the price charged by either monopoly or a competitive market.
   d. less than the price charged by either monopoly or a competitive market.

8. As the number of sellers in an oligopoly increases,
   a. collusion is more likely to occur because a larger number of firms can place pressure on any firm that defects.
   b. output in the market tends to fall because each firm must cut back on production.
   c. the price in the market moves further from marginal cost.
   d. the price in the market moves closer to marginal cost.

9. A situation in which oligopolists interacting with one another each choose their best strategy given the strategies that all the other oligopolists have chosen is known as a
   a. collusion solution.
   b. cartel.
   c. Nash equilibrium.
   d. dominant strategy.

Use the table below for the following four questions. The table shows the demand schedule for tickets to watch amateur baseball games in a medium-sized town. The city provides the ball parks and the players play for free so the marginal cost of providing the games is zero. The city has authorized two companies to provide baseball games in two stadiums and the public considers the games in each stadium to be equivalent.

Price	Quantity
$6	0
5	1,000
4	2,000
3	3,000
2	4,000
1	5,000
0	6,000

10. Under competition, the price and quantity in this market would be
    a. $4; 2,000.
    b. $3; 3,000.
    c. $2; 4,000.
    d. $1; 5,000.
    e. $0; 6,000.

11. If the duopolists in this baseball market collude and successfully form a cartel, what is the price that each should charge in order to maximize profits?
    a. $5
    b. $4
    c. $3
    d. $2
    e. $1

12. If the duopolists in this baseball market collude and successfully form a cartel, how much profit will *each* earn?
    a. $1,500
    b. $3,000
    c. $4,000
    d. $4,500
    e. $9,000

13. If the duopolists are unable to collude, how much profit will *each* earn when the market reaches a Nash equilibrium?
    a. $2,500
    b. $4,000
    c. $4,500
    d. $8,000
    e. $9,000

Use the prisoners' dilemma game in Exhibit 2 to answer the next two questions. It shows the possible profits for duopolists that are the only two restaurants in town. Each firm can choose how many hours to be open for business.

EXHIBIT 2

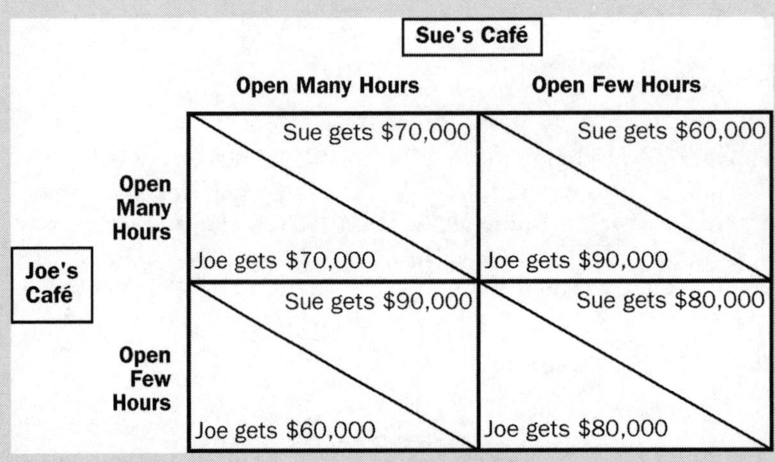

14. The dominant strategy for Sue and Joe is for
    a. both to be open for many hours.
    b. both to be open for few hours.
    c. Sue to be open for many hours while Joe is open for few hours.
    d. Sue to be open for few hours while Joe is open for many hours.
    e. There is no dominant strategy in this prisoners' dilemma game.

15. Suppose Sue and Joe agreed to collude and jointly maximize their profits. If Sue and Joe were to be able to repeatedly play the game shown above and they agreed on a penalty for defecting from their agreement, what is the likely outcome of the game?
    a. Both are open for many hours.
    b. Both are open for few hours.
    c. Sue is open for many hours while Joe is open for few hours.
    d. Sue is open for few hours while Joe is open for many hours.

16. Many economists argue that resale price maintenance
    a. is price fixing and, therefore, is prohibited by law.
    b. enhances the market power of the producer.
    c. has a legitimate purpose of stopping discount retailers from free riding on the services provided by full service retailers.
    d. both (a) and (b)

17. Collusion is difficult for an oligopoly to maintain
    a. because antitrust laws make collusion illegal.
    b. because, in the case of oligopoly, self-interest is in conflict with cooperation.
    c. if additional firms enter of the oligopoly.
    d. all of the above.

Use the following information for the next two questions: Suppose that ABC Publishing sells an economics textbook and accompanying study guide. Bob is willing to pay $75 for the text and $15 for the study guide. Mary is willing to spend $60 for the text and $25 for the study guide. Suppose both the book and study guide have a zero marginal cost of production.

18. If ABC Publishing charges separate prices for both products, its best strategy is to charge prices that, when combined, total
    a. $60.
    b. $75.
    c. $80.
    d. $85.
    e. $90.

19. If ABC Publishing engages in tying, its best strategy is to charge a combined price of
    a. $60.
    b. $75.
    c. $80.
    d. $85.
    e. $90.

20. Laws that make it illegal for firms to conspire to raise prices or reduce production are known as
    a. pro-competition laws.
    b. antitrust laws.
    c. antimonopoly laws.
    d. anticollusion laws.
    e. all of the above.

ADVANCED CRITICAL THINKING

You are watching television. An advertisement begins, "Come on down to Warehouse Electronics. We've got deals so great you won't believe it! National brand 13-inch color television sets for $99. The price is so low that we can't tell you the name of the manufacturer!"

1. Why would Warehouse Electronics be unable to reveal the name of the manufacturer when it advertises its television sets for an unusually low price?

2. Although this activity appears like price fixing, is the objective of this practice to reduce competition? Why?

3. Why would the manufacturer place this type of restriction on the retailers that sell its products?

SOLUTIONS

Terms and Definitions

5 Imperfect competition

7 Oligopoly

2 Monopolistic competition

6 Duopoly

3 Collusion

10 Cartel

9 Nash equilibrium

1 Game theory

8 Prisoners' dilemma

4 Dominant strategy

Practice Problems

1. a. Monopoly, only one firm from which to purchase.
   b. Monopolistic competition, many firms each selling differentiated products.
   c. Monopoly, only one firm can produce it due to copyright laws.
   d. Oligopoly, few firms (Fuji, Kodak) selling similar products.
   e. Perfect competition, many firms selling identical products.
   f. Monopolistic competition, many firms each selling differentiated products.
   g. Oligopoly, few firms (Goodyear, Firestone, Michelin) selling very similar products.
   h. Monopoly, only one firm from which to purchase.
   i. Monopolistic competition, many firms each selling differentiated products.
   j. Oligopoly, few firms (Kellogg's, Post, General Mills, Quaker Oats) selling similar products.
   k. Perfect competition, many firms selling identical products.
   l. Oligopoly, few airlines from which to choose at any one airport, similar product.

Note: While monopoly and competition are more easily distinguished, the line between oligopoly and monopolistic competition is not as sharp. For example, (b) might be considered to be an oligopoly since there are relatively few publishers and economic text books may be considered to be very similar, and (j) might be considered to be monopolistic competition if the products are considered to be differentiated, and so on.

2. a.

Price per Bushel	Quantity (in bushels)	Total Revenue (profit)
$12	0	$ 0
11	5	55
10	10	100
9	15	135
8	20	160
7	25	175
6	30	180
5	35	175
4	40	160
3	45	135
2	50	100
1	55	55
0	60	0

b. In a competitive market, competition reduces the price until it equals marginal cost (which is zero in this case), therefore $P = \$0$ and $Q = 60$.

c. These duopolists would behave as a monopolist, produce at the level that maximizes profit, and agree to divide the production levels and profit. Therefore, $P = \$6$, $Q = 30$ for the market. Profit = $\$6 \times 30 = \$180$. Each firm produces 15 units at $6 and receives profit of $90 (half of the $180).

d. Cheating firm: $20 \times \$5 = \$100$, other firm: $15 \times \$5 = \$75$.

e. Each firm: $20 \times \$4 = \$80$.

f. No, because the profit would fall for the cheater to $25 \times \$3 = \$75$ which is below $80 profit from part (e) above. Therefore, the Nash equilibrium is each firm producing 20 units (40 for the market) at a price of $4, creating $160 of profit for the market and each duopolist receives $80 profit.

g. The Nash equilibrium has a higher price ($4 compared to $0) and a smaller quantity (40 units compared to 60 units). Society is better off with competitive equilibrium.

h. The new Nash equilibrium would have a lower price and a larger quantity. It would move toward the competitive solution.

i. See Exhibit 3.

EXHIBIT 3

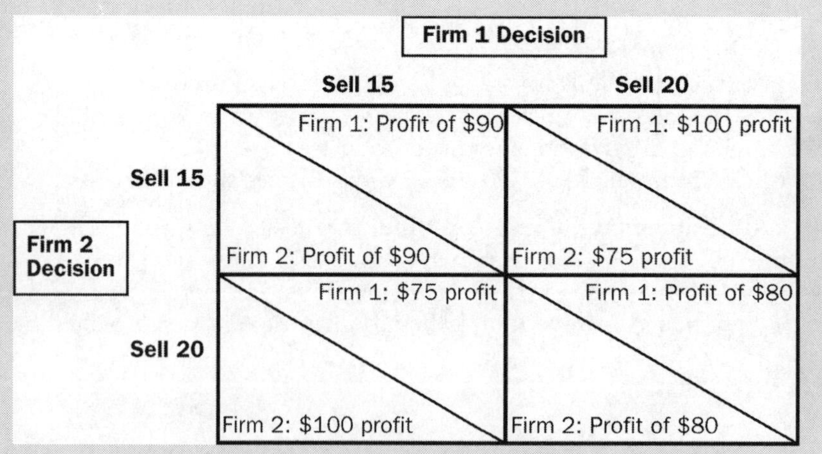

j. The dominant strategy for each is to cheat and sell 20 units because each firm's profit is greater when it sells 20 units regardless of whether the other firm sells 15 or 20 units.

k. They might be able to maintain the cooperative (monopoly) production level of 30 units and each produce 15 units because if the game is repeated, the participants can devise a penalty for cheating. The simplest penalty is "tit-for-tat."

Short-Answer Questions

1. Oligopoly and monopolistic competition. Oligopoly is a market structure in which only a few sellers offer similar or identical products. Monopolistic competition is when many firms sell products that are similar but not identical.

2. Oligopoly, because there are few firms and the products are similar or identical.

3. The outcome is the same as if the market were served by a monopolist. Monopoly profits are divided among the firms and production levels are limited by agreement to the level that a monopoly would produce.

4. The price will be lower than monopoly but higher than competition. The quantity sold will be greater than monopoly but less than competition.

5. The price would fall and the quantity sold would rise. This is because with the addition of another firm, the individual firm's impact on the price is reduced, which causes the output effect to exceed the price effect and the profit-maximizing output level of the group is increased. As members are added, the outcome approaches a competitive solution.

6. Once an agreement to reduce production is made, it is always profitable for the individual firm to cheat and produce in excess of the agreement regardless of whether the others cheat or maintain the agreement. Cheating is a dominant strategy. This is the prisoners' dilemma.

7. It is better if they do not cooperate because the Nash equilibrium is closer to the efficient competitive solution than the monopoly solution would have been. Anti-trust laws make it illegal for firms to make agreements not to compete.

8. Word processing price = $100, spreadsheet price = $200, total = $300. If tying the two together, price = $325. Maybe, because it may be just a method of price discrimination which, recall, increases total surplus (is more efficient) but it moves surplus from the consumer to the producer.

True/False Questions

1. F; an oligopoly is where a few sellers offer similar or identical products.

2. T

3. T

4. F; it raises prices above marginal cost and reduces output below the socially optimal level.

5. T

6. F; it is the same as that generated by a monopoly.

7. T

8. F; the greater the number of firms, the more the market approaches the competitive solution.

9. F; cooperation maximizes the profits of the group and the individual firms if none of the oligopolists violate the agreement. However, once the agreement is made, an individual firm will increase its profits if it cheats and produces more.

10. T

11. T

12. F; the dominant strategy is to increase production regardless of the choices of the other firms.

13. F; sometimes courts view retail price maintenance as price fixing and declare it illegal.

14. T

15. F; repeated games are more likely to generate cooperation because a penalty for cheating can be enforced.

Multiple-Choice Questions

1. c	5. c	9. c	13. b	17. d
2. d	6. a	10. e	14. a	18. b
3. a	7. b	11. c	15. b	19. d
4. b	8. d	12. d	16. c	20. b

Advanced Critical Thinking

1. The manufacturer may be engaging in "resale price maintenance" or "fair trade" practices with its retailers (including Warehouse Electronics). This may restrict the retailer's right to advertise a price below the suggested retail price for the product.

2. No, because any reduction in competition at the retail level generates market power for the retailer and fewer units will be sold. This is not in the interest of the manufacturer.

3. The purpose is to stop discount retailers from free riding on the services provided by full service retailers—retailers with a knowledgeable sales force, a repair shop, and so on.

17

MONOPOLISTIC COMPETITION

GOALS

In this chapter you will

- Analyze competition among firms that sell differentiated products
- Compare the outcome under monopolistic competition and under perfect competition
- Consider the desirability of outcomes in monopolistically competitive markets
- Examine the debate over the effects of advertising
- Examine the debate over the role of brand names

OUTCOMES

After accomplishing these goals, you should be able to

- Show the long-run adjustment that takes place in a monopolistically competitive market when a firm generates economic profits
- Show why monopolistically competitive firms produce at less than efficient scale in the long run
- Discuss the inefficiencies of monopolistically competitive markets
- Provide an argument in support of and in opposition to the use of advertising
- Provide an argument in support of and in opposition to the use of brand names

CHAPTER OVERVIEW

Context and Purpose

Chapter 17 is the final chapter in a five-chapter sequence dealing with firm behavior and the organization of industry. Chapters 14 and 15 developed the two extreme forms of market structure—competition and monopoly. The market structure that lies between competition and monopoly is known as imperfect competition. There are two types of imperfect competition—oligopoly, which we addressed in the previous chapter, and monopolistic competition, which is the topic of the current chapter. The analysis in this chapter is again based on the cost curves developed in Chapter 13.

The purpose of Chapter 17 is to address *monopolistic competition*—a market structure in which many firms sell products that are similar but not identical. Recall, oligopoly differs from perfect competition because there are only a few sellers in the market. Monopolistic competition differs from perfect competition because each of the many sellers offers a somewhat different product. As a result, monopolistically competitive firms face a downward-sloping demand curve while competitive firms face a horizontal demand curve at the market price. Monopolistic competition is extremely common.

CHAPTER REVIEW

Introduction

Monopolistic competition shares some features of competition and monopoly:

- *Many sellers:* This is in common with competition.
- *Product differentiation:* This is in common with monopoly—each firm's product is slightly different so each firm is a price maker and faces a downward-sloping demand for its product.
- *Free entry:* This is in common with competition—firms can enter or exit without restriction so economic profits are driven to zero.

Examples of monopolistically competitive markets are the market for books, CDs, movies, restaurants, and so on. Monopolistically competitive markets are common.

Oligopoly differs from perfect competition because there are only a few sellers in the market. Monopolistic competition differs from perfect competition because each of the many sellers offers a somewhat different product. As a result, monopolistically competitive firms face a downward-sloping demand curve while competitive firms face a horizontal demand curve at the market price.

Competition with Differentiated Products

Similar to a monopolist, a monopolistically competitive firm faces a downward-sloping demand curve for its product. Therefore, it follows the same rule for profit maximization as a monopolist—it produces the quantity at which marginal cost equals marginal revenue and then uses the demand curve to determine the price consistent with this quantity. In the short run, if the price exceeds average total cost, the firm makes economic profits. If the price is below average total cost, the firm generates losses.

As in a competitive market, if the firm is making profits, new firms have incentive to enter the market. Entry reduces the demand faced by each firm already in the market (shifts their demand curves to the left) and reduces their profits in the long run. If the firm is generating losses, incumbent firms have incentive to exit the market. Exit increases the demand faced by each firm that remains in the market (shifts their demand curves to the right) and reduces their losses. Entry and exit continues until the firms in the market are making zero economic profits. In long-run equilibrium, the demand curve facing the firm must be tangent to the average-total-cost curve so that $P = ATC$ and profits are zero.

The long-run equilibrium for a monopolistically competitive firm exhibits the following:

- As in monopoly, price exceeds marginal cost because profit maximization requires that $MR = MC$, and MR is always less than demand if demand is downward sloping.
- As in competition, price equals average total cost so economic profits equal zero because, unlike in monopoly, free entry drives profits to zero.

The long-run equilibrium under monopolistic competition differs from the long-run equilibrium under perfect competition in two ways:

- *Excess capacity:* Monopolistically competitive firms produce in the downward-sloping portion of their average-total-cost curve. Therefore, they produce a quantity that is less than that which would be produced at the *efficient scale* (minimum *ATC*) of the firm. As a result, they are said to have *excess capacity.* Competitive firms produce at the efficient scale.

- *Markup over marginal cost:* A monopolistically competitive firm charges a price that exceeds its marginal cost. A competitive firm charges a price that equals its marginal cost. As a result, if a monopolistically competitive firm could attract another customer, it would increase its profits.

  Monopolistic competition may be inefficient for two reasons:

- Since price exceeds marginal cost, some units that buyers valued in excess of the cost of production are not produced and consumed. This is the standard deadweight loss associated with monopoly. Regulating a monopolistically competitive firm in order to reduce the deadweight loss is not easily accomplished—the task is similar to regulating a natural monopoly.

- The number of firms in the market may not be "ideal" because the entering firm only considers its own profits but its entry generates two external effects:

  (1) *The product-variety externality*: Entry creates consumer surplus in the new market, which is a positive externality.

  (2) *The business-stealing externality*: Entry causes other firms to lose customers and profits and reduces existing surplus, which is a negative externality.

  Therefore, the entry of new firms into a monopolistically competitive market can raise or lower social surplus.

Monopolistically competitive markets do not ensure the maximization of total surplus. However, there is no easy way for public policy to improve the market outcome.

Advertising

Since monopolistically competitive firms sell differentiated products at prices above marginal cost, each firm has incentive to advertise to attract more buyers. Firms that sell highly differentiated consumer products spend 10 to 20 percent of revenue on advertising, firms that sell industrial products spend little, and firms that sell undifferentiated products spend nothing at all. About 2 percent of firm revenue, or about $200 billion per year, is spent on advertising. In 2001, 31 percent of advertising spending was on commercials on television and radio, 24 percent on space in newspapers and magazines, 19 percent on direct mail, 6 percent on the yellow pages, 3 percent on the Internet, and 17 percent on other miscellaneous outlets.

Economists debate the social value of advertising. Critics argue that advertising manipulates people's tastes to create a desire that otherwise would not exist and that advertising impedes competition by increasing the perception of product differentiation, which increases brand loyalty, causes demand to be more inelastic, and allows the firm to charge a greater markup over marginal cost. Defenders of advertising argue that advertising provides information to customers about prices, the existence of new products, and the location of retail outlets. This information increases competition because consumers are aware of price differentials and it provides new firms with the means to attract customers from existing firms. Evidence suggests that advertising increases competition and reduces prices for consumers.

Advertising that appears to contain little information may be useful because it provides a *signal* of product quality. Firms are likely to spend a great deal on advertising only if they think their product is of high quality. Therefore, consumers may be rational to try new products that are expensively advertised because it signals that the product is of high quality. The content of the ad is irrelevant. What is important is that the ad is expensive.

Advertising is related to *brand names*. Critics of brand names argue that brand names cause consumers to perceive differences between goods that do not exist. Defenders of brand names argue that brand names ensure that the product is of high quality because (1) brand names provide *information* about the quality of a product and (2) brand names give firms the *incentive* to maintain high quality.

Conclusion

Monopolistic competition contains characteristics of both monopoly and competition. Like monopoly, firms face downward-sloping demand curves and charge prices above marginal cost. Like competition, entry and exit drives profits to zero in the long run. Many markets are monopolistically competitive. The allocation of resources under monopolistic competition is not perfect but policymakers may not be able to improve on it.

HELPFUL HINTS

1. A source of inefficiency in monopolistic competition is underproduction. That is, some units are not produced that buyers value in excess of the cost of production. The monopolistically competitive firm charges a price that exceeds marginal cost while the competitive firm charges a price equal to marginal cost. However, the higher price charged by the monopolistically competitive firm is not the source of inefficiency. As with monopoly, it is the lower quantity demanded that results from the higher price that is the source of inefficiency. By itself, the higher price simply redistributes surplus from the buyer to the seller but it does not reduce total surplus.

TERMS AND DEFINITIONS

Choose a definition for each key term.

Key terms:

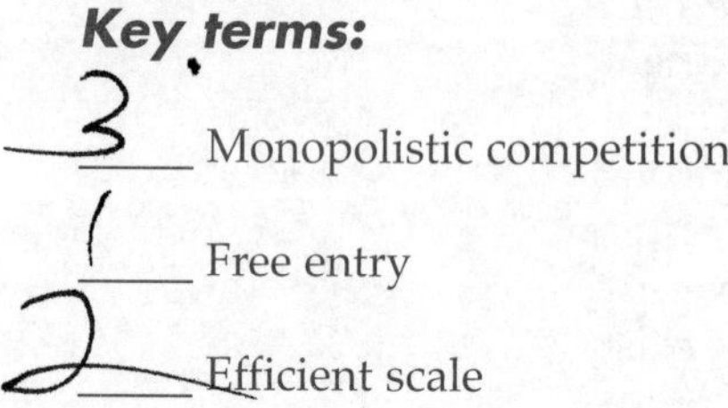

_____ Monopolistic competition

_____ Free entry

_____ Efficient scale

Definitions:

1. A situation where firms can enter the market without restriction
2. The quantity that minimizes average total cost
3. A market structure in which many firms sell products that are similar but not identical

PROBLEMS AND SHORT-ANSWER QUESTIONS

Practice Problems

1. Categorize each of the following markets as either competitive, monopolistic, or monopolistically competitive. Explain.
   a. toothpaste
   b. cable television
   c. gasoline at retail
   d. local newspapers
   e. magazines
   f. wheat
   g. video games
   h. beer

2. Suppose that there are many restaurants in the city and that each has a somewhat different menu.
   a. In Exhibit 1, draw the diagram of the cost curves (average total cost and marginal cost), demand curve, and marginal revenue curve for Mario's Pizza when it is in long-run equilibrium.

EXHIBIT 1

Price

0

Quantity

   b. Is Mario's Pizza profitable in the long run? Explain

   c. Is Mario's Pizza producing at the efficient scale? Explain. Why doesn't Mario's expand its output if it has excess capacity?

   d. In Exhibit 1, show the deadweight loss associated with Mario's level of output. Does this deadweight loss occur because the price is higher than a competitive firm would charge or because the quantity is smaller than a competitive firm would produce? Explain.

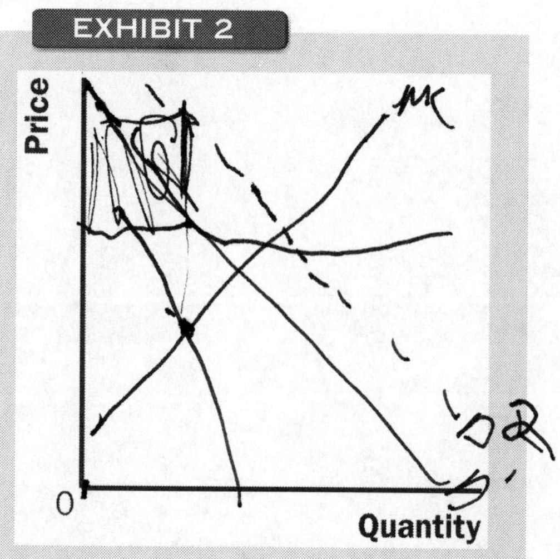

   e. Suppose that Mario's engages in an advertising campaign that is a huge success. In Exhibit 2, draw the diagram of Mario's cost curves, demand curve, and marginal-revenue curve and show Mario's profit in the short run. Can this situation be maintained in the long run? Explain.

3. For each of the following pairs of firms, which firm would likely spend a higher proportion of its revenue on advertising? Explain.
   a. the maker of Bayer Aspirin or the maker of generic aspirin

   b. a firm introducing a low quality ice cream or a firm introducing a high quality ice cream that each cost about the same to make.

   c. John Deere farm tractor division or John Deere lawnmower division

   d. the bakery that bakes Old Home Wheat Bread or a wheat farmer

Short-Answer Questions

1. What characteristics does monopolistic competition have in common with monopoly?

2. What characteristics does monopolistic competition have in common with perfect competition?

3. How does a monopolistically competitive firm choose the quantity and price that maximizes its profits?

4. Is it possible for a monopolistically competitive firm to generate economic profits in the long run? Why?

5. How does the long-run equilibrium in monopolistic competition differ from the long-run equilibrium in perfect competition?

6. Is the long-run equilibrium in monopolistic competition efficient? Explain.

7. Summarize the arguments in support of advertising and brand names.

8. Summarize the arguments in opposition to advertising and brand names.

SELF-TEST

True/False Questions

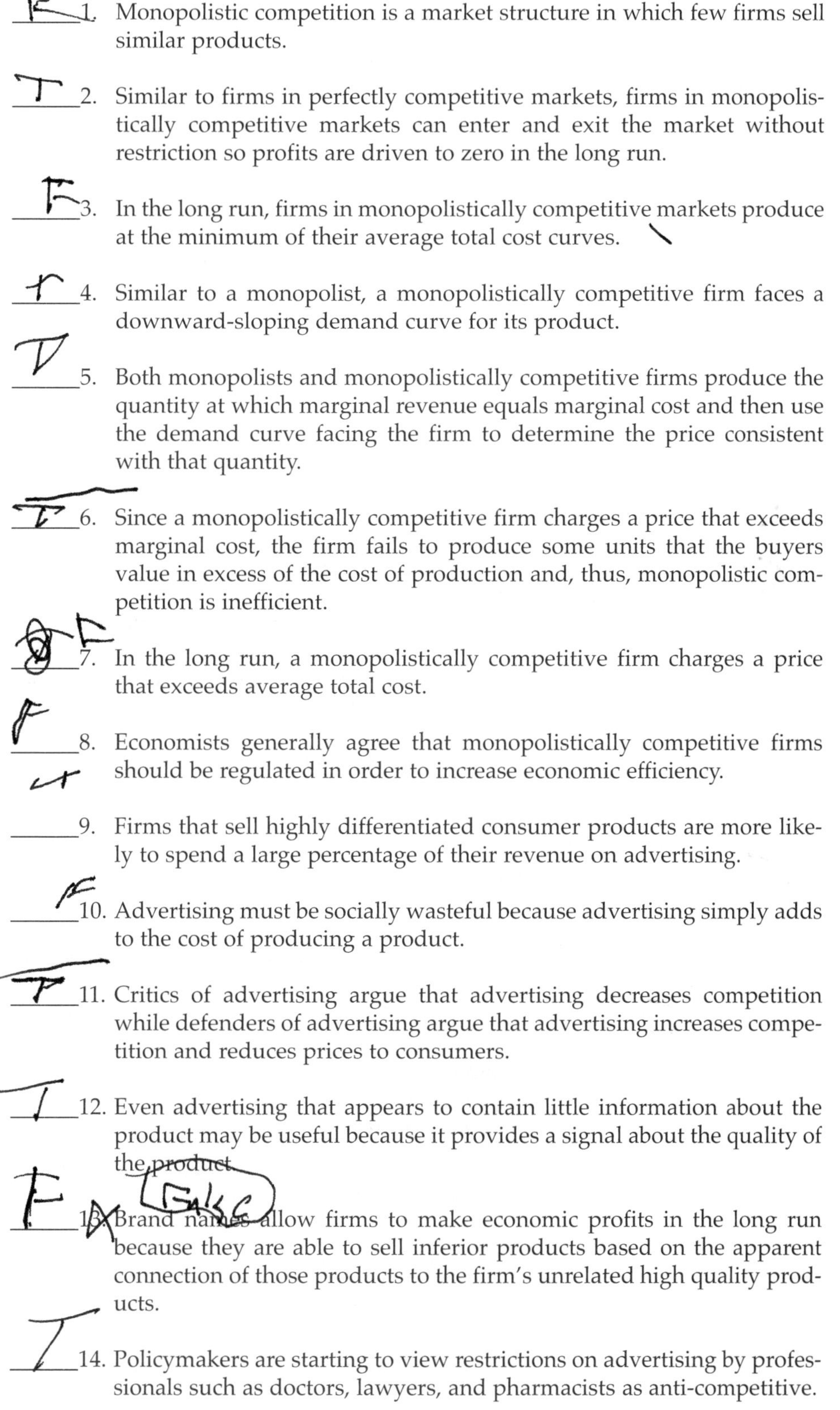

_____1. Monopolistic competition is a market structure in which few firms sell similar products.

_____2. Similar to firms in perfectly competitive markets, firms in monopolistically competitive markets can enter and exit the market without restriction so profits are driven to zero in the long run.

_____3. In the long run, firms in monopolistically competitive markets produce at the minimum of their average total cost curves.

_____4. Similar to a monopolist, a monopolistically competitive firm faces a downward-sloping demand curve for its product.

_____5. Both monopolists and monopolistically competitive firms produce the quantity at which marginal revenue equals marginal cost and then use the demand curve facing the firm to determine the price consistent with that quantity.

_____6. Since a monopolistically competitive firm charges a price that exceeds marginal cost, the firm fails to produce some units that the buyers value in excess of the cost of production and, thus, monopolistic competition is inefficient.

_____7. In the long run, a monopolistically competitive firm charges a price that exceeds average total cost.

_____8. Economists generally agree that monopolistically competitive firms should be regulated in order to increase economic efficiency.

_____9. Firms that sell highly differentiated consumer products are more likely to spend a large percentage of their revenue on advertising.

_____10. Advertising must be socially wasteful because advertising simply adds to the cost of producing a product.

_____11. Critics of advertising argue that advertising decreases competition while defenders of advertising argue that advertising increases competition and reduces prices to consumers.

_____12. Even advertising that appears to contain little information about the product may be useful because it provides a signal about the quality of the product.

_____13. Brand names allow firms to make economic profits in the long run because they are able to sell inferior products based on the apparent connection of those products to the firm's unrelated high quality products.

_____14. Policymakers are starting to view restrictions on advertising by professionals such as doctors, lawyers, and pharmacists as anti-competitive.

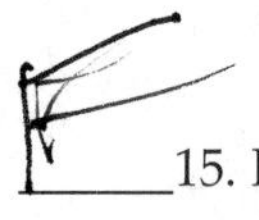

______15. In the long run, a monopolistically competitive firm produces at the efficient scale while a competitive firm has excess capacity.

Multiple-Choice Questions

1. Which of the following is not a characteristic of a monopolistically competitive market?
   a. many sellers
   b. differentiated products
   c. long-run economic profits
   d. free entry and exit

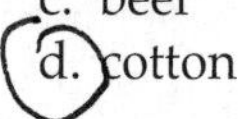

2. Which of the following products is least likely to be sold in a monopolistically competitive market?
   a. video games
   b. breakfast cereal
   c. beer
   d. cotton

3. Which of the following is true regarding the similarities and differences in monopolistic competition and monopoly?
   a. The monopolist faces a downward-sloping demand curve while the monopolistic competitor faces an elastic demand curve.
   b. The monopolist makes economic profits in the long run while the monopolistic competitor makes zero economic profits in the long run.
   c. Both the monopolist and the monopolistic competitor operate at the efficient scale.
   d. The monopolist charges a price above marginal cost while the monopolistic competitor charges a price equal to marginal cost.

4. In the short run, if the price is above average total cost in a monopolistically competitive market, the firm makes
   a. losses and firms enter the market.
   b. losses and firms exit the market.
   c. profits and firms enter the market.
   d. profits and firms exit the market.

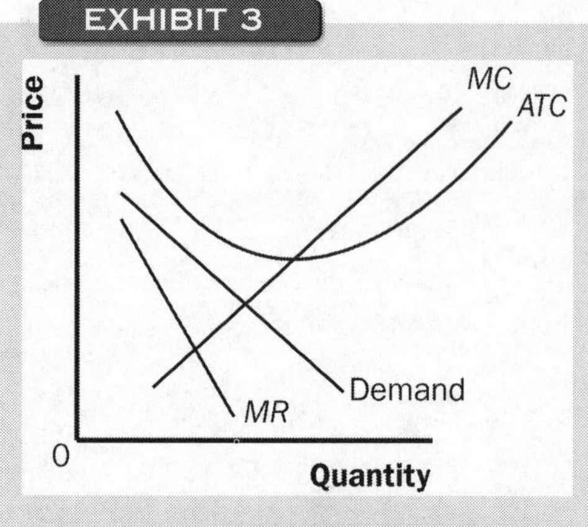

5. If the monopolistic competitor described by Exhibit 3 is producing at the profit-maximizing (loss-minimizing) level of output, it
   a. is generating losses.
   b. is generating profits.
   c. is generating zero profits.
   d. could be generating either profits or losses depending on what quantity it chooses to produce.

6. The monopolistically competitive market shown in Exhibit 3 will, in the long run,
   a. attract new producers into the market, which will shift the demand faced by incumbent firms to the right.
   b. attract new producers into the market, which will shift the demand faced by incumbent firms to the left.
   c. cause producers to exit the market, which will shift the demand faced by incumbent firms to the right.
   d. cause producers to exit the market, which will shift the demand faced by incumbent firms to the left.

7. Which of the following is true regarding the production and pricing decisions of monopolistically competitive firms? Monopolistically competitive firms choose the quantity at which marginal cost equals
   a. average total cost and then use the demand curve to determine the price consistent with this quantity.
   b. marginal revenue and then use the demand curve to determine the price consistent with this quantity.
   c. average total cost and then use the supply curve to determine the price consistent with this quantity.
   d. marginal revenue and then use the supply curve to determine the price consistent with this quantity.

8. Exhibit 4 depicts a monopolistically competitor
   a. generating profits in the short run.
   b. generating losses in the short run.
   c. generating zero profits in the long run.
   d. It is impossible to determine from this graph whether the firm is generating profits or losses.

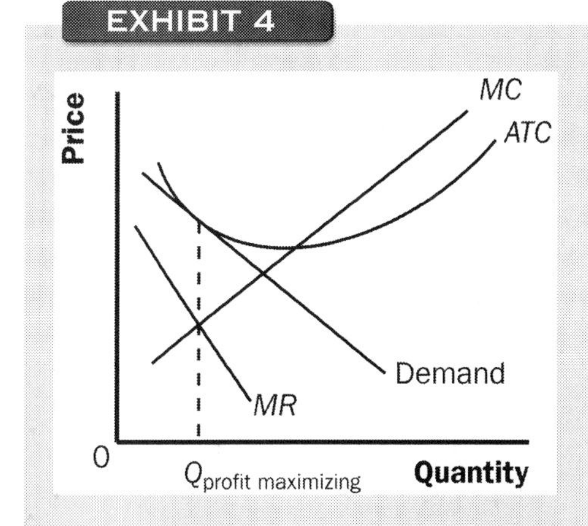

9. Which of the following is true with regard to monopolistically competitive firms' scale of production and pricing decisions? Monopolistically competitive firms produce
   a. at the efficient scale and charge a price equal to marginal cost.
   b. at the efficient scale and charge a price above marginal cost.
   c. with excess capacity and charge a price equal to marginal cost.
   d. with excess capacity and charge a price above marginal cost.

10. One source of inefficiency in monopolistic competition is that
    a. since price is above marginal cost, surplus is redistributed from buyers to sellers.
    b. since price is above marginal cost, some units are not produced that buyers value in excess of the cost of production and this causes a deadweight loss.
    c. monopolistically competitive firms produce beyond their efficient scale.
    d. monopolistically competitive firms earn economic profits in the long run.

11. When firms enter a monopolistically competitive market and the business-stealing externality is larger than the product-variety externality, then
    a. there are too many firms in the market and market efficiency could be increased if firms exited the market.
    b. there are too few firms in the market and market efficiency could be increased with additional entry.
    c. the number of firms in the market is optimal and the market is efficient.
    d. the only way to improve efficiency in this market is for the government to regulate it like a natural monopoly.

12. The use of the word "competition" in the name of the market structure called "monopolistic competition" refers to the fact that
    a. monopolistically competitive firms charge prices equal to the minimum of their average total cost just like competitive firms.
    b. monopolistically competitive firms face a downward-sloping demand curve just like competitive firms.
    c. the products are differentiated in a monopolistically competitive market just like in a competitive market.
    d. there are many sellers in a monopolistically competitive market and there is free entry and exit in the market just like a competitive market.

13. The use of the word "monopoly" in the name of the market structure called "monopolistic competition" refers to the fact that
    a. a monopolistically competitive firm faces a downward-sloping demand curve for its differentiated product and so does a monopolist.
    b. monopolistically competitive markets have free entry and exit just like a monopolistic market.
    c. monopolistically competitive firms charge prices equal to their marginal costs just like monopolists.
    d. monopolistically competitive firms produce beyond their efficient scale and so do monopolists.

14. Which of the following firms is most likely to spend a large percentage of their revenue on advertising?
    a. the manufacturer of an undifferentiated commodity
    b. a perfect competitor
    c. the manufacturer of an industrial product
    d. the producer of a highly differentiated consumer product
    e. the producer of a low quality product that costs the same to produce as a similar high quality product.

15. In 2001, the greatest amount of advertising expenditures was for
    a. commercials on television and radio.
    b. space in newspapers and magazines.
    c. direct mail.
    d. billboards.

16. Which of the following is *not* put forth as a criticism of advertising and brand names?
    a. Advertising manipulates people's tastes to create a desire that otherwise would not exist.
    b. Advertising increases competition, which causes unnecessary bankruptcies and layoffs.
    c. Advertising increases brand loyalty, causes demand to be more inelastic and, thus, increases markup over marginal cost.
    d. Brand names cause consumers to perceive differences between goods that do not exist.
    e. All of the above are criticisms of advertising and brand names.

17. Expensive television commercials that appear to provide no specific information about the product being advertised
    a. are most likely used by firms that are perfect competitors.
    b. should be banned by regulators because they add to the cost of the product without providing the consumer with any useful information about the product.
    c. may be useful because they provide a signal to the consumer about the quality of the product.
    d. only affect the buying habits of irrational consumers.

18. Which of the following is *not* an argument put forth by economists in support of the use of advertising?
    a. Advertising provides information to customers about prices, new products, and location of retail outlets.
    b. Advertising provides a creative outlet for artists and writers.
    c. Advertising increases competition.
    d. Advertising provides new firms with the means to attract customers from existing firms.

19. Defenders of the use of brand names argue that brand names
    a. provide information about the quality of the product.
    b. give firms incentive to maintain high quality.
    c. are useful even in socialist economies such as the former Soviet Union.
    d. all of the above

20. Which of the following firms has the least incentive to advertise?
    a. a manufacturer of home heating and air conditioning
    b. a manufacturer of breakfast cereal
    c. a wholesaler of crude oil
    d. a restaurant

ADVANCED CRITICAL THINKING

You are watching a sporting event on television. An advertisement featuring Tiger Woods (a famous golfer) is broadcast during a commercial break. In the ad, Tiger Woods does nothing but hit golf balls. He never speaks. There is no written copy. At the end of the advertisement, the Nike "swoosh" appears on the screen along with the words "Nike Golf." A short time earlier, you read in a newspaper that Tiger Woods received $40 million to be the spokesperson for Nike golf equipment.

1. A friend watches the Nike advertisement with you and says, "What a waste of society's resources. I didn't learn anything about Nike golf equipment from that ad. I think there should be government regulations requiring ads to be informative in some way." Explain to your friend what you did learn from Tiger Wood's presence in this ad.

___

___

___

2. Did the use of the Nike name and Nike "swoosh" provide any information? Explain.

___

___

___

___

3. In general, does advertising tend to decrease competition and raise prices to consumers or increase competition and reduce prices to consumers? Why?

___

___

___

___

SOLUTIONS

Terms and Definitions

3 Monopolistic competition

1 Free entry

2 Efficient scale

Practice Problems

1. a. monopolistically competitive—many firms, differentiated products, free entry
   b. monopoly—one firm
   c. competitive—many firms, identical products
   d. monopoly—one firm (Could be a natural monopoly because one firm can satisfy the entire market on the downward-sloping portion of its *ATC* curve.)
   e. monopolistically competitive—many firms, differentiated products, free entry
   f. competitive—many firms, identical products
   g. monopolistically competitive—many firms, differentiated products, free entry
   h. monopolistically competitive—many firms, differentiated products, free entry

2. a. See Exhibit 5.
   b. No. Since there is free entry, profit causes firms to enter the industry, which reduces the existing demand faced by profitable firms until $P = ATC$ and profit is zero.
   c. No. Profits attract new firms, which reduces the demand for an incumbent firm's product to the point where its demand is tangent to its *ATC* curve causing $P = ATC$ and profits equal zero. Since the tangency of demand and *ATC* is in the negatively sloping portion of *ATC*, the firm is operating at less than the efficient scale. If Mario's expanded output, *MC* would exceed *MR* and $P < ATC$ so profits would be negative.
   d. See Exhibit 6. The deadweight loss occurs because firms fail to produce units that the buyer values in excess of the cost of production. That is, the loss is due to the reduced quantity in monopolistic competition.
   e. See Exhibit 7. No. Profits attract entry which reduces the demand faced by each firm to the point where it is again tangent to its *ATC* curve.

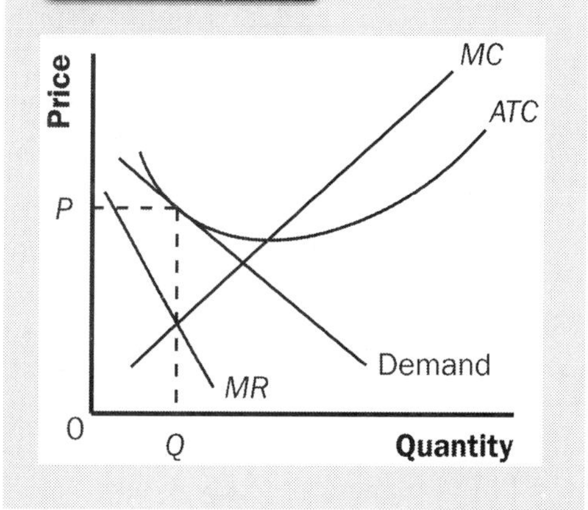

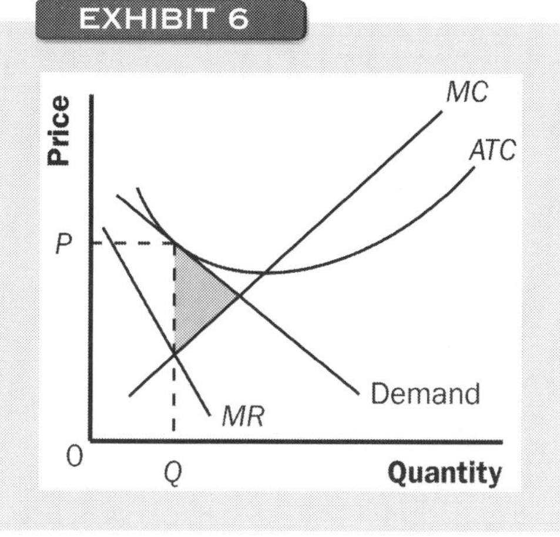

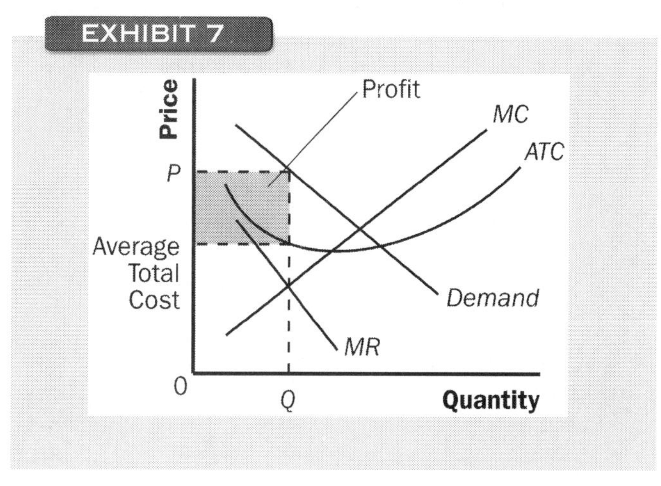

3. a. Bayer Aspirin because it is a branded or differentiated consumer good.
   b. Firm generating high quality ice cream because advertising is more profitable if there are repeat buyers.
   c. John Deere lawnmower division because lawnmowers are sold to consumers as opposed to industry.
   d. Bakery of Old Home Wheat Bread because it is differentiated. Wheat is not differentiated.

Short-Answer Questions

1. Both market structures involve a differentiated product so firms face downward-sloping demand curves, equate *MC* and *MR*, and charge a price above *MC*.

2. Both market structures have many sellers and free entry and exit. Thus, profits are driven to zero in the long run.

3. It chooses the quantity by equating *MC* and *MR* and then uses the demand curve to find the price that is consistent with this quantity (just like a monopolist).

4. No. Profits attract new firms to the market, which reduces the demand faced by each of the incumbent firms until the demand faced by each firm is tangent to its *ATC* curve and profits are zero.

5. Monopolistic competition has excess capacity because monopolistically competitive firms produce at less than efficient scale and they charge prices in excess of marginal cost. Competitive firms produce at the efficient scale and charge prices equal to marginal cost.

6. No. Since price exceeds marginal cost, there is underproduction—some units that buyers value in excess of marginal cost are not produced. Also, the number of firms in the market may not be ideal because entry into the industry creates the positive product-variety externality and the negative business-stealing externality.

7. Advertising provides information about prices, new products, the location of retail outlets, provides new firms with the means to attract customers from existing firms, and can be a signal of high quality. Brand names provide information about the quality of the product and provide incentive for the producer to maintain high quality.

8. The use of advertising and brand names manipulates peoples' tastes, impedes competition, and creates brand loyalty when there is no difference among goods. This allows for a higher markup over marginal cost and increases inefficiency.

True/False Questions

1. F; monopolistic competition is a market structure in which many firms sell differentiated products.

2. T

3. F; monopolistic competitors produce in the downward-sloping portion of their *ATC* curve where the *ATC* curve is tangent to the demand curve faced by the firm.

4. T

5. T

6. T

7. F; monopolistically competitive firms charge a price equal to *ATC*.

8. F; it is not clear how one would regulate a monopolistically competitive firm in order to increase efficiency.

9. T

10. F; advertising may increase competition, which could increase social welfare.

11. T

12. T

13. F; brand names give the firm incentive to maintain high quality.

14. T

15. F; monopolistically competitive firms have excess capacity while competitive firms produce at the efficient scale.

Multiple-Choice Questions

1. c	5. a	9. d	13. a	17. c
2. d	6. c	10. b	14. d	18. b
3. b	7. b	11. a	15. a	19. d
4. c	8. c	12. d	16. b	20. c

Advanced Critical Thinking

1. Viewers learned that Nike was willing to spend an enormous amount of money to promote their new line of golf equipment. This signals that their market research suggests that they have a high quality product that will generate repeat sales.

2. Yes. The use of the brand name provides information that the product is of high quality and that the firm has incentive to maintain high quality. Nike is a multibillion-dollar company that would not want to risk losing existing sales of shoes and athletic ware by marketing poor quality golf equipment marked with the Nike brand name.

3. Advertising tends to increase competition and decrease prices to consumers because it often provides information about prices, the existence of new products, the location of retail outlets, and it provides new firms with the means to attract customers from existing firms.

18

THE MARKETS FOR THE FACTORS OF PRODUCTION

GOALS

In this chapter you will

Analyze the labor demand of competitive, profit-maximizing firms

Consider the household decisions that lie behind labor supply

Learn why equilibrium wages equal the value of the marginal product of labor

Consider how the other factors of production—land and capital—are compensated

Examine how a change in the supply of one factor alters the earnings of all the factors

OUTCOMES

After accomplishing these goals, you should be able to

Explain why the labor demand curve is the value of the marginal product curve for labor

Explain why the labor supply curve is usually upward sloping

Explain why a competitive firm maximizes profit when it hires labor to the point where the wage equals the value of the marginal product of labor

Demonstrate the similarity between the labor market and the market for other factors of production

Explain why the change in the supply of one factor alters the value of the marginal product of the other factors

CHAPTER OVERVIEW

Context and Purpose

Chapter 18 is the first chapter in a three-chapter sequence that addresses the economics of labor markets. Chapter 18 develops and analyses the markets for the factors of production—labor, land, and capital. Chapter 19 builds on Chapter 18 and explains in more detail why some workers earn more than do others. Chapter 20 addresses the distribution of income and the role the government can play in altering the distribution of income.

The purpose of Chapter 18 is to provide the basic theory for the analysis of factor markets—the markets for labor, land, and capital. As you might expect, we find that the wages earned by the factors of production depend on the supply and demand for the factor. What is new in our analysis is that the demand for a factor is a *derived demand*. That is, a firm's demand for a factor is determined by its decision to supply a good in another market.

CHAPTER REVIEW

Introduction

The **factors of production** are the inputs used to produce goods and services. The most important inputs are labor, land, and capital. This chapter provides the basic theory for the analysis of factor markets. We will find that the supply and demand for a factor determines the wage earned by that factor. What is new in our analysis is that the demand for a factor is a *derived demand*. That is, a firm's demand for a factor is determined by its decision to supply a good in another market. In this chapter, we analyze the factor demand of competitive profit-maximizing firms.

The Demand for Labor

The wage of labor is determined by the supply and demand for labor. The demand for labor is a derived demand in that it depends on the firm's decision to supply output in another market. Suppose that a firm is *competitive* in both its output market and in the market for labor. Also, suppose that the firm is *profit-maximizing*. In order to derive the demand for labor, we first have to determine how the use of labor affects the amount of output the firm produces. A **production function** shows the relationship between the quantity of inputs used to make a good and the quantity of output of that good. Since rational decision makers think at the margin, we derive the **marginal product of labor**—the increase in the amount of output from an additional unit of labor holding all other inputs fixed—from the production function. Production functions exhibit **diminishing marginal product,** which is the property whereby the marginal product of an input declines as the quantity of the input increases.

The firm is concerned with the *value* of the output generated by each worker rather than the output itself. Thus, we calculate the **value of the marginal product,** which is the marginal product of an input times the price of the output. Another name for the value of the marginal product is *marginal revenue product*. Since the output is sold in a competitive market, the price is constant regardless of the amount produced and sold and, therefore, the *value* of the marginal product declines in concert with the decline in the marginal product as the quantity of the input increases.

Since the firm is also a competitor in the market for labor, it takes the wage as given. It is profitable for the firm to hire a worker if the value of the marginal product of that worker is greater than the wage. This analysis implies that:

- a competitive, profit-maximizing firm hires workers up to the point where the value of the marginal product of labor equals the wage, and

- the value-of-marginal-product curve *is* the labor demand curve for a competitive, profit-maximizing firm.

Since the demand for labor is the value-of-marginal-product curve, the demand for labor shifts when the value of the marginal product of labor changes due to changes in the following:

- *The output price*: an increase in the price of output increases the value of the marginal product and shifts labor demand right.

- *Technological change*: an advance in technology raises the marginal product of labor and shifts labor demand right.

- *The supply of other factors*: an increase in the supply of a factor used with labor in production increases the marginal product of labor and shifts labor demand to the right.

For a competitive, profit-maximizing firm, the demand for a factor is closely related to its supply of output because the production function links inputs and output. If W is the wage, MC is marginal cost, and MPL is the marginal product of labor, then $MC = W/MPL$. Thus, diminishing marginal product is associated with increasing marginal cost. In terms of inputs, a profit-maximizing firm hires until the value of the marginal product of labor equals the wage or $P \times MPL = W$. Rearranging, we get $P = W/MPL$. Substituting MC for W/MPL from above we get, $P = MC$. Thus, when a competitive firm hires labor up to the point at which the value of the marginal product equals the wage, it also produces up to the point at which the price equals marginal cost.

The Supply of Labor

The supply of labor arises from individuals' tradeoff between work and leisure. An upward-sloping labor supply curve means that people respond to an increase in the wage by enjoying less leisure and working more hours. While labor supply need not be upward sloping in all cases, for now we will assume that it is upward sloping.

The following events will cause the labor supply curve to shift:

- *Changes in tastes*: Changes in attitudes toward working such that women are more likely to work outside the home will shift the supply of labor to the right.

- *Changes in alternative opportunities*: If better opportunities arise in alternative labor markets, labor supply will decrease in the market under consideration.

- *Immigration*: When immigrants come to the U.S., the U.S. supply of labor shifts to the right.

Equilibrium in the Labor-Market

In competitive labor markets:

- The wage adjusts to balance the supply and demand for labor, and

- The wage equals the value of the marginal product of labor.

As a result, any event that changes the supply or demand for labor must change the equilibrium wage and the value of the marginal product by the same amount because these must always be equal.

For example, suppose that immigration causes an increase in the supply of labor (supply of labor shifts right). This reduces the equilibrium wage, increases the quantity demanded of labor because it is profitable for firms to hire additional workers, and reduces the marginal product of labor (and the value of the marginal product of labor) as the number of workers employed rises. In the new equilibrium, both the wage and the value of the marginal product of labor have fallen.

Alternatively, suppose there is an increase in the demand for the output produced by firms in an industry. This causes an increase in the price of the good and increases the *value* of the marginal product of labor. This event increases the demand for labor (rightward shift in the labor demand curve), increases the equilibrium wage, and increases employment. Again, the value of the marginal product of labor and the wage move together (both increase in this case). When there is a change in the demand for a firm's output, the prosperity of firms and their workers move together.

Our analysis of labor demand shows that the wage equals the marginal product of labor. Therefore highly productive workers should earn more than less productive workers. In addition, real wages should increase in relation to the increase in productivity. Statistics support this conclusion. When productivity grows quickly, real wages grow quickly. Over the past 40 years, both productivity and real wages have grown at 2 percent per year. Since 1995, productivity has grown at 2.6 percent per year and real wages at 2.9 percent per year. The surge in productivity in the United States since 1995 may be due to the spread of computers and information technology.

A market with only a single buyer is called a *monopsony*. When a firm is a monopsonist in a labor market, the firm uses its market power to reduce the number of workers hired, reduce the wage it pays, and increase its profits. As in monopoly, the market is smaller than is socially optimal, which causes dead weight losses.

The Other Factors of Production: Land and Capital

A firm's factors of production fall into three categories—labor, land, and capital. **Capital** is the stock of equipment and structures used to produce goods and services. The *rental price* of a factor is the price one pays to use the factor for a limited period of time while the *purchase price* of a factor is the price one pays to own that factor indefinitely.

Since the wage is the rental price of labor, we can apply the theory of factor demand we used for the labor market to the markets for land and capital. For both land and capital, the firm increases the quantity hired until the value of the factor's marginal product equals the factor's price and, thus, the demand curve for each factor is the factor's value of marginal product curve. As a result, labor, land, and capital each earn the value of their marginal contribution to the production process because each factor's rental price is equal to the value of its marginal product.

Capital is often owned by firms as opposed to being owned directly by households. Therefore, capital income is often paid first to a firm. Capital income is later paid to those households that have lent money to the firm in the form of *interest* and to those households that own stock in the firm in the form of *dividends*. Alternatively, the firm retains some of its capital income to buy more capital. This portion of capital income is known as *retained earnings*. Regardless of how capital income is allocated, its total value equals the value of the marginal product of capital.

The purchase price of land and capital is based on the stream of rental income it generates. Thus, the purchase price of land or capital depends on both the current and expected future value of the marginal product of that factor.

Because of diminishing returns, a factor in abundant supply has a low marginal product and a low price while a factor in scarce supply has a high marginal product and a high price. When the supply of a factor changes, however, it has an effect on other factor markets because factors are used together in production. For example, the destruction of capital in an industry increases the rental price of the remaining capital. In the labor market the workers are now working with less capital, which reduces their marginal product. This reduces the demand for labor and reduces the wage of workers. In a real world example, the bubonic plague reduced the labor force by one-third and increased the wage of the remaining scarce workers. This event decreased the rental price of land because the marginal product of land fell due to the reduction in workers available to farm the land.

Conclusion

The theory developed in this chapter of how labor, land, and capital are compensated is known as the *neo-classical theory of distribution*. It suggests that the amount earned by a factor depends on supply and demand and that the demand for a factor depends on its marginal productivity. In equilibrium, each factor earns the value of its marginal product. This theory is widely accepted.

HELPFUL HINTS

1. Your text provides examples of the impact of an increase in the supply of labor and an increase in the demand for labor on the marginal product of labor and the wage. The same logic used in those examples can be applied to the cases of a decrease in the supply of labor or a decrease in the demand for labor. For example, a decrease in the supply of labor (leftward shift in the labor supply curve) increases the equilibrium wage, decreases the quantity demanded of labor because it is profitable for firms to hire fewer workers, and increases the marginal product of labor (and the value of the marginal product of labor) as the number of workers employed decreases. In the new equilibrium, both the wage and the value of the marginal product of labor have risen. Alternatively, suppose there is a decrease in the demand for the output produced by firms in an industry. This causes a decrease in the price of the good and decreases the *value* of the marginal product of labor. This event decreases the demand for labor (leftward shift in the labor demand curve), decreases the equilibrium wage, and decreases employment.

2. The categories of the factors of production are labor, land, and capital. In this context, land is more than just the land on which one might grow crops. Land is generally considered to be "nature's bounty" and is all forms of natural resources that have not yet been altered by people. This would include rivers, oil reserves, minerals, and land itself.

3. To see the impact of a change in the quantity employed of one factor on the earnings of a second factor, always look at the impact on the marginal product of the second factor. For example, an increase in the available capital will reduce the marginal product of capital and its rental rate. The increase in capital, however, will increase the marginal product of labor because workers have additional capital with which to work and their wages will rise accordingly.

TERMS AND DEFINITIONS

Choose a definition for each key term.

Key terms:

3 Factors of production

8 Derived demand

5 Production function

4 Marginal product of labor

1 Diminishing marginal product

7 Value of the marginal product

2 Capital

6 Rental price (of a factor)

Definitions:

1. The property whereby the marginal product of an input declines as the quantity of the input increases
2. The equipment and structures used to produce goods and services
3. The inputs used to produce goods and services
4. The increase in the amount of output from an additional unit of labor
5. The relationship between the quantity of inputs used to make a good and the quantity of output of that good
6. The price a person pays to use a factor for a limited period of time
7. The marginal product of an input times the price of the output
8. The demand for a factor of production which is derived from the firm's decision to supply another good

PROBLEMS AND SHORT-ANSWER QUESTIONS

Practice Problems

1. Suppose that labor is the only variable input in the production process for a competitive profit-maximizing firm that produces coffee mugs. The firm's production function is shown below.

Labor (number of workers)	Output per Hour	Marginal Product of Labor	Value of *MPL* when P = $3	Value of *MPL* when P = $5
0	0	9	27	45
1	9	8	24	40
2	17	7	21	35
3	24	6	18	30
4	30	5	15	25
5	35	4	12	20
6	39	3	9	15
7	42	2	6	10
8	44			

a. Fill out columns three and four of the table above (the marginal product of labor and the value of the marginal product of labor when the price of output equals $3 per mug).
b. Suppose that the competitive wage for workers who can make coffee mugs is $19 per hour. How many workers should this firm hire? Why?

c. Suppose that schools that teach pottery skills increase the supply of workers that can make coffee mugs and that this event lowers the competitive wage for coffee mug workers to $13 per hour. How many workers should this firm hire? Why? Does this represent a shift in the firm's demand for labor or a movement along the firm's demand for labor? Explain.

d. Suppose there is an increase in the demand for coffee mugs and that the price of coffee mugs rises to $5 per mug. Fill out the last column of the table above to show the value of the marginal product of labor when the price of mugs is $5 per mug.
e. Suppose that the competitive wage for coffee mug workers remains at $13 per hour and the price of mugs is $5 per mug. How many workers should this firm now hire? Why? Does this represent a shift in the firm's demand for labor or a movement along the firm's demand for labor? Explain.

2. Suppose there is an increase in the demand for lumber, which raises the price of lumber.
    a. Show the impact of the increase in the price of lumber on the market for lumberjacks in Exhibit 1.
    b. What did the increase in the price of lumber do to the value of the marginal product of lumberjacks and the wage of lumberjacks? Explain.

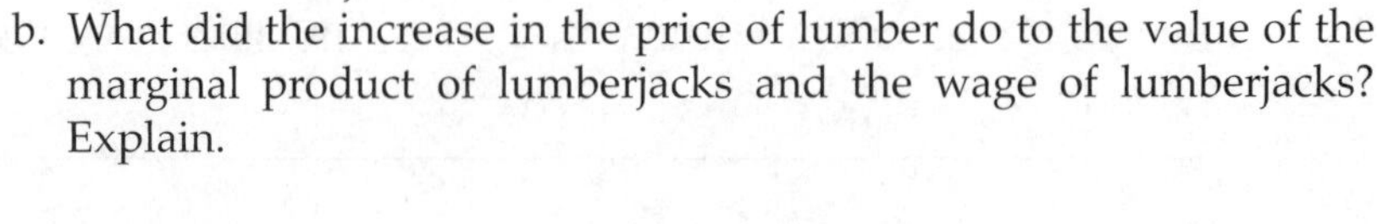

EXHIBIT 1

Wage of Lumberjacks

0

Quantity of Lumberjacks

____

____

____

    c. What will happen to the value of the marginal product and the rental rate for timberland and for capital that is used for cutting and shipping timber? Explain.

____

____

____

    d. How has this event affected the prosperity of the firm and the owners of the factors of production employed by the firm? Explain.

____

____

____

3. Suppose that an enormous amount of forest land is cleared for agricultural use in Brazil.
    a. Show the impact of this event on the market for agricultural land in Brazil in Exhibit 2. What has happened to the marginal product of land and the rental price of land in Brazil?

EXHIBIT 2

Rental Price of Land

0

Quantity of Land

____

____

____

____

____

b. Show the impact of this event on the market for Brazilian farm workers in Exhibit 3. What has happened to the marginal product of farm labor and the wage of farm labor?

EXHIBIT 3

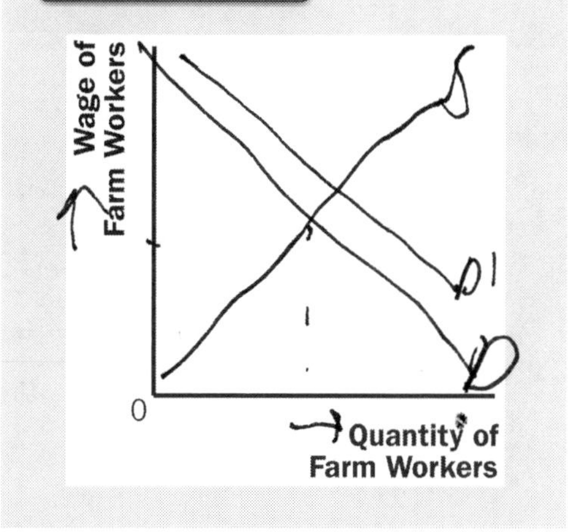

Wage of Farm Workers

0

Quantity of Farm Workers

4. Describe the impact of the following events on the market for auto workers in Tennessee. (Note that Honda operates a factory in Tennessee.)

a. Honda adds on to its factory in Tennessee.

b. *Consumer Reports* declares Honda to be the best-made automobile in its class.

c. Refugees with manufacturing skills from war-torn Bosnia and Kosovo are relocated to Tennessee.

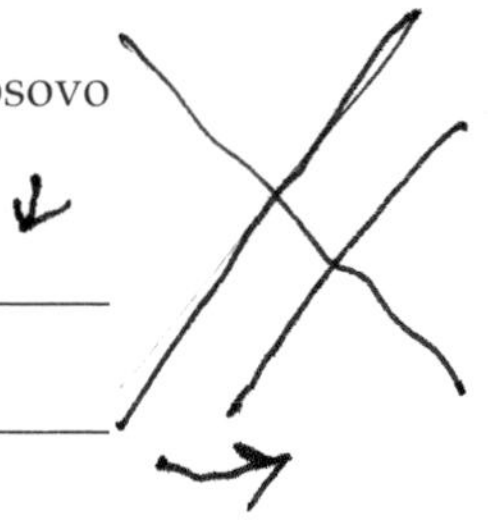

Short-Answer Questions

1. Why is the firm's demand curve for labor the value of the marginal product of labor?

2. Why does the firm's demand curve for labor slope downward (that is, why does it slope negatively)?

3. Prove that when a competitive firm hires up to the point at which the value of the marginal product equals the wage, it also produces up to the point at which price equals marginal cost.

4. Why must the equilibrium wage in the market for labor equal the value of the marginal product of labor for each firm?

5. Suppose there is an increase in college enrollments, which causes an increase in the demand for textbooks. What should happen in the markets for labor and capital employed in the manufacturing of textbooks? Explain.

6. Why does an increase in the amount of capital reduce the rental rate of capital? Why does this same event increase the wage of labor?

7. Explain the difference between the rental price of a factor and the purchase price of a factor. How are they related?

____

____

____

____

____

8. When households own capital directly, capital income is in the form of rental payments to households. In what form is capital income paid when businesses own capital?

____

____

____

9. What events will shift the demand for labor to the right?

____

____

____

____

10. What events will shift the supply of labor to the right?

____

____

____

____

SELF-TEST

True/False Questions

__F__ 1. The factors of production are labor, land, and money.

__T__ 2. The demand for a factor is considered to be a derived demand because it is derived from the firm's decision to supply output in another market.

T ______ 3. For a competitive profit-maximizing firm, the demand curve for a factor is the value of the marginal product curve for that factor.

F ______ 4. A factor exhibits diminishing marginal productivity if employing additional units of the factor reduces output.

T ______ 5. If there is an increase in the equilibrium wage, there must have been an increase in the value of the marginal product of labor.

T ______ 6. An increase in the demand for textbooks will increase the value of the marginal product of textbook writers.

F ______ 7. A decrease in the supply of labor reduces the value of the marginal product of labor, decreases the wage, and decreases employment.

F ______ 8. The only way for the value of the marginal product of a factor to rise is for the price of the output produced by the factor to rise.

T ______ 9. An increase in the demand for pencils will likely improve the fortunes of both the pencil factory and the workers in the pencil factory.

T ______ 10. The demand for labor is downward sloping because the production function exhibits diminishing marginal productivity of labor.

T ______ 11. In equilibrium, when a competitive firm hires labor up to the point at which the value of the marginal product of labor equals the wage, it also produces up to the point at which the price equals marginal cost.

F ______ 12. An increase in the supply of capital will increase the marginal product of capital and the rental rate of capital.

F ______ 13. If capital is owned by firms as opposed to being owned directly by households, then capital income will be in the form of stocks, bonds, and retained interest.

T ______ 14. The value of the marginal product of land is the marginal product of land multiplied by the price of the output produced on the land.

F ______ 15. An increase in the supply of capital decreases the value of the marginal product of capital, reduces the rental rate of capital, and decreases the value of the marginal product of labor, which reduces the wage of labor.

Multiple-Choice Questions

1. The most important factors of production are
   a. money, stocks, and bonds.
   b. water, earth, and knowledge.
   c. management, finance, and marketing.
   d. labor, land, and capital.

D

2. If a factor exhibits diminishing marginal product, hiring additional units of the factor will
   a. generate ever smaller amounts of output.
   b. cause a reduction in output.
   c. have no effect on output.
   d. increase the marginal product of the factor.

Use the following table for the next three questions.

Labor (number of workers)	Output per Hour	Marginal Product of Labor	Value of the *MPL*
0	0		
1	5		
2	9		
3	12		
4	14		
5	15		

3. What is the marginal product of labor as the firm moves from using three workers to using four workers?
   a. 0
   b. 2
   c. 12
   d. 14
   e. none of the above

4. If the price of output is $4 per unit, what is the value of the marginal product of labor as the firm moves from using four workers to using five workers?
   a. $4
   b. $8
   c. $12
   d. $56
   e. $60

5. If this profit-maximizing firm sells its output in a competitive market for $3 per unit and hires labor in a competitive market for $8/hour, then this firm should hire
   a. one worker.
   b. two workers.
   c. three workers.
   d. four workers.
   e. five workers.

6. The value of the marginal product of labor is
   a. the price of the output times the wage of labor.
   b. the wage of labor times the quantity of labor.
   c. the price of the output times the marginal product of labor.
   d. the wage of labor times the marginal product of labor.
   e. none of the above.

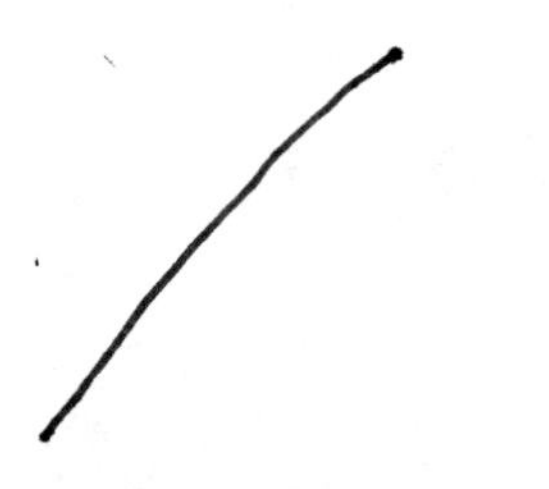

7. For a competitive, profit-maximizing firm, the value-of-the-marginal-product curve for capital is the firm's
   a. production function.
   b. marginal cost curve.
   c. supply curve of capital.
   d. demand curve for capital.

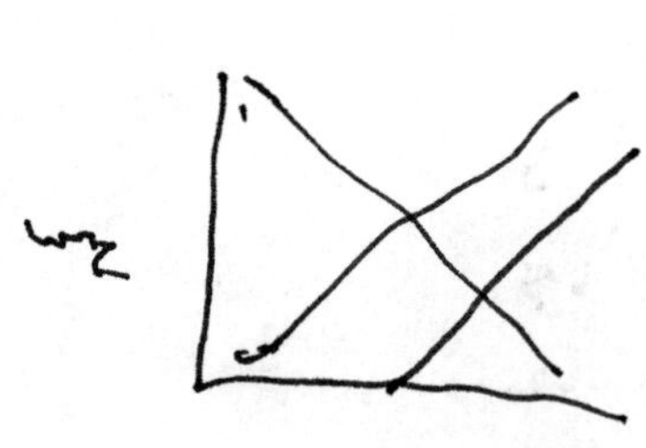

8. An increase in the supply of labor
   a. increases the value of the marginal product of labor and increases the wage.
   b. decreases the value of the marginal product of labor and decreases the wage.
   c. increases the value of the marginal product of labor and decreases the wage.
   d. decreases the value of the marginal product of labor and increases the wage.

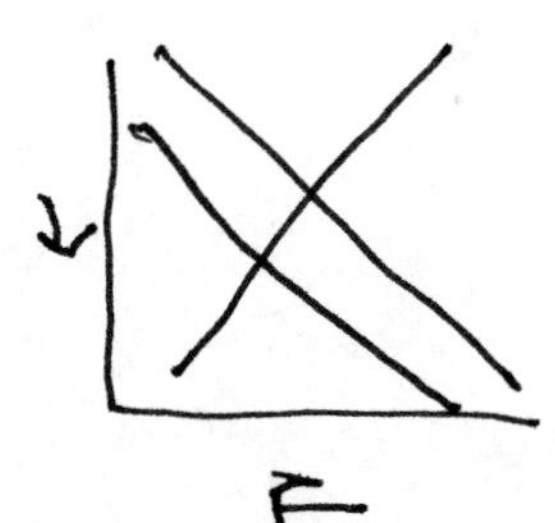

9. A decrease in the demand for fish
   a. decreases the value of the marginal product of fishermen, reduces their wage, and reduces employment in the fishing industry.
   b. increases the value of the marginal product of fishermen, increases their wage, and increases employment in the fishing industry.
   c. decreases the value of the marginal product of fishermen, reduces their wage, and increases employment in the fishing industry.
   d. increases the value of the marginal product of fishermen, increases their wage, and decreases employment in the fishing industry.

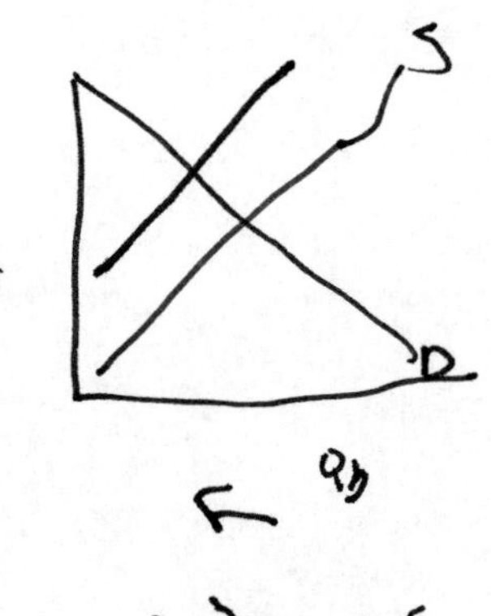

10. What will a decrease in the supply of fishermen do to the market for capital employed in the fishing industry?
   a. increase the demand for fishing boats and increase rental rates on fishing boats
   b. decrease the demand for fishing boats and decrease rental rates on fishing boats
   c. increase the demand for fishing boats and decrease rental rates on fishing boats
   d. decrease the demand for fishing boats and increase rental rates on fishing boats

11. An increase in the demand for apples will cause all but which of the following?
   a. an increase in the price of apples
   b. an increase in the value of the marginal product of apple pickers
   c. an increase in the wage of apple pickers
   d. a decrease in the number of apple pickers employed

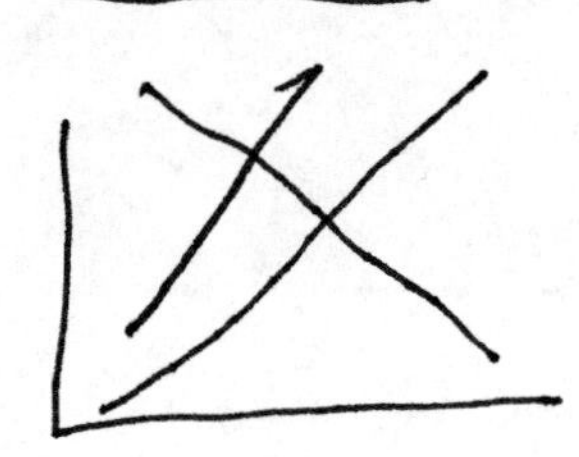

12. A decrease in the supply of farm tractors will cause all but which of the following?
   a. an increase in the rental rate for tractors
   b. an increase in the value of the marginal product of tractors
   c. an increase in the wage of farm workers
   d. a decrease in the rental rate of farm land

13. If both input and output markets are competitive and firms are profit maximizing, then in equilibrium each factor of production earns
    a. an equal share of output.
    b. the value of its marginal product.
    c. the amount allocated by the political process.
    d. an amount equal to the price of output times total output.

14. An individual firm's demand for a factor of production
    a. slopes downward due to the factor's diminishing marginal product.
    b. slopes downward because an increase in the production of output reduces the price at which the output can be sold in a competitive market, thereby reducing the value of the marginal product as more of the factor is used.
    c. slopes upward due to the factor's increasing marginal product.
    d. is perfectly elastic (horizontal) if the factor market is perfectly competitive.

15. An increase in the demand for a firm's output
    a. increases the prosperity of the firm but decreases the prosperity of the factors hired by the firm.
    b. decreases the prosperity of the firm but increases the prosperity of the factors hired by the firm.
    c. increases the prosperity of both the firm and the factors hired by the firm.
    d. decreases the prosperity of both the firm and the factors hired by the firm.

16. A competitive, profit-maximizing firm should hire workers up to the point where
    a. the wage, the rental price of capital, and the rental price of land are all equal.
    b. the marginal product of labor equals zero and the production function is maximized.
    c. the marginal product of labor equals the wage.
    d. the value of the marginal product of labor equals the wage.

17. Which of the following is not true with regard to workers who have a high value of marginal product? These workers
    a. are usually highly paid.
    b. usually have little capital with which to work.
    c. have skills that are in relatively scarce supply.
    d. produce output for which there is great demand.

18. An increase in the price of automobiles shifts the demand for autoworkers to the
    a. right and increases the wage.
    b. left and decreases the wage.
    c. right and decreases the wage.
    d. left and increases the wage.

19. When capital is owned by the firm as opposed to being directly owned by households, capital income may take any of the following forms except
    a. retained earnings.
    b. interest.
    c. dividends.
    d. stock.

20. Suppose that a war is fought with biological weapons. The weapons destroy people but not capital. What is likely to happen to equilibrium wages and rental rates after the war when compared to their values before the war?
   a. Wages rise and rental rates rise.
   b. Wages fall and rental rates fall.
   c. Wages rise and rental rates fall.
   d. Wages fall and rental rates rise.

ADVANCED CRITICAL THINKING

You are watching a debate about immigration on public television with a friend. The participants represent two camps—organized labor and corporate industry. Organized labor argues against open immigration while U.S. industry argues in favor of more open immigration. Your friend says, "I can't believe that these two groups can't get together on this issue. Both firms and workers join forces to produce our industrial output. I would think that their interests would be similar. Maybe a better arbitrator could help these groups find a position on immigration that would satisfy both groups."

1. If there were open immigration, what would happen to the value of the marginal product of labor and the wage?

   ____

   ____

2. If there were open immigration, what would happen to the value of the marginal product of capital and land and their rental rates?

   ____

   ____

3. Are the positions that each group takes on immigration consistent with their interests? Explain. Is there likely to be a solution that satisfies both?

   ____

   ____

SOLUTIONS

Terms and Definitions

3 Factors of production
8 Derived demand
5 Production function
4 Marginal product of labor
1 Diminishing marginal product
7 Value of the marginal product
2 Capital
6 Rental price (of a factor)

Practice Problems

1. a.

Labor (number of workers)	Output per Hour	Marginal Product of Labor	Value of *MPL* when P = \$3	Value of *MPL* when P = \$5
0	0			
		9	\$27	\$45
1	9			
		8	24	40
2	17			
		7	21	35
3	24			
		6	18	30
4	30			
		5	15	25
5	35			
		4	12	20
6	39			
		3	9	15
7	42			
		2	6	10
8	44			

b. Three workers because the value of the marginal product of each of the first three workers exceeds the \$19 wage so each worker adds to profits but the fourth worker only has a value of marginal product of \$18 so hiring the fourth worker would reduce profits.

c. Five workers because the value of the marginal product of each of the first five workers now exceeds the \$13 wage but the sixth worker only has a value of marginal product of \$12 so hiring the sixth worker would reduce profits. This is a movement along the firm's demand curve for labor because the value of the marginal product of labor for each worker is remaining the same but the wage facing the firm has changed.

d. See the fifth column in the table in part (a) above.

e. Seven workers because the value of the marginal product of each of the first seven workers exceeds the \$13 wage but the eighth worker only has a value of marginal product of \$10 so it would be unprofitable to hire that worker. This is a shift in the demand curve for labor because the value of the marginal product of labor has increased for each worker because the price of output rose. Thus, the firm demands more workers at the same \$13 wage.

2. a. See Exhibit 4.
   b. Increase the value of the marginal product of labor and the wage.
   c. When the price of output rises, the value of the marginal product of all of the inputs increases accordingly. Thus, the value of the marginal product of both land and capital will rise and so will their rental rates.
   d. When the price of output changes, the prosperity of the firm and the inputs move together. In this case, the prosperity of the firm and the inputs are increased.

EXHIBIT 4

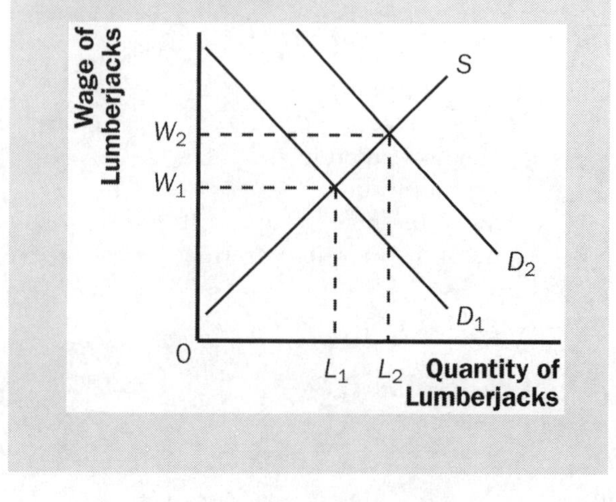

3. a. See Exhibit 5. This event increases the supply of agricultural land and decreases the marginal product of land and the rental price of land.
   b. See Exhibit 6. The increase in the supply of agricultural land increases the marginal product of labor and shifts the demand for farm labor to the right which increases the wage.

EXHIBIT 5

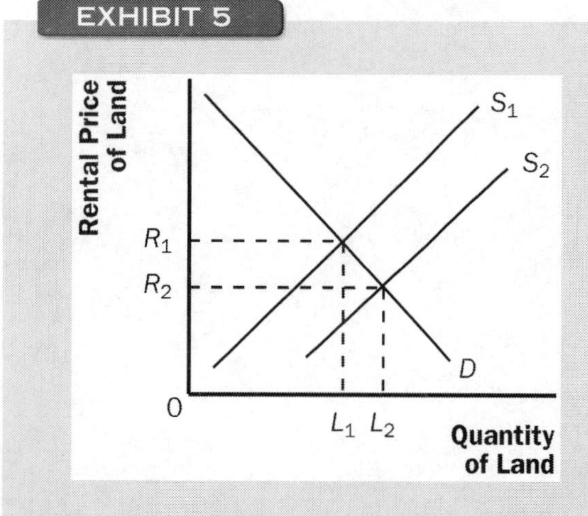

EXHIBIT 6

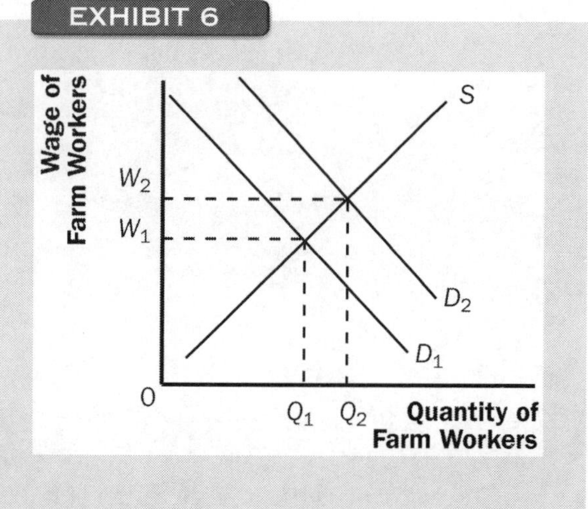

4. a. The increase in capital available for workers increases the marginal product of labor, shifts the demand for labor to the right, and increases the wage.
   b. This event increases the demand for Hondas and increases the price of Hondas. The increase in the price of Hondas increases the value of the marginal product of labor, shifts the demand for labor to the right, and increases the wage.
   c. This event increases the supply of labor, decreases the marginal product of labor, and decreases the wage.

Short-Answer Questions

1. The profit-maximizing firm will hire workers up to the point where the value of the marginal product of labor is equal to the wage. Beyond that point, additional workers cost more than the value of their marginal product and their employment would reduce profit. Since the value of the marginal product curve determines how many workers the firm will hire at each wage, it *is* the demand curve for labor.

2. The marginal product of labor is diminishing as more labor is added to the production process. Since the price of output is given in a competitive market, it follows that the *value* of the marginal product also declines as the quantity of labor is increased.

3. Given: $MC = W/MPL$. If the firm hires up to the point where the wage equals the value of the marginal product, then $P \times MPL = W$, or $P = W/MPL$. Substituting, MC for W/MPL we get $P = MC$.

4. The equilibrium wage is determined by supply and demand for labor in the market for labor. Each firm then hires workers up to the point where that wage equals the value of the marginal product of labor in each firm.

5. The value of the marginal product of both labor and capital employed in the production of textbooks should rise because the price of the output produced by them has risen. Therefore, the wage and rental rate paid to each should also rise.

6. Since there is a declining marginal product of capital as more capital is used, an increase in capital reduces the marginal product of capital and its rental rate. The increase in capital, however, increases the marginal product of labor and increases its wage.

7. The rental price is the price one pays to use the factor for a limited period of time while the purchase price of a factor is the price one pays to own that factor indefinitely. The purchase price of a factor depends on the current and expected future value of the marginal product of the factor.

8. Interest, dividends, and retained earnings.

9. An increase in the price of output produced by labor, an advance in technology used in production, and an increase in the supply of factors used with labor in production.

10. A shift in tastes toward working outside the home, a reduction in alternative opportunities for employment, and immigration.

True/False Questions

1. F; the factors are labor, land, and capital.

2. T

3. T

4. F; a factor exhibits diminishing marginal productivity if the increase in output generated from an additional unit of input diminishes as the quantity of the input increases.

5. T

6. T

7. F; a decrease in the supply of labor increases the value of the marginal product of labor, increases the wage, and decreases employment.

8. F; the marginal product of the factor could rise from a reduction in the supply of the factor (more scarce) or from an increase in the productivity of that factor.

9. T

10. T
11. T
12. F; an increase in the supply of capital will decrease the value of the marginal product of capital and decrease the rental rate.
13. F; capital income will be in the form of interest, dividends, and retained earnings.
14. T
15. F; it increases the value of the marginal product of labor and the wage.

Multiple-Choice Questions

1. d	5. c	9. a	13. b	17. b
2. a	6. c	10. b	14. a	18. a
3. b	7. d	11. d	15. c	19. d
4. a	8. b	12. c	16. d	20. c

Advanced Critical Thinking

1. Labor would be less scarce so the value of the marginal product of labor would decrease and so would the wage.
2. Additional labor could be applied to capital and land, which would increase the value of the marginal product of capital and land and increase their rental rates.
3. Yes. Organized labor wishes to keep the wage of labor high so it hopes to restrict immigration. Corporate interests wish to raise the return to capital and land so it hopes to allow open immigration. No.

19

EARNINGS AND DISCRIMINATION

GOALS

In this chapter you will

Examine how wages compensate for differences in job characteristics

Learn and compare the human-capital and signaling theories of education

Examine why in some occupations a few superstars earn tremendous incomes

Learn why wages rise above the level that balances supply and demand

Consider why it is difficult to measure the impact of discrimination on wages

See when market forces can and cannot provide a natural remedy for discrimination

OUTCOMES

After accomplishing these goals, you should be able to

Explain why an economics professor earns less than a corporate economist of similar age, background, and training

Explain the differing impact of policies aimed at increasing the educational attainment of all workers under the signaling and the human-capital view of education

List the characteristics of a market where superstars can arise

List three reasons why a wage can rise above the equilibrium wage

Explain why differences in wages among groups does not by itself say anything about how much discrimination there is in the labor market

Explain why competitive employers are unlikely to discriminate against groups of employees unless the customers or the government demands it

CHAPTER OVERVIEW

Context and Purpose

Chapter 19 is the second chapter in a three-chapter sequence that addresses the economics of labor markets. Chapter 18 developed the markets for the factors of production. Chapter 19 goes beyond the supply-and-demand models developed in Chapter 18 to help explain the wide variation in wages we find in the economy. Chapter 20 addresses the distribution of income and the role the government can play in altering the distribution of income.

The purpose of Chapter 19 is to extend the basic neoclassical theory of the labor market that we developed in Chapter 18. Neoclassical theory argues that wages depend on the supply and demand for labor and that labor demand depends on the value of the marginal productivity of labor. To address the wide variation in the wages that we observe, we must examine more precisely what determines the supply and demand for various types of labor.

CHAPTER REVIEW

Introduction

Chapter 19 extends the basic neoclassical theory of the labor market that we developed in Chapter 18. Neoclassical theory argues that wages depend on the supply and demand for labor and that labor demand depends on the value of the marginal productivity of labor. To address the wide variation in the wages that we observe, Chapter 19 examines more precisely what determines the supply and demand for various types of labor.

Some Determinants of Equilibrium Wages

Workers differ from one another. Jobs also differ in terms of the wages they pay and their nonmonetary characteristics. These differences affect labor supply, labor demand, and equilibrium wages.

Some jobs are easy, fun, and safe while others are hard, dull, and dangerous. If the wages were the same, most people would prefer to do easy, fun, and safe jobs. Therefore, workers require a higher wage in order to be induced to do a hard, dull, and dangerous job. A **compensating differential** is the difference in wages that arises to offset the nonmonetary characteristics of different jobs. For example, people who work in coal mines or on the night shift receive a compensating differential to compensate for the disagreeable nature of their work.

Capital is a factor of production that itself has been produced. Capital includes the economy's accumulation of equipment and structures and also includes a less tangible form of capital known as human capital. **Human capital** is the accumulation of investments in people, such as education and on-the-job training. Workers with more human capital earn more than those with less for the following reasons: With regard to labor demand, educated workers have a higher marginal product so firms are willing to pay more for them. With regard to labor supply, workers are only willing to educate themselves if they are rewarded for doing so. In effect, there is a compensating differential between educated and uneducated workers to compensate for the cost of becoming educated. In 1980, male college graduates earned 44 percent more than workers with a high school diploma. By 2000, the difference was 89 percent. For women, the differential rose from 35 percent to 70 percent. There are two hypotheses that may explain the increased differential. First, the growth in international trade has allowed the United States to import goods made by unskilled workers in foreign countries where unskilled workers are plentiful, and export goods produced by skilled labor. In the domestic economy, this increases the demand for skilled workers and decreases the demand for unskilled workers. Second, increases in technology have increased the demand for skilled workers and decreased the demand for unskilled workers. Both hypotheses may be true. People gain more than just human capital when they go to college. The greater an individual's educational attainment, the greater the individual's overall satisfaction with life, including satisfaction with one's love life.

Natural ability, effort, and chance help explain wages. Some people are smarter and stronger than others and they are paid for their natural ability. Some people work harder than others and are compensated for their effort. Chance plays a role in that someone's education and experience can be made valueless if there is a change in technology that eliminates that person's job. Beauty may be a natural ability because attractiveness may make an actor or waiter more productive. It may also be a sign of an intelligent person who expends effort to successfully appear attractive and this may suggest that the individual may be successful at other things, too. Alternatively, a wage premium for beauty may simply be a type of discrimination. Attractive people do earn a premium over less attractive people.

The human-capital view of education argues that workers with more education are paid more because the education made them more productive. As an alternative, the *signaling* view of education argues that firms use education as a method of sorting high-ability workers from low-ability workers. Educational attainment signals high ability because it is easier for high-ability people to earn a college degree than it is for low-ability people and firms are willing to pay more for high-ability people. Just as with the signaling theory of advertising where the advertisement itself contains no real information, the signaling theory of education suggests that schooling has no real productivity benefit. According to the human-capital view of education, a policy of increasing educational attainment for all workers should raise all workers' wages. According to the signaling view of education, additional education would not affect productivity or wages. The benefits of education are probably a combination of both human-capital and signaling effects.

A few superstars earn astronomical salaries. These superstars are often performers such as athletes, actors, writers, and so on. Superstars arise in markets that have two characteristics:

- Every customer in the market wants to enjoy the good supplied by the best producer.
- The good is produced with a technology that makes it possible for the best producer to supply every customer at low cost.

So far, we have addressed why workers might earn different *equilibrium* wages. Some workers, however, may earn higher wages because their wages are held above equilibrium due to the following:

- *Minimum-wage laws.* This mostly effects less-experienced and less-skilled workers.
- *The market power of labor unions.* A **union** is a worker association that bargains with employers over wages and working conditions. The union can hold wages 10 to 20 percent above equilibrium because they can threaten to **strike** or withhold labor from the firm.
- *Efficiency wages.* **Efficiency wages** occur when firms choose to hold wages above equilibrium to increase productivity because high wages reduce worker turnover, increase worker effort, and raise the quality of workers that apply for jobs at the firm.

Whenever the wage is held above equilibrium, the result is unemployment.

The Economics of Discrimination

Wages can differ due to discrimination. **Discrimination** is the offering of different opportunities to similar individuals who differ only by race, ethnic group, sex, age, or other personal characteristics. Discrimination is an emotional issue.

Wages differ across races and sexes for a number of reasons. Whites have more human capital on average than blacks due to more years of schooling and better schools. Men generally have more years of education and more job experience than women. In school, women may have been directed away from science and math courses. Men may also receive a compensating differential for doing more unpleasant jobs than women choose to do. While some of the wage differentials are likely to be due to discrimination, there is no agreement with regard to how much. Economists would agree that *because the differences in average wages among groups in part reflect differences in human capital and job characteristics, they do not by themselves say anything about how much discrimination there is in the labor market.*

While it is difficult to measure discrimination, suppose that we have evidence that there is discrimination in the labor market. If some employers discriminate against certain groups of employees, then the demand for the services of those that are discriminated against will be low and their wages will be low while the demand for those workers not discriminated against will be high and their wages will be high. In a competitive market, employers that discriminate against certain groups of employees will be at a competitive disadvantage because their labor costs will be higher. Firms that care only about profits and do not discriminate will tend to replace those that do discriminate because they will be more profitable. The firms that do not discriminate will increase the demand for the labor services of the group that was discriminated against, decrease the demand for the group not discriminated against, and the wages will be equalized across groups. Thus, competitive markets can be a cure for employer discrimination.

If customers or governments demand discrimination, however, then competition and the profit motive of firms may not correct the wage differential. If bigoted customers are willing to pay extra to be served by a certain group in a restaurant and are not willing to be served by another group, then the wage differential can persist even in a competitive market. If the government mandates discriminatory practices, then competition will again fail to equalize a discriminatory wage differential. There is evidence that, in some professional sports, white athletes are paid more than black athletes of comparable ability and that attendance is greater for teams with a greater proportion of white players. This suggests that sports fans are willing to pay a premium to watch white players. Since black players are less profitable, this wage differential can persist even if owners care only about profits. If a wage differential persists in a competitive market, it is because bigoted customers are willing to pay for it or because the government requires it. The wage differential cannot be maintained by a bigoted employer alone.

Conclusion

In competitive markets, workers earn a wage equal to the value of their marginal product. The workers' value of marginal product is higher if they are more talented, diligent, experienced, and educated. Firms pay less to those workers against whom customers discriminate because they are less profitable to the firm.

HELPFUL HINTS

1. The wage is explained by supply and demand. Characteristics of both people and jobs affect supply, demand, and the wage for labor in each labor market. For example, education, experience, and hard work increases the value of the marginal productivity of workers, increases the demand for their services, and increases their wage. An increase in the disagreeable nature of the work, the expense of training, and the required ability to do the job reduces the pool of workers willing and able to do a particular job, reduces the supply of labor in that market, and increases the wage. Even the market for superstars can be explained with supply and demand. Since superstars can satisfy every customer at the same time through television, movies, music CDs, and so on, the value of their marginal product is enormous and so is the demand for their services.

2. Different pay for different groups of people is not, by itself, evidence of labor market discrimination because differences in pay among groups in part reflects differences in human capital and job characteristics. What seems to be discrimination may simply be a compensating differential that

is paid for the disagreeable nature of a job. In addition, a wage differential could be due to a difference in the average productivity across groups of workers.

TERMS AND DEFINITIONS

Choose a definition for each key term.

Key terms:

_____ Compensating differential

_____ Human capital

_____ Union

_____ Strike

_____ Efficiency wages

_____ Discrimination

Definitions:

1. The offering of different opportunities to similar individuals who differ only by race, ethnic group, sex, age, or other personal characteristics
2. A difference in wages that arises to offset the nonmonetary characteristics of different jobs
3. The organized withdrawal of labor from a firm by a union
4. The accumulation of investments in people, such as education and on-the-job training
5. Above-equilibrium wages paid by firms in order to increase worker productivity
6. A worker association that bargains with employers over wages and working conditions

PROBLEMS AND SHORT-ANSWER QUESTIONS

Practice Problems

1. Within each of the following pairs of workers, which worker is likely to earn more and why? (It may be obvious which one is paid more. The real issue is to explain why one is paid more than the other.)
   a. A carpenter working at the top of a 600-foot cooling tower of a nuclear power plant or a carpenter who frames houses?

   ____

   ____

   b. A clerk in a grocery store or a lawyer?

   ____

   ____

   c. A lawyer with one year of experience or a lawyer with six years of experience?

   ____

   ____

d. An attractive salesperson or a homely salesperson?

e. An autoworker in a factory who works the day shift or an autoworker in a factory who works the night shift?

f. An economics professor or a corporate economist?

g. A history professor or an economics professor?

h. Someone trained as a key-punch operator (typist who types input commands on cards to be read by a mainframe computer prior to the existence of computer terminals) or someone trained as a personal computer specialist?

i. Your favorite local blues band that plays regularly at a nearby campus bar or David Bowie?

j. A lazy, stupid plumber or a hardworking, bright plumber?

k. The best carpenter on the planet or the best writer on the planet?

2. a. Explain the human-capital view of education and the signaling view of education.

b. What are the implications for education policy under each view?

c. Which of the above is true? Explain.

3. a. How can a competitive market eliminate discrimination in the labor market?

b. What limits a competitive market's ability to reduce discrimination? Explain.

Short-Answer Questions

1. Why does someone who has a great amount of human capital that was acquired though education earn more than someone with a small amount of human capital?

2. Name some characteristics of a job that might require a positive compensating differential.

3. What has happened to the relative wages of skilled and unskilled workers in the United States over the last 20 years? Why?

4. What are the necessary conditions for a superstar to arise in a market? Explain.

5. Does a difference in average wages among groups, by itself, suggest that there is discrimination in the labor market? Explain.

6. If a discriminatory wage differential persists in a competitive market, is it due to discrimination on the part of the employer or must it be from some other source? Explain.

7. Is there discrimination in professional sports? Is the employer the source of the discrimination? Explain.

8. List the professions of most superstars. What do these professions have in common?

9. Why is a plumber's apprentice paid less than a master plumber?

10. Provide three reasons why wages might be set above the equilibrium wage. Explain.

SELF-TEST

True/False Questions

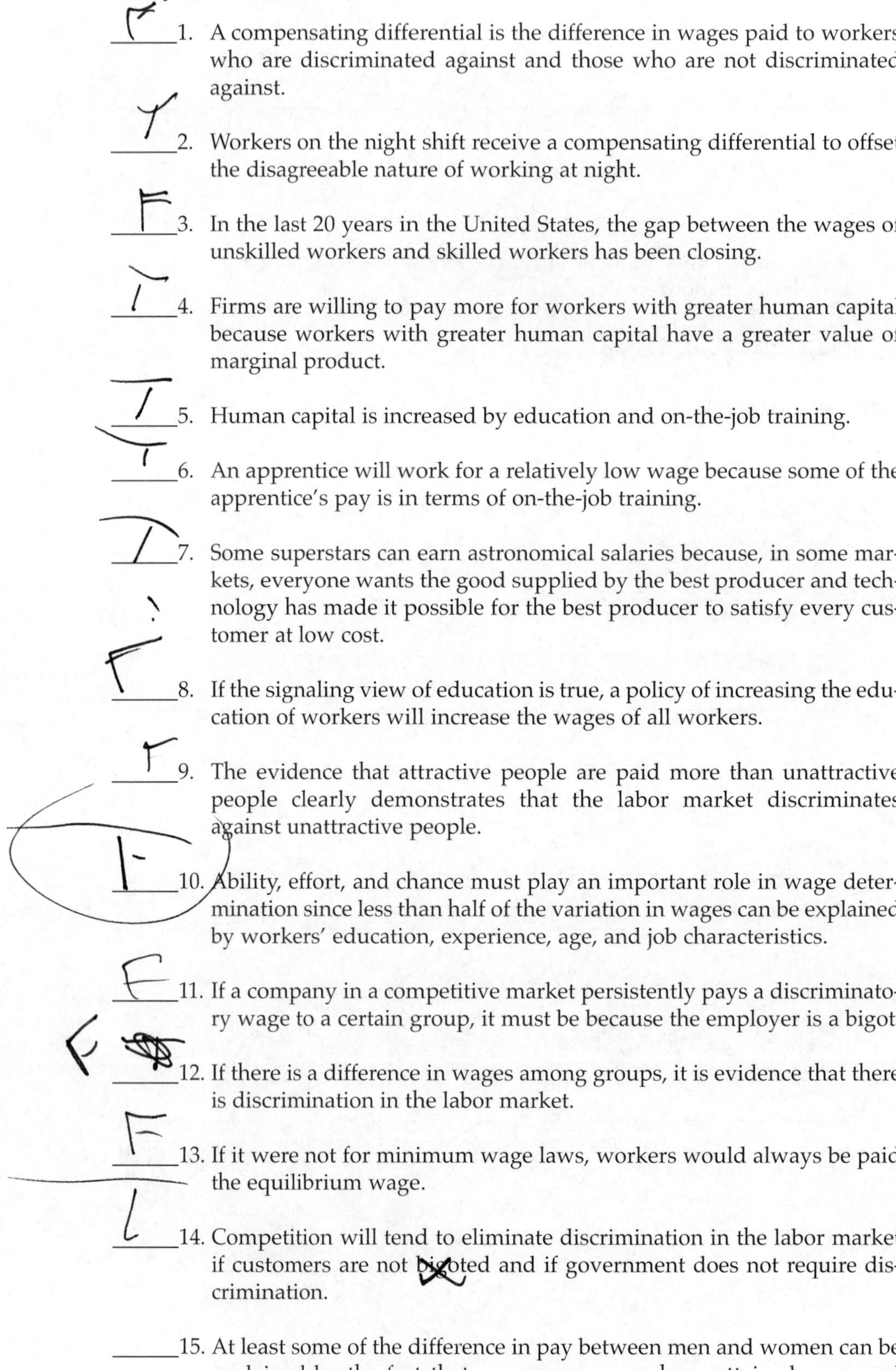

______1. A compensating differential is the difference in wages paid to workers who are discriminated against and those who are not discriminated against.

______2. Workers on the night shift receive a compensating differential to offset the disagreeable nature of working at night.

______3. In the last 20 years in the United States, the gap between the wages of unskilled workers and skilled workers has been closing.

______4. Firms are willing to pay more for workers with greater human capital because workers with greater human capital have a greater value of marginal product.

______5. Human capital is increased by education and on-the-job training.

______6. An apprentice will work for a relatively low wage because some of the apprentice's pay is in terms of on-the-job training.

______7. Some superstars can earn astronomical salaries because, in some markets, everyone wants the good supplied by the best producer and technology has made it possible for the best producer to satisfy every customer at low cost.

______8. If the signaling view of education is true, a policy of increasing the education of workers will increase the wages of all workers.

______9. The evidence that attractive people are paid more than unattractive people clearly demonstrates that the labor market discriminates against unattractive people.

______10. Ability, effort, and chance must play an important role in wage determination since less than half of the variation in wages can be explained by workers' education, experience, age, and job characteristics.

______11. If a company in a competitive market persistently pays a discriminatory wage to a certain group, it must be because the employer is a bigot.

______12. If there is a difference in wages among groups, it is evidence that there is discrimination in the labor market.

______13. If it were not for minimum wage laws, workers would always be paid the equilibrium wage.

______14. Competition will tend to eliminate discrimination in the labor market if customers are not bigoted and if government does not require discrimination.

______15. At least some of the difference in pay between men and women can be explained by the fact that, on average, men have attained more and better schooling, men have more job experience, and men may do more unpleasant jobs.

Multiple-Choice Questions

1. If a person who works in a coal mine gets paid more than a person with a similar background and skills who works in a safer job, then
   a. we have evidence of discrimination against workers outside the coal mine.
   b. we have observed a compensating differential.
   c. coal miners must have greater human capital than others.
   d. coal miners must be more attractive than other workers.

2. According to the human-capital view of education, education
   a. increases human capital and the wages of workers.
   b. only helps firms sort workers into high-ability and low-ability workers.
   c. has no impact on the human capital of workers.
   d. can make any worker into a superstar.

3. Which of the following is not part of a worker's human capital?
   a. education
   b. on-the-job training
   c. experience
   d. effort
   e. All of the above are parts of a worker's human capital.

4. According to the signaling view of education, education
   a. increases human capital and the wages of workers.
   b. only helps firms sort workers into high-ability and low-ability workers.
   c. reduces the wage gap between high-skill and low-skill workers.
   d. can make any worker into a superstar.

5. All of the following would tend to increase a worker's wage except
   a. more education.
   b. working the night shift.
   c. doing a job that is fun.
   d. having a greater amount of natural ability.
   e. working harder.

6. In a competitive market, which of the following is least likely to be the source of a persistent discriminatory wage differential?
   a. the customer
   b. the government
   c. the employer
   d. All of the above could be the source of a persistent discriminatory wage differential.

7. If two jobs require the same amount of skills and experience, the job that pays the most is most likely to be the one that is
   a. unpleasant.
   b. safe.
   c. easy.
   d. fun.
   e. all of the above.

8. In the last 20 years, the gap between the wages of skilled and unskilled workers in the United States has
   a. decreased.
   b. increased.
   c. stayed the same.
   d. first increased and is now decreasing.

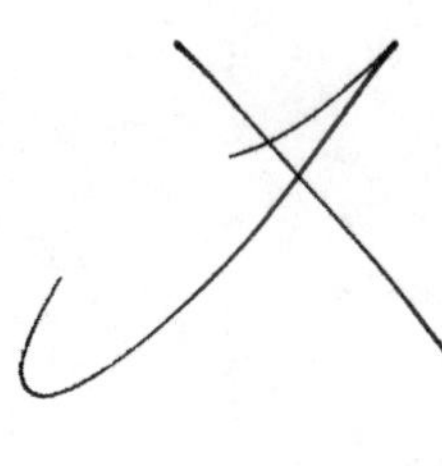

9. Which of the following is true regarding the earnings of attractive versus unattractive workers?
   a. Attractive people tend to earn less because attractive people are viewed as shallow and more self-absorbed and, therefore, as less productive.
   b. Attractive people tend to earn less because attractive people usually have less human capital.
   c. Attractive people tend to earn more because they may actually have a larger value of marginal product.
   d. Attractive people tend to earn more because attractive people usually have greater human capital.

10. The relative wage of unskilled workers has fallen in the United States likely as a result of a relative
    a. increase in the number of unskilled workers available because workers are more poorly educated.
    b. increase in the number of unskilled workers available due to immigration into the United States.
    c. decrease in the demand for unskilled workers because workers are more poorly educated.
    d. decrease in the demand for unskilled workers because of increases in technology and increases in international trade.

11. Which of the following professionals is most likely to be able to generate the income of a superstar?
    a. the best medical doctor.
    b. the best professor.
    c. the best accountant.
    d. the best writer.
    e. All of the above participate in markets that could generate a superstar.

12. It is *not* considered discrimination when an employer offers different opportunities to individuals that differ only by their
    a. race.
    b. sex.
    c. productivity.
    d. age.

13. In order for a market to support superstars it must have which of the following characteristics?
    a. It must be involved in professional athletics.
    b. Every customer must want the good supplied by the best producer and the technology must exist for the best producer to supply every customer at low cost.
    c. Every customer must be willing to pay an enormous amount for the product and the product must be a necessity.
    d. Every customer must be indifferent to the price they pay and the seller must be a competitor in the market for the product.

14. Which of the following statements regarding discrimination is true?
    a. Discrimination cannot exist in a competitive labor market.
    b. Discrimination can only persist in a competitive labor market if customers are willing to pay to maintain the discriminatory practice or the government requires discrimination.
    c. Bigoted employers are the main source of a persistent discriminatory wage differential in a competitive market.
    d. The existence of a wage differential among groups is strong evidence of discrimination in the labor market.

15. Competitive markets tend to
    a. reduce labor market discrimination because non-discriminating firms will employ cheaper labor, earn more profits, and drive discriminating firms out of the market.
    b. have no impact on labor market discrimination.
    c. increase labor market discrimination because bigoted employers can charge any price they want in a competitive market to cover the cost of their discrimination.
    d. increase labor market discrimination because some workers can charge more for their services than other workers in a competitive market.

16. A wage differential among groups may not by itself be evidence of discrimination in the labor market because different groups have
    a. different levels of education.
    b. different preferences for the type of work they are willing to do.
    c. different levels of job experience.
    d. all of the above.

17. Which of the following is *not* a reason why some workers are paid above the equilibrium wage?
    a. minimum-wage laws
    b. beauty
    c. unions
    d. efficiency wages

18. Which of the following is likely to generate a compensating differential?
    a. One employee is more attractive than another.
    b. One employee works harder than another.
    c. One employee is willing to work the nightshift while another is not.
    d. One employee is more educated than another.
    e. All of the above generate compensating differentials.

19. Which of the following explanations of wage differentials is *not* likely to be true?
    a. Men have more human capital than women.
    b. Whites have more human capital than blacks.
    c. Employers in competitive markets are bigots.
    d. Men have more job experience than women.

20. Which of the following could result in women being paid less than men?
   a. customers preferring to deal with men
   b. women preferring to work in pleasant clean safe work places
   c. women entering and leaving the labor force to care for children
   d. women obtaining less human capital because they don't plan to work continuously to the age of retirement
   e. all of the above

ADVANCED CRITICAL THINKING

You are at a political rally with some friends. A candidate for state office states that working women earn about 60 cents for each dollar that working men earn. The candidate says, "This is clearly evidence that employers discrimination against women. This gap between the earnings of men and women will never close because professions women tend to choose are traditionally low paying and the professions men choose are traditionally high paying. I will propose that the government create a panel to decide what jobs should pay so that people of similar skills and education earn the same amount."

1. Suppose a secretary and a truck driver are judged to require the same level of education and skills, yet a secretary earns $30,000 while a truck driver earns $40,000. What would happen to the quantities supplied and demanded in the market for secretaries and truck drivers if the wage for these professions were set by law at $35,000?

____

____

____

2. What would happen to the level of effort and natural ability of the workers available in each market? What would happen to the quality of work generated in each market?

____

____

____

3. Suppose it is true that the skills and education required to do each job are, in fact, nearly identical. What explanation would an economist likely propose to explain why the equilibrium wage differs by $10,000 across these markets?

____

____

____

____

SOLUTIONS

Terms and Definitions

2 Compensating differential

4 Human capital

6 Union

3 Strike

5 Efficiency wages

1 Discrimination

Practice Problems

1. a. The carpenter working at the 600 foot height because he/she will likely require a compensating differential for the danger of the job.
   b. A lawyer because the lawyer has greater human capital from years of education and the lawyer requires a compensating differential to compensate for the cost and effort of becoming educated.
   c. A lawyer with six years of experience because work experience is part of human capital.
   d. An attractive salesperson because they may have a higher value of marginal product due to being attractive or because they have signaled that they may be successful at a variety of things when they succeeded at the task of making themselves look attractive. Alternatively, it may be due to discrimination against homely people.
   e. The nightshift worker because the nightshift is disagreeable and the worker requires a compensating differential.
   f. The corporate economist because the corporate economist requires a compensating differential to compensate for the disagreeable nature of the work. Also, the corporate economist may have a greater value of marginal product.
   g. An economics professor because the market wage for economists is higher due to the economist's higher value of marginal product in the corporate labor market.
   h. A personal computer specialist because, through chance, technology has changed such that key-punch operators are no longer needed while PC specialists are needed.
   i. Superstar David Bowie because through technology he is able to satisfy the entire market at the same time. (He is the first rock star to have a net worth in excess of one billion dollars).
   j. The hardworking bright plumber because the value of the marginal product is higher for people with ability and who work hard.
   k. The best writer because the writer is in a market that can support a superstar while the carpenter is not.

2. a. Education increases human capital and raises the value of the marginal product of labor and, thus, the wage. Alternatively, education is only a signal of high ability.
   b. According to the human-capital view, policies that increase educational attainment for all will increase all wages. According to the signaling view, an increase in educational attainment will not affect wages because education does not increase productivity.
   c. Probably both are true. It is unclear regarding the relative sizes of these two effects.

3. a. Firms only interested in profit will hire the group of workers that is discriminated against. Since their wages are relatively low, the firms that do not discriminate will have a competitive advantage

over the discriminatory firms. As the non-discriminating firms replace the discriminatory firms, the relative demand for workers previously discriminated against will increase, which will remove the discriminatory wage differential.

b. If bigoted customers are willing to pay higher prices to firms that discriminate, or if the government requires discrimination, the competitive market cannot eliminate discrimination.

Short-Answer Questions

1. Because workers with greater human capital are more productive and firms are willing to pay more for workers with a greater value of marginal product. In addition, workers must be compensated for the cost of educating themselves.

2. A compensating differential is paid for the disagreeable, unpleasant nature of a job. Other things being equal, jobs will pay more if they are dirty, noisy, smelly, solitary, unsafe, hard, require travel, require working odd hours such as the nightshift or swing shift, require working with unpleasant people, etc.

3. The gap between skilled and unskilled wages has risen, possibly because the growth in international trade has allowed the United States to import goods made by unskilled workers in countries where unskilled labor is plentiful, and export goods made by skilled workers. This would increase the relative demand for skilled workers. Or it could be that increases in technology have increased the relative demand for skilled workers.

4. Every customer in the market wants to enjoy the good supplied by the best producer and the good is produced with a technology that makes it possible for the best producer to supply every customer at low cost.

5. No. Since average wages among groups are in part based on differences in human capital and job characteristics, a wage differential among groups alone tells us nothing about discrimination.

6. If customers are not bigoted and government does not require discrimination, competition will ensure that employers cannot continuously discriminate. If a wage differential persists, it must be because the customers are willing to pay for it (they are bigoted) or the government requires it. It cannot simply be due to a bigoted employer.

7. Evidence suggests that in some professional sports, white players are paid more than equivalent black players. The source is likely to be the sports fan (the customer).

8. Writers, athletes, television and movie actors, movie directors, musicians, artists, software creators, motivational speakers, etc. Customers want only the best and technology allows the seller to satisfy all customers at low cost.

9. Because the apprentice's value of marginal product is less and because the apprentice is being paid, in part, with on-the-job training that increases the apprentice's human capital and future earnings.

10. Minimum-wage laws (government imposed wage floor), the market power of labor unions (threat of strike raises wage), and efficiency wages (firms pay above equilibrium wage to increase productivity because high wages reduce turnover, increase effort, and raise the quality of job applicants).

True/False Questions

1. F; it is the difference in wages that arises to offset the nonmonetary characteristics of different jobs.

2. T

3. F; the gap has been widening.

4. T

5. T

6. T

7. T

8. F; education would not increase productivity and would have no effect on wages.

9. F; attractive people may have a larger value of marginal product or attractive people may have signaled that since they are good at making themselves attractive they may also be good at other tasks.

10. T

11. F; it must be because the customer is willing to pay for the discrimination or because the government requires it.

12. F; the difference in wages may be due to differences in human capital or job characteristics.

13. F; unions may pressure firms to raise wages above equilibrium, and firms may choose to pay efficiency wages, which are above equilibrium.

14. T

15. T

Multiple-Choice Questions

1. b
2. a
3. d
4. b
5. c
6. c
7. a
8. b
9. c
10. d
11. d
12. c
13. b
14. b
15. a
16. d
17. b
18. c
19. c
20. e

Advanced Critical Thinking

1. There will be a surplus of secretaries and a shortage of truck drivers. That is, it will increase the quantity supplied of secretaries and decrease the quantity demanded while it will decrease the quantity supplied of truck drivers and increase the quantity demanded.

2. Hardworking, high-ability workers would avoid the truck driving market and the quality of truck driving would be reduced. Hardworking and high-ability workers would be attracted to the secretary market and the quality of secretarial services would be increased.

3. An economist would argue that $10,000 is the compensating differential necessary to get someone to undertake the disagreeable nature of truck driving—working alone, overnight travel away from children, less clean and less safe work environment, etc.

20

THE DISTRIBUTION OF INCOME

GOALS

In this chapter you will

Examine the degree of economic inequality in our society

Consider some problems that arise when measuring economic inequality

See how political philosophers view the government's role in redistributing income

Consider the various policies aimed at helping poor families escape poverty

OUTCOMES

After accomplishing these goals, you should be able to

Explain how the women's movement has affected income distribution in the United States

Name some factors that cause the measurement of income distribution to exaggerate the degree of income inequality

Compare and contrast utilitarianism, liberalism, and libertarianism

Explain the concept of a negative income tax

CHAPTER OVERVIEW

Context and Purpose

Chapter 20 is the third chapter in a three-chapter sequence that addresses the economics of labor markets. Chapter 18 developed the markets for the factors of production. Chapter 19 extended the basic supply-and-demand model to help explain the wide variation in wages we find in the economy. Chapter 20 addresses the measurement of the distribution of income and looks at the role the government plays in altering the distribution of income.

The purpose of Chapter 20 is to address income distribution. The discussion proceeds by answering three questions. First, how much inequality is there? Second, what do different political philosophies have to say about the proper role of government in altering the distribution of income? And third, what are the various government policies that are used to help the poor?

CHAPTER REVIEW

Introduction

This chapter addresses the distribution of income by answering three questions. First, how much inequality is there? Second, what do different political philosophies have to say about the proper role of government in altering the distribution of income? And third, what are the various government policies that are used to help the poor? We will find that governments may be able to improve on the distribution of income generated by the market but at the expense of a distortion in incentives and a reduction in efficiency.

The Measurement of Inequality

There are a variety of ways to describe the distribution of income. One way is to show what percent of total before-tax income that is earned by families in each fifth and the top 5 percent of the income distribution. The top fifth earns about 47.4 percent of total income while the bottom fifth earns about 4.3 percent. That is, the top fifth earns about ten times what the bottom fifth earns. The top 5 percent earns more than the bottom 40 percent.

The distribution of income is remarkably stable over time. Over the past 65 years, the bottom fifth has generally earned between 4 percent and 5 percent while the top fifth has earned between 40 percent and 50 percent. However, from 1935 to 1970, the income distribution narrowed slightly and from 1970 to 2000, it has grown slightly wider. The increase in income inequality may be because of increases in international trade and increases in technology have reduced the demand for unskilled workers while raising the demand for skilled workers, which has caused a change in relative wages. In addition, the women's movement has increased income inequality because there has been a greater increase in the labor-force participation of women from already high-income households than from low-income households.

When countries are ranked by inequality, the United States ranks about average. Japan, Germany, and Canada have greater income equality than the United States while Mexico, South Africa, and Brazil have greater income inequality.

Another measure of the distribution of income is the **poverty rate**—the percentage of the population whose family income falls below an absolute level called the **poverty line.** The poverty line is an absolute level of income set by the federal government for each family size below which a family is deemed to be in poverty. It is set at approximately three times the cost of providing an adequate diet. In 2000, the median family had an income of $50,890 while 11.3 percent of the population was in families with incomes below the poverty line of $17,603. The poverty rate fell from 1959 to 1973 but it has not declined since then. Poverty rates demonstrate three facts:

- *Poverty is correlated with race.* Blacks and Hispanics are three times more likely than whites to live in poverty.
- *Poverty is correlated with age.* Children are more likely than average and elderly less likely than average to live in poverty.
- *Poverty is correlated with family composition.* Families headed by females with no husband present are five times as likely to live in poverty as a family headed by a married couple.

There are problems associated with measuring inequality. Although data on the income distribution and the poverty rate are useful in measuring inequality, these measures are not perfect measures of someone's ability to maintain a standard of living for the following reasons:

- **In-kind transfers** are transfers to the poor given in the form of goods and services rather than cash. They are not accounted for in the standard measures of income inequality.

- The economic **life cycle** is the regular pattern of income variation over a person's life. Young and old may earn little income but the young can borrow and the old can live off past saving. Standard measures of income inequality exaggerate the variation in living standards because annual income has greater variation than living standards.

- *Transitory versus permanent income.* Incomes vary due to random and transitory forces. That is, events can cause income to be unusually high or low for any given year. Again, people can borrow and lend so that they can maintain stable living standards even when there is variation in income. A family's living standard depends largely on its permanent income. **Permanent income** is a person's normal, or average, income.

For each of the reasons listed above, standard measures of income distribution exaggerate the inequality of living standards.

Economic mobility in the United States is high. During any ten-year period, 25 percent of families fall below the poverty line in at least one year but only 3 percent of families are poor for eight or more years. At the other extreme, if a father earns income 20 percent above average, his son will earn income only 8 percent above average and his grandson will earn an average income. Further, four out of five millionaires made their money on their own rather than inheriting it. These data suggest that deviations from average income tend to be somewhat temporary and, again, measures of income inequality tend to exaggerate the inequality in living standards.

The Political Philosophy of Redistributing Income

Economics alone cannot tell us whether governments *should* do anything about economic inequality. For this, we must address various schools of political philosophy:

- **Utilitarianism:** the political philosophy according to which the government should choose policies to maximize the total utility of everyone in society. **Utility** is a measure of happiness or satisfaction and it is assumed to be the ultimate objective of all actions. If there is diminishing marginal utility for each additional dollar of income, then taking away a dollar from a rich person and giving it to a poor person lowers the rich person's utility less than the gain in utility received by the poor person. Utilitarians reject complete equalization of income because they realize that people respond to incentives and, thus, taxes create deadweight losses and there is less total income to be redistributed. The founders of this philosophy are the English philosophers Jeremy Bentham and John Stuart Mill.

- **Liberalism:** the political philosophy according to which the government should choose policies deemed to be just, as evaluated by an impartial observer behind a "veil of ignorance." This means that the only objective measure of economic justice is to set the rules for society as if every person were ignorant about the station in life each will end up filling—top, bottom, or middle. John Rawls, the originator of this theory of justice, argues that we would be concerned about being at the bottom of the income distribution so we would create a social rule known as the **maximin criterion**—the claim that the government should aim to maximize the well-being of the worst-off person in society. As a result, redistribution of income is a type of social insurance. Although not equalizing income completely, it would require greater redistribution than utilitarianism. Critics argue that rational people behind a veil of ignorance would not necessarily be so risk averse as to follow the maximin criterion.

- **Libertarianism:** the political philosophy according to which the government should punish crimes and enforce voluntary agreements but not redistribute income. Libertarians, such as Robert Nozick, argue that society earns no income—only individuals earn income. Therefore, income is not a shared resource to be distributed by a social planner. To a libertarian, if the *process* is fair, the *outcome* is fair, no matter how unequal. Thus, the government should punish stealing and cheating to make a fair playing field but should not be concerned with the final score if the rules were fair. Equality of opportunity is more important than equality of incomes.

Policies to Reduce Poverty

Regardless of political philosophy, most people think that the government should help the most needy because the poor are more likely to experience homelessness, drug dependency, domestic violence, health problems, teenage pregnancy, illiteracy, unemployment, low educational attainment, and they are more likely to commit crimes and be victims of crime. Here are some policy options:

- *Minimum-wage laws:* Advocates argue that it helps the poor without any cost to government. Critics argue that it raises the wage above equilibrium for the lowest skill workers and causes unemployment among those workers. Those that keep their jobs gain while those that become unemployed lose. The more elastic the demand for labor, the greater the job loss from a minimum wage. In addition, many minimum-wage workers are teenagers from middle-class families so the program is poorly targeted to the poor.

- *Welfare:* **Welfare** is a broad term that encompasses various government programs that supplement the incomes of the needy. These programs are cash assistance for people who have low incomes and have demonstrated a "need" such as having small children at home (Temporary Assistance for Needy Families, formerly known as Aid to Families with Dependent Children) or have a disability (Supplemental Security Income or SSI). Critics argue that these programs encourage the problems they hope to cure. Eligibility for assistance requires that the father not be in the household. This encourages fathers to abandon their families, causing broken homes, and may encourage unwed women to have illegitimate children. Evidence does not support the claim that welfare caused the decline in the two-parent family.

- *Negative income tax:* A **negative income tax** is a tax system that collects revenue from high-income households and gives transfers to low-income households. Under this tax system, a progressive income tax on the rich would be used to subsidize or provide a "negative tax" to low-income families. Poor families would not have to demonstrate need beyond simply being poor. This would not subsidize the breakup of families or subsidize illegitimate births but it would subsidize those that are just lazy. The Earned Income Tax Credit is similar to a negative income tax but it only applies to the working poor, not the unemployed or sick.

- *In-kind transfers:* In-kind transfers occur when the poor are directly provided goods and services as opposed to being provided cash payments. Food stamps and Medicaid are examples. Supporters argue that this method insures that the poor actually receive what they need as opposed to giving them money that they could spend on alcohol, drugs, and so on. Advocates of cash payments argue that in-kind transfers are inefficient because the government doesn't know what the poor need most. In addition, they argue that it is insulting to the poor to be forced to accept in-kind transfers.

Some antipoverty programs have the unintended effect of reducing the incentive for the poor to work. For example, suppose the government were to guarantee a fixed minimum level of income. If anyone below that income level were to work and earn a dollar, then the government would simply reduce that person's benefits one dollar. As a result, the effective tax rate is 100 percent on any new income and there is no incentive to work. Welfare, Medicaid, food stamps, and the Earned Income Tax Credit are all reduced when a recipient earns more income. This discourages work and may create a "culture of poverty." That is, welfare recipients lose their job skills, their children fail to see the benefits of work, and multiple generations of families become dependent on government. If benefits are reduced gradually as income rises, the incentive to work is not reduced as much. However, this increases the cost of fighting poverty because families above the poverty line will receive some benefits.

Work disincentives created by antipoverty programs can be reduced by *workfare*—programs requiring any person collecting benefits to accept a government-provided job. Another possibility is to limit the number of years a person can collect welfare. This method was used by the 1996 welfare reform bill. Advocates of the 1996 welfare reform cite the falling poverty rate in the late 1990s as evidence of success. Critics argue that falling poverty rates are due to the strong economy and limiting welfare is cruel to the unfortunate.

Universal education should shrink the gap between rich and poor. However, universal education does not mean that it must be provided in government schools. Some economists argue that parents should be given school vouchers provided by the government to purchase the education of their choosing. This would be similar to food stamps—funding is provided by the government but it need not be spent in government food stores. Some economists argue that new private schools would be more efficient and provide improved education. This could help narrow the income distribution.

Conclusion

It is difficult to measure inequality and there is little agreement about what to do about it. If we choose to do something about inequality, we should remember there is a tradeoff between equity and efficiency. That is, the more equally the pie is divided, the smaller the pie becomes.

HELPFUL HINTS

1. People in poverty are more likely to experience homelessness, drug dependency, domestic violence, health problems, teenage pregnancy, illiteracy, unemployment, low educational attainment, and they are more likely to commit crimes and be victims of crime. Note, however, that while it is clear that poverty is associated with these social ills, it is unclear whether poverty causes these social ills or whether these social ills cause poverty. That is, it may be that drug dependency, health problems, having children while young and out of wedlock, illiteracy, and so on are as much a cause of poverty as they are an effect of poverty.

2. There are a variety of reasons why an individual's current annual income can differ from his or her average lifetime income. The individual's income will depend on whether they are young, middle age, or old, and whether they have had an unusually productive or unproductive year. Since people can borrow and lend, standards of living are more stable than incomes and, thus, standard measures of income distribution will exaggerate the degree of economic inequality.

3. An additional reason why some people prefer the government to provide for the poor using in-kind transfers instead of cash payments is that in-kind transfers are thought to generate less fraud. This is because there is little incentive for an individual to file a fraudulent claim to receive medical benefits that the individual doesn't need but there may be a great incentive to file a fraudulent welfare claim to receive cash.

TERMS AND DEFINITIONS

Choose a definition for each key term.

Key terms:

_____ Poverty rate

_____ Poverty line

_____ In-kind transfers

_____ Life cycle

_____ Permanent income

_____ Utilitarianism

_____ Utility

_____ Liberalism

_____ Maximin criterion

_____ Libertarianism

_____ Welfare

_____ Negative income tax

Definitions:

1. A measure of happiness or satisfaction
2. A person's normal income
3. Government programs that supplement the incomes of the needy
4. Transfers to the poor given in the form of goods and services rather than cash
5. The political philosophy according to which the government should choose policies to maximize the total utility of everyone in society
6. The percentage of the population whose family income falls below an absolute level called the poverty line
7. A tax system that collects revenue from high-income households and gives transfers to low-income households
8. The political philosophy according to which the government should choose policies deemed to be just, as evaluated by an impartial observer behind a "veil of ignorance"
9. The political philosophy according to which the government should punish crimes and enforce voluntary agreements but not redistribute income
10. An absolute level of income set by the federal government for each family size below which a family is deemed to be in poverty
11. The claim that the government should aim to maximize the well-being of the worst-off person in society
12. The regular pattern of income variation over a person's life

PROBLEMS AND SHORT-ANSWER QUESTIONS

Practice Problems

1. Use Table 2 from Chapter 20 in your text to answer this question.
   a. In the most recent year available, what percent of income did the bottom fifth of the income distribution earn? What percent of income did the top fifth of the distribution earn? Roughly, what is the relationship between what the bottom fifth earns and what the top fifth earns?

   ____

   ____

   b. What is the range of the percent of income earned by the bottom fifth of the income distribution over the last 65 years? What is the range for the top fifth? Describe the trend for each group over the last 65 years. Provide some explanations for the trends you described.

   ____

   ____

   ____

   ____

   ____

   ____

   c. Describe three reasons why the measure of income distribution expressed in Table 2 in Chapter 20 may not truly measure someone's ability to maintain a certain standard of living. As a result, are the standard measures of income distribution likely to exaggerate or understate the true distribution of the standard of living? Explain.

   ____

   ____

   ____

   ____

d. What is permanent income? Why might we wish to use permanent income when measuring the distribution of income? If we used permanent income instead of current annual income when measuring the distribution of income, would this tend to exaggerate or understate the true distribution of the standard of living? Explain. (Hint: If you are a full-time student, can you borrow as much as you want in order to perfectly smooth out your lifetime consumption?)

2. Susan earns five times as much as Joe.
   a. What would the political philosophy of utilitarianism, liberalism, and libertarianism likely suggest should be done in this situation? Explain.

   b. Compare the degree of redistribution each suggests.

3. Suppose the government has to choose between two antipoverty programs. Each program guarantees that every family has at least $15,000 of income. One scheme establishes a negative income tax where: Taxes = (0.50 of income) – $15,000. The other scheme is for the government to guarantee every family at least $15,000 to spend and if a family falls short, the government will simply make up the difference.
   a. Using the negative income tax scheme described above, fill out the following table.

Earned Income	Taxes Paid	After-tax Income
$ 0	_____	_____
5,000	_____	_____
10,000	_____	_____
20,000	_____	_____
30,000	_____	_____
40,000	_____	_____

b. What is the value of income for which this family neither receives a subsidy nor pays any tax? (That is, how high does income have to be for the family to stop receiving a subsidy?

____

c. Under the second scheme where the government simply guarantees at least $15,000 to every family, what is the level of income at which a family stops receiving a subsidy? Explain.

____

____

d. Which plan is likely to be more expensive to the government? Explain

____

____

e. Suppose a poor family that only earns $5,000 per year decides to plant a garden and sell the produce in a "farmer's market" in the city. Suppose the family earns an additional $5,000 selling the produce. What is the family's final income under each scheme? What is the effective tax rate on the $5,000 earned by family under each scheme? Which scheme promotes a work ethic among the poor and which one discourages work? Explain.

____

____

____

____

____

____

____

Short-Answer Questions

1. How does the income distribution in United States compare with the income distribution in other countries? Explain.

2. Does poverty affect all groups within the population the same? Explain.

3. If the poverty rate is 11 percent, does it mean that about 11 percent of the population live their entire lives in poverty? Explain.

4. Of the three political philosophies discussed in your text, which one differs the most from the other two and why? What does each school of thought suggest about income redistribution?

5. Why don't the political philosophies of utilitarianism and liberalism suggest that income be completely equalized across the population?

6. Suppose there is a minimum wage. Under which of the following conditions is employment of unskilled workers reduced by the greatest amount: When labor demand is relatively inelastic or when labor demand is relatively elastic? Why? Is labor demand likely to be more elastic or inelastic in the long run? Why?

____

____

____

7. How could welfare programs exacerbate the problems they are supposed to cure?

____

____

____

____

8. What are some examples of in-kind transfers? Why do some people prefer that the government provide cash payments to the needy instead of in-kind transfers?

____

____

____

SELF-TEST

True/False Questions

______1. In the United States, the earnings of the top fifth of the income distribution are about ten times the earnings of the bottom fifth of the income distribution.

______2. The income distribution in the United States grew much wider from 1935 to 1970 but has narrowed since 1970.

______3. The poverty line is set at approximately three times the cost of providing an adequate diet.

______4. The increase in the labor-force participation of women that was generated by the women's movement has helped to narrow the income distribution.

______5. Children are more likely than average and the elderly are less likely than average to live in poverty.

______6. Because of in-kind transfers to the poor and because people's incomes vary from year to year and across their lifetimes, standard measures of income distribution exaggerate the degree of inequality in standards of living.

______7. Since about 11 percent of families are below the poverty line, then it follows that about 11 percent of families live their entire lives in poverty.

______8. The political philosophies of utilitarianism and liberalism both suggest that income should be equalized across the population.

______9. Libertarians are more concerned with equal opportunity than with equal outcome.

______10. Robert Nozick argues that economic justice would result if society chose a set of rules for the redistribution of income from behind a "veil of ignorance" and he argues that the set of rules would be the maximin criterion.

______11. If the demand for labor is relatively inelastic, an increase in the minimum wage will increase unemployment among unskilled workers by a relatively small amount.

______12. When compared to other welfare programs such as Temporary Assistance for Needy Families and SSI, a negative income tax would be more costly to the government but it would provide a greater incentive for the poor to work.

______13. Critics of Temporary Assistance for Needy Families argue that since eligibility for this program requires that the father not be in the household, the program encourages families to break up.

______14. It is more efficient for the government to provide in-kind transfers instead of cash payments.

______15. If permanent income were utilized to measure the income distribution instead of current annual income, the income distribution would appear to be wider.

Multiple-Choice Questions

1. In the United States, the top 5 percent of the income distribution earns
   a. more than the bottom 40 percent of the income distribution.
   b. about ten times what the bottom fifth of the income distribution earns.
   c. about the same as the bottom fifth of the income distribution.
   d. about half of all income.

2. The poverty line is set at
   a. two times the price of a new car.
   b. five time the value of average rent.
   c. three times the cost of providing an adequate diet.
   d. one third of average family income.

3. Compared to other countries, the income distribution in the United States is
   a. about average.
   b. a little narrower than most.
   c. the most equal.
   d. the most unequal.

4. Which of the following is *not* an explanation for the slight widening of the income distribution in the United States since 1970?
   a. The increase in technology has decreased the demand for unskilled workers and increased the demand for skilled workers, causing the gap between their wages to widen.
   b. An increase in international trade has decreased the demand for unskilled workers and increased the demand for skilled workers, causing the gap between their wages to widen.
   c. The women's movement has caused an increase in labor-force participation of women from already above-average income households.
   d. An increase in discrimination against unskilled immigrant labor has reduced the demand for unskilled workers and caused an increase in the gap between the wages of unskilled and skilled workers.

5. In the United States, the top fifth of the income distribution earns about
   a. the same as what the bottom fifth earns.
   b. two times what the bottom fifth earns.
   c. five times what the bottom fifth earns.
   d. ten times what the bottom fifth earns.
   e. twenty times what the bottom fifth earns.

6. Which of the following statements about poverty rates is *not* true?
   a. Blacks and Hispanics are three times more likely to live in poverty than whites.
   b. Children are more likely than average to live in poverty.
   c. The elderly are more likely than average to live in poverty.
   d. Families headed by females with no husband present are five times as likely to live in poverty as a family headed by a married couple.

7. Since 1935, the income distribution in the United States has
   a. been unchanged.
   b. narrowed slightly from 1935 to 1970 and then widened slightly from 1970 to today.
   c. widened slightly from 1935 to 1970 and then narrowed slightly from 1970 to today.
   d. slowly widened.
   e. slowly narrowed.

8. Because in-kind transfers are not accounted for in standard measures of income distribution, the standard measures of income distribution
   a. exaggerate the inequality of living standards.
   b. understate the inequality of living standards.
   c. accurately represent the true inequality of living standards.
   d. could exaggerate or understate the inequality of living standards depending on whether the transfers are goods or services.

9. Permanent income is
   a. Social Security income of the elderly and disabled.
   b. equal to the minimum wage.
   c. a person's normal, or average, income.
   d. wages fixed by a union or other labor contract.
   e. none of the above.

10. Because people's incomes vary over the life cycle and because there are transitory shocks to people's incomes, the standard measures of income distribution
   a. exaggerate the inequality of living standards.
   b. understate the inequality of living standards.
   c. accurately represent the true inequality of living standards.
   d. could exaggerate or understate the inequality of living standards depending on whether the transitory shocks are positive or negative.

11. If people can borrow and lend to perfectly smooth out their lifetime living standards, then
   a. current annual income is a good measure of the distribution of living standards.
   b. permanent income is a good measure of the distribution of living standards.
   c. transitory income is a good measure of the distribution of living standards.
   d. life-cycle income is a good measure of the distribution of living standards.
   e. none of the above.

12. Jill earns more than Bob and she came by her income fairly and honestly. Which of the following political philosophies would argue against the redistribution of income from Jill to Bob?
   a. utilitarianism
   b. liberalism
   c. libertarianism
   d. all of the above
   e. none of the above

13. The maximin criterion suggested by Rawl's theory of justice argues that the government should aim to
   a. minimize the difference between the rich and poor.
   b. maximize the total utility of society.
   c. minimize the well-being of the best-off person in society.
   d. maximize the well-being of the worst-off person in society.
   e. maximize the economic freedom of individuals by minimizing government interference in private decision making.

14. Rank utilitarianism, liberalism, and libertarianism in sequence from the political philosophy that would redistribute income the greatest to the one that would redistribute income the least.
   a. utilitarianism, liberalism, libertarianism
   b. libertarianism, liberalism, utilitarianism
   c. liberalism, libertarianism, utilitarianism
   d. liberalism, utilitarianism, libertarianism
   e. All three political philosophies argue for similar degrees of income redistribution.

15. Utilitarianism suggests that the government should choose policies that maximize the total utility of everyone in society by
    a. allowing each individual to maximize their own utility without interference from the government.
    b. redistributing income from rich to poor because, due to the diminishing marginal utility of income, taking a dollar from the rich reduces their utility by less than the gain in utility generated by giving a dollar to the poor.
    c. redistributing income from rich to poor because this would maximize the well-being of the worst-off person in society.
    d. redistributing income from rich to poor because this is what the members of society would choose to do if they were behind a "veil of ignorance."

16. To which of the following policies is the Earned Income Tax Credit most closely related?
    a. minimum-wage laws
    b. welfare
    c. negative income tax
    d. in-kind transfers

17. An increase in the minimum wage will cause a relatively large increase in unemployment among
    a. unskilled workers if the demand for labor is relatively elastic.
    b. unskilled workers if the demand for labor is relatively inelastic.
    c. skilled workers if the demand for labor is relatively elastic.
    d. skilled workers if the demand for labor is relatively inelastic.

18. Current antipoverty programs discourage work because
    a. they make recipients more comfortable than most middle-class Americans.
    b. benefits are reduced at such a high rate when recipients earn more income that there is little or no incentive to work once one is receiving benefits.
    c. antipoverty programs attract naturally lazy people to begin with.
    d. in order to be eligible for benefits, a recipient cannot have a job.

19. The greatest advantage of a negative income tax is that it
    a. reduces the cost to the government of fighting poverty.
    b. generates a smaller disincentive to work than most alternative antipoverty programs.
    c. would not provide benefits to lazy people.
    d. ensures that the poor actually receive what the government thinks they need.
    e. does all of the above.

20. Temporary Assistance for Needy Families
    a. has eliminated poverty in the United States.
    b. provides almost no disincentive to work because the benefits are very gradually reduced as a recipient's income from work increases.
    c. may lead to the break up of families because fathers may not be in the home if single mothers are to receive benefits.
    d. provides in-kind transfers, such as food stamps and Medicaid, to single mothers and their children.
    e. does all of the above.

ADVANCED CRITICAL THINKING

Suppose a friend comments to you, "I think welfare recipients are simply lazy spendthrifts. I have a friend who receives Temporary Assistance for Needy Families and when she was offered a part-time job, she turned it down."

1. What happens to a welfare recipient's benefits if they increase their earnings?

___

___

2. What is the effective tax rate on their additional income if they were to lose $1 in benefits for each dollar of additional income?

___

3. How does this system affect a welfare recipient's incentive to work? Is a welfare recipient necessarily lazy if they turn down a part-time job?

___

___

___

SOLUTIONS

Terms and Definitions

6 Poverty rate

10 Poverty line

4 In-kind transfers

12 Life cycle

2 Permanent income

5 Utilitarianism

1 Utility

8 Liberalism

11 Maximin criterion

9 Libertarianism

3 Welfare

7 Negative income tax

Practice Problems

1. a. Bottom fifth = 4.3 percent. Top fifth = 47.4 percent. The top fifth earns about ten times what the bottom fifth earns.
   b. Bottom fifth range is from 4.1 percent to 5.5 percent. Top fifth range is from 40.9 percent to 51.7 percent. For the bottom fifth, their share grew until 1970 and fell thereafter. For the top fifth, their share fell until 1970 and grew thereafter. Since 1970, the increase in international trade and the increase in technology has decreased the demand for unskilled labor and increased the demand for skilled labor increasing the relative wages of the already higher income workers. The woman's movement has generated an increase in labor-force participation of women from already high-income households.
   c. In-kind transfers are not included, the economic life-cycle is not recognized, and transitory versus permanent income is not recognized. All three problems suggest that standard measures exaggerate economic inequality because the poor receive transfers in the form of goods and services and because the variation in income can be smoothed by borrowing and lending.
   d. Permanent income is a person's normal, or average, income. Using it removes the life-cycle effects and the transitory effects that cause any given year's income to be non-representative of the person's true standard of living. This would probably tend to understate the true distribution of the standard of living because, in reality, we cannot fully smooth our living standards by borrowing when young or when we have a bad year.

2. a. Utilitarianism: Since there is diminishing marginal utility of income as income grows large, it would harm Susan less than it would help Joe if we redistributed income from Susan to Joe. Thus, to maximize total utility, redistribute from Susan to Joe. Liberalism: Both Susan and Joe would agree that if they didn't know their station in life, they would choose to socially insure each other

with a maximin system in case they were to be the one on the bottom end of the income distribution. So, redistribute from Susan to Joe. Libertarian: Since equal opportunity is more important than equal outcome, if each came by their income fairly and honestly, then no redistribution need take place.

b. From least redistribution to most, libertarianism, utilitarianism, liberalism.

3. a.

Earned Income	Taxes Paid	After-tax Income
$0	–$15,000	$15,000
5,000	–12,500	17,500
10,000	–10,000	20,000
20,000	–5,000	25,000
30,000	0	30,000
40,000	5,000	35,000

b. $30,000

c. $15,000. The government simply guarantees that each family has $15,000 so once a family reaches that level, it fails to receive a subsidy.

d. The negative income tax because, under this tax scheme, the government will continue to subsidize families in the $15,000 to $30,000 range.

e. If negative income tax, final income = $10,000 earned income + $10,000 subsidy = $20,000. If $15,000 guarantee, final income = $10,000 + $5,000 subsidy = $15,000. If negative income tax, tax rate equals .50 because when income went up $5,000, take home pay went up $2,500 or $2,500/$5,000 = .50. If $15,000 guarantee, tax rate equals 100 percent, because when income went up $5,000, final take home pay stayed the same at $15,000 because benefits were reduced by $5,000 or $5,000/$5,000 = 100 percent. The $15,000 guarantee discourages work because there is no gain whatsoever from working when income is in the $0 to $15,000 range.

Short-Answer Questions

1. The United States ranks about average. Japan, Germany, Canada, India, United Kingdom, and China have greater income equality than the United States while Russia, Nigeria, Mexico, South Africa, and Brazil have greater income inequality.

2. No. With regard to race, blacks and Hispanics are more likely to live in poverty. With regard to age, young are more likely than average and old are less likely than average to live in poverty. With regard to family composition, families headed by females are more likely to live in poverty.

3. No. There is a great deal of variation in a person's income from year to year and a great deal of variation in a person's income over their lifecycle. There is also variation from generation to generation within a family. As a result, a much larger portion of the population than 11 percent lives some small portion of their lives in poverty and very few live a large portion of their lives in poverty.

4. Libertarianism differs from both utilitarianism and liberalism because libertarianism argues that income is earned only by individuals and not by society so no social planner has the right to alter the distribution of income if it was generated by a fair playing field. Utilitarianism redistributes income because of the diminishing marginal utility of income and liberalism redistributes income because of a maximin criterion for social insurance.

5. Because they recognize that taxes cause disincentives to work so that too much redistribution causes the pie to become so small that both rich and poor lose.

6. When labor demand is relatively elastic because an increase in the wage causes a large reduction in labor demand. More elastic in the long run because firms have time to adjust production in response to the rise in wages.

7. Welfare programs could cause families to break up and unwed mothers to have children. They can cause a disincentive to work. Children fail to see the advantages of work and multiple generations become dependent on government.

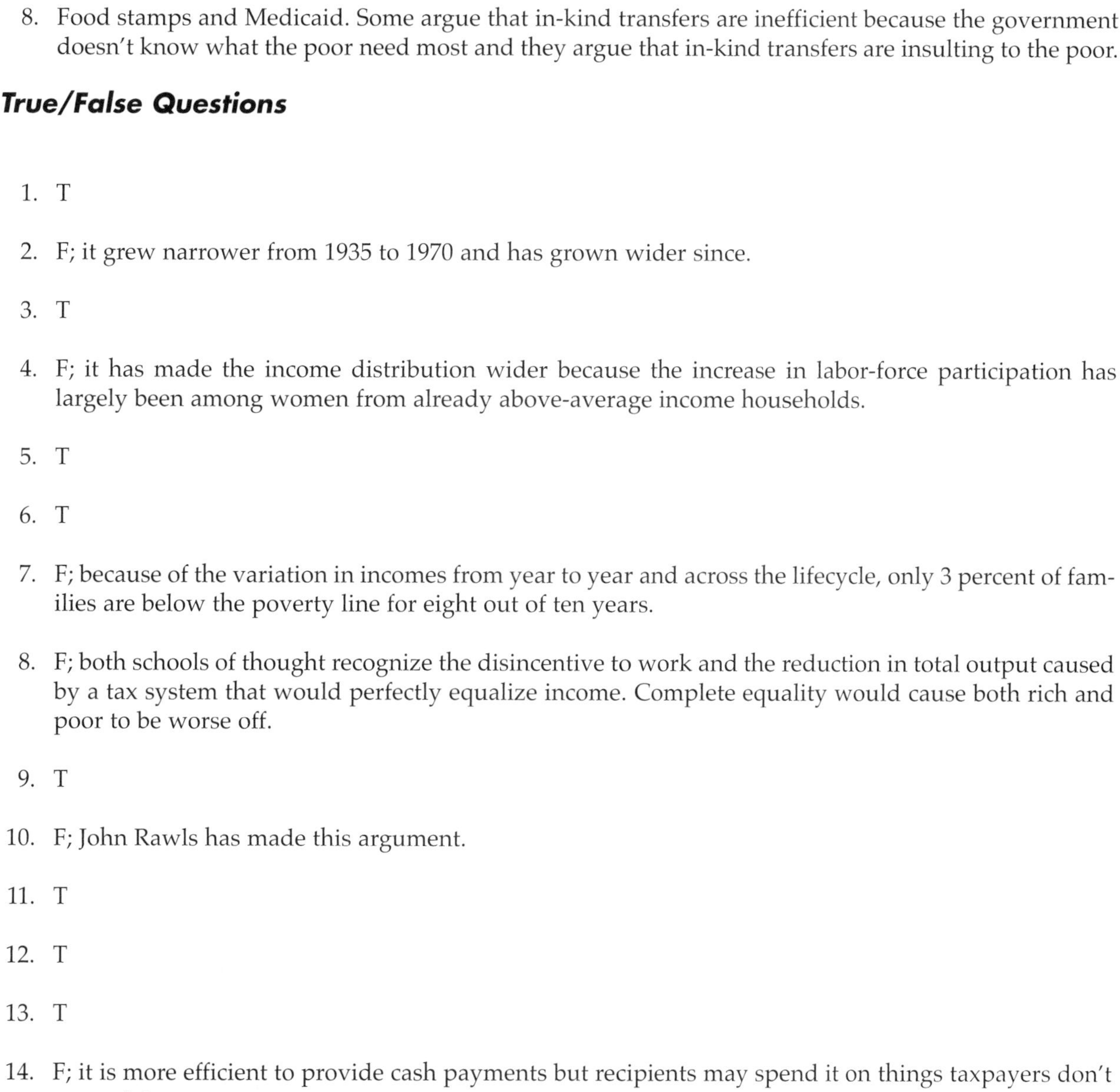

8. Food stamps and Medicaid. Some argue that in-kind transfers are inefficient because the government doesn't know what the poor need most and they argue that in-kind transfers are insulting to the poor.

True/False Questions

1. T

2. F; it grew narrower from 1935 to 1970 and has grown wider since.

3. T

4. F; it has made the income distribution wider because the increase in labor-force participation has largely been among women from already above-average income households.

5. T

6. T

7. F; because of the variation in incomes from year to year and across the lifecycle, only 3 percent of families are below the poverty line for eight out of ten years.

8. F; both schools of thought recognize the disincentive to work and the reduction in total output caused by a tax system that would perfectly equalize income. Complete equality would cause both rich and poor to be worse off.

9. T

10. F; John Rawls has made this argument.

11. T

12. T

13. T

14. F; it is more efficient to provide cash payments but recipients may spend it on things taxpayers don't appreciate.

15. F; income distribution would appear to be narrower.

Multiple-Choice Questions

1. a	5. d	9. c	13. d	17. a
2. c	6. c	10. a	14. d	18. b
3. a	7. b	11. b	15. b	19. b
4. d	8. a	12. c	16. c	20. c

Advanced Critical Thinking

1. They tend to lose benefits at a very high rate.
2. The tax rate would be 100 percent on the additional income.
3. Once one is on welfare, there is little or no incentive to work. Once on welfare, one need not be lazy to remain on it. It may be rational to remain on welfare if every time a person makes a dollar, the person loses a dollar in benefits.

21

THE THEORY OF CONSUMER CHOICE

GOALS

In this chapter you will

- See how a budget constraint represents the choices a consumer can afford
- Learn how indifference curves can be used to represent a consumer's preferences
- Analyze how a consumer's optimal choices are determined
- See how a consumer responds to changes in income and changes in prices
- Decompose the impact of a price change into an income effect and a substitution effect
- Apply the theory of consumer choice to three questions about household behavior

OUTCOMES

After accomplishing these goals, you should be able to

- Draw a budget constraint on a graph if you are given the value of income and the prices of the goods
- Explain why indifference curves must slope downward if the two products considered are "goods"
- Explain the relationship between the relative prices and the marginal rate of substitution between two goods at the consumer's optimum
- Shift the budget constraint when the price of a good increases
- Demonstrate the income and substitution effect on a graph using indifference curves and budget constraints
- Show why someone's labor-supply curve might be backward sloping

CHAPTER OVERVIEW

Context and Purpose

Chapter 21 is the first of two unrelated chapters that introduce you to some advanced topics in microeconomics. These two chapters are intended to whet your appetite for further study in economics. Chapter 21 is devoted to an advanced topic known as the theory of consumer choice.

The purpose of Chapter 21 is to develop the theory that describes how consumers make decisions about what to buy. So far, we have summarized these decisions with the demand curve. We now look at the theory of consumer choice which underlies the demand curve. After developing the theory, we apply the theory to a number of questions about how the economy works.

CHAPTER REVIEW

Introduction

Chapter 21 develops the theory that describes how consumers make decisions about what to buy. So far, we have summarized these decisions with the demand curve. We now look at the theory of consumer choice which underlies the demand curve. After developing the theory, we apply the theory to the following questions:

- Do all demand curves slope downward?
- How do wages affect labor supply?
- How do interest rates affect household saving?

The Budget Constraint: What the Consumer Can Afford

A *budget constraint* is the limit on the consumption bundles that a consumer can afford (given the consumer's income and the prices of the goods the consumer wishes to buy). On a graph that measures the quantity of a consumption good on each axis, a budget constraint is a straight line connecting the maximum amounts that could be purchased of each commodity given the prices of each commodity and the consumer's income. For example, if a consumer has income of $1000 and the price of Pepsi is $2 per pint, the maximum amount of Pepsi that could be purchased is $1000/$2 = 500 pints. If the price of pizza is $10, the maximum amount of pizza that could be purchased is $1000/$10 = 100 pizzas.

The slope of the budget constraint is the *relative price* of the two goods. In this case since a pizza costs five times what a pint of Pepsi costs, the consumer can trade one pizza for five pints of Pepsi. If the quantity of Pepsi is plotted on the vertical axis and the quantity of pizza on the horizontal axis, the slope of the budget constraint (rise/run) is 5/1 which equals the price of pizza divided by the price of Pepsi or $10/$2 = 5. Since the budget constraint always slopes downward or negatively, we often ignore the negative sign.

Preferences: What the Consumer Wants

A consumer's preferences can be represented with indifference curves. If two bundles of commodities suit a consumer's tastes equally well, the consumer is indifferent between them. Graphically, an *indifference curve* is a curve that shows consumption bundles that give the consumer the same level of satisfaction. When drawn on a graph that measures the quantity consumed of each good on each axis, an indifference curve must be downward sloping because if consumption of one good is reduced, the consumption of the other good must be increased for the consumer to be equally happy. The slope at any point on an indifference curve is known as the *marginal rate of substitution* or *MRS*. The *MRS* is the rate at which a consumer is willing to trade one good for another while maintaining a constant level of satisfaction.

There are four properties of indifference curves:

- Higher indifference curves (further from the origin) are preferred to lower ones because consumers prefer more of a good to less of it.
- Indifference curves are downward sloping because if consumption of one good is reduced, the consumption of the other good must be increased for the consumer to be equally happy.
- Indifference curves do not cross because it would suggest that a consumer's preferences are contradictory.
- Indifference curves are bowed inward because a consumer is willing to trade a greater amount of a good for another good if they have an abundance of the good they are trading away and they are willing to trade a lesser amount of a good for another good if they have very little of the good they are trading away.

When it is easy to substitute two goods for each other, indifference curves are bowed inward very little. When it is difficult to substitute two goods for each other, indifference curves are bowed inward a great deal. This is demonstrated by two extreme cases:

- *Perfect substitutes*: two goods with straight-line indifference curves. An example of perfect substitutes is nickels and dimes—two nickels for each dime.
- *Perfect complements*: two goods with right-angle indifference curves. An example of perfect complements is right shoes and left shoes—additional shoes that don't come in pairs do not increase satisfaction.

Optimization: What the Consumer Chooses

When we combine the budget constraint and the consumer's indifference curves, we are able to determine the amount of each commodity that the consumer will buy. The consumer will try to reach the highest indifference curve subject to remaining on the budget constraint. The point where an indifference curve just touches the budget constraint determines the *optimum* amount of purchases of each good. At the optimum, the indifference curve is *tangent* to the budget constraint and the slope of the indifference curve and the budget constraint are the same. Thus, the consumer chooses consumption of the two goods so that the marginal rate of substitution (slope of the indifference curve) equals the relative price of the two goods (slope of the budget constraint). At the optimum, the tradeoff between the goods that the consumer is willing to make (slope of the indifference curve) is equal to the trade off between the goods that the market is willing to make (slope of the budget constraint).

An alternative way to describe preferences and optimization is with the concept of utility. Utility is an abstract measure of the happiness or satisfaction a consumer receives from consuming a bundle of goods. Therefore, an indifference curve is actually an "equal-utility" curve. The *marginal utility* of a good is the increase in utility one gets from consuming an additional unit of that good. Goods exhibit *diminishing marginal utility* as more of any good is consumed. Since the marginal rate of substitution (the slope of the indifference curve) is the trade-off between two goods that the consumer is willing to make, it must also equal the marginal utility of one good divided by the marginal utility of the other good. Therefore, for two goods X and Y, at the optimum:

$$MRS = P_x / P_y = MU_x / MU_y \text{ or,}$$

$$MU_x / P_x = MU_y \,/ P_y.$$

At the optimum, the marginal utility of a dollar spent on X must be equal to the marginal utility of a dollar spend on Y. Similarly, one can say that, at the optimum, the indifference curve is tangent to the budget constraint.

Suppose the income of the consumer were to increase. Because the consumer can now consume more of both goods and because the relative price of the two goods remains unchanged, an increase in income shifts the budget constraint outward in a parallel fashion. The consumer can now reach a new optimum on a higher indifference curve. It is most common that the consumer will choose to consume more of both goods. Thus, a *normal good* is a good for which an increase in income raises the quantity demanded. Alternatively, an *inferior good* is a good for which an increase in income reduces the quantity demanded. Bus rides are an inferior good.

Suppose the price of one of the goods were to fall. If the consumer allocates all of his income to the good whose price has fallen, the consumer can buy more of that good. If the consumer allocates all of his income to the good whose price is unchanged, the maximum amount he can purchase remains unchanged. This causes the budget constraint to rotate outward. That is, the budget constraint only shifts outward on the axis of the good whose price has fallen. The consumer can now reach a new optimum on a higher indifference curve.

The impact of a change in the price of a good can be decomposed into two effects: an income effect and a substitution effect. The *income effect* is the change in consumption that results when a price change moves the consumer to a higher or lower indifference curve. The *substitution effect* is the change in consumption that results when a price change moves the consumer along a given indifference curve to a point with a new marginal rate of substitution. Graphically, the substitution effect is the change in consumption that results from the change in relative prices which rotates the budget line along a given indifference curve. The income effect is the change in consumption that results from the parallel shift in the budget constraint to the new optimum on the new indifference curve.

A demand curve can be derived from the consumer's optimizing decisions that result from the consumer's budget constraint and indifference curves. The combined income and substitution effect shows the total change in quantity demanded from a change in the price of a good. When these values are plotted on a price/quantity graph, the points form the consumer's demand curve.

Three Applications

- *Do all demand curves slope downward?* Theoretically, demand can sometimes slope upward. If an increase in the price of an inferior good has a larger income effect than substitution effect (the good is very strongly inferior) then an increase in the price of the good would cause the quantity demanded to rise. A *Giffen good* is a good for which an increase in the price raises the quantity demanded. Giffen goods are so rare that economists are not certain that one has ever existed.

- *How do wages affect labor supply?* The theory of consumer choice can be applied to the allocation decision between work and leisure. In this case, the two goods are consumption and leisure. The maximum amount of leisure is the number of hours available. The maximum amount of consumption is the number of hours available times the wage. The individual's indifference curves determine an optimum amount of leisure and consumption. Suppose the wage were to rise. The substitution effect induces more consumption and less leisure (more work). However, if both leisure and consumption are normal goods, the income effect suggests that the individual will wish to have both more consumption and more leisure (less work). If the substitution effect outweighs the income effect, an increase in wages will increase the quantity of labor supplied and labor supply is upward sloping. If the income effect outweighs the substitution effect, an increase in wages will decrease the quantity of labor supplied and labor supply slopes backward. Evidence that the work week is getting shorter suggests that the income effect is very strong and the labor supply curve bends backward when measured over long periods of time. Evidence on the behavior of lottery winners and people who receive large bequests suggests that, at high income levels, the labor-supply curve is backward sloping.

- *How do interest rates affect household saving?* The theory of consumer choice can be applied to the decision of how much income to consume today and how much to save for tomorrow. In this case, we measure consumption when young on the horizontal axis and consumption when old on the vertical axis. A person can consume all of his earnings when young and have nothing when old, or consume nothing when young, save all of his income, earn interest on the saving, and consume a greater amount when old. A person's preferences determines the optimal amounts of consumption in each period. If the interest rate rises, the budget constraint becomes steeper because the maximum possible consumption when old increases. When the interest rate rises, the substitution effect suggests that the consumer should increase consumption when old and decrease consumption when young (save more) because consumption when old has become relatively cheaper. However, if consumption in both periods is a normal good, the income effect suggests that the individual should consume more in both periods (save less). If the substitution effect outweighs the income effect, an increase in the interest rate will cause the individual to save more. If the income effect outweighs the substitution effect, an increase in the interest rate will cause the individual to save less. Evidence on this issue is mixed, so there is no clear recommendation for public policy toward the taxation of interest.

Conclusion: Do People Really Think This Way?

While consumers may not literally make decisions in the manner suggested by the theory of consumer choice, the model of consumer choice describes a process that permits economic analysis. The theory is useful in many applications.

HELPFUL HINTS

1. We have noted that the slope of the budget constraint is equal to the relative prices of the two goods represented on the graph. But which price should we put in the numerator and which price should we put in the denominator of the slope? Place the price of the good represented on the horizontal axis in the numerator and the price of the good represented on the vertical axis in the denominator of the slope. For example, if the quantity of popcorn is measured on the horizontal axis and the quantity of candy bars is measured on the vertical axis, and if the price of a bag of popcorn is $2 while the price of a candy bar is $1, then 2 candy bars can be exchanged for one bag of popcorn. The slope of the budget constraint is $2/$1 or 2. (Again, the slope of the budget constraint is always negative so we often ignore the sign.)

2. A mapping of an individual's preferences generates an infinite set of indifference curves. Each indifference curve divides the commodity space into three areas—points preferred to those on the indifference curve (points outside the indifference curve or away from the origin), points inferior to the indifference curve (points inside the indifference curve or toward the origin), or points of equal satisfaction as those on the indifference curve (points on the indifference curve). While there are an infinite set of indifference curves, it is customary to represent on a graph only those indifference curves that are tangent to a budget constraint and, thus, only those indifference curves that determine an optimum.

3. The slope of the indifference curve is the marginal rate of substitution which is the marginal utility of one good compared to the marginal utility of the other good. The slope of the budget constraint is equal to the relative prices of the two goods. Since at the optimum the indifference curve is tangent to the budget constraint, it follows that at the optimum the relative prices of the two goods equals the relative marginal utilities of the two goods. Thus, at the optimum, the additional utility gained by the consumer from an additional dollar's worth of one good is the same as the additional utility gained by the consumer from an additional dollar's worth of the other good. That is, at the optimum, the consumer cannot increase his total satisfaction by moving expenditures from one good to the other good.

TERMS AND DEFINITIONS

Choose a definition for each key term.

Key terms:

_____ Budget constraint

_____ Indifference curve

_____ Marginal rate of substitution

_____ Perfect substitutes

_____ Perfect complements

_____ Normal good

_____ Inferior good

_____ Income effect

_____ Substitution effect

_____ Giffen good

Definitions:

1. The change in consumption that results when a price change moves the consumer to a higher or lower indifference curve
2. The rate at which a consumer is willing to trade one good for another
3. The limit on the consumption bundles that a consumer can afford
4. A good for which an increase in income raises the quantity demanded
5. A good for which an increase in the price raises the quantity demanded
6. Two goods with right-angle indifference curves
7. A curve that shows consumption bundles that give the consumer the same level of satisfaction
8. A good for which an increase in income reduces the quantity demanded
9. Two goods with straight-line indifference curves
10. The change in consumption that results when a price change moves the consumer along a given indifference curve to a point with a new marginal rate of substitution

PROBLEMS AND SHORT-ANSWER QUESTIONS

Practice Problems

1. Suppose a consumer only buys two goods—hot dogs and hamburgers. Suppose the price of hot dogs is $1, the price of hamburgers is $2, and the consumer's income is $20.

a. Plot the consumer's budget constraint in Exhibit 1. Measure the quantity of hot dogs on the vertical axis and the quantity of hamburgers on the horizontal axis. Explicitly plot the points on the budget constraint associated with the even numbered quantities of hamburgers (0, 2, 4, 6 . . .).

b. Suppose the individual chooses to consume six hamburgers. What is the maximum amount of hot dogs that he can afford? Draw an indifference curve on the figure above that establishes this bundle of goods as the optimum.

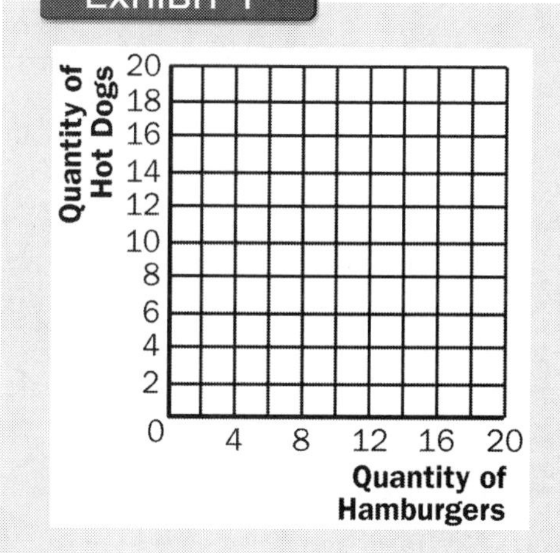

____

____

c. What is the slope of the budget constraint? What is the slope of the consumer's indifference curve at the optimum? What is the relationship between the slope of the budget constraint and the slope of the indifference curve at the optimum? What is the economic interpretation of this relationship?

____

____

____

____

d. Explain why any other point on the budget constraint must be inferior to the optimum.

____

____

____

2. Use Exhibit 2 to answer the following questions.

a. Suppose the price of a magazine is $2, the price of a book is $10, and the consumer's income is $100. Which point on the graph represents the consumer's optimum—X, Y, or Z? What are the optimal quantities of books and magazines this individual chooses to consume?

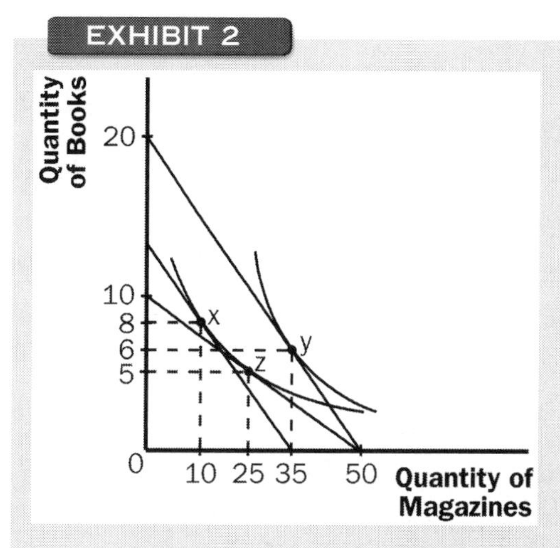

____

____

b. Suppose the price of books falls to $5. What are the two optimum points on the graph that represent the substitution effect (in sequence)? What is the change in the consumption of books due to the substitution effect?

c. Again, suppose the price of books falls to $5. What are the two optimum points on the graph that represent the income effect (in sequence)? What is the change in the consumption of books due to the income effect? Is a book a normal good or an inferior good for this consumer? Explain.

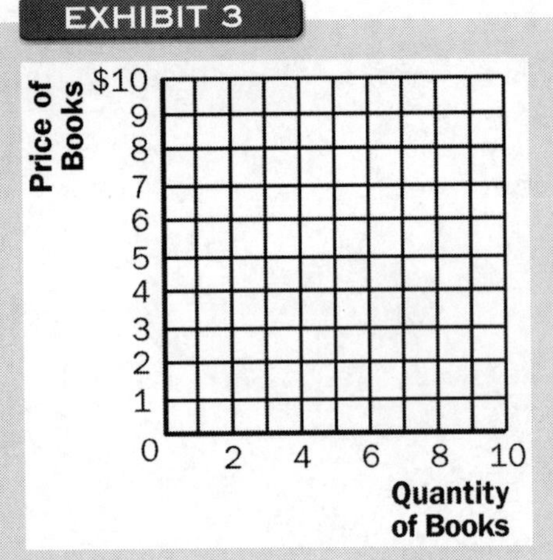

d. For this consumer, what is the total change in the quantity of books purchased when the price of books fell from $10 to $5?

e. Use the information in this problem to plot the consumer's demand curve for books in Exhibit 3.

Short-Answer Questions

1. Suppose that there are two goods available to the consumer—pens and pencils. Suppose that the price of a pen is $2.00 while the price of a pencil is $0.50. If we measure the quantity of pens on the horizontal axis and the quantity of pencils on the vertical axis, what is the slope of the budget constraint? Do you need to know the income of the consumer to answer this question? Why?

2. If we measure "goods" on each axis, is an indifference curve positively (upward) sloped or negatively (downward) sloped? Why? If we measure a "good" on one axis but a "bad" (such as pollution) on the other axis, what type of slope do you think an indifference curve would have? Why?

____

____

____

____

3. Why are most indifference curves bowed inward?

____

____

____

____

4. Consider the following two pairs of goods:
   - Graduation caps and graduation gowns
   - Gasoline at an Exxon station and gasoline at a Shell station

   Which of the pairs of goods above is likely to be nearly perfect substitutes and which is likely to be nearly perfect complements? Explain.

____

____

____

____

5. Referring to question #4 above, what is the shape of the indifference curves that you would expect each pair of goods to generate, straight line or right angle? For which pair of goods would you observe the greatest substitution effect if the relative prices of the two goods were to change? Why?

____

____

____

____

6. Suppose there are two goods available to the consumer—coffee and tea. Suppose that the price of coffee decreases. What impact will the substitution effect and income effect have on the quantity demanded of coffee if coffee is a normal good? Explain. What impact will the substitution effect and income effect have on the quantity demanded of coffee if coffee is an inferior good? Explain.

7. Suppose there are only two goods available to you, apples and oranges. Suppose that the prices of apples and oranges double and that your income also doubles. What will happen to the amount of apples and oranges that you choose to consume? Explain. (Hint: What has happened to the slope of the budget constraint? What has happened to the maximum amount of apples or oranges that you could consume if you allocated all of your income to one good or the other?)

8. Some people argue that the tax rate should be reduced on interest earned from saving because it will increase the after-tax return to saving, increase the quantity of saving supplied, and increase economic growth. Are we certain that a decrease in the tax rate on interest earned from saving will increase the quantity of saving? Explain.

SELF-TEST

True/False Questions

______1. If we measure the quantity of French fries on the horizontal axis and the quantity of hamburgers on the vertical axis, and if the price of

French fries is $0.60 and the price of a hamburger is $2.40, then the slope of the budget constraint is 1/4 (and it is negative).

______2. A budget constraint is a set of commodity bundles that provide the consumer with the same level of satisfaction.

______3. Indifference curves measure the consumer's willingness to trade one good for another good while maintaining a constant level of satisfaction.

______4. When drawn on a graph that measures the quantity of a good on each axis, indifference curves are usually straight lines that slope downward (negatively).

______5. If two goods are perfect complements, indifference curves associated with these two goods would cross each other at the optimum.

______6. Indifference curves tend to be bowed inward because a consumer is willing to trade a greater amount of a good for another if they have an abundance of the good they are trading away.

______7. At the consumer's optimum point, the marginal rate of substitution of apples for oranges is equal to the ratio of the price of oranges to the price of apples.

______8. The more difficult it is to substitute one good for another, the more bowed inward indifference curves become.

______9. If the price of a good falls, the substitution effect always causes an increase in the quantity demanded of that good.

______10. If the price of a good falls and the good is a normal good, the income effect causes a decrease in the quantity demanded of that good.

______11. If the price of a good falls and the good is an inferior good, the income effect causes a decrease in the quantity demanded of that good.

______12. The income effect is measured as the change in consumption that results when a price change moves the consumer along a given indifference curve to a point with a new marginal rate of substitution.

______13. An increase in the interest rate will always lead to a greater amount of saving.

______14. A Giffen good is an extremely inferior good.

______15. The theory of consumer choice can be used to demonstrate that labor supply curves must be upward sloping.

Multiple-Choice Questions

1. The limit on the consumption bundles that a consumer can afford is known as
   a. an indifference curve.
   b. the marginal rate of substitution.
   c. the budget constraint.
   d. the consumption limit.

2. A change in the relative prices of which of the following pair of goods would likely cause the smallest substitution effect?
   a. gasoline from 7-Eleven and gasoline from Quick Stop
   b. right shoes and left shoes
   c. Coke and Pepsi
   d. Bud Light and Coors Light

3. Indifference curves for perfect substitutes are
   a. straight lines.
   b. bowed inward.
   c. bowed outward.
   d. right angles.
   e. nonexistent.

4. Suppose a consumer must choose between the consumption of sandwiches and pizza. If we measure the quantity of pizza on the horizontal axis and the quantity of sandwiches on the vertical axis, and if the price of a pizza is $10 and the price of a sandwich is $5, then the slope of the budget constraint is
   a. 5
   b. 10
   c. 2
   d. 1/2

5. The slope at any point on an indifference curve is known as
   a. the trade-off rate.
   b. the marginal rate of substitution.
   c. the marginal rate of tradeoff.
   d. the marginal rate of indifference.

6. Which of the following statements is *not* true with regard to the standard properties of indifference curves?
   a. Indifference curves are downward sloping.
   b. Indifference curves do not cross each other.
   c. Higher indifference curves are preferred to lower ones.
   d. Indifference curves are bowed outward.

7. The consumer's optimal purchase of any two goods is the point where
   a. the consumer reaches the highest indifference curve subject to remaining on the budget constraint.
   b. the consumer has reached the highest indifference curve.
   c. the two highest indifference curves cross.
   d. the budget constraint crosses the indifference curve.

8. Which of the following is true about the consumer's optimum consumption bundle? At the optimum,
   a. the indifference curve is tangent to the budget constraint.
   b. the slope of the indifference curve equals the slope of the budget constraint.
   c. the relative prices of the two goods equals the marginal rate of substitution.
   d. all of the above are true.
   e. none of the above are true.

9. Suppose we measure the quantity of good X on the horizontal axis and the quantity of good Y on the vertical axis. If indifference curves are bowed inward, as we move from having an abundance of good X to having an abundance of good Y, the marginal rate of substitution of good Y for good X (the slope of the indifference curve)
   a. rises.
   b. falls.
   c. stays the same.
   d. could rise or fall depending on the relative prices of the two goods.

10. If an increase in a consumer's income causes the consumer to increase his quantity demanded of a good, then the good is
    a. an inferior good.
    b. a normal good.
    c. a substitute good.
    d. a complementary good.

11. If an increase in a consumer's income causes the consumer to decrease her quantity demanded of a good, then the good is
    a. an inferior good.
    b. a normal good.
    c. a substitute good.
    d. a complementary good.

Suppose that the consumer must choose between buying socks and belts. Also, suppose that the consumer's income is $100. Use Exhibit 4 to answer the next four questions.

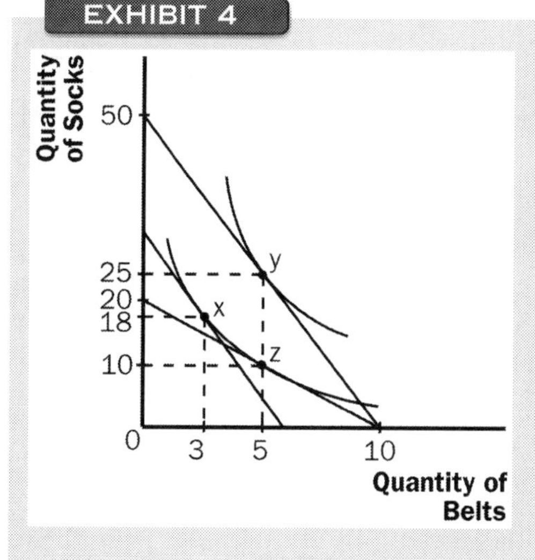

12. If the price of a belt is $10 and the price of a pair of socks is $5, the consumer will choose to buy the commodity bundle represented by point
    a. X
    b. Y
    c. Z
    d. the optimal point cannot be determined from this graph.

13. Suppose that the price of a pair of socks falls from $5 to $2. The substitution effect is represented by the movement from point
    a. Y to point X.
    b. X to point Y.
    c. Z to point X.
    d. X to point Z.

14. Suppose that the price of a pair of socks has falls from $5 to $2. The income effect is represented by the movement from point
    a. Y to point X.
    b. X to point Y.
    c. Z to point X.
    d. X to point Z.

15. A pair of socks is
    a. an inferior good.
    b. a normal good.
    c. a Giffen good.
    d. none of the above.

16. The change in consumption that results when a price change moves the consumer along a given indifference curve is known as the
    a. complementary effect.
    b. normal effect.
    c. income effect.
    d. substitution effect.
    e. inferior effect.

17. If income were to double and prices were to double, the budget line would
    a. shift outward in a parallel fashion.
    b. shift inward in a parallel fashion.
    c. stay the same.
    d. rotate inward.
    e. rotate outward.

18. If leisure is a normal good, an increase in the wage
    a. will always increase the quantity of labor supplied.
    b. will always decrease the amount of labor supplied.
    c. will increase the amount of labor supplied if the income effect outweighs the substitution effect.
    d. will increase the amount of labor supplied if the substitution effect outweighs the income effect.

19. If consumption when young and when old are both normal goods, an increase in the interest rate
    a. will always increase the quantity of saving.
    b. will always decrease the quantity of saving.
    c. will increase the quantity of saving if the substitution effect outweighs the income effect.
    d. will increase the quantity of saving if the income effect outweighs the substitution effect.

20. Which of the following is <u>not</u> true regarding the outcome of a consumer's optimization process?
    a. The consumer has reached his highest indifference curve subject to his budget constraint.
    b. The marginal utility per dollar spent on each good is the same.
    c. The consumer is indifferent between any two points on his budget constraint.
    d. The marginal rate of substitution between goods is equal to the ratio of the prices between goods.
    e. The consumer's indifference curve is tangent to his budget constraint.

ADVANCED CRITICAL THINKING

Suppose you have a wealthy aunt. Your aunt dies and leaves you a great deal of money (potentially). When you attend the reading of the will, you discover that she has bequeathed her millions to a "family incentive trust." As the lawyer reads the will, you discover that you only get the money if you get married, have children, stay with your spouse and raise your children, don't become dependent on drugs or alcohol, and if you *continuously have a full-time job*. (Note: Family incentive trusts are real and becoming very common.)

1. Why might your aunt include the requirement that you continuously have a full-time job?

   ____

   ____

2. Does the evidence about how people behave after they receive an inheritance suggest that your aunt's concerns are well-founded or is she just a control freak who wants to control the lives of her relatives even after she is gone? Explain.

   ____

   ____

   ____

3. What does this evidence suggest about the slope of the labor supply curve? Explain.

   ____

   ____

   ____

   ____

   ____

SOLUTIONS

Terms and Definitions

3 Budget constraint

7 Indifference curve

2 Marginal rate of substitution

9 Perfect substitutes

6 Perfect complements

4 Normal good

8 Inferior good

1 Income effect

10 Substitution effect

5 Giffen good

Practice Problems

1. a. See Exhibit 5.
   b. Eight. For the indifference curve, see Exhibit 5.
   c. Rise over run = 2/1. This is also the price ratio of price of hamburgers to price of hot dogs = $2/$1. The slope of the indifference curve is also 2/1. (Note: all of these slopes are negative.) At the optimum, the indifference curve is tangent to the budget constraint so their slopes are equal. Thus, the tradeoff between the goods that the individual is willing to undertake (*MRS*) is the same as the trade off that the market requires (slope of budget constraint).
   d. Since the highest indifference curve reachable is tangent to the budget constraint, any other point on the budget constraint must have an indifference curve running through it that is below the optimal indifference curve so that point must be inferior to the optimum.

2. a. Point Z. 25 books and five magazines.
   b. From point Z to point X. From five books to eight books.
   c. From point X to point Y. From eight books to six books. Books are inferior because an increase in income decreases the quantity demanded of books.
   d. The quantity demanded increased from five books to six books.
   e. See Exhibit 6.

EXHIBIT 5

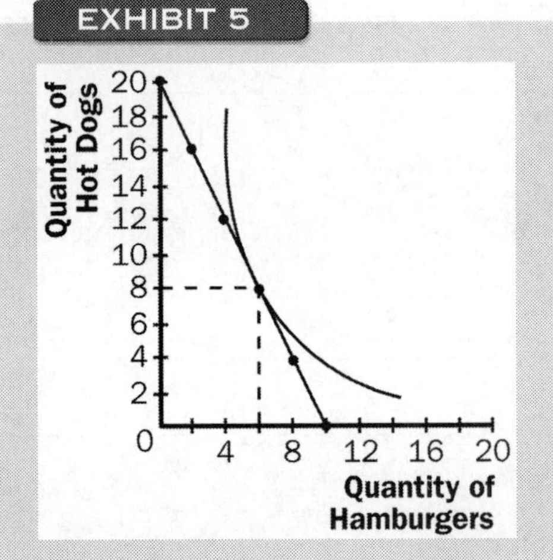

EXHIBIT 6

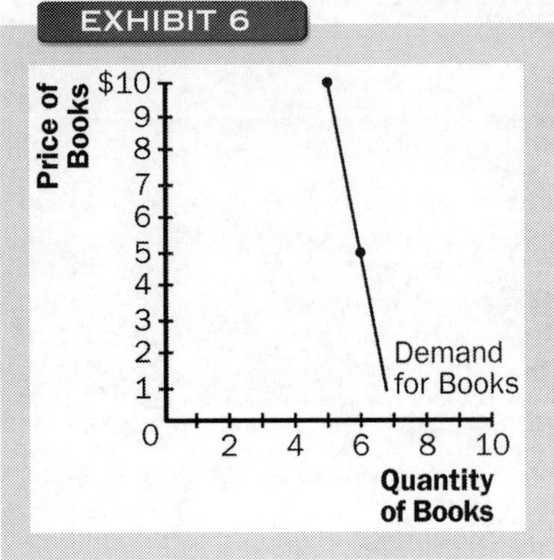

Short-Answer Questions

1. Slope = rise / run = 4 / 1 or 4. It is also the ratio of the price of pens to the price of pencils or $2.00 / $0.50 = 4. (All slopes are negative.) No. Income simply must be any positive amount. A change in income shifts the budget constraint in or out but does not change its slope.

2. Negatively sloped because, for a consumer to be equally happy, if consumption of one good is reduced the consumption of the other good must be increased. Positively sloped because, for a consumer to be equally happy, if consumption of the bad item is increased the consumption of the good item must also be increased.

3. Because the marginal rate of substitution (MRS) is not constant along most indifference curves. A consumer is willing to trade a greater amount of a good for another if they have an abundance of the good they are trading away. They are willing to trade a lesser amount away if they have very little of the good they are trading away.

4. Gasoline at Exxon and at Shell are nearly perfect substitutes because the marginal rate of substitution is fixed at about one—one gallon of Exxon gas for one gallon of Shell gas. Graduation caps and gowns are nearly perfect complements because additional units of caps without gowns or additional units of gowns without caps provide little or no additional satisfaction.

5. Exxon gas and Shell gas would have nearly straight line indifference curves while graduation caps and gowns would have nearly right angle indifference curves. A change in the relative prices of gas would cause a great substitution between gas at each station while a change in the relative prices of caps and gowns would cause little or no substitution of caps for gowns or gowns for caps.

6. The substitution effect will cause an increase in the quantity demanded of coffee regardless of whether coffee is normal or inferior. If coffee is normal, the income effect will cause an increase in the quantity demanded of coffee. If coffee is inferior, the income effect will cause a decrease in the quantity demanded of coffee.

7. There will be no impact because the slope of the budget constraint is unaltered (relative prices are the same so the market tradeoff is the same) and the position of the budget constraint is unaltered (the maximum amount of each good that can be purchased is unaltered so the end points of the budget constraint are the same).

8. No. An increase in the return to saving should increase consumption when old (substitution effect increases saving) but an increase in the return to saving increases income and should increase consumption when young and old (income effect decreases saving). If the income effect outweighs the substitution effect, a greater after-tax return on saving would decrease saving.

True/False Questions

1. T

2. F; a budget constraint is the limit on the consumption bundles that a consumer can afford.

3. T

4. F; indifference curves are negatively sloped but they are usually bowed inward.

5. F; indifference curves for perfect complements are right angles but still never cross another indifference curve.

6. T

7. T

8. T

9. T

10. F; the income effect would cause an increase in the quantity demanded.

11. T

12. F; the income effect is measured as the change in consumption that results when a change in price moves the consumer to a higher or lower indifference curve.

13. F; if the income effect from a change in interest rates outweighs the substitution effect the individual will save less.

14. T

15. F; labor supply curves can be backward sloping if the income effect from a change in the wage outweighs the substitution effect.

Multiple-Choice Questions

1. c	5. b	9. a	13. c	17. c
2. b	6. d	10. b	14. b	18. d
3. a	7. a	11. a	15. b	19. c
4. c	8. d	12. c	16. d	20. c

Advanced Critical Thinking

1. She is probably afraid that her gift of millions would tempt you to be lazy and cause you to lead a less useful life than you would otherwise.

2. Her concerns may be well-founded. People who win lotteries or receive large inheritances often quit work or reduce the hours they work.

3. This evidence suggests that the labor supply curve may be backward sloping. We generally assume that a higher wage increases the quantity supplied of labor (upward sloping labor supply) but, in fact, a higher wage may decrease the quantity of labor supplied (backward sloping labor supply) if leisure is a normal good and the income effect of an increase in the wage outweighs the substitution effect.

22

FRONTIERS OF MICROECONOMICS

GOALS

In this chapter you will

Examine the problems caused by asymmetric information

Learn about market solutions to asymmetric information

Consider why democratic voting systems may not represent the preferences of society

Consider why people may not always behave as rational maximizers

OUTCOMES

After accomplishing these goals, you should be able to

Describe the information asymmetry in the labor market

Explain why insurance companies screen potential customers

Generate an example of the Condorcet voting paradox

Explain why people are willing to sign contracts that require them to contribute a portion of their paychecks to a retirement savings program

CHAPTER OVERVIEW

Context and Purpose

Chapter 22 is the last chapter in the microeconomics portion of the text. It is the second of two unrelated chapters that introduce you to some advanced topics in microeconomics. These two chapters are intended to whet your appetite for further study in economics.

The purpose of Chapter 22 is to give you a taste of three topics on the frontier of microeconomic research. The first topic we address is *asymmetric information,* a situation when one person in an economic relationship has more relevant knowledge than the other person. The second topic is *political economy,* the application of economic tools to the understanding of the functioning of government. The third topic we address is *behavioral economics,* the introduction of psychology into the study of economic issues.

CHAPTER REVIEW

Introduction

The study of economics is always seeking to expand the understanding of human behavior and society. This chapter addresses three areas on the frontier of economic study. The first topic we address is *asymmetric information,* a situation when one person in an economic relationship has more relevant knowledge than the other person. The second topic is *political economy,* the application of economic tools to the understanding of the functioning of government. The third topic we address is *behavioral economics,* the introduction of psychology into the study of economic issues.

Asymmetric Information

A difference in access to relevant knowledge is called an *information asymmetry.* We address two types of information asymmetries: *hidden actions* and *hidden characteristics.*

Hidden Actions and Moral Hazard Hidden actions may occur when a person (called the **agent**) performs some task on behalf of another person (called the **principal**). The agent knows more about his effort and performance than the principal. The problem of **moral hazard** arises if the principal cannot perfectly monitor the agent, so the agent tends to engage in dishonest or undesirable behavior (he shirks his responsibilities). In the employment relationship, the employer is the principal and the worker is the agent. Employers respond to the moral hazard problem with:

- *Better monitoring.* Employers use video cameras to catch irresponsible behavior or workers.
- *High wages.* Firms pay efficiency wages (above equilibrium wages) to raise the cost to the worker of being fired and make the worker less likely to shirk.
- *Delayed payment.* Year-end bonuses and higher pay later in life reduce shirking today.

Insurance can generate moral hazard because the insured may have little incentive to reduce the risk of an accident.

Hidden Characteristics and Adverse Selection **Hidden characteristics** are when a seller knows more than the buyer about the good being sold. Hidden characteristics may generate a problem known as **adverse selection**—the buyer risks selecting goods of low quality. Adverse selection may occur in the market for:

- *Used cars.* Buyers may choose not to buy even slightly used cars because they surmise that sellers know something bad about the cars. This is known as the "lemons" problem.
- *Labor.* If a firm reduces the wage it pays, high productivity workers tend to quit and the firm is left with low productivity workers.
- *Insurance.* People with hidden health problems are more likely to want to buy health insurance than people with average or good health.

When markets suffer from adverse selection, people may continue to drive used cars they would rather sell, firms may pay wages above equilibrium and cause unemployment, and relatively healthy people may fail to purchase health insurance because it is too expensive. That is, markets may become inefficient.

Markets respond to asymmetric information in several ways.

Signaling **Signaling** is when an informed party takes actions to reveal information to an uninformed party. Recall from previous chapters that firms spend money on expensive advertising to signal that they sell high-quality products. Students attend high quality schools to signal that they are high-ability people.

For a signal to be effective, it must be costly, but less costly to the person with the higher-quality product. Signaling is rational for both the buyer and seller. A personal gift qualifies as a signal of love because it is costly (it takes time to purchase) and if someone loves another the most, they know what to buy (takes less time to buy than it would for a simple acquaintance).

Screening **Screening** is when an uninformed party acts to induce an informed party to reveal information. Buyers of used cars may have their mechanic check out a used car. Auto insurers may check a driver's driving history, or offer different policies that have different degrees of appeal to risky and safe drivers so the two kinds of drivers will reveal their driving characteristics.

Although markets may fail to allocate resources efficiently when there is asymmetric information, it is not clear that public policy actions can improve market outcomes because:

- Private markets can sometimes deal with the problem by using signaling and screening.
- The government rarely has more information than private parties so it cannot improve upon the current imperfect allocation or resources. Thus, the market is not first-best, but is second-best.
- The government itself is an imperfect institution.

Political Economy

Political economy, also known as *public choice*, applies the methods of economics to study how the government works. Before we choose to have the government attempt to improve market outcomes, we must recognize that government is also imperfect. Problems with how a government chooses public policy include the following.

The Condorcet voting paradox The **Condorcet voting paradox** is the failure of majority rule to produce transitive preferences for society. *Transitivity* is the property that if A is preferred to B, and B preferred to C, then A must be preferred to C. When society has to choose between more than two outcomes, majority rule democracy may not tell us which alternative society really wants because pairwise voting across three or more alternatives does not guarantee transitivity, a phenomena known as the Condorcet paradox. That is, it is possible under pairwise voting that A is preferred to B, and B preferred to C, yet C preferred to A. Because the property of transitivity is required for majority-rule democracy to accurately aggregate preferences, two conclusions can be drawn: (1) majority-rule voting does not necessarily tell us what society wants and, (2) setting the order in which items are voted can affect the outcome.

Arrow's impossibility theorem Arrow's impossibility theorem is a mathematical result showing that, under certain assumed conditions, there is no scheme for aggregating individual preferences into a valid set of social preferences. Due to the Condorcet paradox, alternative voting systems have been proposed. A *Borda count* allows voters to rank and give points to possible outcomes when there are more than two outcomes—like sports team rankings. However, Arrow has shown that *no voting system* can satisfy the following properties required of a perfect voting scheme:

- *Unanimity*: If everyone prefers A to B, then A should beat B.
- *Transitivity*: If A beats B, and B beats C, then A should beat C.

- *Independence of irrelevant alternatives*: The rankings between any two outcomes should not depend on whether some third outcome is available.
- *No dictators*: There is no person that always gets his way.

For example, majority rule does not always satisfy transitivity and the Borda count does not always satisfy the independence of irrelevant alternatives. While democracy should not be abandoned, all voting schemes are flawed mechanisms for social choice.

The median voter is king. The median-voter theorem is a mathematical result showing that if voters are choosing a point along a line and each voter wants the point closest to his most preferred point, then majority rule will pick the most preferred point of the median voter. The median voter is the voter exactly in the middle of the distribution. Majority rule voting will always generate an outcome that is preferred by the median voter if each voter votes for the outcome that is closest to his most preferred outcome. This outcome will not necessarily be the average preferred outcome or the modal outcome. In addition, minority views are not given much weight.

Politicians may be self-interested. Self-interest may cause politicians to maximize their own well-being as opposed to maximizing the well-being of society. Some politicians may act out greed and others may sacrifice the national interest to improve their local popularity. Therefore, actual economic policy often fails to resemble the ideal policy derived in economic textbooks.

Behavioral Economics

In the field of *behavioral economics,* economists make use of the following basic psychological insights.

People aren't always rational. Economists generally assume that people and firms behave rationally. But people may not act as rational maximizers but instead as *satisficers*. Or people may exhibit "near rationality" or "bounded rationality." People make the following systematic errors:

- People are overconfident
- People give too much weight to a small number of vivid observations
- People are reluctant to change their minds

Regardless of these issues, economic models based on rationality may be good approximations of reality.

People care about fairness. The *ultimatum game* is a game where one player decides what portion of $100 to give to another player. The second player must either accept the split or both get nothing. Rational wealth maximizers would choose $99 and offer $1. The second player would accept because $1 is better than nothing. In experiments, however, the first player tends to give much more than $1 (but less than $50) to the second player and the second player usually rejects small offerings. People may be driven by a sense of fairness as opposed to their normal self-interest. As a result, firms may pay above equilibrium wages during profitable years to be fair or to avoid retaliation on the part of workers.

People are inconsistent over time. People tend to desire instant gratification as opposed to delayed gratification. Therefore, they fail to follow through on plans to do things that are dreary, take effort, or cause discomfort. For example, people often save less than they plan. To help follow through on a plan, people may restrict their future behavior: Smokers throw away their cigarettes, dieters put a lock on the refrigerator, and workers sign up for a retirement plan.

Conclusion

This chapter introduced areas of continuing economic research. Asymmetric information should make us more wary of market outcomes. Political economy should make us more wary of government solutions. Behavioral economics should make us more wary of human decision-making.

HELPFUL HINTS

1. The market for insurance demonstrates many of the problems and market solutions generated by asymmetric information. For auto insurance, firms first screen prospective customers to reduce *adverse selection*—the problem of selling insurance to worse than average drivers. After the sale of the insurance, auto insurance companies require a deductible or co-payment on collision insurance. This reduces *moral hazard*—the problem of insured drivers driving more recklessly once they are insured.

2. No method of economic decision-making is always perfect. Markets may not maximize total surplus due to externalities, public goods, imperfect competition, and asymmetric information. In addition, people and firms may not always rationally maximize their own well-being. But government may not be able to improve upon the situation because governments may not have any better information than markets, all voting schemes are imperfect, and politicians may choose to maximize their own well-being instead of the well-being of society.

TERMS AND DEFINITIONS

Choose a definition for each key term.

Key terms:

_____ Moral hazard

_____ Agent

_____ Principal

_____ Adverse selection

_____ Signaling

_____ Screening

_____ Condorcet paradox

_____ Arrow impossibility theorem

_____ Median voter theorem

Definitions:

1. An action taken by an informed party to reveal private information to an uniformed party
2. The failure of majority rule to produce transitive preferences for society
3. A person for whom another person, called the agent, is performing some act
4. The tendency of a person who is imperfectly monitored to engage in dishonest or otherwise undesirable behavior
5. A mathematical result showing that if voters are choosing a point along a line and each voter wants the point closest to his most preferred point, then majority rule will pick the most preferred point of the median voter
6. A mathematical result showing that, under certain assumed conditions, there is no scheme for aggregating individual preferences into a valid set of social preferences
7. The tendency for the mix of unobserved attributes to become undesirable from the standpoint of an uninformed party
8. A person who is performing an act for another person, called the principal
9. An action taken by an uninformed party to induce an informed party to reveal information

PROBLEMS AND SHORT-ANSWER QUESTIONS

Practice Problems

1. For each of the following situations, identify the principal and the agent, describe the information asymmetry involved, and explain how moral hazard has been reduced.
   a. Dental insurance companies offer free annual check-ups

   ____

   ____

   b. Firms compensate traveling salespersons with commissions (a percent of the value of the sales)

   ____

   ____

   ____

   c. Agricultural seed companies pay migrant workers bonuses if they work the entire summer season

   ____

   ____

   ____

   d. McDonald's pays twice the minimum wage to high school students

   ____

   ____

2. For each of the following situations, describe the information asymmetry involved, name the type of action that has been taken to reduce adverse selection (signaling or screening), and explain how adverse selection has been reduced.
   a. McDonald's only hires high school students with good grades

   ____

   ____

   ____

b. Hyundai (a Korean auto manufacturer) provides a 100,000 mile warranty on its new cars

c. A health insurance company requires prospective customers to take a physical examination

d. Budweiser sponsors the Super Bowl half-time show

3. Answer the questions regarding the Condorcet paradox for the three sets of voting preferences below.

Case 1

	Voter Type		
	Type 1	**Type 2**	**Type 3**
Percent of Electorate	15	40	45
First Choice	C	A	B
Second Choice	A	B	C
Third Choice	B	C	A

a. If voters must choose between A and B, what are the percentages of votes that each outcome receives and which outcome wins?

b. If voters must choose between B and C, what are the percentages of votes that each outcome receives and which outcome wins?

c. If voters must choose between C and A, what are the percentages of votes that each outcome receives and which outcome wins?

d. Do these preferences exhibit transitivity? Explain.

e. If the voters choose between A and B and then compare to C , which outcome wins?

____

If the voters choose between B and C and then compare to A, which outcome wins?

____

If the voters choose between A and C, and then compare to B which outcome wins?

____

Does the order in which items are voted on matter in this case? Why or why not?

____

____

Case 2

	Voter Type		
	Type 1	**Type 2**	**Type 3**
Percent of Electorate	30	15	55
First Choice	A	B	C
Second Choice	B	C	A
Third Choice	C	A	B

a. If voters must choose between A and B, what are the percentages of votes that each outcome receives and which outcome wins?

____

b. If voters must choose between B and C, what are the percentages of votes that each outcome receives and which outcome wins?

____

c. If voters must choose between C and A, what are the percentages of votes that each outcome receives and which outcome wins?

____

d. Do these preferences exhibit transitivity? Explain.

____

____

e. If the voters choose between A and B and then compare to C, which outcome wins?

____

If the voters choose between B and C and then compare to A, which outcome wins?

____

If the voters choose between A and C and then compare to B, which outcome wins?

____

Does the order in which items are voted on matter in this case? Why or why not?

____

____

Case 3

	Voter Type		
	Type 1	**Type 2**	**Type 3**
Percent of Electorate	25	35	40
First Choice	A	B	C
Second Choice	B	A	A
Third Choice	C	C	B

a. If voters must choose between A and B, what are the percentages of votes that each outcome receives and which outcome wins?

____

b. If voters must choose between B and C, what are the percentages of votes that each outcome receives and which outcome wins?

____

c. If voters must choose between C and A, what are the percentages of votes that each outcome receives and which outcome wins?

____

d. Do these preferences exhibit transitivity? Explain.

____

____

e. If the voters choose between A and B and then compare to C, which outcome wins?

____

If the voters choose between B and C and then compare to A, which outcome wins?

____

If the voters choose between A and C and then compare to B, which outcome wins?

____

Does the order in which items are voted on matter in this case? Why or why not?

____

____

Is the winning outcome the first choice of a large portion of the population? How can this be?

____

____

4. a. For Case 1 in problem 3 above, which outcome wins if you use a Borda count to determine the winner among outcomes A, B, and C, and what are the scores for each outcome?

____

____

b. For Case 1 in problem 3 above, eliminate outcome C and use a Borda count to find the winner from the remaining choices of A and B. What property required of a perfect voting system has been violated? Explain

____

____

____

c. Compare the results of Case 1 in problem 3 under simple majority rule, a Borda count with three choices, and a Borda count with two choices. What conclusions can you draw from these results?

____

____

____

5. In each of the following situations, describe the behavior that suggests that people may not always behave as self-interested rational maximizers.
   a. Workers agree to a labor contract that gives them a 5 percent raise for each of the next three years. After one year passes, they discover that the firm's profits have increased by 100 percent. The workers go on strike and receive no income during the strike.

   ____

   ____

   b. A worker plans to start saving 20 percent of his income starting three months from now because he has to first pay off some overdue bills. After three months passes, the worker saves nothing and instead spends all of his monthly income.

   ____

   ____

   c. After a famous rock star dies in a plane crash, many people decide to ride the train rather than fly.

   ____

   ____

   d. Joe wants to go on a Canadian fishing trip and his wife, Sue, wishes to take a different type of trip. The newspaper reports that the size and number of fish being caught in the area where they plan to fish is greater than normal because the temperature has become unseasonally cool. Joe is more sure about his choice of the fishing trip and Sue is more sure about her desire to go on a different type of trip.

   ____

   ____

Short-Answer Questions

1. What is *moral hazard*? What steps might a firm take to avoid moral hazard in the employment relationship?

2. What is *adverse selection*? Would you pay as much for a home that is only a year old (but has been lived in by people that have since built another home in the local area) as you would for a brand new home that has yet to be lived in? Why? What steps might you take to avoid adverse selection?

3. Would you expect the buyers of auto insurance to have a higher or lower than average probability of having an auto accident? Why? How does the insurance company address the adverse selection in this market? How does it address the moral hazard in this market?

4. To reduce adverse selection, firms signal high quality with expensive advertising. What are the necessary characteristics of an effective signal? Why don't firms producing low-quality goods use expensive advertising to falsely signal high quality?

5. Why does choosing a good gift qualify as a signal of love and concern to the recipient?

6. Suppose that 30 percent of the voters want to spend $10,000 on a new park, 30 percent want to spend $11,000, and 40 percent wish to spend $25,000. How much does the average voter want to spend? How much does the median voter want to spend? If each voter chooses the point closest to his most preferred choice, what will be the final choice between these three choices of a majority rule? Does the Condorcet paradox arise?

7. Use the median voter theorem to explain why the Republican presidential nominee is more conservative during the primaries than during the general election and the Democratic nominee is more liberal during the primaries than during the general election.

8. Do politicians always choose policies that maximize the well-being of society? Why?

9. If people were rational wealth maximizers, what result would we expect from the "ultimatum game?" What results do we actually find in experiments? What does this imply about wage determination?

10. The most popular major on campus is economics. Your best friend takes an introductory economics class and tells you that it was the worst class she has ever taken. You avoid taking any economics. Is this rational? Explain.

SELF-TEST

True/False Questions

_____ 1. Asymmetric information is a problem that occurs when one person in a transaction knows more about what is going on than the other.

_____ 2. In the principal agent relationship, the principal performs a task on behalf of the agent.

_____ 3. Employers may pay higher than equilibrium wages to avoid moral hazard in the employment relationship by raising the cost of shirking.

_____ 4. To avoid the problem of adverse selection, insurance companies screen their prospective customers to discover hidden health problems.

_____ 5. Signals to convey high quality are most effective when they are costless to all firms in the industry.

_____ 6. If A is preferred to B, B preferred to C, and A is preferred to C, then these preferences exhibit the property of unanimity.

_____ 7. The Condorcet paradox shows that majority-rule voting always tells us the outcome that society really wants.

_____ 8. Arrow's impossibility theorem shows that no voting system can satisfy the properties required of a perfect voting system.

_____ 9. According to the median voter theorem, majority rule will produce the average preferred outcome.

_____10. Politicians do not always choose the ideal economic policy because some politicians are corrupt and greedy, and others are willing to sacrifice the national interest for local popularity.

_____11. In the real world, people always behave rationally when making economic decisions.

_____12. The ultimatum game demonstrates that people will always make choices according to their self-interest.

_____13. Since people tend to care about fairness, firms may give bonuses during particularly profitable years to be fair and to avoid retaliation from the workers.

_____14. People seem to naturally engage in delayed gratification and they tend to follow through on plans made today to do something unpleasant in the future.

_____15. Since people are reluctant to change their minds in the face of new information, we can conclude that people do not always behave as rational maximizers.

Multiple-Choice Questions

1. John's car is in need of repair so John decides to sell it to avoid the repair bill. Unaware of the problem, Susan buys the car. This is an example of
   a. adverse selection.
   b. moral hazard.
   c. efficiency wages.
   d. hidden actions.

2. Judy wants to avoid buying a car that is a lemon. She takes a car she would like to buy to her mechanic before she purchases it. This is known as
   a. moral hazard.
   b. adverse selection.
   c. signaling.
   d. screening.

3. Chris is a traveling salesman for an apparel company. In this employment relationship, Chris is the
   a. principle.
   b. agent.
   c. signaler.
   d. screener.

4. Which of the following must be true about a signal that is used to reveal private information in order for the signal to be effective?
   a. It must be free to the informed party.
   b. It must be costly to the informed party but less costly to the party with the higher-quality product.
   c. It must be "as seen on TV."
   d. It must be applied to an inexpensive product.

5. Which of the following is an example of a signal that is used to reveal private information?
   a. Bob carefully chooses a special gift for Carolyn.
   b. Lexus advertises its cars during the Super Bowl.
   c. Madelyn earns her MBA from the Harvard Business School.
   d. All of the above are correct.

6. Which of the following is *not* a method firms use to avoid the moral hazard problem in the employment relationship?
   a. pay above equilibrium wages
   b. put hidden video cameras in the workplace
   c. buy life insurance on their workers
   d. pay employees with delayed compensation such as a year-end bonus

7. Which of the following best demonstrates the problem of moral hazard?
   a. Karen doesn't buy health insurance because it is too expensive and she is healthy.
   b. Rachel chooses to attend a well-respected college.
   c. Dick drives more recklessly after he buys auto insurance.
   d. A life insurance company forces Fred to have a physical prior to selling him insurance.

8. Under pairwise majority voting, if A is preferred to B and B is preferred to C, then A should be preferred to C. This is known as the property of
   a. unanimity.
   b. transitivity.
   c. independence.
   d. impossibility.

Use the following set of voter preferences to answer questions 9 through 12.

	Voter Type		
	Type 1	Type 2	Type 3
Percent of Electorate	35	25	40
First Choice	C	A	B
Second Choice	A	B	C
Third Choice	B	C	A

9. What percent of the population votes for A when the choice is between A and B?
   a. 25 percent
   b. 35 percent
   c. 40 percent
   d. 60 percent
   e. 75 percent

10. Under pairwise majority voting, which outcome wins?
    a. A
    b. B
    c. C
    d. These preferences suffer from the Condorcet paradox so there is no clear winner.

11. If we first compare A to C, and then compare the winner to B, which outcome is the winner?
    a. A
    b. B
    c. C
    d. These preferences suffer from the Condorcet paradox so there is no clear winner.

12. Using a Borda count, which outcome is preferred?
    a. A
    b. B
    c. C
    d. These preferences do not exhibit transitivity so there is no clear winner.

13. Which of the following is *not* a property required of a perfect voting system?
    a. the median voter always wins
    b. transitivity
    c. no dictators
    d. independence of irrelevant alternatives

14. Suppose that 40 percent of the voting population wish to spend $1,000 for artwork in City Hall, 25 percent wish to spend $20,000, and 35 percent wish to spend $22,000. What is the median preferred outcome, the average preferred outcome, and the modal preferred outcome?
    a. $1,000; $14,333; $1,000
    b. $20,000; $20,000; $22,000
    c. $20,000; $13,100; $1,000
    d. $1,000; $20,000; $22,000

15. Which of the following is true under pairwise majority rule if people vote for the outcome closest to their most preferred outcome?
    a. The average preferred outcome wins.
    b. The outcome preferred by the median voter wins.
    c. The outcome preferred by the greatest number of voters wins.
    d. There is no clear winner due to Arrow's Impossibility Theorem.

16. Which of the following is *not* true about how people make decisions?
    a. People are sometimes too sure of their own abilities.
    b. People are reluctant to change their minds in the face of new information.
    c. People give too much weight to a small number of vivid observations.
    d. People are always rational maximizers.
    e. All of the above are actually true statements about how people make decisions.

17. In the *ultimatum game*, what split would be rational for both the person proposing the split and the person who must accept or reject the split?
    a. 99/1
    b. 75/25
    c. 50/50
    d. 1/99
    e. There is no rational solution.

18. Which of the following help explain why firms pay bonuses to workers during particularly profitable years to prevent workers from becoming disgruntled?
    a. People are rational maximizers.
    b. People are inconsistent over time.
    c. People care about fairness.
    d. People are reluctant to change their minds.

19. John's friend dies of a sudden heart attack. John rushes to his doctor for an expensive physical examination. This response demonstrates that
    a. people give too much weight to a small number of vivid observations.
    b. people easily change their minds when confronted with new information.
    c. people tend to plan ahead and follow through on their plans.
    d. people enjoy going to the doctor.

20. Which of the following is a response to people's inconsistent behavior over time?
    a. efficiency wages
    b. year end bonuses
    c. forced contributions to a retirement plan
    d. all of the above

ADVANCED CRITICAL THINKING

You are watching a television news story about the AIDS crisis with a friend. Your friend says, "I think it is terrible that people infected with AIDS often can't buy health insurance. People that are ill are the ones that really need health insurance. Even worse, once someone gets health insurance, they often have to pay a deductible equal to 20 percent of the first $3,000 of their medical bills each year. Only then does the insurance company cover the remainder of the medical bills."

1. What problem caused by asymmetric information are insurance companies trying to avoid when they deny coverage to someone who may already be ill? What would happen if the insurance companies did not deny coverage to people who are already ill?

____

____

____

____

____

2. What problem does charging a deductible help solve? What might happen if insurance companies didn't require a deductible?

____

____

____

____

3. How might public policy address the problems in the market for health insurance? What are some of the shortcomings of a public policy solution?

____

____

____

____

SOLUTIONS

Terms and Definitions

4 Moral hazard

8 Agent

3 Principal

7 Adverse selection

1 Signaling

9 Screening

2 Condorcet paradox

6 Arrow impossibility theorem

5 Median voter theorem

Practice Problems

1. a. The insurance company is the principal; the insured is the agent. Only the agent knows how well he takes care of his teeth. By checking the insured's teeth each year, the insurance company can better monitor the behavior of the insured and reduce major future claims.
   b. The firm is the principal; the salesperson is the agent. The firm does not know how hard the salesperson works. By only paying the salesperson a commission, the firm is able to better monitor the salespersons work habits, and the worker is less likely to shirk.
   c. The firm is the principal; the worker is the agent. The firm does not know how hard the migrant worker works. By paying a large bonus for completing the season, the firm raises the cost of shirking and the cost of being fired. The worker is less likely to shirk.
   d. McDonald's is the principal; the student is the agent. McDonald's does not know how hard the student works. By paying above market wages, McDonald's increases the cost of shirking and the cost of being fired. The worker is less likely to shirk.

2. a. McDonald's doesn't know the abilities of the potential workers as well as do the workers. McDonald's *screens* potential workers using past educational performance and it is able to select high-ability workers.
   b. Buyers don't know the quality of Hyundai cars because they are relatively new to this market. Hyundai *signals* high quality with a long warranty and buyers are able to select high quality cars.
   c. The insurance company does not know as much about the health of the insurance buyer as does the buyer. The insurance company *screens* prospective customers with a physical exam to find hidden health problems so its insurance pool is not sicker than average.
   d. Beer buyers don't know the quality of Budweiser as well as Budweiser. Budweiser *signals* high quality with expensive advertising because they could only afford to do it if they could generate repeat buyers. Customers are able to choose a high quality beer.

3. **Case 1:**
   a. A = 15 + 40 = 55, B = 45. A beats B.
   b. B = 40 + 45 = 85, C = 15. B beats C.
   c. C = 15 + 45 = 60, A = 40. C beats A.

d. No. A beats B and B beats C, so transitivity requires that A beats C but, in fact, C beats A.
e. A beats B, so compare A to C and C wins.
B beats C, so compare B to A and A wins.
C beats A, so compare C to B and B wins.
Yes, because these preferences do not exhibit transitivity.

Case 2:

a. A = 30 + 55 = 85, B = 15. A beats B.
b. B = 30 + 15 = 45, C = 55. C beats B.
c. A = 30, C = 15 + 55 = 70. C beats A.
d. Yes. C beats A and A beats B. Transitivity requires that C beats B and it does.
e. A beats B, so compare B to C and C wins.
C beats B, so compare C to A and C wins.
C beats A, so compare C to B and C wins.
No, because these preferences exhibit transitivity.

Case 3:

a. A = 25 + 40 = 65, B = 35. A beats B.
b. B = 25 + 35 = 60, C = 40. B beats C.
c. A = 25 + 35 = 60, C = 40. A beats C.
d. Yes. A beats B and B beats C. Transitivity requires that A beats C and it does.
e. A beats B, so compare A to C and A wins.
B beats C, so compare B to A and A wins.
A beats C, so compare A to B and A wins.
No, because these preferences exhibit transitivity. No, only 25 percent of the population chooses A as their first choice, but most of the population greatly dislikes C and none of the population greatly dislikes A.

4. a. If choosing between A, B, and C, A = 30 + 120 + 45 = 195, B = 15 + 80 + 135 = 230, C = 45 + 40 + 90 = 175 and B wins.
   b. If choosing between only A and B, A = 30 + 80 + 45 = 155, B = 15 + 40 + 90 = 145 and A wins. Independence of irrelevant alternatives: the rankings of A and B shouldn't change when C is removed but the ranking did change.
   c. A wins, then B wins, then A wins again. Thus, majority voting does not necessarily tell us what society wants and deciding the order on which items are voted may affect the outcome.

5. a. People care about fairness and may be willing to accept nothing so that their adversary gets nothing if they think the split was unfair.
   b. People are inconsistent over time. From 3 months away, saving seems like a good idea but as that date approaches, the desire for immediate gratification takes over.
   c. People give too much weight to a small number of vivid observations. The probability of a plane crash has probably not changed yet people are more afraid to fly due to one highly publicized case.
   d. People are reluctant to change their minds. Both Joe and Sue use the same information to defend their original opinion.

Short-Answer Questions

1. The tendency of a person who is imperfectly monitored to engage in immoral behavior. Better monitoring, and paying higher wages or delaying some payment to raise the cost of shirking.

2. When unobserved attributes become undesirable from the standpoint of the uninformed party. No. Because you might assume that the sellers know something bad about the house—flooding, poor con-

struction, bad neighbors or schools, etc. Have the house inspected and check out the neighborhood and schools.

3. Higher, because buyers of insurance know more about their probability of an accident and those with a high probability of having accidents will need insurance. Insurance companies check a driver's driving history and offer policies that appeal differently to risky and safe drivers, and then they charge higher premiums to risky drivers. They require a deductible to avoid moral hazard.

4. It must be costly, but less costly to the individual with the higher-quality product. Since low-quality firms will not generate repeat purchases from their advertising, it is not cost effective for them to engage in expensive advertising.

5. Because it takes time (is costly) but it takes less time for someone that is knowledgeable about the recipient.

6. 0.3($10,000) + 0.3($11,000) + 0.4($25,000) = $16,300. Median voter wants to spend $11,000. $11,000 wins. No. Take any pair, find the winner, and then compare it to the remaining choice and $11,000 always wins.

7. Each candidate first must win the nomination through the primaries. To do that, they must capture the median voter within their party—conservative for the Republicans and liberal for the Democrats. After being nominated, they must capture the overall median voter, which requires each to move to the center—Republicans become more liberal and Democrats become more conservative.

8. No. Some politicians may act out of greed and others may sacrifice the national interest to improve their local popularity.

9. The first person would take $99 and give $1 to the other, and the other would accept. The first person usually offers more than $1 and the second person rejects small offers. Firms that are having particularly profitable years may pay above equilibrium wages to be fair or to avoid retaliation.

10. No. People give too much weight to a small number of vivid observations. In this case, the friend is just one additional observation out of thousands.

True/False Questions

1. T

2. F; the agent performs a task on behalf of the principal.

3. T

4. T

5. F; signals must be costly, yet less costly to the person with the higher-quality product.

6. F; these preferences exhibit transitivity.

7. F; it shows that the order in which items are voted can determine the outcome, therefore majority-rule voting does not always tell us what society wants.

8. T

9. F; it will produce the outcome preferred by the median voter.

10. T

11. F; there is evidence that people are only "near rational."

12. F; it shows that people care about fairness.

13. T

14. F; people tend to seek instant gratification and fail to follow though on unpleasant tasks.

15. T

Multiple-Choice Questions

1. a	5. d	9. d	13. a	17. a
2. d	6. c	10. d	14. c	18. c
3. b	7. c	11. b	15. b	19. a
4. b	8. b	12. c	16. d	20. c

Advanced Critical Thinking

1. Adverse selection. People who are already ill would seek to buy insurance. Their medical bills would be far higher than average, causing premiums to rise. At the artificially high price for insurance, fewer healthy people would buy insurance because the cost would exceed their expected bills. When healthy people drop out of the market, the price rises even further for the remaining participants, further reducing the size of the insurance market.

2. Moral hazard. Without a deductible, people might go to the doctor even if they don't really need medical attention. They also have little incentive to take care of themselves to avoid illness because they bear no cost of the illness. As above, this raises the cost of insurance above the expected bills of healthy people and many will fail to buy insurance.

3. Some people advocate government-provided health insurance where everyone (sick and healthy) would be forced to participate. Majority-rule democratic institutions may not generate the amount of health care that people want. Self-interested politicians may choose to provide an amount of health care that is different than what people actually want.